The Battle for the Soul of Islam

James M. Dorsey

The Battle for the Soul of Islam

Defining the Muslim Faith in the 21st Century

James M. Dorsey
RSIS
Singapore, Singapore

ISBN 978-981-97-2806-0   ISBN 978-981-97-2807-7 (eBook)
https://doi.org/10.1007/978-981-97-2807-7

© The Editor(s) (if applicable) and The Author(s), under exclusive license to Springer Nature Singapore Pte Ltd. 2024

This work is subject to copyright. All rights are solely and exclusively licensed by the Publisher, whether the whole or part of the material is concerned, specifically the rights of translation, reprinting, reuse of illustrations, recitation, broadcasting, reproduction on microfilms or in any other physical way, and transmission or information storage and retrieval, electronic adaptation, computer software, or by similar or dissimilar methodology now known or hereafter developed.
The use of general descriptive names, registered names, trademarks, service marks, etc. in this publication does not imply, even in the absence of a specific statement, that such names are exempt from the relevant protective laws and regulations and therefore free for general use.
The publisher, the authors and the editors are safe to assume that the advice and information in this book are believed to be true and accurate at the date of publication. Neither the publisher nor the authors or the editors give a warranty, expressed or implied, with respect to the material contained herein or for any errors or omissions that may have been made. The publisher remains neutral with regard to jurisdictional claims in published maps and institutional affiliations.

This Palgrave Macmillan imprint is published by the registered company Springer Nature Singapore Pte Ltd.
The registered company address is: 152 Beach Road, #21-01/04 Gateway East, Singapore 189721, Singapore

If disposing of this product, please recycle the paper.

To Tess, Deirdre. Lucas, Djess, and Olaf. Life would be a void without them.

Preface: Why Religion Matters in Geopolitics

Religion was never my focus even though religion-driven players inevitably were part of my decades of reporting and research of the Muslim world. I tuned into the battle for the soul of Islam as a result of having been based among others in Iran, Saudi Arabia, the UAE, Kuwait, Egypt, Turkey, and Israel and regular visits to Malaysia and Indonesia.

A weekend in 2015 in the northeastern Central Java town of Rembang hosted by Yahya Cholil Staquf, a leader of Nahdlatul Ulama, the Muslim world's largest and most moderate Muslim civil society movement, and his international affairs advisor, C. Holland Taylor, alerted me to the fact that there were fundamentally different visions of Islam competing to define what 'moderate' means. I travelled to Rembang to satisfy my curiosity sparked by snippets I heard and read about Nahdlatul Ulama's pluralistic, anti-autocratic vision of Islam that challenged Saudi and Emirati concepts as well as the teachings of Al-Azhar, the more than 1,000-year-old Cairo-based citadel of Islamic learning.

Morals and ethics are at the core of the discussion of the role of religion in politics, policymaking, and international relations. Scholars Amrita Narlikar and Daniel W. Drezner laid the groundwork for a discussion of the neglect of morals and ethics in a special edition of International Affairs, an academic journal, entitled "International relations: the 'how not to' guide."[1]

Responding to former White House chief of staff and one-time Secretary of State and of the Treasury James Baker's observation that policy solutions often create problems that need to be ameliorated at a later stage,[2] Narlikar and Drezner noted that this is an "endemic problem created by the mismatch between the grand arc of international relations and the powerful short-term incentives that political leaders face."

---

[1] Amrita Narlikar and Daniel W. Drezner (eds.). "International relations: the 'how not to' guide." International Affairs, Vol. 98, Issue 5, September 2022.

[2] James A. Baker III and Thomas M. DeFrank. "The Politics of Diplomacy: Revolution, War and Peace 1989-1992." New York: G. P. Putnam's Sons. 1995.

Narlikar and Drezner's edited edition suggested that academics, analysts, and policymakers revisit the maxim of seeking to replicate past policy successes as the basis for the crafting of new policies. Contributors argued that examining how to avoid catastrophic failure might be a better approach. They called implicitly for out-of-the-box thinking. They proposed the application of the medical sector's Hippocratic Oath to international relations. The Oath obliges doctors to avoid doing harm.

"The Hippocratic Oath principle in IR (international relations) serves as a cautionary warning against action merely for action's sake. There is a bias in politics towards 'doing something' in response to an event. Doing something, however, is not the same as doing the right thing… A Hippocratic Oath asks policymakers to weigh the costs and risks of viable policy options before proceeding," Narlikar and Drezner said in their introduction to the special edition.

Inevitably, the search for a moral and ethical yardstick forces one to come to grips with religion, irrespective of whether one is religious or not. Simply put, there is no alternative to religion as a moral and ethical yardstick for societies and systems of governance, whether religious or secular.

Major attempts at creating a secular yardstick, for example, Communism, Kemalism, the philosophy on which Mustafa Kemal Ataturk carved modern Turkey out of the ruins of the Ottoman Empire, or Zionism that sought to transform an amorphous religious, cultural, and/or national identity into a clearly defined national Jewish identity, lost their relevance once they were no longer fit for the purpose.

The attempts drove home that there is no societal moral and ethical yardstick not inspired by religion. Countries like the United States and Saudi Arabia could not be more different. Yet, both societies are undergirded by religiously inspired moral and ethical yardsticks. In the United States, Christianity is the overriding inspiration; in the kingdom, it is Islam.

The difference is the yardstick's positioning. In the United States, the yardstick is a voluntary benchmark rather than a hard and fast rule. Adherence is largely regulated socially rather than legally. In the kingdom, the yardstick is religious law that authorities have historically harshly enforced, even if Crown Prince Mohammed bin Salman has loosened the rules. Perhaps surprisingly, China also fits the bill. It does so in its recognition of religion's centrality by seeking, often brutally, to control, if not repress, expressions of faiths other than Buddhism.

A look at dominant issues, disputes, and conflicts in the last two decades suggests that they involved civilisational choices and policies that often violated international law and challenged a world order based on heterogeneous nation-states and/or propagated exclusionist and supremacist attitudes.[3]

---

[3] James M. Dorsey. "Civilizationism vs the Nation State." The Turbulent World with James M. Dorsey." 24 March 2019. https://www.jamesmdorsey.net/post/civilizationism-vs-the-nation-state

These included the controversy over the 2020 US presidential election; Britain's exit from the European Union; the Russian invasion of Ukraine; ethnoreligious nationalism in Russia, China, Hungary, Serbia, India, and Israel, as well as among American Christian nationalists; and the carnage in the Middle East.

Nahdlatul Ulama, like opponents of Christian nationalism in the United States, Hindu nationalism in India, and Jewish supremacy in Israel, underscore the likelihood that morals and ethics embedded in respect of human dignity and rights as the organising principle of politics and policymaking will have to be grounded in shared values derived from religion.

Moreover, the central role of religion in shaping societies makes an unambiguous re-articulation of religious precepts to avoid faith justifying abuse of human rights and universally recognised freedoms a sine qua non. Inevitably, this requires reform or repositioning of religious law and precepts. The rise of ultra-nationalist, supremacist interpretations of religion has put the struggle for reform into sharp relief. That applies Islam with the rise of Muslim militancy, Christianity with the increasing prominence of Christian nationalism, ultra-conservative and ultra-nationalist Judaism, similar trends in Hinduism Buddhism, and the role of the Russian Orthodox church in framing President Vladimir Putin's anti-Western policy.

The rise of jihadism with the birth of Al-Qaeda and the 2001 9/11 attacks on New York and Washington, the subsequent emergence of the even more virulent Islamic State that declared a caliphate in parts of Syria and Iraq, and the appeal of non-violent political Islam, put a bull's eye on Islam. The focus on Islam was enhanced by geopolitics, especially in the Middle East, a predominantly Muslim part of the world at the crossroads of maritime shipping; rich in oil, gas, and disposable cash; and a magnet as the cradle of Abrahamic faiths.

Moreover, the Middle East, home to Islam's holiest sites, was the Muslim-majority part of the world that twisted the concept of a nation-state that emerged from the 17th-century Peace of Westphalia to suit the elite's autocratic instincts. Westphalia envisioned the separation of church and state and the subordination of religion. With 20th-century decolonisation, the Middle East maintained its long-standing subordination of religion to legitimise autocratic rule but ignored the notion of a separation of church and state. In doing so, it relegated Muslim religious reformers to the margins and prevented the emergence of mass grassroots movements clamouring for change.

That vacuum was filled at the fringes of the Muslim world, particularly in Indonesia, the world's most populous Muslim-majority state with a history of tolerance and pluralism that predates Islam. "The current struggle between the United States and its allies and transnational jihadism is not a simple clash of Islam versus the West. Instead, it is a competition within Islam between a tiny minority of extremists and a much larger mainstream of moderates," said political scientist Jeffrey Haynes.[4] Haynes coined the phrase 'religious soft power.' Yet, at moments of heightened geopolitical tensions between rival Muslim powers like Saudi Arabia and Iran, the quest for religious soft power involves 'sharp power,' defined by Hayne's colleague, Christopher Walker, as information warfare with the aim of sowing discord and fuelling polarisation.[5]

Jihadism, 9/11, and political Islam as well as increasing anti-Muslim sentiment fuelled by rising religious nationalism in multiple faiths put Muslim-majority states and Muslims across the globe in the crossfire. Except for countries like Turkey and Iran that propagated a militant, conservative, and activist interpretation of Islam, Muslim-majority states and Muslim minorities were hard pressed to define a moderate understanding of the faith that demonstrated Islam's compatibility with modernism, human rights, and principles of tolerance and pluralism.

The pressure sparked a battle for the soul of Islam that pitted self-serving autocrats against proponents of a truly inclusive and pluralistic form of the faith based on reform of religious law and precepts rather than a tightly controlled top-down projection of Islam anchored in a ruler's decree or changes to national law. For both sides of the divide, religion became a pillar of how they projected themselves on the international stage. It was also a valuable tool in the pursuit of soft power as conceptualised by political scientist Joseph Nye. Nye defined soft power as "the ability to get what you want through attraction rather than coercion or payment." He said soft power was rooted in "the attractiveness of a country's culture, political ideals, and policies."[6]

To be sure, the pressure also enhanced the rivalry between proponents of a 'moderate' Islam and more traditional, conservative, and activist forms of Islam that has been a prime focus of Islam- and political violence-related research and media coverage. This book zeroes in on the struggle to define what constitutes 'moderate' Islam, about which little has been written, rather than the divide between moderates and militants. To be sure, extensive research exists on individual rivals competing to don the mantle as a beacon of moderate Islam, including Saudi Arabia, the United Arab Emirates, and Indonesia, but few have conducted comparative research or paid attention to the rivalry itself. Nevertheless, the outcome of the battle among moderates is likely to define what Islam stands for in the 21st century.

This book is the product of seven years of looking into the rivalry that amounted to competing quests for the wielding of Muslim religious soft power and leadership of the Muslim world sparked by geopolitical jockeying, particularly in the Middle East, and my eye-opening journey to Rembang. The book

---

[4] Jeffrey Haynes. "Religious Transnational Actors and Soft Power." Abingdon: Routledge. 2012. p. 5

[5] Christopher Walker. ""What Is 'Sharp Power'?" Journal of Democracy Vol. 29 Nbr 3. 2018. p. 9–23

[6] Joseph Nye. "Soft Power: The Means to Success in World Politics." Cambridge: Public Affairs. 2004. p. x

is both a first stab at writing an initial history of the rivalry and a snapshot of an ongoing battle. While this book zeroes in on Saudi Arabia, the UAE, and Indonesia, it also refers extensively to their main rivals, including Qatar, the Muslim Brotherhood, Iran, and Turkey. There are other players such as Morocco, Jordan, and Malaysia that I have not included because they either play bit or regional roles or have little impact beyond their borders.

The problem with Saudi Arabia and the UAE's vision is that it is tailored to suit the two countries' rulers. It advocates autocracy and absolute obedience to the ruler without reform of Islamic jurisprudence while allowing for degrees of religious and pluralism required for economic diversification, development, and growth. That is not to say that Nahdlatul Ulama's propagation of religious and political pluralism, respect for human rights, and democracy is without problems. But in the search for a non-autocratic vision of 'moderate' Islam, Nahdlatul Ulama is the only game in town that has the political, organisational, and religious clout to ensure that its voice cannot be ignored, even if it operates in a decentralised Muslim world in which no player can impose their view.

Chapter 1 of the book seeks to frame the battle for the soul of Islam in a global perspective. Chapters 2–4 detail and contrast the approaches of Indonesia, Saudi Arabia, and the UAE. Chapter 5 discusses the ideological and theological differences between religious scholars backed by the main players as well as Qatar. Chapter 6 portrays Turkey, a geopolitical powerhouse like Iran, that cycles through various chapters. Finally, chapter 7 delves into the gap between Islam as it is projected by governments and elites and popular attitudes towards religion, religiosity, and religious authority. How that gap plays out may be the joker in the deck.

I have a debt of gratitude to the Smith Richardson Foundation, whose generous support made this book possible.

I also have an immense debt to numerous sources who helped me think things through or whose publications informed my thinking. There are too many to list here, including multiple Nahdlatul Ulama leaders among whom first and foremost Yahya Cholil Staquf and C. Holland Taylor. Many others prefer to remain anonymous to avoid repercussions. So, this book is a tribute to them without whom it would never have come to life.

This book would not have seen the day of light without Tess, my wife. Not only is she the rock in my life, she is also the rock of this book. Her input, knowledge, encouragement, understanding, and patience were priceless.

This book will have served its purpose if it empowers readers to make informed judgements of their own and contributes to a long overdue discussion of religious reform not only of Islam but of religions across the board and a rethink of inclusivity and human rights and freedoms.

Time will tell.

Singapore, Singapore   James M. Dorsey

Contents

1 The Battle for the Soul of Islam   1
2 Islam's New Kid on the Block   33
3 The Saudi Sultan's Scholar   63
4 Emirati Gold Loses Its Shine   97
5 Muslim Clerics Battle It Out   123
6 Turkey Seeks Lost Glory   143
7 Trouble Brews in Islam's Backyard   171
8 Epilogue: The Prabowo Presidency   193

Index   197

CHAPTER 1

The Battle for the Soul of Islam

Flying parallel to the Iranian Gulf coast from Islamabad to Riyadh on a US Air Force Boeing 707 in February 1980, National Security Advisor Zbigniew Brzezinski and Assistant Secretary of State Warren M. Christopher knew they could change history. In Pakistan, Saudi Arabia, and Egypt, Brzezinski and Christopher set the stage for an Islamist jihad that, a decade later, forced Soviet troops to withdraw from Afghanistan. The jihad lit a fire that sparked the Soviet Union's demise.

Little did Brzezinski, the father of the anti-Soviet jihad,[1] and Christopher anticipate the holy war that would also change the Muslim world in ways that would haunt the United States and the rest of the world for decades. The two men toured the region amid heightened tensions. Religious zealots had seized the grand mosque in the holy city of Mecca three months earlier. That same month, Iranian militants occupied the US embassy in Tehran. In December, protesters burned the Islamabad US embassy to the ground, and Soviet troops invaded Afghanistan. Anti-US sentiment was rampant. All of that while the Middle East and South Asia reeled from a popular Shiite Muslim revolt that toppled the Shah of Iran, an icon of US power, a year earlier.

For Saudi Arabia, the Afghan jihad was about more than defeating godless communism and earning brownie points in Washington. It was also about countering Shiite revolutionaries who replaced Iran's monarchy with an Islamic republic. Iranian militants promised to repeat the exercise in Saudi

---

[1] Murat Yetkin. "We Owe Radical Islamist Militancy to Brzezinski." Hurriyet Daily News. 20 May 2017. https://www.hurriyetdailynews.com/opinion/murat-yetkin/we-owe-radical-islamist-militancy-to-brzezinski-113539.

Arabia and other Gulf states. The jihad crystallised the kingdom's erstwhile religious soft power strategy and created a release valve for frustrated and radicalised youth, often hailing from parts of Saudi Arabia that turned conservative as the 1970s oil boom passed them by. Saudi Arabia's lagging regional economic and military power tempered ambition. At the time, Saudi Arabia was neither one of the Muslim world's largest economies nor a potent military force or the most populous Muslim-majority state. Its religious soft power drive rested on the kingdom's custodianship of Islam's holiest cities, Mecca and Medina, the most respected accolade in the Muslim world, and its ability to export religious puritanism.

The jihad put Pakistan, the world's second-largest Muslim-majority country and home to the world's most significant Shiite minority, in the bull's eye. So did the South Asian nation's 900-kilometre-long border with Iran. Pakistan was both a launching pad for the jihad and a focal point of Saudi promotion of Sunni Muslim ultra-conservatism as an anti-dote to Iranian Shiite revolutionary zeal. The kingdom funded the jihad with billions of dollars. It steered large sums to anti-Shiite and anti-Iranian Sunni militants, ultra-conservative religious seminaries, pro-Saudi media houses, and cultural institutions. This turned Pakistan into one of the foremost targets of a global effort to promote the kingdom's puritan strand of Islam, and an extremist and jihadist breeding ground.

Brzezinski and Christopher flew home with a sense of accomplishment.[2] The two men agreed with Pakistani President Zia ul-Haq and Saudi King Khaled to support a guerrilla war that would turn Afghanistan into the Soviet Union's Vietnam and potentially weaken the Communist Party's grip on power. A US-backed Saudi-Pakistani joint venture that enlisted the Muslim Brotherhood facilitated the recruitment of up to 35,000 militants from 43 Muslim countries in the Middle East, Africa, and Asia.[3] The militants joined tens of thousands of Pakistani and Afghan volunteers studying at, often Saudi-funded, Pakistani madrassas or religious seminaries.

Abdullah Azzam, a charismatic cleric and former Palestinian fighter, facilitated their arrival. By incorporating Muslim causes in personal jihad, he redefined in a fatwa the religious definition of personal jihad. Azzam's fatwa gave Saudi and other Muslim governments religious cover to enable frustrated young men and thrill seekers in search of meaningful glory to join the Afghan jihad. The Saudi government offered volunteers a one-way US$75 ticket to Afghanistan to encourage them.

Saudi intelligence chief Turki AlFaisal Al Saud frequently visited the volunteers in the Pakistani frontier town of Peshawar, where Azzam and Osama bin Laden welcomed and accommodated them. An Al Saud aide delivered bags of

---

[2] The author accompanied Brzezinski and Warren as a reporter for The Christian Science Monitor.

[3] Olivier Roy. "Afghanistan: From Holy War to Civil War." Princeton, NJ: Darwin Press. 1995. p. 87.

cash while the Muslim World League and other Saudi government-controlled non-governmental organisations opened offices in Peshawar. As governor of Riyadh, Salman bin Abdulaziz Al Saud, who became king in 2015, coordinated private donations. Saudi-backed groups managed Peshawar's mushrooming refugee camps. Millions of refugees registered with Saudi-backed mujahedeen to qualify for food and humanitarian aid, turning the camps into recruitment centres.

Pro-government and more mainstream clerics ridiculed Azzam's fatwa. Influential Saudi cleric Abdulaziz bin Baz sought to limit the obligation to defend Muslim causes to financial and moral support. The large numbers of young Muslims responding to Azzam's call and the government's willingness to assist them drowned out criticism. The fatwa fused religious ultra-conservatism and jihadism. What started as a way station in Peshawar for anti-Soviet foreign fighters became Al-Qaeda's nucleus.

With Al-Qaeda came an energised quest for a caliphate, a global wave of jihadist violence, and the post-9/11 Muslim and non-Muslim scramble for a 'moderate' Islam that would serve as a buffer against militancy, extremism, and ultra-conservative supremacism and intolerance. This ongoing battle for Islam's soul means different things to different people. For the most enlightened, it's about more than faith; it's about humanity and shared values and beliefs that encourage peaceful coexistence. For others, it's about religious integrity. For a third group, the battle is a geopolitical power struggle and part of the ruling elite's survival strategy.

The battle is rooted in centuries of struggle and debate. It is a key facet of the Afghan jihad aftermath, the Iranian revolution, and a militant attack on the Grand Mosque in Mecca.[4] "The radical legacy of 1979…began a process that transformed societies and altered cultural and religious references… The ripples of the rivalry reengineered vibrant, pluralistic countries and unleashed sectarian identities and killings that had never defined us in the past," said journalist and author Kim Ghattas.

Thousands of Muslim fighters emerged from a decade of war in Afghanistan drunk with a sense of defeating a superpower. Little was done to deprive them of the illusion that they were more than proxies on a geopolitical and ideological chessboard and help them reintegrate into society. Bin Laden exploited their stupor to create a jihadist franchise; Al-Qaeda launched attacks across the globe, sparking an even more brutal offshoot, the Islamic State. The jihadists struck US embassies in Africa; American warships in the Gulf; the World Trade Towers in New York and the Pentagon in Washington; public transport in Madrid and London; restaurants, bars, and a music hall in Paris; a theatre in Moscow and hotels and resorts in Indonesia.

The violence sparked a clarion call to define Islam. Muslim autocrats, authoritarians, and illiberals lined up with Western leaders to declare that

---

[4] National Public Radio. "1979: Remembering 'The Siege Of Mecca'." 20 August 2009. https://www.npr.org/templates/story/story.php?storyId=112051155.

jihadism was not part of Islam, even if Islamic law could justify it. Muslim leaders saw the call as an opportunity to solidify their power grip. They projected themselves as icons of religious moderation and allies in a battle against what Al Saud, the former Saudi intelligence chief, dismissively termed in hindsight "young people of little intelligence, minimal education and absolutely no understanding of the complexities of the world, who have to believe they have a mission to change the world through violence… The origin of this way of thinking in recent times lies with Al-Qaida."[5]

For many of Al Saud's simpletons, the battle for Islam's soul was a fallout of the 1924 abolition of the Caliphate by Mustafa Kemal Ataturk, the visionary who carved modern Turkey out of the ruins of the Ottoman empire, which ruled much of the Muslim world and large chunks of the non-Muslim world for more than half a millennium. The Caliphate's demise left a political, theological, and civilisational void at a time when empires, kingdoms, and tribal confederations dominated the world. The abolition strengthened colonial rule and produced rulers considered illegitimate and corrupt by many. It sparked a century of geopolitical and religious soft power struggles. For the longest time, the contest involved countries and groups competing to be the most purist in doctrine. Today's battle for Islam's soul is the competition's latest manifestation. Instead of focusing on purity, the battle is about adjusting to modernity and twenty-first-century norms in a world grappling with defining morality, ethics, and values in a new order. In some ways, the battle is a throwback to the era of Prophet Mohammed, a Meccan trader concerned with ethics and creating a pathway to a just and pure life.

Jordanian ruler Abdallah I bin Al-Hussein, a descendant of the Prophet, gloated when he heard of the Ottoman Caliphate's demise. "The Turks have committed suicide. They had in the Caliphate one of the greatest political forces and have thrown it away… I feel like sending a telegram thanking Mustapha Kemal. The Caliphate is an Arab institution. The Prophet was an Arab, the Koran is in Arabic, the Holy Places are in Arabia, and the Khalif should be an Arab of the (Prophet Mohammed's) tribe of Khoreish. Now the Khaliphate has come back to Arabia,"[6] Abdullah said. He spoke as his father, Hussein bin Ali, the Hashemite emir of Mecca, declared himself a short-lived caliph.

Abdullah responded in the interview to a seven-hour uninterrupted speech by justice minister and professor of Islamic jurisprudence Seyyid Bey in the new Turkish Parliament. Seyyid's speech laid the groundwork for abolishing the caliphate and challenging a centuries-old alliance between the state and religious scholars or ulama. For much of Islam's history, the ulama lent states

---

[5] Prince Turki AlFaisal Al Saud. "The Afghanistan File." Isle of Wight: Arabian Publishing. 2021. p. xviii.

[6] The Manchester Guardian. "Hussein The New Khalif: Special Interview In His CAMP in TrandJordania. Arab Claims to Moslem Leadership. Dangers to Hedjaz From Arabia: Reproach For the Allies. Emir Abdullah Confident." 13 March 1924, ProQuest Historical Newspapers: The Guardian and The Observer.

religious legitimacy, countered unorthodox and alternative schools of thought, and limited the influence of private sector merchants and an independent private sector that enabled and funded the Golden Age of Islam's intellectual flourishing before the eleventh century.[7]

One of a small band of 20th-century Muslim intellectuals who favoured degrees of separation of religion and state and argued that a caliphate was not religiously mandated, Seyyid advocated popular sovereignty. He believed nations could shape their political institutions. Seyyid quoted Prophet Mohammed as predicting a true caliphate would exist in the first three decades following his death. After that, it would become a corrupt sultanate. "To sum up…the issue of the Caliphate, rather than being a religious matter, is a worldly issue," Seyyid said.[8]

Unlike Mohammed, Abdullah's prediction proved wrong. The caliphate did not return to Arabia. A century later, it is not the caliphate that Muslim powerhouses fight about. Instead, they are engaged in a deepening religious soft power struggle for geopolitical influence and dominance in which the concept of the caliphate is in dispute. This battle for Islam's soul pits major players that purport to be religiously moderate, such as the UAE, Saudi Arabia, and Indonesia, against one another in sharp contrast to Iran, Turkey, Islamists, and jihadists. The two Gulf states and Indonesia may be the leading contenders seeking to define moderate Islam. However, they also compete with other Muslim-majority states like Morocco, eager to enhance, regionally rather than globally, their religious soft power in the name of moderate Islam and proponents of more hardline interpretations like Turkey and Iran.

Iran's 1979 Islamic revolution marked the moment Saudi religious diplomacy and funding were no longer unchallenged in a class of their own. It heralded the next phase in the Saudi-Iranian rivalry that engulfed the Middle East, North Africa, the non-Arab Muslim world, and the international community. It moved the rivalry beyond Islam's historic divide between Sunni and Shiite Muslims. The revolution produced an alternative form of religious governance that initially recognised a degree of popular sovereignty and challenged monarchical rule.

Like Saudi Arabia, Iran is driven by geopolitics. However, contrary to Saudi Arabia, Iran opted for asymmetric hard power bolstered by revolutionary zeal and hampered by US and international sanctions that limited its access to sophisticated weaponry. It supported religious militants initially in Lebanon and subsequently in Iraq, Syria, and Yemen.[9] The war against Iraq

---

[7] Ahmet T. Kuru. "Islam, Authoritarianism, and Underdevelopment." Cambridge: Cambridge University Press. 2019. pp. 3–6.

[8] Michelangelo Guida. "Seyyid Bey and the Abolition of the Caliphate." Middle Eastern Studies. Vol. 44, Issue 2. pp. 275–289.

[9] Claire Parker and Rick Noack. "Iran Has Invested in Allies and Proxies Across the Middle East. Here's Where They Stand After Soleimani's Death." The Washington Post. 3 January 2020. https://www.washingtonpost.com/world/2020/01/03/iran-has-invested-allies-proxies-across-middle-east-heres-where-they-stand-after-soleimanis-death/.

in the 1980s, in which Gulf states funded Iraqi leader Saddam Hussein's war machine, fuelled Iran's pursuit of asymmetric hard power. The quest was also in response to rising Iranian nationalism as a result of the war and, at times, served as a vehicle for Iranian efforts to export its revolution. It deepened the cleavage between the Islamic Republic and the conservative Gulf monarchies. Iran saw its nurturing of Shiite militias as its primary forward line of defence, driven by a belief that the United States and its Gulf allies sought to topple its Islamic regime. Iran's detractors viewed the militias as vehicles to undermine conservative monarchies and spread the revolution.

Like in the 1980s, geopolitics could in the 21st century shift the paradigm in the battle for Islam's soul, particularly if the United States succeeds in engineering formal Saudi recognition of Israel. It could put moderate Islam's leadership competition on par with the struggle between moderates and militants. Establishing relations between the custodian of Islam's two holiest cities and the Jewish state could prompt Iran to attack Saudi Arabia, where it is most sensitive. Saudi Arabia has long viewed Iranian efforts to challenge the Saudi administration of Mecca and Medina and the haj, a pillar of the kingdom's international standing, as a significant threat. Iran wants to replace Saudi control with an international Muslim administration. Iran has downplayed its assault on Saudi legitimacy since the kingdom and the Islamic Republic reestablished diplomatic relations in 2023. Saudi Arabia broke off relations in 2016 after Iranian protesters attacked Saudi diplomatic missions in response to the kingdom's execution of a prominent Shiite cleric. "If Saudi Arabia embraces Israel, Iran will likely throw everything but the kitchen sink at the Saudis," said Middle East analyst Bilal Y. Saab.[10]

The Iranian shift to nationalism in the early 1980s was evident in emotive debates in parliament about the utility of the 444-day occupation of the US embassy at a time when Iran was at war with Iraq. Men like Hojatoleslam Hashemi Rafsanjani, the parliament speaker and later president of Iran, Ayatollah Mohammed Beheshti, the Iranian political hierarchy's number two, and chief jurist Ayatollah Sadegh Khalqali, known as the hanging judge for his penchant for the death penalty and hatred of cats, unsuccessfully argued in favour of a quick resolution of the embassy crisis so that Iran could concentrate on the defence of its territory and revolution. The debates signalled a move from ideological rivalry to a geopolitical fight with Saudi Arabia that continues today while, at the same time, both countries strive to prevent it from spinning out of control. Hampered by its primary reliance on Arab Shiite allies and unable to transcend the Sunni-Shiite divide, Iran fared better in its asymmetric hard power approach than in its attempts to garner religious soft power through cultural and religious outreach and militant support for popular Muslim causes like the Palestinian plight.

---

[10] Bilal U. Saab. "Peace With Israel Means War with Iran." Foreign Policy. 30 August 2023. https://foreignpolicy.com/2023/08/30/saudi-arabia-israel-deal-iran/.

In the end, no clear winner may emerge from the battle for Islam's soul. Yet, the course of the battle could determine the degree to which Islam will be defined by one or more competing statist forms of the faith that support autocracy, preach absolute obedience to political rulers, and reduce religious establishments to pawns of the state or open the door to a more politically pluralistic and democratic interpretation of the faith. More broadly, it pits the interventionism of illiberal and authoritarian leaders, who envision a civilisational world where borders are defined by civilisation, against proponents of the rule of law and respect for international law.

Implicit in the rivalry is a broader debate across the Muslim world that speaks to the heart of the relationship between state and religion. At the core of the discussion is whether and what role the state should play in enforcing religious morals and the place of religion in education, judicial systems, and politics. As the battle for religious soft power intensifies, the lines dividing the state and religion become increasingly blurred, particularly in more autocratic countries. This struggle has and will affect the prospects for the emergence of a truly more tolerant and pluralistic interpretation of one of the three Abrahamic religions.

The battle kicked into high gear in the wake of the September 11, 2001, Al-Qaeda attacks on New York and Washington. It was further energised by popular Arab revolts a decade later that toppled Tunisia's, Egypt's, Libya's, and Yemen's leaders. The 9/11 attacks shifted the litmus test of moderation from attitudes towards Israel to definitions of Islam that rejected violence and extremism, supported the War on Terror, and paid lip service to religious tolerance and pluralism. The attacks initially enhanced religious moderation's importance in branding Muslim-majority states aligned with the West. It allowed Middle Eastern autocrats to denounce jihadism as a deviation from and misinterpretation of Islam that only they can counter. Advocacy of moderate Islam retained its significance as the battle, over time, became a facet of the global tug of war, shaping a new 21st-century world order.[11] Rivals employed religion to garner favour, empathy, and goodwill, or what political scientists term soft power[12] among influential Muslim, Jewish, Christian, Buddhist, and Hindu communities across the globe.

The 2011 revolts reinforced autocrats' quest for control of the definition of Islam. "God was a force to contend with during the Arab Spring... Islamist movements, populist uprisings, entrenched regimes, rebellious youth, desperate breadwinners, and secular intellectuals were among those who found themselves – in some form or fashion – reckoning with God in these tumultuous times," said Islam scholar Joud Alkorani. Protesters invoked God in their chants. "God is with us," they chanted as they recited their demands,

---

[11] James M. Dorsey. "The Battle for the Soul of Islam." Current Trends in Islamist Ideology, Vol. 27, 2020. pp. 106–127.

[12] Joseph S. Nye. "Soft Power: The Means to Success in World Politics." New York: Public Affairs, 2005.

and "God is Great" when security forces attacked them. "The question of God's place in the Muslim world's travails coupled with an increasingly critical attitude of Muslim youth toward traditionally state-aligned religious authority bolstered autocrats' need to define Islam," Alkorani said.[13]

Some of the battle's contenders project themselves as protagonists of purportedly moderate forms of Islam that are religiously tolerant and pluralistic. They engage in interfaith dialogue but stop short of institutionally and legally reforming outdated, obsolete, and discriminatory concepts in Muslim religious law. Others promote more militant expressions of the faith. As a result, the battle is a struggle to define what Islam represents and how Muslims worldwide will practice their religion. It is a battle at multiple levels and across numerous platforms ranging from the world's corridors of power to mosques and villages in Africa and Asia to mainstream and social media. The significance of this battle lies in what is at stake. At stake is which Muslim-majority country or countries will be recognised as leaders of the Islamic world and the degree to which moderate Islam incorporates principles of tolerance, pluralism, gender equality, secularism, and human rights as defined in the Universal Declaration of Human Rights. In some ways, the battle mirrors the Cold War, at the core of which were notions of popular sovereignty, democracy, the rule of law, transparency, accountability, and human and minority rights.

For Saudi Arabia and the UAE, the battle is about control of religion, a powerful and emotive mobiliser, regime legitimacy, soft power projection, deflection of criticism of repressive domestic policies, and support for autocracy and authoritarianism. Saudi and Emirati concepts of moderate Islam frame Saudi Crown Prince Mohammed bin Salman and UAE President Mohammed bin Zayed's strategies to manage their international, regional, and domestic challenges and reshape their nations.

For Turkey, the battle is about exploiting and reviving past imperial glory to project power globally and influence Diaspora constituencies, particularly in Europe. Iran, locked with Saudi Arabia in a battle for Muslim hearts and minds for more than four decades, has faced an uphill battle. Creeping corruption, mismanagement of the economy, and support for Syrian President Bashar al-Assad's brutal regime have severely diminished its revolutionary appeal and ability to project itself as a regional alternative.

Unlike Indonesia, an underrated powerhouse, Saudi Arabia and the UAE have geopolitics in their sails, even if Indonesian Islam is far more embracing of pluralistic and democratic values such as the separation of state and religious authority, equality before the law, and religious and political pluralism. US Secretary of State Hilary Clinton recognised this on a 2009 visit to the

---

[13] Email exchange with the author, 21 August 2023.

archipelago state. "If you want to know whether Islam, democracy, modernity, and women's rights can co-exist, go to Indonesia," Clinton said.[14] To be sure, Clinton spoke six years before Bin Salman's rise and a decade before far-reaching social reforms in the UAE.

Developments in the years since Clinton's remark should have enhanced Indonesia's significance. While the Middle East reverted to autocracy, Indonesia and Nahdlatul Ulama, the world's largest and most moderate Muslim civil society movement, increasingly articulated a genuinely pluralistic and more democratic vision of Islam. The contrast could not have been starker. Nahdlatul Ulama adopted Humanitarian Islam as the UAE and Saudi Arabia supported the rollback of the 2011 revolts' achievements, cracked down on dissent, and intervened militarily in Yemen. The adoption also coincided with Turkish President Recep Tayyip Erdogan's hollowing out of his country's democracy in response to a 2016 failed military coup and Saudi Arabia's 2018 killing of journalist Jamal Khashoggi.

Even so, the United States and much of the world prioritised Saudi Arabia as Islam's heartland, the faith's cradle, and home to its holiest cities. Moreover, the international community attributes greater strategic value to the energy and cash-rich Gulf states, geographically located along some of the world's most vital waterways and capable of wielding influence in crucial parts of the world. Minus the geopolitical firepower, Indonesia, the world's third largest democracy and among its top 20 economies, has many of those attributes. It has Asia Pacific's third largest natural gas reserves. It is the world's foremost biofuel producer and boasts significant manganese, copper, gold, tin, bauxite, and nickel deposits. Yet, a US News & World ranking of the world's best countries listed the Southeast Asian nation as number 32 on the political influence totem pole and 45th in terms of cultural influence. By comparison, the UAE ranked 9th in political and economic power and 14th culturally. Saudi Arabia occupied 11th place in political and economic impact and 36th culturally.[15]

The leading contenders in the battle for Islam's moderate soul—Saudi Arabia, the UAE, and Indonesia, in association with Nahdlatul Ulama—have more in common than just economic assets. They all support a socially more liberal society but reject Western liberal social norms such as LGBTQ rights. They oppose political Islam. Yet, what divides them is what defines Islam in the twenty-first century.

Contrary to the kingdom and the Emirates, Nahdlatul Ulama argues, in a radical break with tradition, that Islam needs to reform Sharia to remove outdated, obsolete, and problematic legal concepts. Indonesia's quest for reform of Muslim jurisprudence threatens a vital pillar of how Gulf autocrats

---

[14] Arshad Mohammed and Ed Davies. "Indonesia Shows Islam, Modernity Coexist: Clinton." Reuters, 18 February 2009. https://www.reuters.com/article/us-indonesia-clinton-idUSTRE51H15A20090218.

[15] U.S. News & World Report. "U.S. News Best Countries." 7 September 2022. https://www.usnews.com/news/best-countries/rankings.

position themselves on the international stage. Echoing world leaders, who are careful not to hold Islam as a faith responsible for jihadism and Muslim extremism, men like Bin Salman, his predecessors, and Bin Zayed catered to their narrative by arguing that radicalism is alien to Islam. They skilfully exploited fears of Islamic militancy fuelled by the Iranian revolution, 9/11, and attacks by jihadists and religious zealots, in Europe, Africa, and Africa. The rulers insisted that only they and their state-aligned clerics can counter jihadism, extremism, and religion-driven political violence and promote 'moderate' Islam on religious grounds. The focus on "moderate" Islam allowed much of the international community, with the United States in the lead, to draw attention away from popular discontent with autocratic and abusive rule in the Arab world that created an extremist breeding ground. Joining the fight against terrorism allowed Arab rulers to don the mantle of religious moderation and garner favour in world capitals.

By contrast, Nahdlatul Ulama was willing to expose problems in Islamic jurisprudence. It did not shy away from admitting that Islamic law can be interpreted to justify jihadism and extremism, much like other religions embrace texts that legitimise radicalism. In contrast to Gulf rulers and clerics, Nahdlatul Ulama maintained that countering Islamic extremism meant tackling problematic Muslim religious precepts that often contradicted the Qur'anic notion of Wasatiyyah or centrism and Prophet Mohammed's multiple calls for moderation. The group argued that religious reform was a central plank in ensuring adherence to human rights, embracing pluralism, and preserving the rule of law.

The Indonesian approach went against the grain of traditional Islamic scholars who opt to ignore outdated, obsolete, and problematic provisions of Islamic law rather than amending the law. In that way, scholars ensured that rulers retained their grip on religion. Autocrats and state-aligned scholars' rejection of Nahdlatul Ulama's approach is reinforced by the movement's advocacy of political pluralism and unambiguous embrace of human rights. As a result, Indonesian governments and Nahdlatul Ulama have, unlike Saudi Arabia and the UAE that designated the Muslim Brotherhood and its many affiliates as terrorists, not called for the outlawing of the country's Brotherhood-affiliated political party, the Prosperous Justice Party (PKS). Even so, critics took President Joko Widodo's government to task for rolling back Islamist influence in politics and society with investigations and prosecutions, the closure of websites and social media pages, and the proscription of militant Islamist organisations. Opinion polls suggested the measures enjoyed public support.[16]

Without exception, all players in the battle for Islam's soul are haunted by their dark sides. Their records on freedom of religion and minority protection are mixed. They employ religious favouritism and counterterrorism to suppress

---

[16] Greg Fealey and Sally White. "The Politics of Banning FPI." New Mandala. 18 June 2021. https://www.newmandala.org/the-politics-of-banning-fpi/.

other religious and philosophical strands. Saudi Arabia's counterterrorism law criminalises "anyone who challenges, either directly or indirectly, the religion or justice of the King or Crown Prince" and prohibits "the promotion of atheistic ideologies in any form." Except for Indonesia, they control mosque sermons and require preachers to abstain from discussing politics.[17]

Nonetheless, Nahdlatul Ulama leaders have shown scant remorse for the participation of their paramilitary force in the 1965 mass killings of alleged Communists, who challenged their power and control of land in Java. At the time, the Indonesian Communist Party was the non-Communist world's largest Communist Party. Nahdlatul Ulama leaders authorised the rounding up of suspects by its paramilitaries in coordination with the military, the slaughter's instigator.[18] Some older figures involved in the killing as youth leaders still pride themselves on an operation they see as preventing Communists from gaining power.[19] Abdurrahman Wahid, a widely respected visionary former Nahdlatul Ulama leader and one-time Indonesian president, who turned blind in the late 1990s, emerged as one of the movement's few figures to express regret for the group's role in the massacres. He was abroad at the time of the killings. As president, Wahid sparked controversy when he proposed lifting the 1965 ban on Communism and Marxist Leninism.[20]

In 2022, Saudi Crown Prince bin Salman and Yahya Cholil Staquf, the Nahdlatul Ulama central board chairman, expressed their rival visions in separate but almost simultaneously published interviews. While the timing of the interviews was coincidental, they neatly laid out the parameters of the rivalry among major Middle Eastern and Asian Muslim-majority powers to dominate the discourse on Islam's place in the world. Unsurprisingly, the two leaders' visions mirrored the struggle, epitomised by the Russian invasion of Ukraine, between an autocratic, civilisationalist, and a more democratic and pluralistic image of the world in the twenty-first century. At the heart of the differences between Bin Salman and Staquf lie whether Islam needs reform or a return to basics, who can interpret or reinterpret the faith, and what constitutes appropriate Islamic governance.

Speaking to The Atlantic, Bin Salman left no doubt that the authority to interpret Islam was his and his alone. A law graduate from King Saud University who prides himself on being a student of Islamic jurisprudence who has

---

[17] Pew Research Center, A Closer Look at How Religious Restrictions Have Risen Around the World, 15 July 2019.

[18] Kenneth R. Young. "Local and National Influences in the Killings of 1965." In Robert Cribb (ed.), The Indonesian Killings, 1965–1966: Studies from Java and Bali, 1990. Clayton, Victoria: Monash University. p. 82.

[19] Mass Violence and Resistance—Research Network. "Hasyim, Yusuf." Science Po. 4 August 2009. https://www.sciencespo.fr/mass-violence-war-massacre-resistance/en/document/hasyim-yusuf.html.

[20] Andrée Feillard. "Indonesian Traditionalist Islam's Troubled Experience with Democracy (1999–2001)." Archipel 64. July 2002. pp. 117–144. https://www.persee.fr/doc/arch_0044-8613_2002_num_64_1_3728.

bent the kingdom's religious establishment to his will, Bin Salman laid out the principle of the autocrats' notion of moderate Islam: absolute obedience to the ruler. He insisted he had the authority and power to interpret the faith as he saw fit and determine what implementation of Islamic law should entail. In line with universally accepted dogma, Bin Salman said he could not change rules enshrined in the Qur'an, viewed as God's word, but was free to reinterpret most Islamic legal provisions derived from Prophet Mohammed's reported sayings and deeds.[21]

Bin Salman's self-appointment reflected the Al Sauds' long-standing view of the clerics' place in the kingdom's pecking order. Citing Islamic jurisprudence, AlFaisal Al Saud, the former intelligence chief and subsequent ambassador to Britain and the United States, insisted in an op-ed in 2002 that the kingdom's rulers had the sole right to demand total allegiance and obedience. Scholars merely "advise and guide" rulers, AlFaisal, who now heads the Riyadh-based King Faisal Center for Research and Islamic Studies, said.[22] Like many autocratic rulers and clerics, AlFaisal quoted the Qur'an's Verse of Obedience or Surat An-Nisa (4:59), which obliges the faithful to "obey God and obey the Messenger and those in authority among you."[23] With his subjugation of the clergy, Bin Salman followed in his predecessors' footsteps. In the 1920s, Bin Salman's grandfather, King Abdulaziz, modern Saudi Arabia's founder, sidelined ultra-conservative scholars opposed to trade and development. "The history of the modern Saudi state has shown that at key junctures where it could have acted otherwise, the leadership within the royal family has made decisions that maintained their political supremacy over and against any contestation from religious elites or individual clerics," said Middle East scholars Kristian Coates Ulrichsen and Anelle R. Sheline.[24]

Elaborating on Bin Salman's assertion, Middle East scholar Bernard Haykel argued the crown prince was "short-circuiting the tradition…in an Islamic way. He's saying that there are very few things that are fixed beyond dispute in Islam. That leaves him to determine what is in the interest of the Muslim community. If that means opening movie theatres, allowing tourists, or women

---

[21] Graeme Wood. "Absolute Power." The Atlantic. April 2022. https://www.theatlantic.com/magazine/archive/2022/04/mohammed-bin-salman-saudi-arabia-palace-interview/622822/.

[22] Prince Turki Al Faisal. "الولاة هم الحكام وطاعتهم واجبة أما العلماء فهم مستشارون" (The Rulers Are the Rulers, and Obedience to Them Is Obligatory. The Scholars Are Advisors)." Ash-Sharq al-Awsat. 20 January 2002. https://archive.aawsat.com/details.asp?section=17&article=83764&issueno=8454#.VoPA1kp97Dc.

[23] Seyyed Hossein Nasr, Caner K. Dagli, Maria Massi Dakake, Joseph E. B. Lumbard, and Mohammed Rustom. "The Study Quran. A New Translation and Commentary." New York: Harper Collins. 2015. https://archive.org/details/thestudyquran_201909/mode/2up?q=4%3A59.

[24] Kristian Coates Ulrichsen and Anelle R. Sheline. "Mohammed bin Salman and Religious Authority and Reform in Saudi Arabia." Baker Institute for Public Policy. 19 September 2019. https://www.bakerinstitute.org/sites/default/files/2019-09/import/bi-report-092319-cme-mbs-saudi.pdf.

on the beaches on the Red Sea, then so be it." Expressing a less benign view, Gulf scholar Christopher M. Davidson defined Bin Salman and Bin Zayed's sultanism as "an extreme form of autocracy" in which rulers rather than consulting the elite "treat the state as their 'personal' instruments... and – more generally –...are able to act arbitrarily beyond any traditional constraints."[25]

Putting their mouth where their money is, prominent ultra-conservative clerics such as Saleh al-Luhaidan, a former Saudi judiciary head, and Grand Mufti Abdulaziz al-Sheikh, a member of the influential family of clerics descended from Mohammed Ibn Abd al-Wahhab, the 18th preacher of a puritan interpretation that shaped the kingdom for much of its history, set aside their long-standing ultra-conservative beliefs that contradict Bin Salman's reforms to support the crown prince publicly. They called for obedience to the ruler and warned against public criticism. In 2017, Al-Sheikh issued at least eight fatwas and statements asserting the need to maintain allegiance to the ruler.[26] In return, Bin Salman's arrest of scholars with significant social media followings, who long called for the kind of change he propagates, removed the ultra-conservative religious challengers and strengthened their allegiance to the kingdom's de facto ruler.

Some incarcerated figures threatened Bin Salman and the ultra-conservatives by arguing that free choice supersedes religious requirements. Exploiting the Wahhabi movement's three-way split, their detention eliminated religious actors and narratives operating beyond the government's control.[27] Al-Lohaidan belongs to a centrist wing, dubbed 'the sultan's scholars' by the movement's more liberal faction, which advocates civil rights and a constitutional monarchy. A more hardline bloc hews closer to jihadism. "The state has strengthened the Wahhabi centre through neutralising the Wahhabi left and right, which each represented a threat to state authority and legitimacy … As for the civic rights innovations of the Wahhabi left exemplified by al-Awdah, it is precisely this discourse that the state wants to shut down," said Saudi Arabia scholar Andrew Hammond. He was referring to Salman al-Awdah, a popular but controversial religious scholar who has lingered in solitary confinement since 2017.[28]

Bin Salman's views clash with what Staquf, the Nahdlatul Ulama leader, calls the need to "recontextualise" Islam to bring its legal concepts and philosophy into line with the twenty-first century. Recontextualisation would involve

[25] Christopher M. Davidson. "From Sheikhs to Sultanism, Statecraft and Authority in Saudi Arabia and the UAE." London: Hurst. 2021. p. 20.

[26] Abdulaziz Bin al-Sheikh. https://mufti.af.org.sa/ar/search/node/طاعة20%ولي20%الأمر.

[27] Ola Salem and Abdullah Alaoudh. "Mohammed Bin Salman's Fake Anti-Extremist Campaign." Foreign Policy. 23 June 2019. https://foreignpolicy.com/2019/06/13/mohammed-bin-salmans-fake-anti-extremist-campaign/.

[28] Andrew Hammond. "Reordering Saudi Religion: MBS Is Defanging Wahhabism, Not Dethroning It." Maydan. 20 September 2021. https://themaydan.com/2021/09/reordering-saudi-religion-mbs-is-defanging-wahhabism-not-dethroning-it/.

revision or removal of "obsolete" elements of Islamic jurisprudence that are supremacist or discriminatory such as concepts of the kafir or infidel; dhimmi or people of the book, Jews and Christians who enjoy a protected but second-class status under Islamic law; slavery which has been abolished across the Muslim world in secular law but has yet to be removed from Sharia, and the divvying up of the world into a House of Islam (Dar al-Islam), a House of Infidels (Dar al-Kufr), and a House of War (Dar al-Harb).

"If we implement without questioning any provision of fiqh (the body of Islamic law) ... then we may ... butcher people according to the rules of fiqh that still exist today. This is a problem," Staquf said in one of many conversations with the author. His international affairs advisor, C. Holland Taylor, aka Mohammed Cholil, an American national and convert to Islam, added, "Nahdlatul Ulama highlights that elements within classical Islamic law explicitly enjoin discrimination against certain classes of human beings based on religion. Nahdlatul Ulama scholars examine how problems facing humanity are connected to Islamic law and teachings and how these might be reconceptualised."

Insisting that 7th-century Islam was perfect, Bin Salman rejected using the term 'moderate Islam' because it "would make terrorists and extremists happy." His positioning of the faith justified his anchoring of social reforms in civil but not religious law. It also allowed him to hew closer to orthodox Islamic jurisprudence as he saw fit, like with the kingdom's adoption of a first-ever personal status.

A 2023 Amnesty International analysis suggested the kingdom's first-ever personal status law was rooted in classical Islamic jurisprudence. The law codified problematic practices of the kingdom's religion-based male guardianship system. It entrenched gender-based discrimination in most aspects of family life, including marriage, divorce, child custody, and inheritance, even though it set a minimum age for marriage. Under the law, women must obtain their male legal guardian's consent to marry. The law obliges a wife to "obey" her husband. It conditions her right to financial support, food, and accommodation on her "submit(ting) herself" to her husband. Moreover, men can initiate divorce without conditions, while women face legal, financial, and practical barriers. In divorce, a mother does not have equal rights to her children; the father is granted guardianship as a matter of principle.[29]

By contrast, Staquf noted that Nahdlatul Ulama founder Haji Hasyim Asy'ari conceived the mystic Sufi movement a century ago as a vehicle for "consolidating the universe." At the time, that meant filling the void created by Ataturk's abolition of the caliphate and the conquest of Mecca and Medina by the Al Sauds' Wahhabi army and challenging the notion that the caliphate underpinned Islamic civilisation. "From the existing records, Nahdlatul Ulama

---

[29] Amnesty International. "Saudi Arabia: New Personal Status Law Codifies Discrimination Against Women." 8 March 2023. https://www.amnesty.org/en/documents/mde23/6431/2023/en/.

was established to forge a new path for future civilization, to replace the old civilizational construct that was lost," Staquf said. Malay civilisation, uninhibited by the constricts of orthodox Islam, had "developed a spiritual view of Islam that tends to view Islamic law as a set of universal principles that all religions recognize and acknowledge, rather than an inflexible set of rules developed by classical Muslim jurists for running a pre-modern state."[30]

Rooted in Indonesian Islam and Nahdlatul Ulama's history, Staquf branded the group's religious precepts 'Humanitarian Islam' that offered an alternative to state-backed, less tolerant, and less pluralistic notions of moderate Islam propagated by Saudi Arabia and the UAE, as well as expressions of political Islam represented by Turkey, Iran, and the Muslim Brotherhood. Staquf has one advantage few Muslim religious reformers have. Indonesia and Nahdlatul Ulama rely on diverse indigenous religious authorities that do not need to take their cue from Middle Eastern seats of Islamic learning like Al-Azhar in Cairo or the Islamic University of Medina.

Staquf sees himself as the embodiment of the vision of Wahid, the former Nahdlatul Ulama leader, who was impeached by parliament on charges of incompetence and corruption two years into his presidency. Affectionately known as Gus Dur, Wahid's presidency constituted a new era in which Nahdlatul Ulama re-engaged in politics against some of its leaders' instincts. A soft-spoken, yet at times fiery orator, prominent Islamic scholar, and Wahid disciple, Staquf said he sought to forge "a new path towards the development of a new civilization. We must strive to establish a universal consensus that respects the equal rights and dignity of every human being." [31]

Like Seyyid Bey, the post-Ottoman Turkish justice minister, Nahdlatul Ulama's proposition challenged the Middle East and North Africa's paradigm of autocratic rule based on an alliance between the state and religious scholars. This alliance has long hindered economic and political development in much of the Muslim world. It created an initial template for a civilisational state built on the caliphate concept. The alliance has since shaped contemporary debate about what Islam stands for.

The alliance witnessed its 20th-century heyday in the 1970s and 1980s when religion played a more significant public role in countries like Egypt and Pakistan, and Iran's revolution handed power to the mullahs. The 1973 Arab oil boycott jacked up oil prices and gave Gulf states the cash to fund global propagation of religious ultra-conservatism. In Saudi Arabia, the clergy's influence was reinforced. Ironically, autocratic alliance proponents, donning the cloak of religious moderation, have much in common with extremists and jihadists. They insist there is only one religious and political truth. They control religious institutions, strive for religious legitimacy to cement their grip on power, and attempt to squash any potential challenge.

---

[30] Multiple conversations with the author, 2017–2023.
[31] Multiple conversations with the author 2015–2023.

Nahdlatul Ulama's proposition introduced a new paradigm designed to force state authorities to cede control of religious knowledge and production, something they have jealously guarded for decades. It would open the door to discussions that challenge theological assumptions underlying a body of law that justifies coercion in the name of Islam. To meet 21st-century requirements and ensure regime survival, conservative Gulf states, revolutionary Iran, and Islamist-led Turkey have updated their existing paradigm. "Today, most Muslim countries are under the influence of ulema-state alliances and rentier economies. The dismantling of these alliances and the restructuring of economies will be important for these countries' ability to achieve democracy and development," said Ahmet Kuru, author of an acclaimed study of the relationship between Muslim rulers and religious scholars.[32]

Kuru traced the alliance's origins to the eleventh century when Muslim clerics lost their economic independence as the Abbasid caliphs in Baghdad unified Sunni orthodoxy to counter Shiite states in northern Syria and Mesopotamia and emerging powerful military states elsewhere in the Muslim world. These states took control of the economy and undermined the merchant class that funded religious scholars and guaranteed their independence. The teachings of Abu Hamid Al-Ghazali, one of Islam's foremost theologians, Abu al-Hasan al-Mawardi, a polymath and legal theoretician, and 13th-century jurist Taqi ad-Dīn Ahmad ibn Taymiyyah, provided them with religious legitimacy.

Al-Ghazali and Al-Mawardi's principle of "commanding right and forbidding wrong" survives until today with the policing of public spaces in Iran and elsewhere in the Muslim world to enforce 'proper' moral behaviour and adherence to rituals. In Saudi Arabia, Bin Salman has defanged but not disbanded the kingdom's religious police. They have largely disappeared from Saudi streets but continue to monitor social media. Known as the Mutaween, the religious police emerge from the playbook in one of Al-Mawardi's most influential works, the Ordinances of Government. Al-Mawardi prescribed volunteer forces that would force men to perform the Friday noon prayer, prevent men and women from speaking to one another in public, ban musical instruments, and ensure that men do not dye their grey hair.[33]

Tenth-century free-thinking philosophers like Al-Farabi, a musicologist, and Ibn Sina, a physician, who made strides in mathematics, physics, and medicine and developed the modern Arabic number system and a forerunner of the camera challenged Al-Ghazali and Al-Mawardi's principles. State-aligned religious scholars, led by Al-Ghazali, labelled them posthumously apostates because they were allegedly influenced by Greek philosophy

---

[32] Ahmet T Kuru. "The Ulema-State Alliance: A Barrier to Democracy and Development in the Muslim World." Tony Blair Institute for Global Change. 2 September 2021. https://institute.global/policy/ulema-state-alliance-barrier-democracy-and-development-muslim-world.

[33] Al-Mawardi. "Ordinances of Government." Reading: Garnet Publishing. 2000.

and Shiite Muslim thought.[34] Al-Ghazali's reasoning remains at the core of modern-day repression of those challenging religious conservatism and/or political authority. "Questioning religious orthodoxy and political authority wasn't merely dissent – it was apostasy," Kuru said.

Taking Kuru's paradigm a step further, political economist Timur Kuran suggested that the state-ulama alliance, particularly in the Middle East, impeded the evolution of a civil society capable of countering, if not preventing, arbitrary governance. "Islamic law casts a dark shadow on social capabilities... Insufficient experience holds back grassroots politics. That legacy is rooted in Islamic institutions. Meanwhile, personal freedoms remain limited because of inabilities, also grounded in legal history, to assert and defend individual rights," Kuran said.[35]

Indonesia never adopted Kuru's paradigm. It has long hosted powerful, independent religious civil society movements with significant political influence. Founded as Turkey abolished the caliphate, movements like Nahdlatul Ulama and Muhammadiyah, Indonesia's second-largest Muslim civil society movement, echoed Seyyid Bey, the Turkish justice minister, and shared much with Ali Fuad Basgil, a 20th-century conservative Turkish legal scholar. Following in Seyyid Bey's footsteps, Basgil insisted Turkey's Directorate for Religious Affairs, known as Diyanet, the government's vehicle for control of the clergy and the global promotion of Turkish religious thought, should be autonomous and financially independent.[36]

Decades later, Mehmet S. Aydin, a liberal theologian, philosophy professor, member of Turkish President Recep Tayyip Erdogan's ruling Justice and Development Party (AKP), and one-time state minister responsible for Diyanet, asserted Turkey could only unleash the intellectual creativity needed to develop a modern Islamic theology if the directorate was independent and enabled free-flowing discourse.[37]

In the early 2000s, Aydin organised consultations to reconceptualise Islamic law. In his first brainstorm, he wanted to reshape thinking about women's role in society based on gender equality.[38] The consultation concluded Sharia

---

[34] Ahmet T. Kuru. "Islam, Authoritarianism, and Underdevelopment." New York: Cambridge University Press. 2019, Kindle edition.

[35] Timur Kuran. "Freedoms Delayed: Political Legacies of Islamic Law in the Middle East." New York: Cambridge University Press. 2023. Kindle edition.

[36] A. F. Basgil. "Din ve laiklik (Religion and Secularism)." Istanbul: Yagmur Yayinevi. 2007. https://kupdf.net/download/ali-fuad-basgil-din-ve-laiklik_58eefd1bdc0d600b4fda981c_pdf.

[37] Günter Seufert. "Religion: Nation-Building Instrument of the State or Factor of Civil Society? The AKP Between State- and Society-Centered Religious Politics." In Hans-Lukas Kieser (ed.), Turkey Beyond Nationalism. Towards Post-Nationalist Identities. London: I.B. Tauris. 2006, Kindle edition.

[38] Raoul Motika, Stefan Reichmuth, Mehmed Nuri Yilmaz, Ali Toksari, Şamil Dağci, Mehmet Aydm and Hamza Aktan. "Current Religious Issues Consultation Meeting—I Final Communiqué: May 18, 2002 Istanbul." Die Welt des Islams. Vol. 44, Issue 2. 2004. pp. 281–289.

precepts that entitle a woman to only half a man's share of an inheritance, attribute less weight to a woman's testimony, and subjugate her to a man's will needed to be understood in their historical context and no longer reflect universal Muslim values.[39] In addition, Aydin's Diyanet commissioned 85 theologians to create a new collection of Prophet Mohammed's doctrinal sayings and deeds that ensured Islam stayed relevant in the twenty-first century.[40]

Indonesia would have served Aydin as a model had the Southeast Asian state been on his radar. It wasn't, signalling obstacles to Indonesia and Nahdlatul Ulama's quest to gain traction for religious reform beyond the 17,000 islands that make up the archipelago state. Geography is one obstacle. Indonesia is located at the far end of the Muslim world. Conservatives perceive it as practising a syncretic form of Islam. Moreover, conservatives were not the only ones rejecting religious institutions' independence. So did diehard secularists, including followers of Ataturk, the founder of modern Turkey, who believed religion should be tightly controlled.

Proponents and opponents of Muslim jurisprudential reform base their positions on centuries of legal debate and long-entrenched opinions. Opponents have dominated the discussion since the eleventh century. They favour limiting Islamic law sources to the Qur'an, hadiths (records of Prophet Muhammad's words and actions), religious scholars' consensus, and analogical reasoning. Rationality and empirical observation are excluded. In other words, interpreting the Qur'an and the hadiths is the prerogative of a self-appointed religious elite, and reality is irrelevant. Inevitably, these scholars produced literal interpretations of the law that served the interests of those in power and/or groups like the Muslim Brotherhood that advocated implementing Islamic law. "Sharia has remained essentially frozen for centuries, unable to respond to the needs of contemporary Muslim societies. Sharia has failed to update to modern conditions due to the limitations of the dominant legal method, which rejects people's participation, rational argumentation, and empirical observation," Kuru said.[41]

By contrast, Nahdlatul Ulama's justification for the development of new jurisprudence that breaks with tradition to accommodate political, social, and economic change is rooted in the notion that Islamic law was designed to

---

[39] Mehmet Bulut (ed.), "Güncel Dini Meseleler İstişare Toplantısı - I (15–18 Mayıs 2002) (Current Religious Issues Consultation Meeting—I (15–18 May 2002)." Ankara: Diyanet Isleri Bakanligi. 2004.

[40] Son Peygamber.info. "Prof. Dr. Mehmet Görmez "Konulu Hadis Projesi"nin İlk Örneklerini Açıkladı (Prof. Dr. Mehmet Görmez Presents the First Results of the 'Hadith-Project'." 31 July 2011. https://www.sonpeygamber.info/prof-dr-mehmet-gormez-kon ulu-hadis-projesi-nin-ilk-orneklerini-acikladi.

[41] Ahmet T. Kuru. "Muslim Politics Between Sharia and Democracy." Muslim Politics Review. Vol. 1, Issue 1. 2022. pp. 23–39. https://journal.uiii.ac.id/index.php/mpr/art icle/view/50/89.

achieve five objectives or maqashid al-shari'a to ensure people's well-being—protection of religion, life, intellect, progeny, and property. The concept was first articulated by Al-Ghazali, the 12th-century theologian who stopped short of suggesting that achieving this could justify legal thinking that contradicts the Qur'an and the Prophet's sayings and deeds. The suggestion that traditional sources of Islamic law, particularly analogical reasoning, no longer adequately addressed Muslims' needs was initially left to Andalusian jurist Abu Ishaq al-Shatibi, who argued three decades later that Al-Ghazali's goals should get more weight in 14th-century Spanish rules and laws.[42]

In its groundbreaking reforms of Islamic law, Nahdlatul Ulama (Awakening of the Ulama, Arabic for religious scholars) invoked Al-Ghazali's and Shatibi's principles. A 2023 Nahdlatul Ulama discussion paper argued that maintaining the notion of infidels would not serve Al-Ghazali's objectives. "These consequences would be directly counter to the purposes of Sharia because they would entail the widespread destruction of religious institutions and places of worship, of human life, of rational behavior, of families and property. If choosing to retain the set of established fiqh (the body of Islamic law) views regarding kuffar (infidels) and normative Muslim conduct in engaging with infidels does not serve the purposes of…maqashid al-sharia, then it is not a legitimate choice from the perspective of Sharia itself," the paper argued.[43]

In contrast to Nahdlatul Ulama, Bin Salman and Bin Zayed employed an updated version of Kuru's paradigm. They subjugated clerics and insisted on absolute obedience. Western officials disregarded Bin Salman and Bin Zayed's autocratic definition of moderate Islam. They acquiesced to lumping together violent and non-violent Islamism because of non-violent Islamists' attitudes towards women and minorities and advocacy of the death penalty for apostasy, blasphemy, and adultery. "The problem is that Emirati and Saudi reformist thinking is stuck at the elite and intellectual level. It doesn't' trickle down," said a European counterterrorism official. Ignoring the illiberal components of Bin Salman and Bin Zayed's version of moderate Islam, the official praised their social reforms.[44]

Bin Salman and Bin Zayed's insistence on the religious principle of absolute obedience is a pillar of their top-down efforts to forge a national identity centred on nationalism rather than religion and tribal allegiance. In Saudi Arabia, this involves replacing the portrayal of the Al Sauds as rulers of an ultra-conservative Islamic utopia. Instead, Bin Salman and Bin Zayed see religion as a policy tool to further their nationalist aspirations and reaffirm their religious credentials. To bolster national identity, the Saudi government declared February 22, 1927, when Muhammad bin Saud, founder of the first

---

[42] Muhammad Khalid Masud. "Shatibi's Philosophy of Islamic Law." New Delhi: Kitab Bhavan. 1998.

[43] "Is There a Need to Establish an Islamic Legal (Fiqhi) Foundation for Global Peace and Harmony?" Nahdlatul Ulama Draft Discussion Paper, 6 February 2023.

[44] Interview with the author, 27 July 2023.

Saudi state, captured the town of Diriyah as the kingdom's 'Founding Day.' Bin Saud first met Mohammed ibn Abd al-Wahhab, the Islamic scholar whose teachings produced Wahhabism, in Diriyah. Founding Day replaced the kingdom's annual commemoration of Bin Saud's power-sharing agreement with Abd al-Wahhab concluded in 1745. The deal shaped Saudi Arabia.

Like the rivalry sparked by Ataturk's elimination of the caliphate a hundred years ago, this century's battle for the soul of Islam is as much a battle for geopolitical and religious soft power as it is a struggle to prevent the collapse or disintegration of norms, values, meanings, and explanations that ground individuals and cement communities in a world in which multiple forces compete to shape a new world order. In many ways, the battle is as much about Islam as it is about religion in an era where the breakdown of the moral order fuels intolerance, xenophobia, scapegoating, migration, and attacks on religious minorities. "Religion, religious language, justification, affiliation, not only serves as an effective boundary between us and the other, but it also promises a clarity and a foundation to restore, return, rebuild on… This is…why religions are intrinsic to violence. You could very well argue that violence lies at the heart of religions, not as something they promote, but as something they have emerged from," said analyst Ziya Meral.[45] Meral studies religion's role in the Arab world since the Ottoman Caliphate's demise.

Mohamed Sid-Ahmed, a left-wing intellectual and activist introduced to communism by Egyptian Jewish militants, recalled Muslim Brothers visiting his family home in 1946 to negotiate a solution to a political crisis with his uncle, Ismail Sidqi, King Farouk's prime minister. The Brotherhood offered to help the government. "The Brotherhood developed supportive slogans a day after the visit. They knew that an Islamic identity would express their anti-imperialism. It would prove more effective than a Marxist analysis of imperialism," Sid-Ahmed recalled in interviews in the 1970s and 1980s. He argued that Gulf oil wealth bolstered the Brotherhood by fuelling the region's religious focus. "It brought with it religious modes of political expression that ran the gamut from fanatic and retrograde forces to enlightened and progressive forces. The masses started to speak the language of religion to express themselves politically, not the language of politics we had inherited from Europe," Sid-Ahmed said.

Nahdlatul Ulama hoped to break that cycle by confronting problematic myths and religious tenets to ensure religion served as a conflict resolution mechanism. Staquf, the movement's leader, sees those myths and precepts as the Ottoman Caliphate's legacy. "While the Ottoman Caliphate collapsed nearly a century ago, its operational assumptions and the classical corpus of Islamic jurisprudence, or fiqh, through which it was governed have remained

---

[45] Ziya Meral. "Religion, Identity, and Politics in the 21st Century." Foreign Policy Research Institute. 30 November 2020. https://www.fpri.org/article/2020/11/religion-identity-and-politics-in-the-21st-century/.

deeply embedded within Muslim societies. As a result, obsolete and problematic elements of classical Islamic law are still taught by most orthodox Sunni and Shiite institutions worldwide. Even when not enshrined in statutory law, these teachings retain considerable religious authority and social legitimacy among Muslims. They enable key state actors, including Iran, Turkey, Saudi Arabia, Qatar, and Pakistan, to weaponize problematic tenets of Islamic orthodoxy in pursuit of their respective geopolitical agendas," Stacuf said.[46]

In November 2022, as Indonesia handed India the rotating chairmanship of the Group of 20 (G20) that brings together the leaders of the world's largest economies, it elevated the battle for the soul of Islam to a struggle for the soul of religion as such. Indonesia sought to put its stamp on the G20 by institutionalising religion as an official engagement track. It created the Religion Forum 20 or R20, an annual summit of religious leaders. The first summit was in Bali on the eve of the Indonesia-chaired G20 meeting of heads of state and government. The passing of the baton to India unleashed a struggle between Muslim and Hindu groups as well as the governments of India, Saudi Arabia, the UAE, and Indonesia to determine the role of religion in global politics and whether religion needed reform. The struggle effectively turned the battle for the soul of Islam into a fight for the soul of religion. Like with Islam, it was about what constitutes religious moderation, the state's role in defining what religion stands for, and whether a change should involve jurisprudential and doctrinal reform aimed at erasing concepts of supremacy and enhancing principles of pluralism and greater freedom.

The Bali R20 set the stage for the struggle. Nahdlatul Ulama benefitted from establishing close ties to major non-Muslim players, including the World Evangelical Alliance, which claims to represent 600 million believers in 143 countries; the Simon Wiesenthal Center; the feuding factions of the Anglican church, the right-wing Centrist Democrat International (CDI), the world's largest alliance of political parties with 109 right-wing member parties in 83 countries; and India's far right-wing, Hindu nationalist Rashtriya Swayamsevak Sangh (RSS), Prime Minister Narendra Modi's ideological cradle. The R20 positioned Nahdlatul Ulama, the world's largest and most moderate Muslim civil society organisation, as a leading force in defining moderate Islam, just like the G20 summit positioned Indonesia as a rising power. With the R20, the Indonesian government sought to ensure the Southeast Asian state had a seat at the table as its 2022 G20 chairmanship moved in 2023 to India, the world's largest Hindu country, and in 2024 to Brazil, the world's most populous Catholic nation. Nahdlatul Ulama hoped the Bali gathering would offer religious reformers an institutional base and spark a movement promoting moderation and religious and political pluralism based on shared civilisational values. That proved easier said than done.

In his opening address at the R20, Stacuf invited religious leaders to openly and honestly discuss "what values our respective traditions need to relinquish,

---

[46] Multiple conversations with the author, 2017–2023.

to ensure that religion functions as a genuine and dynamic source of solutions, rather than problems, in the twenty-first century." He argued that "we need to conduct a thorough review of our religious teachings, and — if we find elements that can endanger coexistence and peace between our communities — then we must have the courage to consider new interpretations that grant us all the possibility of living together in peace."

Staquf's invitation targeted decades of state-sponsored interfaith dialogue that religion scholar Alberto Melloni described as a "useless exercise" destined for failure. "If theologies merely endorse the agendas of those who are most powerful in society…this will ignite rebellion. If religious pluralism is nothing but a facile sermon on fraternity to be kindly preached, it will never become reality," Melloni said.

Nahdlatul Ulama proved to be no pushover for powerful Arab governments. On the back of an estimated 90 million followers, a five million-strong militia, 18,000 religious seminaries, 27 universities, tens of thousands of Muslim scholars that constitute a religious authority independent of traditional centres in the Middle East, and a political party that was part of Indonesian President Joko Widodo's coalition government, Nahdlatul Ulama threw down a gauntlet for proponents of state-controlled, autocratic Islam as well as militant religious nationalists in other faith groups. Like Muhamadiyya, Nahdlatul Ulama has no equivalent mass movement, elsewhere in the Muslim world. Nahdlatul Ulama defines itself as religious and nationalist rather than religious its blend of nationalism and faith is rooted in the movement's DNA and encapsulated in its anthem:

"Oh, fellow citizens!
Love of nation is integral to faith.
And it's not forbidden [in Islam] to defend one's country.
Oh, fellow citizens! Awake and realize (your duty to God and country)
Indonesia is my nation and my homeland.
My sacred inheritance and source of pride
Whoever comes to threaten you shall certainly perish beneath your thorns," the march's lyrics say.[47]

In early 2020, US Secretary of State Mike Pompeo visited Indonesia at the invitation of Nahdlatul Ulama, not the Indonesian government, showing its influence on the global stage. Pope Francis accepted the group's invitation to the archipelago state but postponed his travel because of the COVID-19 pandemic. Similarly Staquf joined Policy Exchange, a London-based think tank with close ties to the Conservative Party's leadership, in 2020 to formulate Britain's Indo-Pacific strategy. Members of the commission included former Canadian Prime Minister Stephen Harper, Parliamentary Private Secretary to

---

[47] Bayt ar-Rahmah. "Nahdlatul Ulama Centennial March." 7 February 2023. https://baytarrahmah.org/2023_02_07_nahdlatul-ulama-centennial-march.

then Chancellor Rishi Sunak, former Australian Foreign Minister Alexander Downer, and former British Defence Minister Michael Fallon.[48]

In sharp contrast to most Muslim-majority states, including Saudi Arabia and the UAE, that have remained silent, if not endorsed, China's brutal crackdown on Turkic Muslims in the northwestern province of Xinjiang, Nahdlatul Ulama offered Pompeo an Asian platform to denounce the People's Republic.

Pompeo landed in Jakarta days after signing the Geneva Consensus Declaration on Promoting Women's Health and Strengthening the Family. Endorsed by 34 countries, including Indonesia, Saudi Arabia, and the UAE, the declaration sought to promote women's rights and health and strengthen the family but emphasised that "in no case should abortion be promoted as a method of family planning." It asserted there is "no international right to abortion, nor any international obligation on the part of States to finance or facilitate abortion." Many of the signatories were members of the Group of Friends of the Family, a block of 25 nations in the United Nations that aims to pre-empt expansion of rights for girls, women, and LGBT people and weaken international support for the Beijing Declaration. This landmark 1995 agreement is an internationally recognised progressive blueprint for women's rights. C-Fam, an influential far-right American group that focuses on abortion, sexual orientation, and gender identity, coordinates the group. C-Fam has worked with the State Department since the George W. Bush administration.

The Centrist Democratic International backed Pompeo's socially conservative agenda and Nahdlatul Ulama's call for religious reform. Muhaimin Iskandar, the Nahdlatul Ulama-affiliated National Awakening Party (PKB) leader, is one of 16 CDI vice presidents. Even so, CDI deals primarily with Nahdlatul Ulama through C. Holland Taylor, Staquf's advisor, rather than the party. The network urged its members "to cooperate in securing recognition of the R20 as a permanent G20 Engagement Group"[49] after India refused to integrate the R20 and Nahdlatul Ulama in preparations for the 2023 G20 Delhi summit.[50]

Indian Prime Minister Narendra Modi opposed the religious gathering, fearing it would attack his government and ruling Bharatiya Janata Party (BJP) over anti-Muslim policies. Modi and the party stand accused of hollowing out Indian democracy, undermining secularism, and fuelling violence against

[48] Policy Exchange. "Policy Exchange Announces New Indo-Pacific Commission." Bayt-ar-Rahmah. 20 July 2020. https://www.baytarrahmah.org/media/2020/Policy-Exchange_Policy-Exchange-announces-new-Indo-Pacific-Commission_07-20-20.pdf.

[49] IDC-CDI. "Resolution on Infusing the World's Geopolitical and Economic Power Structures with Universal Ethics and Humanitarian Values Through the G20 Religion Forum (R20), in Keeping with the Vision and Traditions of IDC-CDI." Bayt-ar-Rahmah. 18 May 2023. https://www.baytarrahmah.org/media/2023/CDI_Resolution-on-G20-Religion-Forum-(R20).pdf.

[50] James M. Dorsey. "US Secretary of State Pompeo Set to Boost Indonesian Religious Reform Efforts." The Turbulent World with James M. Dorsey. 25 October 2020. https://www.jamesmdorsey.net/post/us-secretary-of-state-pompeo-set-to-boost-indonesian-religious-reform-efforts.

India's 200 million Muslims, the world's largest Muslim minority. Modi was also concerned that opting for the R20 would put him at odds with Saudi Arabia and the UAE, who promoted government-aligned Nahdlatul Ulama competitors like the Muslim World League and the G20 Interfaith Forum Association. The Forum, the G20's unofficial religious interlocutor, was sidelined during Indonesia's presidency, but has since made a comeback thanks to UAE support. As a result, the rivalry shaping the G20's religious engagement temporarily shifted the focus of the battle for Islam from Islamic centres such as Mecca, Medina, and Jakarta to Hindu nationalist Delhi. The BJP and the RSS, Modi's Hindu nationalist ideological cradle, resembled a maiden courted by competing Muslim suitors.

Even so, thinking in Delhi aligned more with Riyadh and Abu Dhabi than Jakarta. Barely back from the Bali summit, Ram Madhav, an RSS national executive member, and close Modi associate, who was the point man for Hindu nationalist interaction with Nahdlatul Ulama, fired the first salvo in the post-Bali interfaith power struggle. Madhav maintained that India would decide whether to recognise the Nahdlatul Ulama-controlled R20 as an official G20 engagement group. Putting a different spin on the Indonesian initiative, he insisted that the Forum was intended to address "global issues… The focus of this…religious forum was and will not be religions alone… It will be not religion-centric but humanity-centric. So, an effort to bring religions together on larger issues."[51]

Madhav's redefinition of the R20 fit a pattern. In an essay published ten months earlier in Open,[52] an Indian current affairs weekly, and an interview,[53] Madhav called on Indian Muslims to embrace Nahdlatul Ulama's concept of Islam. "Eastern civilizations (and) Eastern religions all share the same civilizational value system, including an Islam with an Eastern value system like Indonesian Islam," Madhav said. He asserted the embrace would counter the Indian Muslim leadership's alleged adherence to Wahhabism, the puritan interpretation of Islam long dominant in Saudi Arabia. Violent elements, whether "Muslim or Hindu, do not and should not represent our respective mainstream communities," Madhav said. He claimed RSS had distanced itself from "violent language and talk of annihilation of an entire community." Madhav described such language as "un-Hindu." He added that Hinduism was "very inclusive and very open. No ideological or philosophical movement that proclaims exclusivity exists in Hinduism."

As Madhav wrote and spoke, riots erupted in the Delhi working-class neighbourhood of Jahangirpuri when participants in a Hindu procession brandished

---

[51] News X. "RSS Leader Ram Madhav on Religion as a Part of Solution. Cover Story with Priyal Sahgal." YouTube. 13 November 2022. https://www.youtube.com/watch?v=PxagsTVY1bY.

[52] Ram Madhav. "Indian Muslims Need to Emulate the Indonesian Model." Open. 18 February 2022. https://openthemagazine.com/cover-stories/indian-muslims-need-to-emulate-the-indonesian-model/.

[53] Interview with the author, 9 May 2022.

weapons and chanted anti-Muslim slogans as they passed through predominantly Muslim areas. "There was chaos," said Sudarshan Prasad, a 71-year-old Hindu. "I've always lived here in peace. This has not happened in the last 40 years."[54] Days later, authorities imposed a curfew and cut off Internet connections in Jodhpur, the capital of Rajasthan, following altercations between Hindus and Muslims.[55] The crackdown occurred as Muslims celebrated Eid al Fitr, a holiday at the end of Ramadan, and Hindus commemorated the festival of Parshuram Jayanti. At about the same time, tension rose in Maharashtra, home to India's financial capital, Mumbai, after Hindu leaders demanded that Muslims remove loudspeakers from their mosques because the call to prayer created noise pollution.

Madhav first met senior Nahdlatul Ulama leaders on the sidelines of an executive committee meeting of Centrist Democratic International in early 2020 in the Javan city of Yogyakarta hosted by Nahdlatul Ulama's political party. Madhav attended the meeting as an observer. Despite the recurring inter-communal violence, Nahdlatul Ulama officials welcomed Madhav's endorsement of Humanitarian Islam "as an opportunity to place humanitarianism at the heart of interaction between different faith groups — regardless of religion and across different sectors of society, ranging from mass organizations to governments — in order to promote peaceful coexistence and enshrine equal rights before the law."

In concert with Saudi and Emirati intentions, Madhav's redefinition of the R20's purpose avoided exploring explosive issues and troublesome questions posed by Nahdlatul Ulama. Like Madhav, Indian journalist, politician, and Modi associate Sri Swapan Dasgupta sought to spin Nahdlatul Ulama's thrust by seemingly embracing the movement's approach. He acknowledged that "obfuscation and denial (of traumatic historical events) has only worsened the situation." Dasgupta, steeped in Hindutva ideology first coherently articulated a century ago by politician and writer Vinayak Damodar Savarkar, was referring to Hindu nationalist grievances dating back to the Muslim conquests in the Indian subcontinent in the 13th to seventeenth centuries that fuelled Hindutva ideology. Describing Muslims as Mohammedans, Savarkar saw them as foreign implants and potential traitors hostile to Hindus.[56] What Dasgupta did not say was that Hindu nationalist India needed to come to grips with

---

[54] Jyotsna Singh and Benjamin Parkin. "'Politics Has Been Turned on Its Head': India Reels from Wave of Religious Violence." Financial Times. 29 April 2022. https://www.ft.com/content/cb195e8b-8a7f-4a2d-ba6e-7d4654973ede.

[55] Al Jazeera. "India: Curfew Imposed in Jodhpur following Hindu-Muslim Clashes." 3 May 2022. https://www.aljazeera.com/news/2022/5/3/india-curfew-imposed-in-jodhpur-following-hindu-muslim-clashes.

[56] V. D. Savarkar. "Essentials of Hindutva." Savarkar.org. 23 May 2017. https://savarkar.org/en/encyc/2017/5/23/2_12_12_04_essentials_of_hindutva.v001.pdf_1.pdf.

the subcontinent's history in ways that did not boil down to a campaign of revenge against Indian Muslims.[57]

Madhav and Dasgupta's spin suggested that several years of dialogue, which Nahdlatul Ulama hoped would nudge them towards a Hindu equivalent of its Humanitarian Islam, had come to naught. If anything, Nahdlatul Ulama's follow-up to the R20 magnified the need for groups like the RSS and Muslim proponents of autocracy to control the G20's religious tack and sideline, if not co-opt, the Indonesian movement. To flesh out its religious reform skeleton, the R20 secretariat established working groups to formulate detailed responses to the Bali summit questions. The working groups were tasked with addressing historical grievances, truth-telling, reconciliation, and forgiveness; the recontextualisation of obsolete and problematic tenets of religious orthodoxy; and new 21st-century values.[58]

For UAE President Mohammed bin Zayed, the Bali R20 and the Muslim World League's prominent role constituted a wake-up call. Having gone to great lengths to position the UAE as the beacon of moderate Islam by loosening social norms at home, welcoming Jews, and recognising Israel, Bin Zayed moved swiftly to ensure he would not be left out in the competition for Indian favour. Within weeks of the R20, Bin Zayed's representatives teamed up with W. Cole Durham, a law professor at Brigham and Young University and head of the Mormon-led Interfaith Forum , to ensure the UAE's voice would be heard. Left out in the cold by the R20, IF20 found a sponsor with financial muscle and convening power in the UAE.

Weeks after the R20, the IF20, under Bin Zayed's sponsorship, banded together with the Interfaith Alliance for Safer Communities, an obscure UAE-based group, to gather Muslim, Jewish, Christian, Hindu, and Buddhist figures in Abu Dhabi for a conference entitled "Engaging Faith Communities: G20 Agendas and Beyond." The conference aimed to take the wind out of Nahdlatul Ulama's sails and position the UAE as an autocratic player alongside the Muslim World League.

Nahdlatul Ulama and Saudi scholars were conspicuously absent. More surprisingly, organisations created by the UAE to promote its autocratic notion of moderate Islam, such as the Forum for Promoting Peace in Muslim Societies led by Abdallah bin Bayyah, a Mauritanian Islamic scholar, and Hamza Yusuf, one of the most prominent Western Muslim figures, remained in the background. They were also missing from follow-up conferences in India, organised by the Interfaith Alliance.

The IF20 hewed closely to Madhav's agenda. In contrast to Nahdlatul Ulama's R20 focus on shared religious and civilisational values, historical

---

[57] Bayt ar-Rahmah. "G20 Religion Forum (R20) Plenary Session 3: Historical Grievances, Truth-Telling, Reconciliation, and Forgiveness." 2 November 2022. https://baytarrahmah.org/2022_11_02_r20-plenary-session-3/.

[58] Bayt ar-Rahmah. "2023_01_19_Launch of the R20 Website." 19 January 2023. https://baytarrahmah.org/2023_01_19_launch-of-the-r20-website/.

grievances, truth-telling, reconciliation, and forgiveness, IF20's Abu Dhabi agenda reflected Western nations and Middle Eastern autocracies' priorities. These included interfaith dialogue, tolerance, conflict resolution, freedom of religion, refugees, the food crisis, human trafficking, health care, and social protection.[59] As a result, Madhav and the Indian government supported a religious gathering in the southern Indian city of Pune, 1,200 kilometres south of Delhi, on the eve of the Group of 20 summit in the Indian capital, organised by IF 20 rather than Nahdlatul Ulama's Religion Forum 20.

Not to be left behind, Muslim World League Secretary-General Mohammed al-Issa echoed Madhav on a five-day visit to India, where he was celebrated as an icon of moderate Islam. Indian officials rolled out the red carpet. Al-Issa met the country's top leaders, including Modi, President Draupadi Murmu, minority affairs minister Smriti Irani, external affairs minister S. Jaishankar, national security advisor Ajit Doval, and prominent Hindu, Buddhist, and Muslim figures. In Madhav's mould, Al-Issa said he discussed with Modi "ways to further human-centric development and the importance of promoting understanding and harmony among the followers of faith and culture." Echoing Saudi endorsement of China's crackdown on Turkic Uyghur Muslims in the northwestern province of Xinjiang, the cleric sought to shield Modi from criticism of his handling of anti-Muslim sentiment by praising the prime minister's "passionate perspective towards inclusive growth" and describing India as "an inspiration to the rest of the world for being open to dialogue."[60]

India's embrace of Al-Issa and refusal to carry the R20 forward as a G20 engagement group called into question the effectiveness of Nahdlatul Ulama's interactions with rivals like the Muslim World League and organisations such as the RSS, even though the latter facilitated its access to Hindu religious leaders. In both cases, Nahdlatul Ulama failed to advance its cause. Nahdlatul Ulama invited the League to co-host the Bali summit after Saudi Arabia asked the Indonesian government to give the group a prominent place at the conference. The Indonesian movement hoped the cooperation would persuade the League to break ties with Indonesia's Muslim Brotherhood-inspired Prosperous Justice Party (PKS). Instead, Al-Issa used the League's co-hosting to brandish its credentials. Nahdlatul Ulama helped him by recognising the League as a 'non-governmental organisation,' even though it is government-controlled and funded. Its staff, including Al-Issa, are public servants.

Nahdlatul Ulama's gesture didn't prevent Al-Issa from taking full credit for the R20 and writing the Indonesian movement out of the story. "Leaders

---

[59] IF20. "The UAE G20 Interfaith Forum on Engaging Faith Communities: G20 Agendas and Beyond." 13 December 2022. https://www.g20interfaith.org/press-release-uae-g20-agendas-and-beyond/.

[60] Sravasti Dasgupta and Faiyaz Ahmad Wajeeh. "India Hosts Muslim World League Chief Al Issa: Outreach or Image Building PR Exercise?" The Wire. 24 July 2023. https://thewire.in/diplomacy/india-hosts-mwl-chief-outreach-or-pr.

participating in the #R20Summit express their appreciation of the great efforts and quality work of the Muslim World League, under the leadership of His Excellency the Secretary General, Sheikh Dr. @MhmdAlissa, the founder of R20, whose efforts contributed to its success," the League said in a tweet immediately after the Bali conference.[61] For Al-Issa, dealing with R20 and Nahdlatul Ulama boiled down to public relations. Like claiming R20 ownership, Al-Issa declared early on that moderate Islam was an issue of using appropriate language rather than reform. "All religious institutions must modernise their speech to be compatible with the times," Al-Issa said.[62]

Bin Zayed had more arrows in his quiver than Saudi Arabia. The UAE president recognised Indonesia as a potential religious soft power rival and a lucrative investment target several years before the Bali R20. He befriended President Joko Widodo during the Indonesian leader's 2015 Middle East tour. Strolling five years later through the tropical gardens next to Indonesia's summer Presidential Palace, Bin Zayed offered to build a US$20 million replica of Abu Dhabi's Sheikh Zayed Mosque, named after the founder of the UAE, in Widodo's hometown of Solo. Bin Zayed wasted no time. Emirati officials travelled to Solo a day later to find mosque sites. At the same time, Bin Zayed built the President Joko Widodo Mosque in Abu Dhabi on a street renamed after the Indonesian leader. The Bin Zayed mosque, Indonesia's largest, set the stage for Emirati investment in Widodo's ambitious US$400 billion infrastructure program, the world's largest floating photovoltaic solar power plant, and the expansion of the UAE's presence in fast-growing Asian markets.

Crowning the UAE's economic engagement as the largest Gulf investor in the archipelago state, Bin Zayed agreed to chair a committee overseeing the construction of a new Indonesian capital at an estimated cost of $34 billion. Jokowi envisioned the new capital as a city of seven million people on Borneo Island, a region rich in coal and gas some 1,200 kilometres from the current overcrowded government seat in Jakarta.

Bin Zayed's committee included SoftBank Chief Executive Officer Masayoshi Son and former British Prime Minister Tony Blair. Bin Zayed brought more than money to the table. The UAE's rapid development of Dubai and Abu Dhabi as cutting-edge 21st-century cities is a model for others. In addition, real estate developer Emaar Properties gained valuable urban planning experience by drafting the master plan for Saudi Arabia's King Abdullah Economic City.

---

[61] Muslim World League. Twitter. 22 November 2022. https://twitter.com/MWLOrg_en/status/1589992749171818496.

[62] Benjamin Barthe. "Au sein du clergé wahhabite, la montée d'une jeune garde, plus moderne et docile (The Rise of a Young Guard in the Wahhabi Clergy, More Modern and Docile)." Le Monde. 9 June 2017. https://www.lemonde.fr/proche-orient/article/2017/06/09/au-sein-du-clerge-wahhabite-la-montee-d-une-jeune-garde-plus-moderne-et-docile_5141260_3218.html.

In 2020, Indonesia and the UAE signed a memorandum of understanding to "promote concepts of religious moderation, values of tolerance and raise public awareness of the risks of extremism."[63] A year later, on a visit to Abu Dhabi, Widodo threw Bin Zayed a bone by saying he wanted to explore religious cooperation "because we both share the closeness in the vision and characters of moderate Islam that propagate tolerance."[64] Despite carefully crafted statements and stage-managed events, Widodo ensured that the UAE did not enhance its religious influence in the archipelago state or drive a wedge between the president and Nahdlatul Ulama. Widodo cemented his relationship with Nahdlatul Ulama months after the garden stroll when he appointed a senior leader of the movement and brother of the group's chairman as religious affairs minister.

Widodo did not spell out what cooperation with the UAE would entail, but Indonesian officials pointed to sharing expertise in Qur'an memorisation, translation, and publishing; promoting discussions among scholars, politicians, and academics on ways to strengthen religious moderation; and cooperating on the development of digital education programs for madrassas or religious seminaries.[65] So far, the cooperation has involved little more than 50 Indonesian imams preaching in Emirati mosques[66] and the inclusion of prominent Indonesian scholars on advisory boards of Emirati religious institutions. In addition, Widodo facilitated US$100 million in Emirati funding for a newly established Mohammed bin Zayed Center for Future Studies at Nahdlatul Ulama's Yogyakarta University.

A UAE foreign ministry official noted that Widodo and Bin Zayed had much in common. Both opposed political Islam, shared concepts of religious tolerance and interfaith understanding, represented Sufi Muslim traditions, rejected religious ultra-conservatism, and believed that tough measures were needed to combat radicalism and terrorism.[67] The suggestion of a common approach overlooked differences between Widodo and Bin Zayed's philosophy and policy. As president, Widodo banned two hardline Islamist groups

---

[63] Dream.co.id. "Indonesia dan UAE Teken MoU Cegah Radikalisme (Indonesia and UAE Sign MoU to Prevent Radikalism)." 13 January 2020. https://www.dream.co.id/stories/indonesia-dan-uae-jalin-kerja-sama-moderasi-agama-dan-wakaf-200113z.html#.

[64] WAM. "Indonesia, UAE 'Like Brothers,' Can Work Together to Promote Moderate Islam: Joko Widodo." Khaleej Times. 5 November 2021. https://www.khaleejtimes.com/government/indonesia-uae-like-brothers-can-work-together-to-promote-moderate-islam-joko-widodo.

[65] James M. Dorsey. "How Much Is Religious Soft Power Worth? Indonesian President Jokowi Searches for Answers in Abu Dhabi." The Turbulent World with James M. Dorsey. 6 November 2021. https://www.jamesmdorsey.net/post/how-much-is-religious-soft-power-worth-indonesian-president-jokowi-searches-for-answers-in-abu-dhab.

[66] Embassy of the republic of Indonesia in Abu Dhabi. "15 Imam Asal Indonesia Siap Bertugas di Persatuan Emirat Arab (15 Imams from Indonesia Ready to Serve in the United Arab Emirates)." 31 October 2021. https://kemlu.go.id/abudhabi/id/news/17288/15-imam-asal-indonesia-siap-bertugas-di-persatuan-emirat-arab.

[67] Interview with the author, 1 November 2021.

but did not outlaw a Muslim Brotherhood-affiliated political party that commands seven to eight percent of the vote. Moreover, Widodo has repeatedly supported Nahdlatul Ulama's religious reform agenda. Bin Zayed, like Bin Salman and other Middle Eastern autocrats, denies that Islamic jurisprudence is problematic and needs recontextualisation. Instead of reforming Wahhabi doctrine and teachings, Bin Salman has sought to repurpose religion to serve his interests.

So far, the battle for Islam's soul has failed to spark Muslim polarising culture wars like the struggles fought in the United States, Israel, and India. Repression of freedom of expression, subjugation of the clergy, and criminalisation of blasphemy and apostasy make publicly fought culture wars in the Arab world virtually impossible, even if polls suggest greater public religiosity, piety, and renewed support for political Islam.[68] "In most countries surveyed, young and old citizens demonstrate a clear preference for giving religion a greater role in politics. While youth ages 18–29 have led the return to religion across MENA (the Middle East and North Africa), the rise in support for religion in politics is more widespread across society. In most countries, both older and younger members of society are shifting their views in concert," said Michael Robbins, director and co-principal investigator of Arab Barometer.[69] The group regularly surveys public opinion in the Middle East. Muslim democracies at the other end of the Islamic world witnessed similar shifts. Anwar Ibrahim, an Islamist politician, capped a dramatic political career by becoming Malaysia's prime minister in 2022 after three failed attempts and time spent in prison on sodomy charges many believed were trumped up. In Indonesia, politicians with close ties to religious conservatives, including the Muslim Brotherhood, gained popularity in 2023 as the country geared up for presidential and parliamentary elections in 2024.

Over two decades after the fateful Brzezinski Warren trip to Pakistan, Saudi Arabia, and Egypt, war gamers entered uncharted territory as they gathered in 2003 at the National Defense University in Washington for their first-ever strategic communications exercise. The exercise anticipated the battle for hearts and minds in the Muslim world. It's a battle that the United States seems incapable of winning even if the initial war games were designed to flip the coin so that Osama bin Laden would no longer emerge in opinion polls in the Muslim world two years after 9/11 and months after the US-led invasion of Iraq as a more trusted figure than then-President George W. Bush.

Attended by White House crisis managers, State Department officials, and Pentagon specialists in psychological operations, the exercise involved a scenario in which anti-American protests, hailing jihadists as heroes, swept the Muslim world, and pro-democracy students were killed. US government

---

[68] James M. Dorsey. "Arab Youth Seek Certainty in Religion and Tradition." The Turbulent World with James M. Dorsey. 13 August 2023. https://www.jamesmdorsey.net/post/arab-youth-seek-certainty-in-religion-and-tradition.

[69] Interview with the author, 6 June 2023.

information warriors were tasked with countering anti-American narratives, improving America's image, and helping foster democracy in Iraq as a model for the Arab and Muslim world. Participants in the exercise gave up halfway. The imaginary scenario was so dysfunctional and convoluted that it made no sense to play it out to the end.[70]

Two decades later, things are no less dysfunctional and convoluted. They may be even more complex. The 2003 exercise marked the early days of a psychological warfare campaign comparable in scope and size to America's information war with the Soviet Union. The campaign sought to shape Islam's future. While the CIA prepared to play its part in attempting to reshape Islam, the State Department spearheaded the development of a national strategic communications and public diplomacy strategy published in 2007.[71] The administration initially tasked a newly appointed deputy national security adviser for strategic communication and global outreach to coordinate US public diplomacy, particularly regarding Islam.

The administration ploughed hundreds of millions of dollars, if not billions, into the campaign. It funded public broadcasters focused on the Muslim world, Islamic radio and TV shows, coursework in Muslim schools, Muslim think tanks, political workshops, and other initiatives that promoted 'moderate' Islam in more than 20 countries. US aid helped restore historic mosques in Egypt, Pakistan, and Turkmenistan and a major Sufi shrine in Kyrgyzstan; saved ancient Qur'ans and ancient Islamic texts, some dating to the eleventh century; and built Islamic schools. Programming of broadcasters such as Alhurra TV, a satellite-TV news network targeting an Arab audience, Radio Sawa, a pop music and news station, and Iran-focused Radio Farda aimed to "broaden and deepen overall coverage of Islam and foster interfaith dialogue, including discussion of Islam and modernity and Islam and democracy."[72]

The public diplomacy strategy encouraged US officials to "participate in events that resonate with local populations, including visits to important religious and cultural sites and hosting events such as Iftar dinners (that break the fast during Ramadan) to demonstrate respect for different faiths. Special efforts should be made by USG officials to highlight mainstream Muslim voices that condemn extremist violence." The strategy advised officials to speak about 'mainstream' or 'majority' rather than 'moderate' Muslim voices. "Moderate…is a political word which, when extended to the world of faith, can imply these individuals are less than devout and faithful," the paper cautioned.

---

[70] David E. Kaplan. "Hearts, Minds, and Dollars." Global Issues. 25 April 2005. https://www.globalissues.org/article/584/hearts-minds-and-dollars.

[71] Strategic Communication and Public Diplomacy Policy Coordinating Committee, U.S. National Strategy for Public Diplomacy and Strategic Communication, US Department of State, June 2007. https://2001-2009.state.gov/documents/organization/87427.pdf.

[72] Ibid. Strategic Communication and Public Diplomacy Policy Coordinating Committee.

The US National Strategy for Combating Terrorism published in 2003, which gave birth to a plan for Muslim World Outreach that President Bush approved, informed the CIA's strategy and operations.[73] It built on the administration's 2002 national security strategy that positioned the Muslim world as caught up in "struggle of ideas" and a "clash inside a civilisation."[74] The counterterrorism plan asserted that the United States had a national security interest in what happens in the Muslim world and within Islam itself. The strategy called for partnering with allied Muslim states, private foundations, and non-profit groups that shared common values like democracy, women's rights, and tolerance.

The strategy and outreach were doomed to failure. Rather than sparking a reformation, they fuelled anti-American sentiment as the United States invaded Iraq, incarcerated suspected militants in Guantanamo Bay without due process, and employed divisive and inflammatory language in its War on Terrorism, widely perceived by Muslims as a War on Islam. Moreover, the Bush administration's strategy and outreach misread religion's place in the Muslim world. Unlike communism, religion is carved into the Muslim world's DNA in ways secular ideologies can only dream of.

To be fair, President Barack Obama shied away from his predecessor's confrontational approach, instead emphasising engagement and promotion of notions of tolerance, pluralism, and minority rights. Yet, like Bush, Obama missed the mark, by failing to pay sufficient attention to issues foremost on Muslim minds like Guantanamo and a resolution of the Israeli-Palestinian conflict that has haunted the United States with the 2023 Gaza war. Even so, Donald J. Trump's clash-of-civilisations worldview rolled back whatever goodwill Obama generated in his effort to repair the damage caused by America's wars.

Nonetheless, if there is a silver lining in this, it is the United States' fuelling of the battle for Islam's soul.

---

[73] US General Accounting Office. "Combating Terrorism: Observations on National Strategies Related to Terrorism." 3 March 2003. https://www.gao.gov/assets/a109686.html#:~:text=National%20Strategy%20for%20Combating%20Terrorism%3B%20Issued%20by%20the%20President%2C%20February,strengthen%20security%20at%20home%20and.

[74] The White House. "The National Security Strategy of the United States of America." September 2002. https://georgewbush-whitehouse.archives.gov/nsc/nss/2002/.

CHAPTER 2

Islam's New Kid on the Block

Nahdlatul Ulama went on alert in 2007 when some 100,000 people packed Jakarta's Bung Karno Stadium to attend an International Caliphate Conference organised by Hizb ut-Tahrir or the Party of Liberation, the Indonesian chapter of a global movement founded in 1953 that calls for the peaceful creation of a unitary Muslim state. Participants, often women and children, came from across Indonesia. They waved black flags as they listened to celebrity preachers. "After the destruction of the Caliphate, tragedy after tragedy has descended on the Muslim world. Our (Muslim) nation has been divided into 50 (states), and the infidel colonialists picked rulers in each of these countries," Hizb ut-Tahrir Muhammad Ismail Yusanto bellowed. Islam's golden age when Islam, Christianity, and Judaism coexisted peacefully in Andalusia was evidence that non-Muslims had nothing to fear from a resurrection of the Caliphate, Yusanto asserted.[1]

The conference did not revive a transnational caliphate to replace the autocratic, illiberal, corrupt, and/or failing nation-states that populate the Muslim world. On the contrary, it sparked developments that challenged Hizb ut-Tahrir's aspiration, leading to its banning in Indonesia in 2017. The ban came on the heels of various Arab and Central Asian countries outlawing the group. With the Jakarta gathering, Hizb ut-Tahrir threw down a gauntlet for Nahdlatul Ulama. Banners at a series of subsequent rallies in Java, Nahdlatul Ulama's heartland, proclaimed that Nahdlatul Ulama members

---

[1] Nava Nava. "Divided Muslims: Militant Pluralism, Polarization and Democratic Backsliding." In Thomas Power and Eva Warburton (eds.) Democracy in Indonesia: From Stagnation to Regression? Singapore: ISEAS-Yusof Ishak Institute. pp. 81–100.

longed to restore the caliphate.[2] A showdown became inevitable as Hizb ut-Tahrir made inroads into Nahdlatul Ulama territory by taking mosques and distributing literature. Haysim Muzad, Nahdlatul Ulama's chairman at the time, warned that "transnational Islamic ideologies" threatened Indonesian unity and Pancasila, the country's foundational ideology that propagates monotheism, civility, fairness, democracy, and social justice.

A year later, black-clad, club-wielding militants of the Islamic Defenders Front (FPI), a hardline Muslim group supported by elements in the military and prominent political figures, attacked a rally of the 57-member National Alliance for the Freedom of Faith and Religion (AKKBB) at Jakarta's National Monument, a 132-metre-high obelisk celebrating Indonesia's struggle for independence. Prominent members of Nahdlatul Ulama and the National Awakening Party (PKB), the political party associated with the movement, were among 34 people injured in the attack.[3]

The incident occurred amidst mounting attacks on Indonesia's minuscule Ahmadi minority. Muslims widely denounce Ahmadis as heretics for believing that Mirza Gulam Ahmad, the sect's 19th-century founder, was a prophet. Mainstream Islam sees Prophet Mohammed as the last prophet and condemns as blasphemy any effort to recognise subsequent prophets. Despite numbering only 400,000 adherents in the archipelago, a negligible percentage of Indonesia's 270 million population, Ahmadis emerged as a flashpoint in clashes between Muslim moderates and conservatives. Militants attacked the group as the government of President Sunilo Bambang Yudhonyo, which included ministers representing the Muslim Brotherhood-inspired Prosperous Justice Party (PKS), prepared a mandate to restrict Ahmadi proselytisation but stopped short of banning the group or declaring it non-Muslim.

The mandate, the attacks, and the confrontation with Nahdlatul Ulama, a century-old reformist movement founded in 1926 as an anti-dote to Saudi Arabia's one-time, austere, ultra-conservative version of Islam and to fill the vacuum in Muslim leadership created by the abolishment in 1924 of the Ottoman Caliphate, were at the heart of a perennial battle to define Indonesia and Islam. The 1998 fall of the Suharto dictatorship rekindled the debate. It gave conservatives, who dominated the Indonesian Ulama Council's Sharia committee space to assert themselves. Suharto founded the Council in 1975 as a quasi-independent clerical institution. The Council denounced secularism, 'liberal Islam,' 'deviant' Islamic groups, and pluralism as incompatible with Islam. It condemned interfaith marriage and empowered 'anti-vice' militias to impose their moral code in ways not always checked by the government. The

---

[2] Liputanislam.com. "HTI Catut NU Logo (HTI Deleted NU Logo)." 21 February 2014. https://liputanislam.com/tabayun/hti-catut-logo-nu/.

[3] Fatima Astuti. "Fallout from Jakarta's Monas Incident: What Is to Be Done with Fringe Groups?" RSIS Commentary. 11 June 2008. https://www.rsis.edu.sg/rsis-publication/rsis/1084-fallout-from-jakartas-monas/.

2014 election of Joko Widodo as president on the back of pledges of moderation, pluralism, and support for Nahdlatul Ulama sharpened the debate. On the flipside of his crackdown on proponents of a Sharia-based state, like Hizb ut-Tahrir and the Islamic Defenders Front, Widodo restricted institutional religious freedoms, including the right to build houses of worship and freedom of expression.[4] Widodo banned the Front in 2020.

The confrontation with Hizb ut-Tahrir reinforced Nahdlatul Ulama's reformatory zeal written into the movement's DNA. Nahdlatul Ulama leaders believed the time was ripe for Indonesia to harness its unique culture and history to spark theological, legal, political, intellectual, and moral change that would fuse Muslim traditions with modern notions of freedom, democracy, human rights, and gender equality. The paradigm shift would secure Indonesia's place in a new, multilateral 21st-century world order. "Indonesia is capable of leveraging its remarkable depth of human capital in the fields of culture and religion to attain a high degree of geopolitical influence," said A. Mostafa Bisri, one of the movement's most respected religious scholars and an acclaimed poet and painter, and C. Holland Taylor, a former American telecommunication executive, convert to Islam, and the movement's international affairs advisor.[5] Bisri and Taylor noted that the 16th-century Muslim founders of the second Mataram dynasty introduced freedom of conscience two centuries before the Virginia Statute for Religious Freedom and the Bill of Rights separated church and state in the United States. Nahdlatul Ulama's push for a pluralistic interpretation of Islam largely resonated with the introduction of concepts of 'moderate' Islam into Indonesia foreign policy[6] in the wake of 9/11 and the 2002 Bali bombings that targeted tourists and killed 202 people. Al-Qaeda-linked Jemaah Islamiyah claimed responsibility for the attacks.[7]

Not lacking ambition, Nahdlatul Ulama believed it could leverage Indonesia's moral capital to build a global coalition that would unite the 'humanitarian left' and 'national security-oriented right' and forge a societal consensus capable of discrediting Islamist extremism and countering Islamophobia. To do so, the group created in 2021 the Jakarta-based Centre for Shared Civilisational Values (CSCV) tasked with founding a global grassroots movement. That was easier said than done. Nahdlatul Ulama scored its greatest success by

---

[4] Thomas Seal, Zawawi Ibrahim, Pradana Boy Zulian and Imran Mohd Rasid. "South and Southeast Asia: Deep Diversity Under Strain." Religion, State and Society. Vol. 50, Issue 4. November 2022. pp. 452–468.

[5] A. Mostafa Bisri and C. Holland Taylor. "Indonesia's 'Big Idea': Resolving the Bitter Global Debate on Islam." Strategic Review. Vol. 2, Issue 3, July to September 2012. Strategic-Review_Indonesia-s_Big_Idea.pdf (iiqs.org).

[6] Ahmad Rizky Mardhatillah Umar. "A Genealogy of Moderate Islam: Governmentality and Discourses of Islam in Indonesia's Foreign Policy." Studia Islamika. Vol. 23, Issue 3. 2016. pp. 399–434.

[7] BBC News. "Bali Death Toll Set at 202." 19 February 2003. http://news.bbc.co.uk/2/hi/asia-pacific/2778923.stm.

garnering the support of Centrist Democrat International (CDI), the world's largest network of conservative political parties that run the gamut from centre to far right. While it has yet to forge ties to influential centre-left groups, its relations with right-wing organisations, such as the Muslim World League, a Saudi entity controlled by Crown Prince Mohammed bin Salman, religious groupings that answer to Emirati strongman Mohammed bin Zayed, and India's Hindu nationalist Rashtriya Swayamsevak Sangh (RSS), Prime Minister Narendra Modi's ideological cradle, proved difficult and often contentious.

Nahdlatul Ulama's ambition was not tempered by the fact that the movement acknowledged that to realise its potential, Indonesia needed to clean its own house. "It is a sad commentary on Indonesia's state of moral and cultural decay – and a damning indictment of its leadership - that our population at large should retain a greater appreciation of and commitment to the values and traditions of their ancestors than do many of our governing elites… As a consequence, a nation once renowned for religious pluralism and tolerance is now better known for savage attacks upon its Christian, Ahmadiyya, and Shiite minorities, while government officials stand idly by or even persecute the victims of such attacks," Bisri and Taylor said in their 2012 essay.

Critics charged that little had changed in the decade since, despite Nahdlatul Ulama's alliance with President Widodo. Journalist Haeril Halim noted that a decade of submissions to the United Nations Human Rights Commission showed lagging Indonesian compliance with the International Covenant on Civil and Political Rights (ICCPR). The submissions documented hundreds of violations of religious freedom and attacks on minorities. Government and law enforcement officials often blame attacks on minorities, whom they view as deviants rather than victims, and accuse them of blasphemy.[8] Moreover, Indonesia's Constitutional Court in 2023 upheld a nearly five-decade-old ban on interfaith marriages.[9]

Debates in the early 2010s within Nahdlatul Ulama produced the group's concept of Humanitarian Islam, an adaptation to the modernity of what Abdurrahman Wahid, the movement's former leader and a former Indonesian president, perceived as "the pristine beauty and truth of Islam's original message, as revealed by the Quran and the life of the Prophet Muhammad." In contrast to purportedly moderate but autocratic interpretations of the faith, Humanitarian Islam unambiguously embraced the Universal Declaration of Human Rights and propagated religious and political pluralism.

For Nahdlatul Ulama chairman Yahya Cholil Staquf, a soft-spoken cleric and politician in his late fifties, this was a battle for the soul of Islam with global

---

[8] Haeril Halim. "Indonesia Still Denies Religious Minorities Freedom to Worship." The Jakarta Post. 1 February 2023.

[9] UCA News. "Indonesia Upholds Ban on Interfaith Marriage." 1 February 2023. https://www.thejakartapost.com/paper/2023/02/01/indonesia-still-denies-religious-minorities-freedom-to-worship.html.

ramifications. "Preserving Indonesia's unique civilizational heritage and multi-religious and pluralistic nation-state requires the successful implementation of a global strategy to develop a new Islamic orthodoxy that reflects the actual circumstances of the modern world in which Muslims must live and practice their faith," Staquf said. "This global effort is not just an inevitable corollary of efforts to defeat Islamist subversion of Indonesia. It is vital to the well-being and preservation of virtually every other nation in the world, whose laws are derived from modern political processes and whose people and governments do not wish to be subsumed in a universal Islamic caliphate or exhausted by the struggle to prevent its establishment."[10]

Nahdlatul Ulama spelled out its thinking in a series of conferences and declarations, preceded by the 2009 publication of a book, the Illusion of the Islamic State.[11] Edited by Wahid, the book challenged Salafis, Wahhabis, and the Muslim Brotherhood for importing to Indonesia 'Arab Islam.' Nahdlatul Ulama followed up with a 2016 International Summit of Moderate Islamic Leaders (ISOMIL) Nahdlatul Ulama Declaration that was co-sponsored by Indonesia's National Agency for the Eradication of Terrorism (BNPT),[12] the 2016 First Global Unity Forum Declaration[13]; the 2017 Gerakan Pemuda Ansor Declaration on Humanitarian Islam[14]; and the 2018 Nusantara (Archipelago) Manifesto.[15]

Nahdlatul Ulama's concept shares much with a trend towards "Islamic modernism" or "Islamic progressivism," articulated by Islam scholars such as Mustafa Akyol,[16] Ebrahim Moosa,[17] Mohammed Arkoun,[18] Nasr Hamid

---

[10] Multiple conversations with the author, 2017–2023.

[11] H. E. Kyai Haji Abdurrahman Wahid (Editor). "The Illusion of an Islamic State: How an Alliance of Moderates Launched a Successful Jihad Against Radicalization and Terrorism in the World's Largest Muslim-Majority Country." Yogyakarta: Gading Publishing. 2009.

[12] Bayt ar-Rahmah. "ISOMIL Nahdlatul Ulama Declaration." 10 May 2016. https://baytarrahmah.org/2016_05_10_isomil-nahdlatul-ulama-declaration/.

[13] Bayt ar-Rahmah. "Global Unity Forum and Ansor Declaration." 12 May 2016. https://baytarrahmah.org/2016_05_12_global-unity-forum-and-ansor-declaration/.

[14] Ibid. Bayt ar-Rahmah. Gerakan Pemuda Ansor Declaration on Humanitarian Islam.

[15] Bayt ar-Rahmah. "The Nusantara Manifesto." 25 October. 2018. https://www.baytarrahmah.org/media/2018/Nusantara-Manifesto.pdf.

[16] Mustafa Akyol. "Islam without Extremes: A Muslim Case for Liberty." New York: W. W. Norton & Company. 2015.

[17] Ebrahim Moosa. "The Sunni Orthodoxy." Critical Muslim. Vol. 10. 2014. https://www.criticalmuslim.io/the-sunni-orthodoxy/.

[18] Mohammed Arkoun. "Islam: To Reform or to Subvert?" London: Saqi Books. 2007.

Abu Zayd,[19] Fazlur Rahman,[20] and Muhammad Shahrour.[21] In what historian Christopher de Bellaigue described as the Islamic Enlightenment[22] dating to the nineteenth century, Islamic modernists seek to re-read Islam's fundamental sources—the Qur'an and the Sunna, or the practice of the Prophet—by placing them in their historical context and then reinterpreting them in a modern context. Moosa argued that the failure to do so "suggests that Muslims can act confidently in the present only if the matter in question was already prefigured in the past." Put differently, he asserted that "Muslims discredit the legitimacy of their experience in the present and refuse to allow this experience to be the grounds of innovation, change and adaptation."[23]

Nevertheless, Islam scholar Ruediger Lohlker cautioned, "The extent to which the statements of those calling for Humanitarian Islam will succeed in avoiding political instrumentalization, in the context of a highly partisan political scene, will be decisive for the ultimate success or failure of the movement as it develops."[24] Cognisant of that, Nahdlatul Ulama put its money where its mouth is in 2019. Its religious scholars issued a fatwa or religious opinion, entitled "Transform the Prevailing 'Muslim Mindset,' for the Sake of World Peace and to Achieve a Harmonious Communal Life for All Mankind," that eliminated the notion of the kafir or infidel in Sharia law.

To be fair, the principle of viewing non-Muslims as fully-fledged citizens rather than infidels had already gained ground in the Muslim world. Ahmad al-Tayyeb, the grand imam of Cairo's Al-Azhar, Islam's 1,050-year-old constitutionally recognised theological citadel of religious learning, recognises it in a Declaration of Human Fraternity issued with Pope Francis in Abu Dhabi in 2019. Moreover, contrary to the fatwa, the declaration sidestepped the need to anchor the concept of citizenship in religious law by focusing on declaratory statements. The declaration did not detail its recognition of non-Muslim rights

---

[19] Nasr Hamid Abu Zayd. "Reformation of Islamic Thought: A Critical Historical Analysis." Amsterdam: Amsterdam University Press. 2006.

[20] Fazlur Rahman. "Islamic Methodology in History." Islamabad: Islamic Research Institute. 1965. http://ebooks.rahnuma.org/religion/Fazlur_Rehman/Fazlur_Rehman-Islamic-Methodology-in-History.pdf.

[21] Muhammad Sharour and Makram Abbes. "Pour un islam humaniste." Paris: Les éditions du Cerf. 2019.

[22] Christopher De Bellaigue. "The Islamic Enlightenment: The Struggle Between Faith and Reason: 1798 to Modern Times." New York: Liveright Publishing, Kindle edition. 2017.

[23] Ebrahim Moosa. "The Debts and Burdens of Critical Islam." In Omid Safi (ed.) Progressive Muslims: On Justice, Gender and Pluralism. Oxford: Oneworld Academic. 2003. pp. 111–128.

[24] Rüdiger Lohlker. "Introducing a Concept: Humanitarian Islam." In Katharina Ivanyi and Rüdiger Lohlker (eds.) Humanitarian Islam. Reflecting on an Islamic Concept. Paderborn: Brill Schoenigh. 2023. pp. 1–21.

but rejected "the discriminatory use of the term minorities which engenders feelings of isolation and inferiority."[25]

The fatwa filled in the void. It stipulated that non-Muslims were full citizens and did not belong to any of Sharia's classifications, including kafir; mu'ahad, non-Muslims who are subjects of a non-Muslim ruler who has concluded peace with Muslims; dhimmi, non-Muslims living in a Muslim state who pay a head tax; and Harbi, non-Muslims at war with Muslims who can be killed on sight. "These four categories were conceived within a context where state and religion were absolutely fused together. Differences of opinion and religion can no longer justify hostility between one person and another," the fatwa noted.[26]

A book on the findings of the conference at which the fatwa was adopted included a decree issued by a commission of senior Nahdlatul Ulama clerics that declared the nation-state theologically legitimate and affirmed that the legal category of kafir did not exist. The decree instructed Muslims to obey the laws of the state in which they lived. It emphasised a Muslim's religious obligation to foster peace with non-Muslims rather than automatically joining their co-religionists in case of conflict.[27]

The Indonesian government integrated the fatwa and declarations into public school curricula. It trained hundreds of thousands of teachers in teaching compassion, moderation, and peace. The government introduced project-based learning focused on religious tolerance and harmony. Schools celebrate holidays for the six state-recognised religions: Islam, Protestantism, Catholicism, Buddhism, Hinduism, and Confucianism. Tolerance and Pancasila, the state ideology, are mandatory parts of a university student's first year of study.

Students are encouraged to spend a semester at an Indonesian university located in a different cultural and religious setting. In addition, Indonesia's education ministry annually surveys schools on intercultural and interreligious tolerance. The data are shared with school principals, teachers, and local governments. "Principals are faced with the responsibility of improving their scores on religious and intercultural tolerance… For the first time, the government of Indonesia is telling every single principal and teacher that (tolerance)

---

[25] Pope Francis and Ahmad Al-Tayyeb. "A Document on Human Fraternity for World Peace and Living Together." The Holy See. 4 February 2019. https://www.vatican.va/content/francesco/en/travels/2019/outside/documents/papa-francesco_20190204_documento-fratellanza-umana.html.

[26] Ibid. Bayt ar-Rahmah. NU Rejects the Relevance of Infidel.

[27] Bayt-ar-Rahmah. "Decree, Bahtsul Masa'il ad-Diniyyah Maudluiyyah." 2019. https://www.baytarrahmah.org/media/2019/2019-Munas_Findings-of-Bahtsul-Masa'il-Maudluiyyah.pdf.

is being measured in your school," said Education Minister Nadiem Anwar Makarim.²⁸

In a manifestation of the government's Nahdlatul Ulama-inspired vision, Indonesian schoolchildren chose Jai Ho, a song composed by renowned Indian composer and musician A. R. Rahman (Allah Rakha Rahman) for the Oscar-winning film 'Slumdog Millionaire,' to practice for their country's 2023 Independence Day celebration. Gulzar, an acclaimed Indian poet, lyricist, and film director, wrote the song's lyrics:

> You are my destiny,
> Jai Ho, o-o-o-oh!
> No, there is nothing that can stop us,
> Jai Ho!
> Nothing can ever come between us,
> Jai Ho!.²⁹

While symbolically significant, the fatwa, like all religious opinions in Islam, was not legally binding and has not been adopted by other major Muslim groups. Yunahar Ilyas, chairman of Muhammadiyah, Indonesia's second-largest Muslim civil society movement with an estimated 30 million followers, insisted that the term kafir was theologically justified because the Qur'an categorises non-Muslims as infidels or polytheists. However, he rejected the term in the sociological sense of the word. "We have to look at the context, if it's a societal relationship, yes, we call them brothers who are not Muslim. Non-Muslim brothers and sister are not to be greeted as infidels," Ilyas said. Ilyas used the Arabic word muamalah to describe societal relations. In Islamic jurisprudence, muamalah means transactional, primarily relating to commercial dealings.³⁰

Ilyas represented one extreme of the debate in Indonesia. Former Muhammadiyah chairman Ahmad Syafi'i Maarif hewed closer to Nahdlatul Ulama's analysis. Maarif recognised that Sharia was the product of "centuries-old human reasoning, and thus time-bound." He argued that Islamic governance in the modern era was not possible "without rethinking the basis of our ideas about Sharia... We need big minds that understand the fundamental message

---

[28] TVNU. " الوزير نديم: إندونيسيا مستعدة لرفع مركز الآسيان العالمي بروح التنوع "(Minister Nadim: Indonesia Is Ready to Raise ASEAN's Global Standing in the Spirit of Diversity)." YouTube. 7 August 2023. https://www.youtube.com/watch?v=Zx3EUsrH62I.

[29] Sufi Musafir. "Indonesian School Children Practicing for Their Independence Day Celebration on Indian Songs ARRAhman." YouTube. 17 August 2023. Accessed August 18, 2023. https://www.youtube.com/watch?v=gLf70dJz4Kc.

[30] Andrian Saputra. "PP Muhammadiyah: Istilah Kafir Itu Lihat Konteksnya (PP Muhammadiyah: The Term Infidel Depends on the Context)." Republika. 3 March 2019. https://khazanah.republika.co.id/berita/pnsusd384/pp-muhammadiyah-istilah-kafir-itu-lihat-konteksnya.

of the Quran as rahmatan lil 'alamin - a source of love and compassion for all humanity," Maarif said.[31]

The fatwa and decree were rooted in the teachings of the Wali Songo, or Nine Saints, revered by Javanese society for propagating Islam in the fifteenth and sixteenth centuries. Their teachings allowed Muslims in a region dominated by Hinduism and Buddhism to blend their faith with local beliefs and traditions and build a tolerant, pluralistic society. In doing so, the Wali Songo shaped Indonesian Islam. Sunan Kalijogo, the most prominent of the saints, for example, broke with Islamic orthodoxy by teaching Islam's message using pre-Islamic shadow puppet theatre performances accompanied by orchestras playing brass gongs.

Indonesia's national motto, embraced by Nahdlatul Ulama, Bhinneka Tunggal Ika, Unity in Diversity, reflects the Wali Songo tradition. Mpu Tantular, a 14th-century Javanese court poet and nephew of King Rajasanagara of the syncretic Hindu-Buddhist Majapahit Empire, coined the phrase in his epic, Kakawin Sutasoma. "Buddha and Siva are different in essence, they are indeed different but how one can recognise, the truths of Buddha and Siva (Hindu) are one. They may be divided, but they are one. No conflict lies in truth," the epic reads.[32] The shadow puppet stories served Kalijogo's purpose and infused Nahdlatul Ulama's understanding of itself and its role in politics. The stories revolve around a king who, when receiving a sage, vacates his throne for him so that he can advise the ruler on good governance and how to achieve self-transcendent awareness.

"For over 1,200 years prior to the dissolution of the Ottoman Caliphate, the majority of the world's Muslims lived under political systems that sought to embody the orthodox ideal of a unified Muslim community, led by a pious Muslim ruler who adhered to the basic tenets of Islamic orthodoxy and led his community in a state of permanent warfare with neighboring non-Muslims. These tenets of classical Islamic jurisprudence are still taught by most orthodox Sunni and Shiite institutions as authoritative and correct, and thus continue to shape what may be described as the 'prevailing Muslim mindset' worldwide. One of the few regions of the Muslim world where these orthodox legal teachings were not historically dominant is the Indo-Malayan Archipelago, the territory of modern-day Indonesia, which we call Nusantara," Staquf the Nahdlatul Ulama leader, and Taylor, Staquf's international affairs advisor, wrote in an essay in 2022.[33] For Archipelago Islam, that meant in the pre-industrial age in which travel and communication were difficult, clerics engaged in the reinterpretation of classical legal precepts and the

---

[31] Interview with the author, 14 February 2016.

[32] Toshi's Homepage. "The Sutasoma Story (from Chapter 4)." In History and Culture of Java. http://www.maiguch.sakura.ne.jp/ALL-FILES/ENGLISH-PAGE/JAVA-HISTORY/default-java-history-e.html.

[33] KH Yahya Cholil Staquf and C. Holland Taylor. "The Civilizational Origins of Indonesia's Nahdlatul Ulama and Its Humanitarian Islam Movement." Hudson Institute. 22 January. https://www.hudson.org/node/44724.

creation of new religious rules and norms, or ijtihad, long after the practice was abandoned in the Middle East.

"Islam in the Middle East is seen as a socio-religious and political system that is complete, final, and authoritative. People have no choice but to comply with the dictates of that final construction. Islam in the archipelago is in a state of constant learning. For more than 600 years, its practitioners studied social reality to ascertain the most elegant means of achieving their goals, while maintaining harmony in a diverse and pluralistic society," Staquf said.[34] He argued that Indonesian rulers, unlike Middle Eastern potentates who used discrimination against non-Muslims to retain power, maintained social cohesion through magnanimity and compromise. Staquf, Taylor, and other Nahdlatul Ulama officials frequently cite the example of the sixteenth century-Dekam Sultanate that banned cow slaughter out of respect for its Hindu subjects.

In what some historians suggest may be an idealisation of history,[35] Nahdlatul Ulama sees the Wali Songo as aligning themselves with a pre-Islamic civilisation that conceived religion as a way to develop human potential physically, materially, and spiritually. Their peaceful proselytisation contrasted sharply with Islam's spread in the Middle East, North Africa, and Central Asia through military conquest, political control, and enforced religiosity. Nahdlatul Ulama asserts that they personify the Wali Songo tradition reflected in its support of Indonesia as a multi-religious and pluralistic nation-state rather than an Islamic state. Pancasila, Indonesia's founding philosophy, incorporates the Wali Songo spirit with belief in God, humanitarianism, national unity, democracy, and social justice as its principles.

Ivanyi and Lohlker, the Islam scholars, downplayed the importance of idealisation. "The point is not so much the degree to which this image conforms to actual fact... What matters is the purpose to which arguments such as those of Staquf are fielded: a particular, highly idealized experience of the past is invoked to overcome the challenges of the present – conflict, violence, and strife... A negatively essentialized 'Middle Eastern model' is thus juxtaposed to the 'Indonesian model,' which is presented as a way out for the future," Ivanyi and Lohlke said.[36]

Bisri, the prominent Nahdlatul Ulama cleric and Staquf's uncle, argued that "by reliving the Wali Songo's teachings, we invite others to join us in a mental revolution to reconceptualize our entire understanding of the world. What is our concept of God? What is our concept of humanity? We need to change

---

[34] KH Yahya Cholil Staquf. "How Islam Learned to Adapt in 'Nusantara'." NU Online. 15 October 2015. https://www.nu.or.id/column/how-islam-learned-to-adapt-in-039nus antara039-obo7w.

[35] Martin Slama. "From Wali Songo to Wali Pitu: The Travelling of Islamic Saint Veneration to Bali." In Brigitta Hauser-Schäublin and David D. Harnish (eds.) Between Harmony and Discrimination: Negotiating Religious Identities Within Majority-Minority Relationships in Bali and Lombok. Leiden: Brill. 2014. pp. 112–143.

[36] Idem. Ivanyi and Lohlker. Introducing a Concept.

our entire worldview by reexamining the nature and purpose of life."[37] Nahdlatul Ulama's call for a revival of Wali Songo teachings, like the drivers of the movement's founding, was a response to the industrial age's improved transportation and communication that allowed ever more Indonesian Muslims to perform the haj in Mecca and Medina where they were exposed to the Islamic orthodoxy that prevailed elsewhere in the Muslim world. The pilgrims often returned with an appreciation for orthodox Islam infused with Saudi Arabia's puritan interpretation of the faith.

Aceh, an ultra-conservative, semi-autonomous region on the northwestern tip of Sumatra, the only Indonesian province to implement Sharia, is Nahdlatul Ulama's nightmare. Devastated by a tsunami in 2004, Aceh, from where Islam initially spread in the archipelago, was granted autonomy in 2005 as part of a deal that ended an independence insurgency. Aceh's landscape is dotted with Saudi donations: schools, orphanages, mosques, and hospitals. In 2007, the Islamic and Arabic College of Indonesia or LIPIA, a Saudi university affiliate whose flagship branch in Jakarta is a tentpole of Saudi influence in the country, opened a campus in Aceh. Public caning for offences such as homosexuality, pre- or extramarital sex, alcohol consumption, gambling, and improper dress is a fixture of daily life in the province.

To varying degrees, moderate Islamist thinkers and politicians, like Rachid Ghannouchi, the leader of Tunisia's initially Muslim Brotherhood-inspired Ennahada Party and a former parliament speaker, shared Nahdlatul Ulama's quest. Yet, for Ghannouchi a theologian and agricultural engineer educated at the University of Damascus, the Sorbonne in Paris, and Tunisia's Zaytuna College, as for Ilyas, the Muhammadiyah leader, anchoring societal change in Sharia reform was one step too far. Even so, Ghannouchi, like Nahdlatul Ulama, argued that "there needs to be a genuine reconciliation between Islamists and secularists, between Muslim and non-Muslim. Dictatorship feeds off confrontation between all parties. This only leads to chaos and civil war, where no one will be the winner, and everyone will be a loser."[38]

Ghannouchi was a product of the post-Ottoman Caliphate void in which many Muslims sought refuge in political and/or ultra-conservative Islam. He arrived at his vision of a moderate Islam at the end of an intellectual journey that took him from Egyptian President Gamal Abdel Nasser's Arab nationalism, the flavour of the day in the 1950s and 1960s, to joining the controversial Pakistani Tablighi Jamaat proselytising movement to the Muslim Brotherhood with which he parted ways in 1981 when he first formed an Islamist group that called for democratic pluralism and power sharing in government. In 2016, at Ennahada's tenth party congress, Ghannouchi

---

[37] International Institute of Quranic Studies. "The Divine Grace of Islam Nusantara—Trailer." YouTube. 19 November 2015. https://www.youtube.com/watch?v=aLEi5ED-Xw.

[38] David Hearst. "Rached Ghannouchi Q&A: Thoughts on Democratic Islam." Middle East Eye. 13 June 2016. https://www.middleeasteye.net/news/rached-ghannouchi-qa-thoughts-democratic-islam.

announced an end to the party's proselytisation efforts. "Our objective is to separate the political and religious fields," he said. In Foreign Affairs, Ghannouchi declared that Ennahda was now best understood not as an Islamist movement but as a party of "Muslim democrats." Ghannouchi also implicitly acknowledged that jihadists justified their violence with tenants of Islamic law by recognising them as Muslims rather than deviants but denouncing them as criminals.[39]

Coining the phrase Muslim rather than Islamic democracy, Ghannouchi broke ground by abandoning references to sovereignty, particularly God's sovereignty, which shaped Islamist thinking and raised questions about Islam's compatibility with democracy because it rejected notions of popular sovereignty. Ghannouchi "begins by saying, the people exist, whether they include leftists, communists, feminist, old regime, or conservative figures. They all are necessary parts of creating politics. So, the idea of a sovereign entity is abandoned, and the logic of politics is adopted. It's a way of prioritising politics and recognising the political legitimacy of your opponents. They are not enemies. They may be antagonistic, they may have different agendas, they may be competitors, but their legitimacy as political agents is recognised," said Andrew March, an Islamic law scholar who has engaged in lengthy discussions with the Tunisian leader. In 2023, March published Ghannouchi's essays on democracy that had not been translated into English.[40]

Algerian philosopher Malik Bennabi was one of a handful of more secular Arab intellectuals to recognise early on the potential challenge posed by Asian nations that converted to Islam centuries after the faith's conquest of the Middle East. Bennabi, whose thinking influenced Ghannouchi, believed Indonesia would be one of two Asian nations that liberated Islam. Writing less than a decade after Pakistan's creation in 1947 and Indonesia's liberation from Dutch colonial rule in 1949, Bennabi's notion of a uniform Asian Islam that would liberate the faith from its Arab shackles proved to be only partially correct. Pakistan and Indonesia have bookended Islam at both extremes.

The product of decades of struggling with its identity reinforced by religious ultra-conservatism promoted by Saudi Arabia prior to the rise in 2015 of King Salam and his son, the crown prince, Pakistan makes headlines with militant Muslim mobs that lynch alleged blasphemers, burn churches, and wield street rather than parliamentary power while Indonesia's Nahdlatul Ulama propagates moderate Islam. Bennabi described Indonesia and Pakistan as "new and young countries…Islam is called upon to renovate and activate itself and to learn again to live." He predicted Asian Islam would replace Arab Islam, which was "dynastic through the pasha and his feudal overlords, tribal and

---

[39] Rached Ghannouchi. "From Political Islam to Muslim Democracy." Foreign Affairs. September/October 2016. https://www.foreignaffairs.com/articles/tunisia/political-islam-muslim-democracy.

[40] Interview with the author, 22 September 2023.

nomadic at the level of the Arab-Berber emir, dogmatic and imprisoned in the close vase of its decomposition under the authority of the Sheikh."[41]

The 2008 Hizb ut-Tahrir attack paved the way for the election two years later of a Nahdlatul Ulama leadership determined to counter Islamists more forcefully. Nahdlatul Ulama's newly appointed deputy leader, As'ad Said Ali, seemed perfect for the job. A fluent Arabic speaker who spent 12 years in Saudi Arabia and Syria representing Indonesia's State Intelligence Agency before becoming its deputy director, Ali was deeply suspicious of Sunni Muslim militants and purists as well as Indonesian Shiites, a minuscule minority whom he viewed as revolutionary Iran's fifth wheel. Ali's fears were fuelled by the number of young Indonesians who adopted Shiism in the early days of the 1979 Iranian revolution. Although never implicated in the killing, Ali was a senior intelligence official when the agency allegedly poisoned human rights activist Munir Said Thalib.[42]

Together with other senior intelligence officials, Ali believed non-violent Islamists posed a more significant threat than jihadists because they had greater public appeal. He saw Hizb ut-Tahrir and the Muslim Brotherhood-inspired Prosperous Justice Party (PKS) as Nahdlatul Ulama's foremost threats. Ali co-drafted an intelligence agency memo warning that Hizb ut-Tahrir had followers among military officers and senior bureaucrats. At the same time, PKS participation in elections allowed it to gain control of branches of government.[43]

To bolster Nahdlatul Ulama's resolve, Ali made nationalism alongside religion a centrepiece of consolidating the movement's identity. His training of cadres sought to prepare them for what he called a "war of faith." Nahdlatul Ulama activists needed to be ideologically reinvigorated and incentivised to implement the group's social, political, and religious agenda.[44] At Nahdlatul Ulama gatherings, Ali preached religious tolerance, nationalism, and rejection of foreign ideologies. He warned of the danger posed by radicalism and communism as well as liberalism.

"Communism still exists, and we need to be aware of it. It is against religion and against Islam. It seeks to replace the ideology of Pancasila ideology with communism. Then there is liberalism, a belief that wants freedom, including

---

[41] Asma Rashid. "Translation of Malek Bennabi's 'Vocation de l'Islam.'" Islamic Studies. Vol. 24, Issue 4. Winter 1985. pp. 455–492.

[42] Andreas Harsono. "Sixteen Years on, Still No Justice for Munir's Death." Human Rights Watch. 7 September 2020. https://www.hrw.org/news/2020/09/07/sixteen-years-still-no-justice-munirs-death.

[43] Multiple interviews with the author in 2018, 2019 and 2020.

[44] Ibid. Multiple interviews/Majalah Madani, Setrategi Mutakhir Dengan PKPNU (An Absolute Strategy for PKPNU). 2 January 2018. https://www.majalahmadani.com/2018/01/setrategi-mutakhir-dengan-pkpnu.html. NUOnline, Perkuat Gerakan, Pimpinan Pusat Pergunu Gelar PKPNU (Strengthen the Movement, Pergunu Central Leadership Holds PKPNU). 24 July 2018. https://www.nu.or.id/post/read/93337/perkuat-gerakan-pimpinan-pusat-pergunu-gelar-pkpnu.

freedom of religion. They want to rule the country with a philosophy of irresponsible freedom. They tamper with the law to exploit this country," Ali told some 12,000 Nahdlatul Ulama activists dressed in white tunics and waving green Nahdlatul Ulama flags at a rally in Central Java.[45]

Nahdlatul Ulama's five million-strong paramilitary militia, Multipurpose Ansor Front, better known as Banser, one of the Islamic world's largest with multiple times the combined personnel of the Indonesian armed, security, and law enforcement personnel, initially hosted Ali's training program. Dressed in fatigues, Banser trainees, learning martial arts, are mostly young and physically fit men and women.

An officer of the Indonesian army's Military District Command 0818 said the Nahdlatul Ulama training was "intended to instill a sense of patriotism and nationalism…in the younger generation so that they are prepared to enter society in the context of regional resistance against external threats."[46] Ideologically, the training was grounded in Nahdlatul Ulama's assertion that patriotism was an integral part of faith. "Those who lack a native land will be devoid of history," the movement declared.[47]

By 2019, some 750,000 militia members had gone through Ali's training program, swearing an oath to confront "the enemies and traitors of traditional Sunni Islam," Nahdlatul Ulama, Pancasila, Indonesia's foundational philosophy, and the 1945 constitution.[48] The program was complemented by a ramping up of Nahdlatul Ulama's social services with the opening of new hospitals and clinics, and the revival of dormant chapters and establishment of new ones.[49]

Banser has a mixed history. It participated in large-scale killings in 1965 and 1966 of alleged members of the Indonesian Communist Party (PKI),[50] and more recently, it confronted Hizb ut-Tahrir, leading to the government's 2017 banning of the Islamist group.[51] In 2017, H. Alfa Isnaeni, a

[45] Bangitmedia, Kader NU Harus Waspada terhadap Musuh Agama dan Negara (NU Cadres Must Be Alert to Enemies of Religion and the State). 16 April 2017. https://bangkitmedia.com/kader-nu-harus-waspada-terhadap-musuh-agama-dan-negara/.

[46] Rudi Setiono. "Wasbang bagi anggota PKPNU Kec.Turen (Wasbang Education for PKPNU Members, Turen district)." Kommando District Militer 0818. 7 October 2018. https://kodim-0818.id/pendidikan-wasbang-bagi-anggota-pkpnu-kec-turen/.

[47] Ibid. Bayt ar-Rahmah. ISOMIL.

[48] Khoirun Mukri. "Ikrar kesetiaan kader penggerak NU (NU Active Cadres Pledge Alleigance)." YouTube. 18 April 2017. https://www.youtube.com/watch?v=z4buKCOStFM.

[49] NU Online. "Keberhasilan Program NU karena Kaderisasi PKPNU (The Success of the NU Program Is Due to PKPNU Regeneration)." 21 April 2018. https://www.nu.or.id/post/read/89188/keberhasilan-program-nu-karena-kaderisasi-pkpnu.

[50] Greg Fealy and Katharine McGregor. 2010. "Nahdlatul Ulama and the Killings of 1965–66: Religion, Politics, and Remembrance." Indonesia, Issue 89. April. pp. 37–60.

[51] Andreas Harsono. 2017. "Indonesia's Ban of Islamist Group Undermines Rights." Human Rights Watch. 19 July. https://www.hrw.org/news/2017/07/19/indonesias-ban-islamist-group-undermines-rights.

Banser commander, recalled intercepting a bus convoy ferrying Hizb ut-Tahrir supporters to a rally. "Most people on the buses were villagers. Military officers, who paid them to board the busses, told them that they were travelling to a religious gathering. Hizbut-Tahrir successfully targets the military," Isnaeni said.[52]

Three years later, the government, circumventing legal proceedings like in the case of Hizb ut-Tahrir, banned the Islamic Defenders Front (FPI), a militant group headed by Muhammad Rizieq Shihab, a Saudi-educated Muslim scholar.[53] Nahdlatul Ulama's 'militant pluralism'[54] paid dividends and benefitted the Indonesian president. The banned groups enjoyed the support of Widodo's foremost rivals.

During Abdurrahman Wahid's presidency, Banser frequently intimidated the Indonesian leader's critics.[55] These days, Banser protects Nahdlatul Ulama gatherings as well as Indonesia's non-Muslim minorities, provides security for Nahdlatul Ulama leaders in cooperation with Indonesian police, engages in humanitarian work, demonstrates the movement's power in displays to visitors, and organises marches with hundreds of thousands of participants.

Riyanto, a 25-year-old Banser member, became the movement's poster boy and a national hero. Riyanto died in 2000 guarding the Eben Haezer Church in Mojokerto, East Java, during Christmas Eve services. He was killed when he grabbed a suspicious package with protruding cables and wires and ran towards a ditch where he hoped to dump it. The bomb blew up in his hands as he called on worshippers to lie down. It sent his body flying over 100 metres.[56] The bombing was one of multiple Al-Qaeda and Jemaah Islamiyah attacks that night on Christian churches across Indonesia.

Riyanto's image has become a symbol of modern Indonesia, much like an imposing, 1.8-meter-tall painting by Dutch artist John van der Sterren. The painting portrays the country's founding father, Sukarno, cradling a dead, barefoot rebel killed by Dutch colonial forces in the rice fields and smouldering volcanoes of late 1940s Java. A Christian cross dangles from the body of a martyr in the Muslim nation's independence war. Riyanto is Banser's first and only casualty. But his mission's importance and symbolism has not diminished.

---

[52] Interview with the author, 21 May 2017.

[53] Marcus Mietzner. "Fighting Illiberalism with Illiberalism: Islamist Populism and Democratic Deconsolidation in Indonesia." Pacific Affairs. Vol. 91, Issue 2. June 2018.

[54] Nava Nuraniyah. "Divided Muslims: Militant Pluralism, Polarisation and Democratic Backsliding." In Thomas Power and Eve Warburto (eds.) Democracy in Indonesia: From Stagnation to Regression. Singapore: ISEAS—Yusof Ishak Institute, 2020.

[55] Zamira Loebis. "Wahid's Army of Loyal Believers." Time Asia. 3 July 2000. http://edition.cnn.com/ASIANOW/time/magazine/2000/0703/indonesia.muslims.html.

[56] Coconuts Jakarta. "Remembering Riyanto, the Muslim Youth Who Sacrificed Himself to Save a Church from a Bomb on Christmas Eve." 8 December 2016. https://coconuts.co/jakarta/features/remembering-riyanto-muslim-youth-who-sacrificed-himself-save-church-bomb-christmas-eve/.

Attacks on non-Muslim houses of worship and Muslim sects considered heretical are on the rise. Some 200,000 Banser militia personnel guard Christian churches each Christmas Eve. Often, local police support them. The Setara Institute, a human rights group, counted 50 attacks on Christian houses of worship in 2022.[57] In addition, conservatives increasingly block the construction of new non-Muslim houses of worship based on a 2006 decree by the religious affairs and interior ministries. The decree stipulates that at least 90 worshippers and 60 other locals approve the construction of a new house of worship. Religious Affairs Minister Yaqut Cholil Qoumas, a brother of Nahdlatul Ulama leader Staquf and a former head of Banser, has not responded to calls for the decree to be annulled.

Similarly, red tape makes life difficult for the Indonesian Buddhist Intellectual Association. Whenever it wants to organise an activity at Borobudur, a centuries-old Buddhist temple in Java, it must "get permission, deal with a very complicated mechanism" and pay a steep rental fee, according to Eric Fernando, the association's executive director. To avoid accusations of proselytisation, the association includes a disclaimer in its publications that "they're written for our own circle, not to try to persuade other people to embrace our religion."[58]

The battle lines between religious moderates and hardliners were entrenched in 2017 when mass protests led to the arrest and sentencing to two years in prison on blasphemy charges of former Jakarta governor Basuki Tjahaja Purnama, an ethnic Chinese Christian better known as Ahok. The protests laid bare fault lines between Nahdlatul Ulama and Islamists and within the movement itself.

The anti-Islamist campaign helped Nahdlatul Ulama's reformist wing, dubbed the Rembang establishment after Staquf's hometown, gain the upper hand against rivals like Said Aqil Sirajd, Staquf's immediate Saudi-educated predecessor as secretary-general of Nahdlatul Ulama, and National Awakening Party (PKB) leader Muhaimin Iskandar as well as more conservative elements in the movement, including 80-year-old Ma'ruf Amin, the head of the Ulama Council of Indonesia and a driving force in the anti-Ahok protests. Staquf defeated Siraj in an electoral battle for Nahdlatul Ulama leadership in December 2021.

A descendant of a prominent Javan cleric who was imam at Mecca's Grand Mosque, Amin was sidelined when he was nominated as Widodo's

---

[57] Haris Prabowo. "Indonesia. Equivalent: 50 Places of Worship Disturbed During 2022, Most Churches." The Muslim Times. 1 February 2023. https://themuslimtimes.info/2023/02/02/indonesia-equivalent-50-places-of-worship-disturbed-during-2022-most-churches/.

[58] Neo Chai Chin and Lewa Pardomuan. "No 'Fuss About Each Other's Religion': Where Lies Indonesia's Guard Against Extremism? CNA Insider. 3 June 2023. https://www.channelnewsasia.com/cna-insider/indonesia-presidential-election-politics-religion-islam-identity-3533436.

vice president in the 2019 election. Widely viewed as an influential conservative religious scholar, Amin was known for his fatwas against religious and gender minorities, including a 2005 denunciation of Ahmadis, a sect viewed by orthodox Muslims as heretics. Violent attacks on Ahmadis escalated because of the fatwa with mob killings and the razing to the ground of homes.[59] A Nahdlatul Ulama member since childhood, Amin served as head of the National Sharia Committee of the Indonesian Ulama Council when hardline conservatives, including representatives of the since-banned Hizb ut-Tahrir, dominated it.

Staquf's strained relations with Iskandar persuaded the PKB leader to join Anies Baswedan as his vice presidential candidate in the 2024 election. Iskandar's move sparked debate within Nahdlatul Ulama because Baswedan was backed by the movement's arch-enemy, the Prosperous Justice Party (PKS).

Nahdlatul Ulama's internal struggles were coloured by the Rembang group's long-standing hostility towards Iskandar, dating to his 2008 takeover of the party after he emerged victorious in legal battles against Wahid, a charismatic co-founder of the party, a prodigious intellect and scion of one of Indonesia's most prominent traditionalist Muslim families. Even so, Iskandar enjoyed the continued support of Siraj and prominent East Javan Nahdlatul Ulama scholars.[60]

Wahid had no formal training beyond Islamic sciences but was a passionate autodidact of Catholicism. He learned Indonesian, Javanese, and Arabic as part of his religious education and taught himself French, Dutch, and German.[61] In his brief term in office, Wahid established press freedom, extended civil and political liberties to Indonesia's ethnic Chinese population and other minorities, and restored civilian control of the military. "Abdurrahman Wahid presented young Indonesian Muslims with a vision of Islam that was both relevant to their experience and possessed the poetry and heft of (Indonesia's) long history. ... Wahid's example signaled permission for thoughtful Muslims to view the faith not through the paradigm of religious conviction but as a part of history," said Islam scholar Mark Cammack.[62]

Widodo rewarded Nahdlatul Ulama for its support with US$12 million in government funding for its microfinancing scheme and a significant portion

---

[59] Amy Chew. "Indonesian President Jokowi's Running Mate: A Muslim Cleric Once Seen as a Hardliner." CAN. 12 August 2018. https://www.channelnewsasia.com/asia/indonesian-election-jokowi-running-mate-muslim-cleric-maruf-amin-803126.

[60] Ahalla Tsauro and Fakhridho Susilo. "NU Factionalism on Show After Anies-Muhaimin Surprise." New Mandala. 12 September 2023. https://www.newmandala.org/nu-factionalism-on-show-after-anies-muhaimin-surprise/.

[61] Greg Barton. "Abdurrahim Wahid: Muslim Democrat, Indonesian President." Honolulu: University of Hawaii Press. 2002.

[62] Mark Cammack. "Islamic Law as Hermeneutic: Developments Within Traditionalist Islam in Indonesia." Southwestern Journal of International Law. Vol. 29, Issue 1. May 2023. pp. 53–76.

of 12 million hectares of land allocated to religious seminaries of mainstream Muslim organisations.[63] Moreover, the agriculture ministry partnered with Nahdlatul Ulama for corn production.[64] In addition, Widodo appointed Staquf as a member of his presidential advisory council, from which he resigned in 2019 to run for the Nahdlatul Ulama chairmanship. At the same time, to stymie criticism from other influential Muslim groups, Widodo appointed Din Syamsuddin, a former chairman of Nahdlatul Ulama rival Muhammadiyah, to the newly created position of Special Presidential Envoy for Interfaith Dialogue and Cooperation.

A disciple of Wahid, Staquf belongs to the Nahdlatul Ulama nobility. He was Wahid's spokesman during the cleric's short-lived presidency from 1999 to 2001. Staquf's father, Cholil Bisri, co-founded the National Awakening Party, the Nahdlatul Ulama-affiliated political party. His uncle, Mustofa Bisri, a cleric and poet, was a Wahid confidant.

From the outset, Staquf partnered with Taylor, the former American telecommunications executive and a close associate of Wahid. Wahid, Taylor, and Bisri established LibForAll (Liberty for All) Foundation in Taylor's home state of North Carolina. US President George W. Bush's Deputy National Security Advisor for Combating Terrorism, Juan Zarate, praised the foundation as "the loadstar in efforts to defeat the ideology of radical Islam."[65] A decade later, Staquf and Taylor founded another non-profit, North Carolina-based Bayt ar-Rahmah or House of Mercy, to promote 'humanitarian Islam' by "addressing obsolete and problematic elements within Islamic orthodoxy that lend themselves to tyranny, while positioning these efforts within a much broader initiative to reject any and all forms of tyranny, and foster the emergence of a global civilization endowed with nobility of character."[66]

In 2010, Staquf set out to steer Nahdlatul Ulama towards reforms anticipated by a 1992 board meeting chaired by Wahid and rooted in the indigenisation of Islam in the Malay Archipelago in the late Middle Ages. The board noted that "the changing context of reality necessitates the creation of new interpretations of Islamic law and orthodox Islamic teaching."[67] To achieve that, the Nahdlatul Ulama cadre needed different training than that offered by As'ad Said Ali, the movement's deputy leader. Staquf intended to mobilise Nahdlatul Ulama followers in support of religious reform. Five years

[63] Thomas P. Power. "Jokowi's Authoritarian Turn and Indonesia's Democratic Decline." Bulletin of Indonesian Economic Studies. Vol. 54, Issue 3. December 2018. pp. 307–338.

[64] Ministry of Agriculture. "Kementan dan NU Berdayakan 91 Juta Umat (Ministry of Agriculture and NU Empower 91 Million People)." 2018. https://www.pertanian.go.id/home/?show=news&act=view&id=2589.

[65] LibForAll. "Who We Are." https://libforall.org/who-we-are/.

[66] Bayt ar-Rahmah. "Humanitarian Islam." https://baytarrahmah.org/humanitarian-islam/.

[67] Ibid. Bayt Ar-Rahmah. Gerakan Pemuda Ansor Central Board Bayt-Ar-Rahmah Board of Directors Joint Resolution and Decree.

later, Nahdlatul Ulama's national congress adopted the concept of Nusantara (Archipelago) or Humanitarian Islam that provided a roadmap for reconciling Islam with a modern world that significantly differs from the early days of Islam when classical Islamic law was crafted.

Based on the teachings of Wahid and other Nahdlatul Ulama clerics, Nusantara Islam called for political and religious pluralism, the embrace of the Universal Declaration of Human Rights, and tolerance. It was designed to advance Nahdlatul Ulama's mission of "consolidating the universe" as conceived by the movement's founder, Haji Hasyim Asy'ari. Asy'ari's universe collapsed with the abolition of the caliphate by Mustafa Kemal Ataturk, the visionary who carved modern Turkey out of the ruins of the Ottoman Empire.

A century later, the vacuum created by the abolition continues to shape Nahdlatul Ulama and the struggle to define Islam. "Nahdlatul Ulama was established to forge a new path for future civilization, to replace the old civilizational construct that was lost," Staquf said. Nahdlatul Ulama's logo expresses that mission with nine stars representing the Prophet, his four immediate successors, the Wali Songo and the earth bound by a rope signifying God's 99 names. The movement positions Nusantara Islam as an anti-dote to political and militant expressions of the faith that seek restoration of the caliphate. Nusantara Islam's credibility stems from its roots in the archipelago's history and culture and Nahdlatul Ulama's status as an independent civil society movement with its own clerical authority. At the same time, Nusantara Islam enabled Indonesia to project itself as a beacon of moderate Islam and Muslim democracy.

"Our Islam is Nusantara Islam," Widodo told a 2015 Nahdlatul Ulama congress attended by some 20,000 clerics and followers that launched Nusantara Islam.[68] Sporting a black jacket and a red sarong commonly worn by Indonesian religious scholars, Widodo asserted that Nahdlatul Ulama's emphasis on human solidarity would make Indonesia the reference for an Islam that stands for tolerance, progress, and peace.[69]

A declaration issued a year later at an international conference of Muslim scholars convened by Nahdlatul Ulama to introduce Humanitarian Islam laid the groundwork for the movement's celebration of the nation-state as a way of countering militancy, justified by the quest for a caliphate, a unitary Islamic state. The declaration insisted that "love for the motherland is part of faith." It asserted that Islam encourages the faithful to become noble characters who

---

[68] JPNN. "Jokowi: Alhamdulillah, Islam Kita Islam Nusantara (Jokowi: Alhamdulillah, our Islam Is Islam Nusantara)." 14 June 2015. https://www.jpnn.com/news/jokowi-alhamdulillah-islam-kita-islam-nusantara.

[69] Cabinet Secretary Republic of Indonesia. "Buka Muktamar, Presiden Jokowi: NU Menjadi Garda Terdepan Menjaga NKRI Dan Pancasila (Opening the Congress, President Jokowi: NU Is the Frontline Protecting the Republic of Indonesia and Pancasila)." 1 August 2015. https://setkab.go.id/buka-muktamar-presiden-jokowi-nu-menjadi-garda-terdepan-menjaga-nkri-dan-pancasila/.

adhere to principles of balance, harmony, gentleness, and compassion rather than violence and coercion to conquer the world.

Throwing down the gauntlet, the declaration suggested that "certain governments in the Middle East derive their political legitimacy from...problematic interpretations of Islam that underlie and animate religious extremism and terror. These governments need to develop an alternate source of political legitimacy if the world is to overcome the threat of religious extremism and terror... The realities of economic and political injustice also contribute to the spread of religious extremism and terror." Nahdlatul Ulama was referring to countries like Saudi Arabia, the UAE, Iran, and Turkey that have championed sectarianism, political Islam, and/or autocracy.[70]

In 2017, a conference convened by Ansor, Nahdlatul Ulama's young adults organisation, in a religious seminary in Jombang in East Java, the movement's birthplace, seemed to draw the battles lines. A conference statement left no doubt that Nahdlatul Ulama challenged ultra-conservatives, Islamists, jihadists, and Saudi Arabia. The conference's 8,000-word declaration, Gerakan Pemuda Ansor's Declaration on Humanitarian Islam, spelled out Nahdlatul Ulama's understanding of Islam and Muslims' choices. "Muslims face a choice between starkly different visions of the future. Will they strive to recreate the long-lost ideal of religious, political and territorial unity beneath the banner of a Caliphate—and thus seek to restore Islamic supremacy—as reflected in their communal memory and still firmly entrenched within the prevailing corpus, and worldview, of orthodox, authoritative Islam? Or will they strive to develop a new religious sensibility that reflects the actual circumstances of our modern civilization and contributes to the emergence of a truly just and harmonious world order, founded upon respect for the equal dignity and rights of every human being?" the declaration asked.

The declaration asserted that "social and political instability, civil war and terrorism all arise from the attempt, by ultra-conservative Muslims, to implement certain elements of fiqh (Islamic jurisprudence which addresses how a Muslim state should be governed and conduct international affairs) within a context that is no longer compatible with...classical norms." It charged that "various actors—including but not limited to Iran, Saudi Arabia, ISIS (another acronym for the Islamic State), Al-Qaeda, Hezbollah, Qatar, the Muslim Brotherhood, the Taliban and Pakistan—cynically manipulate religious sentiment in their struggle to maintain or acquire political, economic and military power, and to destroy their enemies. They do so by drawing upon key elements of classical Islamic law (fiqh), to which they ascribe divine authority to mobilize support for their worldly goals." Fiqh is the body of jurisprudence that applies Shariah to everyday life.

---

[70] Bayt ar-Rahmah. "International Summit If Moderate Islamic Leaders (ISOMIL). Nahdlatul Ulama Declaration." 10 May 2016. https://www.baytarrahmah.org/media/2016/Nahdlatul-Ulama-Declaration_05-10-16.pdf.

In a frontal assault on Saudi Arabia, the statement argued that "it is false and counterproductive to claim that the actions of Al-Qaeda, ISIS, Boko Haram, and other such groups have nothing to do with Islam, or merely represent a perversion of Islamic teachings. They are, in fact, outgrowths of Wahhabism and other fundamentalist streams of Sunni Islam… The Wahhabi view of Islam—which is embraced not only by Saudi Arabia and Qatar but also by al-Qaeda and ISIS—is intricately wedded to those elements of classical Islamic law that foster sectarian hatred and violence. Wahhabism is characterized by extreme animosity towards Shi'ites. It is also characterized by antipathy—at times violent—towards Christians, Jews, Hindus, Buddhists, and Sunni Muslims who do not share the Wahhabis' rigid and authoritarian view of Islam… Saudi opposition to Iran, ISIS, and al-Qaeda does not and should not absolve it from responsibility for promoting the very ideology that underlies and animates Sunni extremism and terror," the statement said.[71]

Critics charged that the Nahdlatul Ulama leadership failed to persuade its grassroots to adopt Humanitarian Islam. Scholars Marcus Mietzner and Burhanuddin Muhtadi concluded, based on a 2019 survey, that 54% of the poll's Nahdlatul Ulama-affiliated respondents objected to a non-Muslim becoming a provincial governor. Thirty-four per cent opposed non-Muslim events being held in their neighbourhood and 50% rejected having a non-Muslim house of worship in their vicinity. "This should come as a sobering reminder to NU, as well as to those who have viewed it as a key promoter of tolerance and democracy in Indonesia," Mietzner and Muhtadi said.

Moreover, the Humanitarian Islam declaration sidestepped some of the most controversial tenets of classical Islam and their fallout, such as blasphemy. Pakistani researcher Nazish Brohi warned that "the issue of blasphemy is destroying whatever strands of pluralism remain in the Muslim world." Saudi Arabia and other Muslim-majority nations, including Indonesia, have long lobbied for blasphemy criminalisation in international law. Unanimously adopted by parliament in 2022, Indonesia's criminal code[72] defines blasphemy as a crime punishable by up to five years in prison. The Saudi-led effort enabled autocratic governments to brandish their religious credentials.[73] It has become part of the Muslim world's response to rising anti-Muslim sentiment, Islamophobia, and criticism of human rights abuses.

---

[71] Gerakan Pemuda Ansor, Humanitarian Islam, and Bayt ar-Rahma. "Gerakan Pemuda Ansor's Declaration on Humanitarian Islam." Bayt ar-Rahmah. 22 May 2017. https://www.baytarrahmah.org/media/2017/Gerakan-Pemuda-Ansor_Declaration-on-Humanitarian-Islam.pdf.

[72] National Legal Development Agency, Ministry of Law and Human Rights of the Republic of Indonesia, Draft laws of the Republic of Indonesia Number… Year… Regarding Criminal Law Book, Undated. https://bphn.go.id/data/documents/draft_ruu_kuhp_final.pdf.

[73] Courtney Brooks. "Calls for Blasphemy Ban Resurface at UN." Radio Free Europe/Radio Liberty. 27 September 2012. https://www.rferl.org/a/un-hears-calls-for-blasphemy-ban/24721995.html.

Liberals, human rights activists, and journalists also took Nahdlatul Ulama to task for associating itself with a government that curtailed democracy with the criminal code and the circumvention of due process in the banning of Hizbut-Tahrir and the Islamic Defenders Front. "The president's assaults on democracy are manifold," The Economist said. The magazine cited steps to suppress dissident voices, including asserting the power to disband civil society organisations on national security grounds, levelling criminal charges against online critics, and blocking websites. The Economist further asserted that Widodo had "surrounded himself with generals and relies ever more on the armed forces to help execute domestic policy, such as in increasing rice production."[74] The criticism implicitly raised fundamental chicken-and-egg questions about the relationship between religious and political reform, including what comes first and whether one is possible without the other.

Critics further asked how Nahdlatul Ulama's acquiescence in the criminal code squared with the group's unconditional endorsement of the Universal Declaration of Human Rights—a significant differentiator in its rivalry with state-sponsored autocratic versions of moderate Islam. The code, enacted with the support of the PKB, the Nahdlatul Ulama-affiliated party, bans extramarital sex and curbs freedom of expression by outlawing insulting the president, even though it severely restricts who can file a complaint. Privately, influential Nahdlatul Ulama officials defended the socially restrictive aspects of the law but conceded freedom of expression concerns were legitimate. Even so, scholars Sana Jaffrey and Eve Warburton warned that provisions of the law "threaten political dissent with prison sentences and have the potential to muzzle public debate about the purview of the state in citizens' private and political lives."[75]

Initially, Widodo envisioned his government spearheading Indonesia's positioning as the guiding light of a truly moderate Islam. Speaking in 2018 of the laying of the ground stone of the International Islamic University (UIII) on the outskirts of Jakarta, Widodo challenged the Middle East's icons of Islamic learning. It was "natural and fitting that Indonesia should become the (authoritative) reference for the progress of Islamic civilization,"[76] the president declared.

Widodo saw the university as an anti-dote to traditional centres of Islamic learning that propagated orthodox Islam and legitimised autocratic rule, such as the Islamic University of Medina, a pillar of Saudi Arabia's decades-long, well-funded religious soft power campaign, and Cairo's Al-Azhar University.

---

[74] The Economist. "Indonesia's President Promised Reform. Yet It Is He Who Has Changed." 19 August 2021. https://www.economist.com/asia/2021/08/19/indonesias-president-promised-reform-yet-it-is-he-who-has-changed.

[75] Sana Jaffrey and Eve Warburton. "Indonesia's New Criminal Code Turns Representatives into Rulers." New Mandala. 9 December 2021. https://www.newmandala.org/representatives-into-rulers/.

[76] Fabian Januarius Kuwado. "Harapan Jokowi pada Universitas Islam Internasional Indonesia." Kompas. 5 June 2018. https://nasional.kompas.com/read/2018/06/05/12232491/harapan-jokowi-pada-universitas-islam-internasional-indonesia.

The university is "a promising step to introduce Indonesia as the global epicentre for 'moderate' Islam.' If UIII can successfully attract students from Europe and the Middle East, I think it's a promising step to introduce Indonesia as the global epicentre for 'moderate' Islam,'" said Islamic philosophy scholar Amin Abdullah.[77]

To do so, Widodo's powerful secretary of state, Pratikno, asked Staquf to chart a strategy. Staquf's strategy centred on persuading Middle Eastern religious institutions and religious figures to adopt Indonesia as a model for religious reform. It called on Indonesia to position itself as a United Nations thought leader and engage with governments, the intelligentsia, and the media. The strategy further envisioned Indonesian initiatives to resolve conflicts "on the basis of dialogue with commitment to human values." Staquf suggested Policy Exchange, an influential conservative British think tank with close ties to the Conservative Party and the UAE, would support the strategy.[78]

Indonesian Foreign Minister Retno Marsudi shot down Staquf's proposal because she feared it would upset Saudi Arabia, the UAE, and Qatar. "You will make a mess if you do this," the minister told Staquf. Acting on Retno's advice, Widodo played both ends against the middle. On the one hand, he outsourced Indonesia's religious soft power efforts to Nahdlatul Ulama. Re-elected for a second term in 2019, Widodo appointed Staquf's younger brother, Yaqut Cholil Qoumas, the head of Nahdlatul Ulama's powerful young adults wing and a proponent of its concept of Humanitarian Islam, as minister of religious affairs. He also appointed ambassadors empathetic to Nahdlatul Ulama to key diplomatic posts in London, Riyadh, Abu Dhabi, and Cairo and allocated funds for translating into Arabic and distributing key Nahdlatul Ulama religious texts.[79]

The appointments and translations as well as plans for an Arabic-language Nahdlatul Ulama website seek to address Humanitarian Islam's failure to gain traction in much of the Muslim world, and particularly among a broad swath of Arabs, who pride themselves on being 'authentic' Muslims. Many Arab Muslims discount Indonesian Islam as syncretic and insufficiently rigorous. Moreover, despite a strong tradition of religious scholarship, few Indonesian scholars have been translated into foreign languages, especially Arabic and English. Scholar Martin van Bruinessen noted that Malaysia was the only country outside of Indonesia where he found works authored by Indonesian Muslim thinkers. Van Bruinessen suggested one reason Indonesian scholars failed to have an impact beyond the archipelago was their lack of originality.

---

[77] Luthfi T. Dzulfikar. "How Indonesia's New International Islamic University Will Host Global Research for 'Moderate Islam'." The Conversation. 16 December 2019. https://theconversation.com/how-indonesias-new-international-islamic-university-will-host-global-research-for-moderate-islam-128785.

[78] Yahya C. Staquf. "Indonesia Rujukan Islam Dunia (Indonesia Reference Islamic World)." Unpublished. Undated.

[79] Author's interviews with two Nahdlatul Ulama leaders, 2 March 2021.

Indonesia's strength, he argued, was its "broad degree of acceptance of critical Islamic thought," resulting in an emphasis on rational analysis of state-run Islamic institutes that produce "enlightened religious officials."[80]

Indonesia's handicap did not stop Widodo from capitalising on his friendship with UAE President Bin Zayed to attract tens of billions of dollars in Emirati investment in energy, technology, infrastructure, and Indonesia's sovereign wealth fund. As a result, the UAE emerged as Indonesia's largest Gulf investor. The two countries also tightened security cooperation by exchanging defence attaches, exploring potential cooperation in manufacturing drones, weapons, and munitions, collaboration in aerospace, and cross-training in counterterrorism operations.

As an aside, Widodo engineered a US$100 million Emirati donation to expand the campus of Nahdlatul Ulama's university in Yogyakarta and create a Mohammed bin Zayed Center for Future Studies. Some worried the movement might be on a slippery slope. "Nahdlatul Ulama needs to maintain its commitment to moderate Islamic and democratic values no matter what," said a scholar who empathises with the movement.[81] Nahdlatul Ulama leaders insisted the movement could not be bought. At the same time, the university's rector, Widya Priyahita Pudjibudjo, described tough negotiations with UAE officials in which he rejected Emirati demands to control the appointment of the centre's dean and faculty as well as its curriculum.[82]

Similarly, Staquf turned down tens of millions of dollars dangling in front of him during a gathering of religious leaders in Bali in 2022 by the Muslim World League, the Saudi government-controlled entity promoting Crown Prince Mohammed bin Salman's autocratic version of moderate Islam. In parallel, Staquf overhauled Nahdlatul Ulama's administrative procedures to ensure enhanced transparency and accountability. Illustrating his determination to implement change, Staquf appointed women to the movement's leadership board for the first time.

Simultaneously, Staquf challenged the power of the Indonesian Ulama Council, a bastion of traditional and conservative Islam, that was often headed by successive Nahdlatul Ulama clerics, including Ma'ruf Amin, Widodo's vice president. The Council was seen as Indonesia's top religious institution. Staquf's attack kicked off with the resignation of Miftachul Akhyar, a prominent Nahdlatul Ulama cleric, as council chairman. Qoumas, the religious affairs minister and Staquf's younger brother, simultaneously targeted the council's primary source of revenue. The minister ended the council's monopoly on halal certification by allowing the government's Halal Product Assistance Agency to recognise fatwas from others as a basis for certification

---

[80] Martin van Bruinessen. "Indonesian Muslims and Their Place in the Larger World of Islam." In Anthony J. S. Reid (ed.) Indonesia Rising: The Repositioning of Asia's Third Giant. Singapore: Iseas-Yusof Ishak Institute. 7 May 2012.

[81] Interview with the author, 16 May 2022.

[82] Interview with the author, 9 August 2023.

of companies in a wide range of sectors, including food, fashion, education, pharmaceuticals, cosmetics, tourism, media, health care, culture, and finance.[83]

In a similar vein, Staquf addressed the Simon Wiesenthal Center in Los Angeles, named after a prominent conservative Austrian Nazi hunter, on International Holocaust Day, in his first remarks to an overseas audience weeks after his election. "The international community…is faced with a momentous choice. Shall we indulge the all-too-human instinct to feel anger, hatred, and revenge, and thus perpetuate the cycle of animosity and violence…? Or shall we choose compassion and embrace 'the better angels of our nature,' which urge us to love and respect one another, and unite in striving to create a more dignified and noble future for all humanity? We do not have time to wait for anger, hatred, and a collective yearning for revenge to subside. Our actions will determine what kind of world our children and grandchildren inherit," Staquf said in his videotaped address.[84]

Speaking four years earlier at a conference in Jerusalem at the invitation of the American Jewish Committee (AJC), one of the oldest and most influential Jewish advocacy groups in the United States, Staquf argued that reform of Islamic, as well as Jewish law, was the key to resolving problems between Muslims and Jews. "We have to acknowledge that there are problems in the relationship between Islam and Judaism. Some of the problems lay within the teachings of religion itself. People of religion, including Islam and Judaism, need to find a new…moral interpretation of religion that will guide people of religion to have more harmonious relations with one another," Staquf said.[85]

Without spelling it out, Staquf argued that, like Islam, Judaism has yet to confront concepts of Jewish supremacy in the Halakha, Jewish religious law[86] and harsh commandments of conquest codified by Maimonides, a prolific legal scholar, in the twelfth century[87] that go a long way explaining the nature of the Israeli occupation of Palestinian lands. Even so, Staquf was applauded in Jerusalem, where the Committee and Israelis attached greater importance to his willingness to visit Israel, address a major Jewish audience, and meet

---

[83] James M. Dorsey. "Autocratic vs. Democratic Islam=UAE vs. Indonesia." The Turbulent World with James M. Dorsey. 23 March 2022. https://www.jamesmdorsey.net/post/autocratic-vs-democratic-islam-uae-vs-indonesia.

[84] Bayt ar-Rahmah. "International Holocaust Remembrance Day." 27 January 2022. https://baytarrahmah.org/2022_01_27_international-holocaust-remembrance-day/.

[85] American Jewish Committee. "Conversation with Yahya Cholil Staquf." 10 June 2018. https://www.ajc.org/news/conversation-with-yahya-cholil-staquf.

[86] Menahem Klein. "Israel's Rule over the Palestinians Has Created a New Judaism." Haaretz. 8 April 2023. https://www.haaretz.com/opinion/2023-04-08/ty-article-magazine/israels-rule-over-the-palestinians-has-created-a-new-judaism/00000187-5d43-dde0-afb7-7f53f63f0000.

[87] Rachel Furst. Undated. "The Mishna Torah, Maimonides' Halachic Magnum Opus." My Jewish Learning. https://www.myjewishlearning.com/article/the-mishneh-torah/.

with Prime Minister Binyamin Netanyahu than to what he had to say. Indonesia's mood in the run-up to presidential and parliamentary elections was very different. "The controversy quickly turned into a struggle between competing visions of Islam," said a Nahdlatul Ulama official.[88]

Staquf was not in uncharted territory. Wahid, his mentor, visited Israel three times as leader of Nahdlatul Ulama and addressed the American Jewish Committee's annual forum in 2002 in Washington. The Wiesenthal Center, together with the Wahid Institute and LibForAll, organised a Holocaust conference in Bali five years later attended by Nahdlatul Ulama clergymen, rabbis, Hindu guru Sri Sri Ravi Shankar, and Japanese Buddhist leader Yoichi Kawada. The conference was intended to push back against widespread Holocaust denial in the Muslim world at a time when Iranian President Mahmoud Ahmadinejad was giving it a microphone. "Although I am a good friend of Mahmoud Ahmadinejad, I have to say he is wrong," Wahid said. He said he declined an invitation to attend a Holocaust denial conference in Tehran. In an op-ed published by The Wall Street Journal on the day the Bali conference opened Wahid and Israel Lau, a former Israeli chief rabbi and Holocaust survivor, called on religious leaders to "defend the rights of others to worship differently," and "face up frankly to the evils of Holocaust denial."[89]

Nahdlatul Ulama put the American Jewish Committee in a bind. The Committee welcomed the Indonesians' outreach but struggled with Nahdlatul Ulama's independence and refusal to endorse the establishment of diplomatic relations with the Jewish state without a settlement of the Israeli-Palestinian conflict. Committee officials privately asserted that Staquf had not paid sufficient attention to the Holocaust in his Wiesenthal Center remarks.[90] One official accused Nahdlatul Ulama in an email of "actively thwarting the work of advancing our shared goals in promoting religious freedom and countering antisemitism and misinformation about Jews, Judaism, and Israel in Indonesia."[91]

The official was referring to Committee pressure on the religious affairs ministry to add Judaism to the list of officially recognised religions. Indonesia recognises Islam, Protestantism, Catholicism, Buddhism, Hinduism, and Confucianism. Although not opposed in principle, Nahdlatul Ulama officials cautioned that pushing for official acknowledgement would shine a spotlight on a tiny community of a few hundred Jews in a country of 270 million in which pro-Palestinian sentiment is widespread and often evokes anti-Jewish feelings. Staquf sought to illustrate the point in an interview defending his 2018 visit to Israel. "Even though I've just come from Jerusalem and talking

---

[88] Interview with the author, 22 September 2023.

[89] Abdurrahman and Israel Lau. "The Evils of Holocaust Denial." The Wall Street Journal. 12 June 2007. https://www.wsj.com/articles/SB118161023016032027.

[90] Author's conversation with an AJC executive, 28 February 2022.

[91] Email from AJC executive to American Jewish leader, 27 September 2022.

about compassion, I myself still have ingrained prejudice against Jews (from a lifetime of anti-Semitic conditioning)," Staquf said.[92]

A 2022 study by research firm Saiful Mujani showed 51% of Indonesians prefer not to have Jews as their neighbours, while 61% said they do not want Jews as public officials.[93] American Jewish Committee officials viewed Staquf's remark as an unvarnished reflection of his views rather than an honest admission of prejudice in the context of a defence of his engagement with Israel and Jews.

Even so, Masorti Jews, followers of a conservative strand of Judaism, may be Staquf's closest non-Muslim soul mates. Masorti Jews believe Jewish law and tradition emanate from widespread acceptance rather than divine revelation. Staquf described a 29-page document compiled by 20 Masorti rabbis as "an inspiration for all of us." Entitled 'The Status of Non-Jews in Jewish Law and Lore Today,' the document declared "that all rules discriminating against Gentiles in matters of a civil nature and moral actions are no longer to be considered authoritative in Judaism not only because of the harm they cause to the image of Judaism and relations with non-Jews but because they are intrinsically immoral and deter us from attaining the honest virtues to which we aspire."

The significance of the Nahdlatul Ulama and the Masorti Jewish reform calls went beyond Islam and Judaism. Their push for the removal of supremacist religious concepts amounted to a defence of the nation-state as opposed to an increasing number of civilisationalist states that define their boundaries and policies in civilisational rather than international legal terms. In 2020, the Centrist Democrat International (CDI), the world's largest network of political parties, adopted a Nahdlatul Ulama-drafted resolution condemning "the emergence of authoritarian, civilizationalist states that do not accept the rules-based post-WWII order, whether in terms of human rights, the rule of law, democracy or respect for international borders and the sovereignty of other nations."[94] Indian Prime Minister Narendra Modi took note of the resolution adopted at a CDI executive committee meeting in the Javan city of Yogyakarta. A close associate of the Indian leader was in Yogyakarta as an observer.

---

[92] Heru Triyono. 'Kyai Yahya Staquf: "I Still Have Ingrained Prejudice Against Jews." Bayt ar-Rahmah. 2 July 2018. https://www.baytarrahmah.org/media/2018/Beritagar_Kyai-Yahya-Staquf_I-still-have-ingrained-prejudice-against-Jews_07-02-18.pdf.

[93] Saidiman Ahmad. "Saiful Mujani: Intoleransi pada Yahudi terkat dengan sikap diskriminatif negara (Saiful Mujani: Intolerance Toward Jews Related to State Discriminatory Attitude)." Saiful Mujani. 7 July 2022. https://saifulmujani.com/saiful-mujani-intoleransi-pada-yahudi-terkait-dengan-sikap-diskriminatif-negara/.

[94] IDC-CDI. "Draft Resolution on Promoting a Rules-Based International Order Founded Upon Universal Ethics and Humanitarian Values." 23 January 2020. https://www.idc-cdi.com/wp-content/uploads/2020/04/Resolution-on-promoting-a-rules-based-international-order-founded-uponuniversal-ethics-and-humanitarian-values.pdf.

Three years later, Modi refused as chairman of the Group of 20 to follow Indonesia's example of including religion as a G20 engagement track. Modi's refusal failed to stymie Nahdlatul Ulama, whose bold agenda is centred on religion but extends beyond to influence the shaping of a rules-based, multipolar 21st-century international order. As Modi closed its door, Southeast Asia opened another door. The ten-nation Association of Southeast Asian Nations (ASEAN) embraced an Indonesian government's push for a Southeast Asian return to values rooted in an ancient Indo civilisation.[95] Nahdlatul Ulama envisions the re-emergence of South and Southeast Asia as a cohesive, vital, and proactive civilisational sphere, which functions as a powerful, independent pillar of support for a rules-based international order founded upon shared civilisational values.[96]

The government's push cemented Widodo's alliance with Nahdlatul Ulama, making religion and intercultural and interreligious dialogue key themes of its 2022 G20 and 2023 ASEAN chairmanships. Religious reform was at the core of the Religion Forum 20. It focused on modifying religious laws, confronting historical grievances, truth-telling, and forgiveness as a basis for identifying shared civilisational values. "This work has been taken beyond the realm of Islam to other religions and the world at large," said Timothy Samuel Shaw, a senior executive of the Center for Shared Civilisational Values (CSCV).

In his opening remarks at the ASEAN dialogue, Widodo suggested that a driver of the dialogue was a concern that religion may be losing its relevance in parts of the world. "The people of ASEAN…have an increasing religious spirit. Indonesia, for example, is a country where the people most believe in God, and the number is the highest in the world. According to the Pew Research Center, 96 percent of respondents in Indonesia believe that good morals are determined by belief in God," Widodo said. The president noted that "in the religious field, the world community is becoming less and less religious. A survey from Ipsos Global Religion 2023 of 19,731 people from 26 countries in the world showed that 29 percent stated that they were agnostics and atheists."

The conference declaration argued that the Indosphere stretching from South to Southeast Asia "consists of countries that have traditionally shared a similar set of civilizational values, deeply rooted within their respective societies. These values foster a culture of tolerance and harmony while reducing conflict between groups." The declaration asserted that "it is of the upmost importance that ASEAN Member States cooperate to revitalize the civilizational mentality or worldview, which was long characteristic of Southeast Asia prior to the modern era. This civilizational mentality is characterised by a

---

[95] James M. Dorsey. "Indonesia Pushes a Civilizational Approach to Countering Polarization." The Turbulent World with James M. Dorsey. 9 August 2023. https://www.jamesmdorsey.net/post/indonesia-pushes-a-civilizational-approach-to-countering-polarisation.

[96] Timothy Samuel Shah and C. Holland Taylor. "The "Ashoka Approach" and Indonesian Leadership in the Movement for Pluralist Re-Awakening in South and Southeast Asia." The Review of Faith & International Affairs. Vol. 19, Issue 2. 2021. pp. 56–71.

willingness to accept differences while preserving and strengthening harmony among society's diverse elements."

ASEAN's civilisational approach is rooted in what the Center for Shared Civilisational Values describes as the Ashoka approach. A third-century Indian Buddhist emperor, Ashoka renounced armed conquest after years of bloody warfare to champion compassion, extensive dialogue, and interchange among followers of diverse religious paths, interfaith tolerance, mutual understanding, and respect for others' dignity. Ashoka fostered an Indianised civilisational worldview throughout South and Southeast Asia, a vast geographical and cultural zone shaped by Hinduism and Buddhism and home to 2.5 billion people whose cultural and spiritual heritage is equal to those of the Sinosphere, Europe, and the Middle East.

The Indosphere boasts the world's greatest religious diversity, with far more Muslims, Hindus, and Buddhists than any other region. The Ashoka approach, according to Staquf, builds on the Indonesian archipelago's traditional culture that in his words, "is about prioritizing harmony with others, above one's own self-interest; spiritual self-confidence, which allows one to experience and embrace new ideas and teachings; seeking nobility of character, rather than purely material achievements; knowing that differences of opinion (and religion) are not harmful."

Like Nahdlatul Ulama's call for Islamic law reform, its Ashoka approach is grounded in the fact that the original Muslim proselytisers did not seek the erasure of Java's pre-Islamic past. Instead, they sought to build on the region's millennium-old traditions. "Within the regions dominated by 'classical Islam' – the Middle East, North Africa, the Persian and Turkish cultural basins and much of South Asia – Islam arrived in the form of a 'judge' by subduing, imposing order and adjudicating disputes. In Nusantara, Islam arrived as a guest and was later adopted into the family," Staquf noted. He argued that "military conquest was the essential prerequisite, and catalyst, for the development of classical Islamic civilization… It was precisely in this atmosphere that the classical teachings (ie, interpretation) of Islam evolved."[97]

The Ashoka approach aims to create an "alternate pillar of support for a rules-based international order founded upon respect for the equal rights and dignity of every human being" by "reawaken(ing) the ancient spiritual, cultural, and socio-political heritage of the Indianized cultural sphere, or 'Indosphere' — a civilizational zone that pioneered, long before the West, key concepts and practices of religious pluralism and tolerance."[98]

More immediately, the approach is designed to counter the weaponisation of ethnic, religious, and cultural identities that threaten the post-World War

---

[97] Yahya Cholil Staquf. "How Islam Learned to Adapt in 'Nusantara'." Strategic Review. Vol. 5, Issue 2. April–June 2016.

[98] Center for Shared Civilisational Values. "The 'Ashoka Approach' and Indonesian Leadership in the Movement for Pluralist Re-Awakening in South and Southeast Asia." Undated. https://civilizationalvalues.org/the-ashoka-approach/#:~:text=This%20strategy%20seeks%20to%20reawaken,from%20268%20to%20232%20BCE.

II international order built on a philosophical and moral framework encapsulated in the Universal Declaration of Human Rights. It stems from a belief that Western nations and cultures cannot on their own sustain a rules-based international order that safeguards national sovereignty and fundamental human rights. "The result is an anti-pluralist maelstrom that is sucking much of South and Southeast Asia into a downward spiral or black hole of zero-sum conflicts," Shah and Taylor warned.[99]

In effect, the approach constitutes a repudiation of politicised religion and Western efforts to impose values such as LGBTQ rights that counter deeply held beliefs in non-Western nations. "The question is whether South and Southeast Asia should submit to cultural, ideological, economic, and political dominance by external actors, such as China, the Middle East, and Western countries, or should we defend our interests as independent cultures and nations," said Staquf, the Nahdlatul Ulama chairman.

---

[99] Ibid. Shah and Taylor. The Ashoka Approach.

CHAPTER 3

The Saudi Sultan's Scholar

Mohammed Abdelkarim al-Issa shined in his absence as religious leaders discussed historical grievances, truth-telling, reconciliation, and forgiveness at a gathering he co-hosted in Bali in November 2022. The conference, dubbed Religion Forum 20 or R20, was one of several engagement tracks of the Group of 20 (G20) in advance of a summit of the leaders of the world's largest economies chaired by Indonesian President Joko Widodo, the group's annual rotating chair.

A 59-year-old former justice minister, senior cleric, and law graduate of Riyadh's Imam Muhammad bin Saud Islamic University imbued with a sense of self-importance and grandeur, Al-Issa, the general secretary of the Saudi government-controlled Muslim World League, was in two minds about the summit. Co-hosting enhanced Al-Issa and the League's value for Saudi Crown Prince Mohammed bin Salman. It projected Saudi Arabia, for much of its history, a secretive kingdom that adhered to an ultra-conservative, austere, and supremacist interpretation of Islam, as religiously moderate and engaged in dialogue with non-Muslims. That imagery helped Bin Salman position Saudi Arabia as a religious, cultural, political, and economic leader of the Muslim world. Bin Salman needed the positioning to attract foreign investment and expertise to help diversify his country's economy, reduce its dependence on oil exports, and expand the haj, the pilgrimage to Mecca, as a source of tourism revenue.

To spread the message of Saudi Arabia's newfound religious tolerance, Bin Salman repurposed the League, created in 1962 to propagate Wahhabism and Salafism, the puritan Muslim worldview on which the kingdom was founded in 1932. Buzzwords like tolerance, peace, and human fraternity pepper Al-Issa and the League's pronouncements. The scion of a prominent Najdi clerical family, Al-Issa is the most significant of a coterie of younger, more compliant clerics willing to do Bin Salman's bidding, initially promoted by King Abdullah before the monarch died in 2015.

Al-Issa has served Bin Salman well. He has defended the crown prince's reforms, including the subjugation of the once-powerful clergy, the curbing of religious police powers, the lifting of a ban on women's driving, the loosening of gender segregation, and the nurturing of modern-day entertainment like cinemas and concerts. He also legitimised Bin Salman's refusal to entertain reform of religious jurisprudence by distinguishing between religion and religiosity. Al-Issa argued that religion, Islam, was faultless while religiosity was defined by human interpretation.[1]

Al-Issa had no choice but to attend the Bali conference after the Saudi government asked Indonesia to give the League pride of place. Indonesia hoped the meeting would institutionalise dialogue between religious figures and leaders of the world's most powerful countries. Al-Issa's problem was that the conference's main organiser, Nahdlatul Ulama, the world's largest and most moderate Muslim civil society movement, was taking it in a theological and political direction that challenged Bin Salman's autocratic version of a socially more liberal but politically more restrictive Islam.

Al-Issa did not hide his discomfort. Wearing a Wahhabi-style headdress with no cord to hold it in place, he delivered prepared remarks at a news conference a day before the summit but declined to entertain journalists' questions. The summit's main organiser, Nahdlatul Ulama Secretary-General Yahya Cholil Staquf, was forced to exit the room with Al-Issa immediately after they delivered their statements. They left their subordinates to field journalists' questions. Seemingly uninterested, Abdurrahman Mohammad Amin al-Khayyat, the League's representative in Indonesia and a former Saudi ambassador to the archipelago state, spent much of his time on stage fiddling with his mobile phone.

Beyond platitudes and lofty words, Al-Issa and Al-Khayyat had no incisive response to Nahdlatul Ulama's concept of Humanitarian Islam that embraces religious and political pluralism and unambiguously endorses democracy and the United Nations Declaration of Human Rights. Bin Salman's transition from austere ultra-conservatism inspired by Muhammad ibn Abdul Wahhab, an eighteenth-century theologian, preacher, and activist, whose thinking shaped Saudi Islam for much of the kingdom's existence, to a socially more liberal but autocratic interpretation of the faith,[2] was transactional. Bin Salman was driven by political and economic needs rather than a genuine desire for reform for the greater good. The crown prince introduced change without

---

[1] Bellaty Hiya Ahsan. "Season 1: Episode 23." MBC Shahid. 16 May 2020. https://shahid.mbc.net/en/shows/Billaty-Hiya-Ahsan-season-1-episode-23/episode-415566.

[2] Besnik Sinani. "Post-Salafism: Religious Revisionism in Contemporary Saudi Arabia." Religions. Vol. 13, Issue 4. 2022. https://www.mdpi.com/2077-1444/13/4/340.

anchoring it in religious law reform or taking responsibility for the kingdom's decades-long propagation of supremacism, racism, sectarianism, and religious militancy.

As a result, Bin Salman has subjugated the kingdom's religious establishment and brushed aside social norms they imposed on society. However, he stopped short of denouncing Salafism or Wahhabism. In contrast to Nahdlatul Ulama, a decentralised movement with multiple power centres and factions, Bin Salman sits at the top of the pyramid. He demands absolute obedience. In Bin Salman's world, religious scholars like Al-Issa, dubbed 'the sultan's scholars' by their critics, bend to the crown prince's will to avoid arrest or worse. In Bin Salman's world, there is no place for Nahdlatul Ulama's anchoring in religious law of equal rights for Muslims and non-Muslims, endorsement of separation of mosque and state, and recognition of political freedoms and political pluralism.

Instead, Bin Salman expected clerics like Abdulrahman al-Sudais, one of nine imams of Mecca's Grand Mosque and a Muslim World League council member, to sing his praises and lend religious legitimacy to his policies. In 2018, days after journalist Jamal Khashoggi's killing in the Saudi consulate in Istanbul, Al-Sudais anointed Bin Salman a "muhaddath," a reformer sent by God, in a prayer session broadcast live on cable television and social media from where Prophet Mohammed delivered his last sermon. Muhaddath was the title Mohammed bestowed on Umar Ibn al-Khattab, his companion and Islam's second caliph. In line with the command for absolute obedience, Al-Sudais gave Bin Salman religious legitimacy by defining patriotism as a religious obligation.[3]

Al-Sudais "delivered a troubling sermon, violating the sanctity of the sacred space he occupied... Saudi clerics had never weaponized the podium of the prophet at the Grand Mosque so brazenly to serve the monarchy. No imam of the Grand Mosque had ever anointed a Saudi ruler as the mujaddid of the age or dared to imply as much... The sanctified podium of the prophet in Mecca is being desecrated and defiled," thundered Islamic law scholar Khaled M. Abou El Fadl.[4]

Bin Salman publicly paraded his subjugation of the clergy by appointing Turki Al-Sheikh, a descendant of Abdul Wahhab, to oversee the development of a Western-style entertainment sector.

In Bin Salman's Saudi Arabia, preaching absolute obedience helps keep clerics in the crown prince's good books but is no guarantee. Abd al-Aziz-al-Rayes, an ultra-conservative religious scholar, graphically insisted that even if the crown prince "fornicates in public on television for half an hour each

---

[3] Millichronicle. "Makkah Imam Sudais Emphasizes Significance of Celebrating National Day." 19 September 2023. https://www.millichronicle.com/2023/09/makkah-imam-sudais-emphasizes-significance-of-celebrating-national-day.html.

[4] Khaled M. Abou El Fadl. "Saudi Arabia Is Misusing Mecca." The New York Times. 12 November 2018. https://www.nytimes.com/2018/11/12/opinion/saudi-arabia-mbs-grandmosque-mecca-politics.html.

day, you are still required to bring people together around the ruler, not to aggravate people against him."[5] That didn't shield Al-Rayes from arrest when a five-year-old video clip surfaced in which he denounced Western-style entertainment as "disobedience of Allah" and encouragement of immodesty and mixing of the sexes.[6]

Bin Salman's politically autocratic, socially more liberal version of moderate Islam resonates with autocracies like Russia and China and populists such as India with significant Muslim minorities. Muslim and non-Muslim autocrats and populists share a desire to control religion in general, and Islam in particular, and a rejection of Muslim ultra-conservatism and political Islam. Saudi Arabia failed to take umbrage when Ramzan Kadyrov, president of the Russian republic of Chechnya in 2016, hosted a UAE-organised gathering of 200 prominent Sunni Muslim scholars. The conference "identified Wahhabism, Salafism, and the Muslim Brotherhood as 'misguided' interpretations of Islam, much like the Islamic State."[7] Instead of protesting, Al-Issa three years later brought Muslim scholars from 43 countries to the Chechen capital of Grozny to discuss religious peace and coexistence. The Muslim World League said it had chosen Grozny as the venue because Russia was a model of ethnic harmony.[8] Similarly, Saudi Arabia, like the UAE, has endorsed, at times brutal Chinese efforts to Sinicize Islam, which ensuring "its compliance with (Chinese Communist) Party ideology."[9]

Nahdlatul Ulama's Bali proposition to confront historical grievances and embrace truth-telling, reconciliation, and forgiveness was a slippery slope for Bin Salman. It threatened to force him to acknowledge the effect on Muslims worldwide of the Faustian bargain between the Al Sauds, the clan that rules the kingdom, and the Wahhabis, Abdul Wahhab's followers, on which the kingdom was built. Saudi funding for religious ultra-conservatism often

---

[5] The Middle East Media Research Institute. "Saudi Islamic Scholar and University Lecturer Dr. Abdulaziz Al-Rays: People Must Not Rebel Against a Ruler Even if He Flogs Them or Commits Adultery and Homosexual Acts." 30 October 2019. https://www.memri.org/tv/saudi-islamic-scholar-abdulaziz-rays-people-support-unite-leader-even-unjust-protect-society.

[6] Meem Magazine English. "Arrest of Saudi Scholar Even After His Fatwa Calling for Blind Obedience to…." Facebook. 1 April 2022. https://www.facebook.com/watch/?v=511997230517330.

[7] Samuel Ramani. "Russia and the UAE: An Ideational Partnership." Middle East Policy. Vol. 27, Issue 1. Spring 2020. pp. 125–140.

[8] Saudi Press Agency. "Muslim World League Makes History with Moscow Summit." Arab News. 30 March 2019. https://www.arabnews.com/node/1475061/saudi-arabia.

[9] Lucille Greer and Bradley Jardine. "The Chinese Islamic Association in the Arab World: The Use of Islamic Soft Power in Promoting Silence on Xinjiang." Middle East Institute. 14 July 2020. https://www.mei.edu/publications/chinese-islamic-association-arab-world-use-islamic-soft-power-promoting-silence.

tore communities and families apart; promoted intolerance, supremacism, and sectarianism; and created breeding grounds for militancy and extremism.[10]

In Pakistan, a Sunni Muslim journalist remembered handing sweets and water to Shiite villagers as a youth as they celebrated their holidays. That changed with the arrival of a Pakistani preacher trained in a Saudi-funded seminary. The cleric denounced Shiites as heretics and loose Sunni Muslim mores. Women who used to cover their heads with a shawl started covering themselves from head to toe. Militants attacked kiosks selling music CDs and bombed a local shrine. Families were divided. "In the past, we had economic issues, but as a family, we were culturally on the same path. Now we are deeply divided about what constitutes the correct path of Islam," the journalist said.

Saudi soft power centred on Abdul Wahhab's worldview before the rise in 2015 of King Salman and his son, the crown prince. It was at the core of the clan's survival strategy. Without reliable data, analysts estimate that Saudi Arabia spent up to US$100 billion propagating its austere interpretation of Islam, far more than the United States or the Soviet Union allocated for propaganda and psychological warfare operations during the Cold War. Together with the foreign and Islamic affairs ministries, Al-Issa's Muslim World League and other government-controlled non-governmental organisations distributed funds with no oversight or control of recipients' use of the monies. So did members of the ruling family and the business community.[11]

Donations by ruling family members and wealthy businesspeople were often channelled through a department of numbered accounts at the National Commercial Bank, Saudi Arabia's largest bank. Account holders would contact Khaled bin Mahfouz, the bank's majority shareholder and one of three executives authorised to access the numbered accounts. They would instruct him to transfer money to a specific country. Bin Mahfouz decided who the beneficiaries would be. In one instance, Prince Sultan bin Abdulaziz Al Saud, Saudi Arabia's longest-serving defence minister, directed Bin Mahfouz in the mid-1990s to wire US$5 million from his account to war-ravaged Bosnia Herzegovina. Sultan did not identify a beneficiary. Bin Mahfouz sent the money to the Saudi High Commission for Aid to Bosnia, a Saudi-funded charity in Sarajevo controlled by jihadists.

Bosnian security forces and NATO peacekeepers raided the charity's offices after the September 11, 2001, Al-Qaeda attacks. The group's computer discs contained files on crop duster aircraft, instructions on faking US State Department identification badges, photographs and maps of Washington marking government buildings, and anti-Semitic and anti-US children's literature. Authorities arrested six men, including an administrator, six weeks after the raid on suspicion of planning to blow up the US embassy in Sarajevo.

---

[10] James M. Dorsey. "Creating Frankenstein: The Saudi Export of Wahhabism." The Turbulent World of Middle East Soccer. 7 March 2016. https://www.jamesmdorsey.net/post/creating-frankenstein-the-saudi-export-of-wahhabism.

[11] Ibid. Dorsey. "Creating Frankenstein."

They were handed over to US officials and flown to Camp X-Ray, the US detention centre in Guantanamo Bay, Cuba.[12]

Saudi intelligence long suspected the commission of jihadist links. At one point, intelligence tentatively identified one of the commission's operatives as a member of Egypt's Islamic Jihad, a group aligned with Al-Qaeda. The Saudis sent a representative to Sarajevo to investigate. The investigator confronted the Egyptian national, saying, "We hear that you have these connections, and if that is true, we need to part ways." The man put his hand on his heart and denied the allegation. That settled the issue for the Saudis. But once Bosnian authorities deported the suspect to Egypt, he described how easy it had been to fool the Saudis in court testimony.[13]

Wahhabi and Salafi proselytising served the Al Sauds' purpose. In the 1960s and 1970s, it helped them counter Arab nationalism's anti-monarchical appeal. In the 1980s, Sunni Muslim ultra-conservatism provided an anti-dote to the Iranian revolution. The revolution challenged the Al Sauds' religious legitimacy by toppling the Shah, a monarchical icon of US influence, recognising a degree of popular sovereignty, and installing a cleric as the country's spiritual guide. The revolution, and before it, Arab nationalism, redrew the Middle East and North Africa's political map in ways that potentially threatened the survival of the kingdom's rulers and other Western-backed Middle Eastern monarchs. Reassuringly, the United States, like Saudi Arabia, saw Islam as a Cold War bulwark against communism and Arab nationalism spearheaded by Egypt, the Arab world's foremost military power, and other Middle Eastern republics aligned with the Soviet Union.

Perceptions changed with the 9/11 attacks. Post-9/11, Saudi Arabia strictly regulated charitable donations abroad. However, the source and channelling of continued funding to militants that served the kingdom's geopolitical purpose often remained unclear. Militant Pakistani bagmen described the flow of large amounts to ultra-conservative madrassas that dot Pakistan's borders with Iran and Afghanistan in interviews in 2017 and 2018. They said the monies were channelled through Saudi nationals of Baloch origin and often arrived in suitcases in an operation they believed had tacit Saudi government approval.[14]

The monies were transferred at a time when Saudi Arabia publicly hinted[15] it may support US proponents, like John Bolton, President Donald J. Trump's former national security adviser, of destabilising Iran by supporting ethnic

---

[12] Based on copies of hard drives in the author's possession.

[13] James M. Dorsey. "The Saudi Export of Ultra-Conservatism in the Era of MbS—An Update." The Turbulent World of Middle East Soccer. 19 April 2018. https://www.jamesmdorsey.net/post/the-saudi-export-of-ultra-conservatism-in-the-era-of-mbs-an-update.

[14] James M. Dorsey. "Pakistan Caught in the Middle as China's OBOR Becomes Saudi-Iranian-Indian Battleground." The Turbulent World of Middle East Soccer. 5 May 2017. https://mideastsoccer.blogspot.com/2017/05/pakistan-caught-in-middle-as-chinas.html.

[15] Ibid. Dorsey. "Pakistan Caught in the Middle."

insurgencies.[16] Initially, Saudi backing of anti-Iranian Pakistani militants in the twenty-first century was a throwback to the Cold War when the kingdom backed anti-communist religious ultra-conservatives that constituted a pillar of the US struggle against the atheist Soviet Union.[17] That support faded in the early 2020s as Saudi Arabia sought to negotiate with Iran and, in 2023, reestablished diplomatic relations with the Islamic Republic in a Chinese-mediated deal. The deal aimed to enable Saudi Arabia and Iran to manage their differences, ensure tensions did not spiral out of control, and allow the two countries to focus on economic cooperation. In 2016, Saudi Arabia broke off relations with Iran after Iranian protesters ransacked Saudi diplomatic missions in the Islamic Republic in response to the kingdom's execution of a prominent Saudi Shiite cleric.

Promoting a 'moderate' form of Islam became the name of the game. The Saudis, initially shell-shocked by the revelation that 15 of the 19 9/11 perpetrators were Saudi nationals, worked with the United States to project a softer image of Islam or what some analysts dubbed 'Wahhabism-lite' but stopped short of bringing about real change in the kingdom until Bin Salman's rise 14 years later.[18] Ultra-conservatism represented everything the young prince no longer wished to project. Ultra-conservative social restrictions inhibited his effort to reform and diversify the Saudi economy and cater to the aspirations of a population in majority below the age of 35. Bin Salman needed the kingdom and its religious culture to be perceived as tolerant, forward-looking, and outward rather than inward-looking.[19] He facilitated increased social liberalism by emphasising nationalism rather than religion as the core of Saudi identity and introducing far-reaching social and economic reforms. The reforms lifted a ban on women driving, eased gender segregation, enhanced women's social and professional opportunities, and introduced Western-style entertainment. Bin Salman's redefinition of identity responded to soul-searching in the kingdom sparked by the 9/11 attacks and the popular Arab revolts a decade later.

---

[16] Ibid. Dorsey. "Pakistan Caught in the Middle."

[17] Toby Matthiesen. "Saudi Arabia and the Cold War." In Madawi al-Rasheed (ed.) Salman's Legacy, The Dilemmas of a New Era in Saudi Arabia. London: Hurst & Co. 2018. pp. 217–233.

[18] Salwa Ismail. "Producing 'Reformed Islam': A Saudi Contribution to the US Projects of Global Governance." In Madawi Al-Rasheed (ed.) Kingdom Without Borders. Saudi Arabia's Political, Religious and Media Frontiers. New York: Columbia University Press. 2008. pp. 113–131 / Paul. "Saudi Arabia: More Room for Wahhabism Lite?" Qatar: Gulf Studies Center, Gulf Insights Series 23. https://www.qu.edu.qa/static_file/qu/research/Gulf%20Studies/documents/Gulf%20Insights%2023.pdf.

[19] Martin Chulov. "I Will Return Saudi Arabia to Moderate Islam, Says Crown Prince." The Guardian. 24 October 2017. https://www.theguardian.com/world/2017/oct/24/i-will-return-saudi-arabia-moderate-islam-crown-prince.

In 2014, Badr al-Ibrahim, an epidemiologist, writer, and dual US-Saudi national, noted that "Saudi Arabia has a national identity crisis. In the absence of a collective identity, people define themselves through sectarian, regional, and tribal identities." For Al-Ibrahim, national identity was a prerequisite for social harmony and a transition to democracy. He asserted that Saudi Arabia's identity crisis was the result of Saudis having to choose between a Salafi identity imposed on them by a regime that reduced identity to identification with the state.[20] Al-Ibrahim, one of several targeted journalists, commentators, and bloggers, was arrested five years later on terrorism-related charges. He was released in 2019 and tried in 2021.

With the reforms in the backdrop, Al-Issa travelled to Bali with two goals in mind: bask in the limelight as co-convener of a major interfaith gathering under the auspices of the G20 and co-opt Nahdlatul Ulama to ensure it does not challenge Bin Salman's autocratic concept of Islam. Bali was Al-Issa's third attempt to grapple with Nahdlatul Ulama. Initially, he thought ignoring the movement would work. In 2018, Al-Issa dismissed a suggestion by an American interlocutor that he meet Staquf, the Nahdlatul Ulama leader, in Mecca. "As for the Indonesian Imam Pak Yahya, I have never heard of him before… I regret to inform you that it would be difficult for me to meet with Pak Yahya due to an extremely previous busy schedule of meetings with international Islamic personalities," Al-Issa said.[21] The cleric's standoffishness stemmed as much from refusing to acknowledge Nahdlatul Ulama's challenge as from an ingrained perception that Arabs hailing from Islam's cradle were real Muslims unlike syncretic forms of the faith like that prevalent in Indonesia. "It's religious racism," said Azyumardi Azra, an Islamic scholar.[22]

Indonesian-Saudi relations turned downhill from there. Within months of Al-Issa's refusal to meet Staquf, Indonesia quietly persuaded Saudi Arabia to withdraw its ambassador, Osama bin Mohammed Abdullah Al-Shuaib. The government objected to Al-Shuaib's alleged interference in the 2020 presidential election by denouncing on Twitter the Ansor Youth Movement, Nahdlatul Ulama's young adult organisation and a pillar of the Humanitarian Islam movement, as "heretical." Al-Shuaib falsely accused Ansor supporters of burning a flag symbolising Muslim unity.[23]

---

[20] Badr al-Ibrahim. " مفهوم الإصلاح (1): أزمة الهوية الوطنية السعودية ," (Concept of Reform (1): The Saudi National Identity Crisis)." Al-Maqal. 15 January 2014. https://www.almqaal.com/?p=3235.

[21] Private exchange of text messages.

[22] Interview with the author, 30 January 2022.

[23] Coconuts Jakarta. "NU and Netizens Demand Saudi Ambassador to Indonesia Leave the Country over Pro-212 Tweet." 4 December 2018. https://www.baytarrahmah.org/media/2018/coconuts-jakarta_nu-netizens-demand-saudi-ambassador-indonesia-leave-country-pro-212-tweet_12-04-18.pdf.

Al-Issa changed tactics two years later when, in early 2020, he knocked on Nahdlatul Ulama's door in Jakarta. It was the first visit to the world's largest Muslim civil society movement by a Muslim World League leader in six decades. The visit got off to a wrong start because Al-Issa brought Hidayat Nur Wahid with him, a League Supreme Council member and former leader of Indonesia's Prosperous Justice Party (PKS). Bitterly opposed to political Islam, Nahdlatul Ulama sees the PKS as a Muslim Brotherhood affiliate. A month earlier, Hidayat brandished his Islamist credentials by refusing to join Al-Issa on a groundbreaking visit by Muslim leaders to Auschwitz, the Nazi extermination camp in Poland that symbolises the Holocaust.

Java's mosque landscape illustrates the rivalry between Nahdlatul Ulama and the PKS. Mosques with three-tiered tiled roofs resemble traditional Javanese cultural houses of worship. They outnumber the rapidly growing number of Saudi-funded, PKS-built mosques sporting a dome rather than tiles as the third tier of their roof. The construction of a new mosque in a village in Central Java, Nahdlatul Ulama's heartland, tells the story. Contrary to Javanese tradition, the mosque was named after its Saudi benefactor, who funded its construction through the World Assembly of Muslim Youth (WAMY). Like the Muslim World League, WAMY is a Saudi government-controlled non-governmental organisation used for almost half a century to finance Islamic ultra-conservatism globally. WAMY has since become another arrow in Bin Salman's quiver.

A plaque at the mosque's entrance featured the Saudi flag and the emblem of Vision 2030, Bin Salman's plan to reform and diversify the Saudi economy. The plaque thanked WAMY for funding. "We don't name mosques after human beings," complained a Nahdlatul Ulama villager. Villagers suggested the mosque advanced the PKS' political agenda. They complained that a Palestinian flag suddenly flew from the roof of a nearby pickup truck hub from where farmers transport their produce to the market. Initially, only some residents knew what the flag represented. PKS made significant progress in 2019 in the first election after the mosque's construction. The party won over 20% of the vote in a village where, historically, one could count its votes on the one hand.

The mosque signifies Saudi recognition of Indonesia as a challenger to religious soft power in the Muslim world. It suggests that Bin Salman sees religion as a tool to win Indonesian hearts and minds, even if he has largely halted global Saudi religious funding. Finally, the mosque indicates Bin Salman's willingness to work with Brotherhood affiliates despite the kingdom designating the group as a terrorist organisation in 2014. With his support for Javan mosques, Bin Salman followed in his father's footsteps. Welcomed in 2017 by tens of thousands lining Jakarta streets, King Salman committed to building five mosques for the Indonesian military and three new satellite campuses of the Saudi-funded Institute for Islamic and Arabic Studies (LIPIA).

Bahasa Indonesia, Indonesia's official language, was long virtually nonexistent on LIPIA's campus, traditionally a bastion of Saudi religious culture dedicated to teaching Arabic and Saudi-style Islam in association with the Imam Muhammad ibn Saud Islamic University in Riyadh.[24]

In Bali, Al-Issa's moment under the Indonesian sun was short-lived. He quickly discovered that money buys a lot but only some things when the Indonesian group turned down millions of dollars in Saudi funding. Al-Issa also found that in Nahdlatul Ulama, he faced a competitor determined to pursue an independent agenda that potentially threatened Saudi efforts to monopolise the definition of moderate Islam in ways that would reinforce Bin Salman's grip on power and aspirations for leadership of the Muslim world.

In contrast to Al-Issa's vision and marching orders, Nahdlatul Ulama positioned the Religion Forum 20 as the beginning of a process of reflection by major faith groups, including Islam, on their often-problematic histories and tenets. The movement argued that confronting 'ugly truths' was a prerequisite for positioning religion as a provider of solutions rather than an aggravator of the world's problems. Nahdlatul Ulama's track record of addressing problematic tenets of Islamic law made it difficult to ignore its proposition. So did the movement's willingness to acknowledge Muslims' role in violence against non-Muslims in Africa and Asia. Yet, Nahdlatul defends its role in the killing in 1965 and 1966 of at least 500,000 alleged Communists, leftists, trade unionists, ethnic Chinese, and atheists in a purge instigated by the Indonesian military.

To emphasise its sincerity in advocating religious reform and willingness to point the finger at Islam alongside other major religions, Nahdlatul Ulama spotlighted at the R20 Archbishop Henry Ndukuba, the primate of the Church of Nigeria, the largest Anglican Church in the world with 25 million worshippers, rather than leaders of the Church of England. Ndukuba didn't mince his words in his keynote speech as he described Muslim violence against Christians in Nigeria. "Attacks in Northern and Central and other parts of Nigeria are a clear attempt to terrorize and displace local populations of Christians so that they flee and leave their land and property," Ndukuba told his audience. The archbishop went on to say, "Nigeria is now one of the most dangerous countries to be a Christian. Thousands of people have been killed by these well-organized, well-equipped, and well-funded extremist groups, and over 150 villages have been sacked. There are over 2 million internally displaced people, and thousands more have been kidnapped for sex and ransom. Churches are now forced to pay millions of Naira for ransom for kidnapped church members, and over a dozen pastors have been martyred by these extremists."[25]

---

[24] James M. Dorsey. "Indonesia: A Major Prize in the Battle for the Soul of Islam." The Turbulent World with James M. Dorsey. 30 July 2020. https://www.jamesmdorsey.net/post/indonesia-a-major-prize-in-the-battle-for-the-soul-of-islam.

[25] Henry Ndukuba. "Address by the Archbishop of Nigeria to the G20 Religious Forum Meeting in Bali 2 Nov 2022." Anglican.ink. 8 November 2022. https://anglican.ink/2022/11/08/address-by-the-archbishop-of-nigeria-to-the-g20-religious-forum-meeting-in-bali-2-nov-2022/.

Lamenting efforts in the West to portray violence in Nigeria as the fall out of tribal groups fighting over economic resources rather than religious militancy, Ndukuba spoke as the US State Department dropped the African country for the second year running from its list of "countries of particular concern" for their violations of religious freedoms and weeks before African leaders gathered in Washington for a summit with President Joe Biden. "Politically correct disinformation seems to be strategically pushed forward by Nigerian politicians and other groups who benefit from these undeclared massacres through various corrupt monetary and security budgets and the perpetuation of a radical ideology," the archbishop said.

Ndukuba's exposure of Muslim violence and strained relationship with the Church of England served Nahdlatul Ulama's agenda in multiple ways. It underlined the need for a reform of Islamic jurisprudence that would deprive extremists like Boko Haram, the militant Islamists in Nigeria responsible for many attacks on Christians, Al-Qaeda, and the Islamic State, of a doctrinal justification for their ideology and violence. Moreover, the archbishop's dispute with the Church of England over homosexuality corresponded with the Indonesian group's rejection of Western attempts to impose recognition of LGBTQ rights, even if Nahdlatul Ulama, unlike Ndukuba, endorses informal live-and-let-live arrangements. The dispute erupted after Justin Welby, archbishop of Canterbury, condemned Ndukuba's virulent denunciation of homosexuality.[26] Ndukuba described homosexuality as a "deadly virus" and likened it to "yeast that should be urgently and radically expunged and excised lest it affects the whole dough."

Nahdlatul Ulama's proposition put Al-Issa, the League, and their state backers in an uncomfortable position. It challenged the kingdom, the League, and Al-Issa to confront their ultra-conservative, supremacist past rather than studiously ignoring it. It's a past that haunts them. Al-Issa's condemnation in 2022 of a brutal attack in New York state on writer Salman Rushdie that cost the 75-year-old India-born British-American writer an eye as "unacceptable,"[27] rang hollow. The condemnation would have been more credible had Al-Issa used the opportunity to annul a 1989 fatwa declaring Rushdie an apostate, a crime punishable with death under Sharia law, for publishing The Satanic Verses, a controversial novel inspired by Prophet Mohammed's life. At the time, the League's Islamic Law Academy demanded that Rushdie be prosecuted in a British court and tried in absentia under Sharia law in

---

[26] The Archbishop of Canterbury. "Statement by the Archbishop of Canterbury Regarding Comments by the Primate of Nigeria." 5 March 2021. https://www.archbishopofcanterbury.org/news/news-and-statements/statement-archbishop-canterbury-regarding-comments-primate-nigeria.

[27] Francesco Bangarra. "Salman Rushdie Attack 'Unacceptable' to Islam, Says MWL Chief Al-Issa." Arab News. 21 August 2022. https://www.arabnews.com/node/2147271/world.

an Islamic country.[28] The League issued its fatwa days after Iranian spiritual leader Ayatollah Khomeini condemned Rushdie to death and called on Muslims to kill him. Khomeini put a US$2.8 million bounty on Rushdie's head.[29]

Al-Issa's declaration would also have garnered greater credibility had he cancelled statements by the League calling for killing or disciplining other writers and intellectuals like Mahmoud Mohammed Taha and Rashad Khalifa. In 1975, the League demanded that Taha, a 76-year-old Sudanese religious thinker and engineer, be sentenced to death on charges of apostasy for opposing Islamic law. Taha was tried and executed ten years later.[30] Judith Miller, a New York Times reporter, remembers Taha's execution. "I shall never forget his expression: His eyes were defiant, his mouth firm. He showed no hint of fear," she recorded in her book, 'God Has Ninety-nine Names.'[31]

A withdrawal of those statements would have offered solace to Taha's family and Khalifa's heirs, whom the League excommunicated in 1998. The League stopped short of calling for Khalifa's death but accused the Egyptian-born American imam and biochemist of rejecting the Sunnah, Prophet Mohammed's traditions and practices. Khalifa preached that Muslims should base their beliefs and practices exclusively on the Qur'an and ignore the Sunnah and the hadith, a record of the Prophet's sayings and actions. In a fatwa, the League urged Muslims to be aware of Khalifa's evilness and not to cooperate with him or recognise him as an imam. Two years later, one of Khalifa's students stabbed him to death in an Arizona mosque.[32]

Al-Issa has preached religious tolerance since 2015. He set a new tone with visits to the Holocaust Museum in Washington, a Paris synagogue, and Auschwitz in 2020, where more than one million men, women, and children, mostly Jews, were killed.[33] On videos of his death camp tour, he appears visibly

---

[28] Richard C. Martin (ed.). "Rushdie, Salman (1947–)." In Encyclopedia of Islam and the Muslim World, Volume 2 M-Z. New York: Macmillan. 2004. p. 603.

[29] Agence France-Press. "February 14, 1989: The Fatwa Against Salman Rushdie." 12 August 2022. https://www.france24.com/en/live-news/20220812-february-14-1989-the-fatwa-against-salman-rushdie.

[30] George Packer. "The Moderate Martyr: A Radically Peaceful Vision of Islam." The New Yorker. 11 September 2006. https://www.newyorker.com/magazine/2006/09/11/the-moderate-martyr.

[31] Judith Miller. "God Has Ninety-Nine Names." New York: Simon & Schuster. 1996. p. 12.

[32] Muhammad Abu Samra. "Liberal Critics, ʿUlamaʾ and the Debate on Islam in the Contemporary Arab World." In Meir Hatina (ed.) Guardians of Faith in Modern Times: ʿUlamaʾ in the Middle East. Leiden: Brill. 2009. p. 284.

[33] Arab News. "Muslim World League Chief Leads Delegation to Auschwitz for Holocaust Memorial." 23 January 2020. https://www.arabnews.com/node/1617381/world.

shaken.³⁴ A year earlier, Al-Issa warned in an interview with Arab News that "he who denies the Holocaust seeks to repeat it... Rational human beings must unite and work together to restrain the advocates of murder and extermination; otherwise, the lessons of history won't be useful."³⁵ In a Washington Post op-ed, Al-Issa argued that Holocaust denial "has only helped those who continue to perpetuate hateful ideas of racial, ethnic, or religious purity, such as the genocidal killers of the Rohingya people in Myanmar. The lessons of the Holocaust are universal, and Muslims around the world have a responsibility to learn them, heed the warnings, and join the international commitment to ensure 'never again.'".³⁶

Al-Issa sought to ensure US and European support for an autocratic Saudi version of moderate Islam by highlighting its utility. In 2020, he repeatedly sought to calm emotions after a Pakistani-born Muslim militant stabbed two staffers of the French satirical weekly Charlie Hebdo because it published cartoons depicting Prophet Mohammed. It was the second such attack on the paper. Five years earlier, militants stormed Charlie Hebdo's office and killed 12 staffers. Al-Issa called on Muslims to ignore the cartoons much like the Prophet ignored ridiculers. In statements, the Muslim World League³⁷ and the Senior Scholars Council, Saudi Arabia's highest religious body, of which Al-Issa is a member, urged the faithful to disregard cartoons because the Prophet was above such depictions.

At times, Al-Issa is one step ahead of Bin Salman. His Auschwitz visit and acknowledgement of the Holocaust enhanced the kingdom's projected commitment to a moderate and religiously tolerant form of Islam. Al-Issa travelled to the Polish camp two years after suggesting a Muslim-Christian-Jewish interfaith delegation travel to Jerusalem to promote peace.³⁸ The proposal

---

³⁴ Vanessa Gera. "Islamic Leaders Make 'Groundbreaking' Visit to Auschwitz." Yahoo News. 24 January 2020. https://www.yahoo.com/now/islamic-leaders-groundbreaking-visit-auschwitz-152516116.html.

³⁵ Mohammed Al-Sulami, Rawan Radwan, and Jennifer Bell. "Holocaust a Crime Against All Humanity, Says MWL Chief." Arab News. 28 January 2019. https://www.arabnews.com/node/1442951/world.

³⁶ Mohammad Al-Issa. "Why Muslims from Around the World Should Remember the Holocaust." The Washington Post. 25 January 2019. https://www.washingtonpost.com/opinions/2019/01/25/why-muslims-around-world-should-remember-holocaust/.

³⁷ Jaber al-Maliki. " ، أي مع التعامل في حكمة أكثر يجعلنا الإسلامي وعُيننا :إسلامي" (Muslim World League: Our Islamic Awareness Makes Us Wiser in Dealing with Attempts to Insult Religion)." Al-Madina. 25 October 2020. https://www.al-madina.com/article/705500/-حكمة-أكثر-يجعلنا-الإسلامي-وعينا-الإسلامي-العالم-رابطة/الأخبار-خر
الإساءة-و-للتطاول-محاولة-أي-مع-التعامل-في .

³⁸ Hollie McKay. "Islamic Group Chief Calls for Muslims to Join Christians, Jews in Jerusalem Meeting." Fox News. 5 October 2018. https://www.foxnews.com/world/islamic-group-chief-calls-for-muslims-to-join-christians-jews-in-jerusalem-meeting.

signalled early in Bin Salman's reign his willingness to expand relations with Israel but would not do so unconditionally and not without Israeli moves to resolve the Jewish state's conflict with the Palestinians. In an interview six months earlier, Bin Salman crossed a red line by becoming the first Saudi leader to acknowledge "Israelis have the right to have their own land."[39] Bin Salman has since made a resolution of the Palestinian conflict a pre-condition in US-led efforts to negotiate diplomatic relations with Israel.

Al-Issa prides himself on his interfaith outreach and support for social reforms. "I have travelled to the Vatican to elevate interfaith understanding with His Holiness Pope Francis. I visited the Grand Synagogue of Paris and the United States Holocaust Memorial Museum. I welcomed the highest-level delegation of U.S. evangelical Christian leaders ever to visit Saudi Arabia… Among my proudest achievements (as justice minister) was licensing Saudi Arabia's first women lawyers. I also reformed the Saudi judiciary system," he wrote in a Newsweek op-ed, written to coincide with a meeting of the UAE-backed Muslim Council of Elders to which he had not been invited.[40]

Powerful groups like the American Jewish Committee (AJC) uncritically embraced Al-Issa. They wanted to encourage Saudi Arabia's unprecedented break with its past. The AJC and others hoped the break would be the death knell for Islamic extremism and spark tectonic geopolitical shifts such as Saudi recognition of Israel. They feared pressure, for example, to lift the ban on non-Muslim houses of worship could undermine reforms.

Even so, some of Al-Issa's interlocutors in Washington were unsure what to make of the cleric. A Saudi intellectual rhetorically asked Saudi Arabia scholar Stephane Lacroix, "How can one take Mohammed al Issa's statements seriously when religious bookstores in Riyadh are full of books advocating the exact opposite?"[41] Moreover, allegations that Bin Salman had ordered religious scholars to issue a fatwa, justifying the extrajudicial, extraterritorial killing in Canada of a fugitive Saudi intelligence official called the crown prince's moderation into question as did the murder of journalist Jamal Khashoggi in the kingdom's consulate in Istanbul in 2018.[42]

---

[39] Jeffrey Goldberg. "Saudi Crown Prince: Iran's Supreme Leader 'Makes Hitler Look Good'." The Atlantic. 2 April 2018. https://www.theatlantic.com/international/archive/2018/04/mohammed-bin-salman-iran-israel/557036/.

[40] Mohammed Al-Issa. "I Lead the Muslim World League. Here Is Why I Broke Taboos to Acknowledge the Holocaust." Newsweek. 30 January 2019. https://www.newsweek.com/holocaust-muslims-vatican-interfaith-responsible-leadership-1311860.

[41] Stephane Lacroix. "Saudi Arabia and the Limits of Religious Reform." Transatlantic Policy Network on Religion and Diplomacy. 25 February 2019. https://sharepoint.ucl ouvain.be/sites/cismodoc/Articles/S.%20Lacroix,%20Saudi%20Arabia%20and%20the%20L imits%20of%20Religious%20Reform,%20CIRIS,%2025%20f%C3%A9vrier%202019.pdf.

[42] In the United States District Court for the District of Columbia, Saad AlJabri vs Mohammed bin Salman bin Abdul Aziz Al Saud et all. 6 August 2020. https://www.cou rthousenews.com/wp-content/uploads/2020/08/Aljabri-Complaint.pdf.

For his part, Al-Issa has never explained what persuaded him to abandon his earlier supremacist and anti-Semitic views. In 2014, the year before Bin Salman came to power, Al-Issa, as justice minister and member of the Senior Scholars Council, was unequivocal in his denunciations of Jews, Christians, and witchcraft defined as astrology, plant medicine, palm-reading, and animal calling.[43]

"Jews have harsh hearts, harsh as stones, even harsher... Jews distorted the Torah. They distorted it intentionally and wickedly... The truth is that those who know about how Jews describe God won't see any greater ignorance and ugliness of ideas. They, may God protect us, describe the God Almighty with characteristics that they lied and fabricated of Almighty in their distorted Torah," Al-Issa said in a commentary on Riyadh-based Qur'an Radio on 16 August 2014. Al-Issa was referring to the first five books of the Bible by their Hebrew name. Al-Issa asserted that Christians "spoke lies and fabrications, that God has a son, Jesus, The Messiah, the son of Mary" and "abused the needs of people in poor and impoverished countries. They come to them, treat them, and give them money, so they accept" Christianity.[44]

Similarly, when asked in 2011 by religious freedom scholar and activist Nina Shea why a Saudi textbook on the sayings and deeds of Prophet Mohammed referenced the Protocols of the Elders of Zion, a notoriously anti-Semitic tract fabricated during the Russian revolution, Al-Issa argued that it was part of Islamic culture and widely available in the kingdom. The former justice minister recalled that his father had a copy in his library.[45] Saudi Arabia has since revised its textbooks to eliminate anti-Semitic and anti-Christian references.

Nahdlatul Ulama put Al-Issa back in the hot seat barely two months after the Bali summit. In an assault on Islamic orthodoxy, the group invited the Saudi cleric to participate in an international conference of Islamic scholars convened in the Javan city of Surabaya to discuss abolishing the concept of a caliphate under Islamic law. Instead, Nahdlatul Ulama proposed introducing the notion of the nation-state and the United Nations, structures without a base in Muslim religious legal tradition. The proposal legitimised modern nation-states' constitutional and legal systems instead of Sharia-based rule. The conference was held a day before Nahdlatul Ulama celebrated its centenary according to the Hijri calendar.

---

[43] James M. Dorsey. "Papal Visit Boosts UAE Effort to Redefine Concepts of Tolerance." The Turbulent World with James M. Dorsey. 4 February 2019. https://www.jamesmdorsey.net/post/papal-visit-boosts-uae-effort-to-redefine-concepts-of-tolerance.

[44] Ali Al-Ahmad. "Official Pipeline of Hate, from Grade School to the Military, to Public Broadcasting." Institute for Gulf Affairs. September 2020. https://www.gulfinstitute.org/wp-content/uploads/2020/10/the-Saudi-Pipeline-of-Hatred.pdf.

[45] Nina Shea. "Saudi Arabia's Troubling Educational Curriculum." House Committee on Foreign Affairs, US Congress. 19 July 2017. https://www.congress.gov/115/meeting/house/106289/witnesses/HHRG-115-FA18-Wstate-SheaN-20170719.pdf.

Initially, Al-Issa said he would attend the gathering but backed out because it would have been more challenging to duck the issue if he were there in person. Instead, he opted for a video statement that ignored the proposed reform because it would open the door to questioning autocratic rule in Saudi Arabia and the Muslim world based on Muslim religious law. Al-Issa was not alone among state-aligned religious scholars caught between a rock and a hard place. Their response to Nahdlatul Ulama's invitation suggested how the Indonesian group threatened proponents of an autocratic definition of moderate Islam. Like Al-Issa, Abdullah Bin Bayyah, the head of the UAE's Fatwa Council, Egyptian Grand Mufti Shawki Allam, and his predecessor, Ali Goma, who religiously justified the killing by security forces in 2013 of some 800 Muslim Brotherhood protesters,[46] initially said they would attend but also backed out.

The call for abolishing the caliphate threatened to force men like Allam, Bin Bayyah, and Goma to confront their past. They were among 126 prominent state-aligned Islamic scholars, including many associated with Al-Azhar, the Cairo-based 1,053-year-old citadel of Islamic learning, who, in 2014, signed an open letter to Abu Bakr al-Baghdadi, the late Islamic State leader. They wrote the letter after Al-Baghdadi declared a caliphate in parts of Syria and Iraq with himself as caliph. The clerics insisted "there is agreement (ittifaq) among scholars that a caliphate is an obligation upon the Ummah (Muslim community)" but emphasised that Al-Baghdad's declaration failed to meet Islamic law requirements, including consensus.[47]

The letter illustrated the need for jurisprudential reform to clarify and update legal concepts, eliminate outdated precepts, and reduce confusion about the law's spirit and attempt. It served as an example of problems inherent in legal texts in which state-aligned conservative scholars and Islamist militants recognised themselves. "We...realized that the ulama's interpretations of apostasy, al-jihad, and al-qital (sacrifice of life for ends and values) were in fact not too different from the Islamists' positions and that the deviation from the spirit of Allah's Book did not just come with the Islamist movement but that it had occurred much earlier in history, namely during the formative period of Islamic scholarship!" said Muhammed Shahrur, a prominent Syrian philosopher years before the scholars agreed with Al-Baghdadi on the legitimacy of the caliphate.[48]

---

[46] Usaama al-Azami. "Rabaa Massacre and the Death of Middle East Democracy." Middle East Eye. 15 August 2022. https://www.middleeasteye.net/opinion/egypt-rabaa-massacre-middle-east-democracy-death.

[47] Shawqi Allam, Abdullah Bin Bayyah, Ali Goma et al. "Open Letter to Dr. Ibrahim Awwad Al-Badri, Alias 'Abu Bakr Al-Baghdadi,' and to the Fighters and Followers of the Self-Declared 'Islamic State'." Royal Islamic Strategic Studies Centre. 19 September 2014. https://rissc.jo/wp-content/uploads/2019/04/Letter_to_Baghdadi-EN.pdf.

[48] Andreas Christmann. "Political Islam." In Andreas Christmann (ed.) The Qur'an, Morality and Critical Reason: The Essential Muhammad Shahrur. Leiden: Brill. 2009. p. 329.

Indonesian conservatives and Islamists backed the Middle Eastern clerics' rejection of the Nahdlatul Ulama proposition. "We'll never reject a caliphate concept. Rejecting the caliphate is apostasy," declared Novel Bamukmin, a leader of the Islamic Brotherhood Front, a group viewed as the reincarnation of the Islamic Defenders Front. The government banned the Defenders Front in 2020. The group raided bars and brothels and targeted non-practising Muslims and religious minorities. Referring to Nahdlatul Ulama, Bamukmin asserted that reformists "can never voice the truth. They have no self-worth; they've destroyed religious values, Islamic values."

Privately, state-aligned conservative Gulf clerics agreed with their Indonesian and Islamist counterparts, even if they were not willing to publicly challenge Humanitarian Islam authenticity beyond evading Nahdlatul Ulama's call for judicial reform. "Indonesian Islam is not Islam. Indonesian Islam positions itself as different from Islam in the Arab world. They are deviants. Indonesian Islam rejects Islam's universality. Muslims are united by one God, one Qur'an, and one Messenger. Indonesian Islam is like the Islamic State. It deems Muslim terrorists. They are like the Islamic State. They are both evil. They disgrace Islam," thundered a conservative Gulf cleric.[49]

Students at Al-Azhar saw the university's teachings as confirming jihadism's grounding in Islamic law. "The Islamic State didn't emerge out of thin air. The texts that the group cites are exactly what we are taught. The only difference with Al-Azhar is that the Islamic State acts on these precepts," said a student. He refused to be identified because he was about to join Islamic State. Another student argued that "it's all about sacred texts. We follow neither Al Azhar nor the Islamic State. However, the fact is that the Islamic State adheres to the text in the most consequential form."

Al-Azhar and other prominent state-aligned scholars' refusal to excommunicate jihadists reinforced perceptions of their legitimacy. "No believer can be declared an apostate, regardless of his sins," Al-Azhar said repeatedly.[50] Even so, the scholars insisted Islamic jurisprudence did not require reform because jihadist ideology was not rooted in religious law. Jihadism misrepresented and misconstrued the faith, the scholars said.[51] By blaming deviants rather than Islam for the violence, the scholars helped Muslim autocrats maintain their grip on power by reducing religious law problems to security issues and stymieing debate that could question autocrats' legitimacy on religious grounds.

---

[49] Interview with the author, 20 January 2020.

[50] Veto. "وكيل «الأزهر»: لهذه الأسباب لم نُكفر «داعش»(Al-Azhar Trustee: For These Reasons, We Did Not Declare ISIS to Be an Unbeliever)." 12 December 2014. https://www.vetogate.com/1374000.

[51] Al Jazeera. "السيسي يدعو لثورة دينية ضد نصوص تم تقديسها لقرون(Al-Sisi Calls for a Religious Revolution Against Texts Sanctified For Centuries)." 2 January 2015. https://1-a1072.azureedge.net/news/2015/1/2/%D8%A7%D9%84%D8%B3%D9%8A%D8%B3%D9%8A-%D9%8A%D8%AF%D8%B9%D9%88-%D9%84%D8%AB%D9%88%D8%B1%D8%A9-%D8%AF%D9%8A%D9%86%D9%8A%D8%A9-%D8%B6%D8%AF-%D9%86%D8%B5%D9%88%D8%B5-%D8%AA%D9%85.

Nahdlatul Ulama called for abolishing the caliphate a day after the Surabaya conference at a commemoration of the group's centennial in the East Javan city of Sidoarjo, attended by more than a milion people and Indonesian President Joko Widodo. "Nahdlatul Ulama believes it is essential to the well-being of Muslims to develop a new vision capable of replacing the long-established aspiration, rooted in Islamic jurisprudence (fiqh), of uniting Muslims throughout the world into a single universal state, or caliphate," the group said in a declaration read out at the rally.[52] "It is neither feasible nor desirable to reestablish a universal caliphate that would unite Muslims throughout the world in opposition to non-Muslims. As recently demonstrated by the Islamic State in Iraq and Syria, or ISIS, attempts to do so will inevitably be disastrous and contrary to the purposes of Sharia (Islamic law): i.e., the protection of religion, human life, sound reasoning, family, and property," the declaration said.

The declaration asserted that Islam faces a choice: maintaining the obligation to create a caliphate or reforming Islamic jurisprudence so that it would "embrace a new vision and develop a new discourse regarding Islamic jurisprudence, which will prevent the political weaponization of identity; curtail the spread of communal hatred; promote solidarity and respect among the diverse peoples, cultures, and nations of the world; and foster the emergence of a truly just and harmonious world order."

Nahdlatul Ulama argued in a paper published during the Surabaya conference that "Muslims should acknowledge that a socio-political construct (or imperium) capable of operationalizing these normative views (of a Caliphate) across the Muslim world no longer exists" and that "as a consequence of choosing to retain the established fiqh view and norms associated therewith it would automatically be a religious duty incumbent upon Muslims to revive the imperium. This, in turn, would necessarily entail dissolving any and all existing nation-states, under whose governance Muslims currently live." The group asserted that the view that Muslims "should have a default attitude of enmity towards non-Muslims and that infidels...should be subject to discrimination is well established within turats al-fiqh (the tradition of Islamic jurisprudence)."[53]

The paper reasoned that "texts that legitimize or actively encourage suspicion, segregation, discrimination, and enmity towards – as well as conflict with – those legally classified as 'infidels' ...may be found scattered throughout the corpus of classical Islamic jurisprudence or fiqh. Many Muslim communities throughout the world continue to embrace these teachings... Muslim

---

[52] Religion 20, Nahdlatul Ulama, and Satu Abad NU. "Nahdlatul Ulama Centennial Proclamation." 7 February 2023. https://g20religion.org/media/2023/Nahdlatul-Ulama-Centennial-Proclamation.pdf.

[53] Religion 20, Nahdlatul Ulama, and Satu Abad NU. "Is There a Need to Establish an Islamic Legal (Fiqhi) Foundation for Global Peace and Harmony?" Center for Shared Civilizational Values. February 2023. https://g20religion.org/media/2023/Is-There-a-Need-to-Establish-an-Islamic-Legal_Fiqhi_Foundation-for-Global-Peace-and-Harmony.pdf.

groups involved in conflict generally defend their conduct, including the use of violence and terror, by citing passages from these classical fiqh texts." In 2019, the Indonesian movement first put its money where its mouth is when 20,000 of its scholars issued a religious finding that eliminated the category of kafir in Islamic law.[54]

The paper argued further that religious legitimisation of the United Nations was necessary to ensure that it "even remotely begin(s) to fulfill the world's hopes and expectations" of providing "a guarantee of protection to each identity group, ensuring that its members will be treated justly, and thereby prevent identity-based hatred and conflict" and guaranteeing "territorial boundaries that are definitive and more or less certain for each nation-state."

As a result, the paper suggested Muslim scholars needed to assess "to what extent are the Charter of the United Nations and the United Nations Organization valid, from the perspective of fiqh (the body of Islamic law), as agreements…that are legally binding upon Muslims, on the basis of the validity of the parties — i.e., the states and heads of state — that claimed the authority to serve as their (Muslims') representatives at the time they agreed to the UN Charter?"

Nahdlatul Ulama's call for abolishing the caliphate was no less controversial than when Egyptian scholar, judge, and government minister Ali Abdel Raziq put forward a similar argument just shy of a century ago. In a book published in 1925, the year after Turkish leader Mustafa Kemal Ataturk abolished the Ottoman Caliphate, the world's last acknowledged unitary Islamic state, Raziq reasoned that neither the Qur'an nor the Sunna, the traditions of the Prophet, advocate the establishment of a caliphate. "Islam does not advocate a specific form of government," Raziq wrote.[55] Much like Nahdlatul Ulama charges today, Raziq argued that rulers asserted religious justifications for a caliphate "so that they could use religion as a shield protecting their thrones against the attacks of rebels."

As a result, Muslim autocrats and their surrogates had good reasons to reject religious reform, including the call for abolishing the notion of the caliphate. Reform would deprive them of their ability to project autocracy as necessary to combat extremism and promote moderate Islam. It would also undermine autocrats' use of counterterrorism to justify squashing criticism of their rule. Moreover, with Islamophobia on the rise, religious legitimisation of the nation-state constituted a double-edged sword for Muslim autocrats and Islamists. It potentially weakened their argument in favour of a global ban on blasphemy because it helped take the wind out of the sails of often whipped-up anti-Muslim sentiment that questions Muslim attitudes and loyalty towards

[54] Nahdlatul Ulama. "Nahdlatul Ulama Rejects the Relevance of "Infidel" as a Legal Category Within the Context of Modern Nation States." Bayt ar-Rahma. 16 October 2019. https://baytarrahmah.org/2019_10_16_world-first-nahdlatul-ulama-abolishes-the-legal-category-of-infidel-within-islamic-law/.

[55] Ali Abdel Raziq. "Islam and the Foundations of Political Power" (Edited by A. Filali-Ansary). Edinburgh: Edinburgh University Press. 2012.

the state and Islam's compatibility with democracy. That sentiment was, for example, evident when an anchor on India's controversial Hindu nationalist, Hindi-language Zee news channel recently asked whether "Muslims who sing the national anthem become kafirs." The anchor was using the Arabic word for an infidel.[56]

Most importantly, anchoring the United Nations and its charter in Islamic religious law would increase pressure to respect human rights. The charter obliges member states to honour "fundamental human rights…the dignity and worth of the human person, (and)…the equal rights of men and women." Muslim-majority states couched their acceptance in the Islamic jurisprudential language employed by the Organisation for Islamic Cooperation (OIC) rather than the UN charter. The OIC groups 57 Muslim-majority countries. Introducing the concept of the nation-state and the UN into religious law would oblige Muslim-majority states to recognise human rights as legally framed by the UN charter. So far, various Muslim-majority states have used the OIC's legal framework to monopolise the right to interpret Islamic law and bend it to their will, violating the charter and human rights. In Saudi Arabia, like the UAE, that included a demand for absolute obedience to the ruler.

In response to the 1948 Universal Declaration of Human Rights and the 1966 International Covenants on Civil and Political Rights (ICCPR)[57] and Economic, Social, and Cultural Rights (ICESCR),[58] Muslim-majority states adopted the 1990 Cairo Declaration on Human Rights in Islam. The declaration neglected gender and non-Muslim rights. It allowed OIC members to criminalise blasphemy and lobby the United Nations to classify it as a violation of human rights and hate speech. The declaration was revised two decades later to strengthen women's rights protection and remove supremacist language. The revisions removed Sharia references from operational articles but kept them in the preamble. The revised document emphasised national law primacy over human rights. It disregarded the need to protect freedoms of expression, association, assembly, political participation, and universal suffrage. The declaration insisted that freedom of expression "should not be used to violate sanctities of the dignity of prophets, religions, religious symbols or to undermine moral and ethical values of society."[59]

[56] Listening Post. "India: Why Is Gautam Adani so Interested in NDTV?" Al Jazeera. 17 December 2022. https://www.aljazeera.com/program/the-listening-post/2022/12/17/india-why-is-gautam-adani-so-interested-in-ndtv.

[57] United Nations Human Rights Office of the Commissioner. "International Covenant on Civil and Political Rights." 16 December 1966. https://www.ohchr.org/en/instruments-mechanisms/instruments/international-covenant-civil-and-political-rights.

[58] United Nations Human Rights Office of the Commissioner. "International Covenant on Economic, Social and Cultural Rights." 16 December 1966. https://www.ohchr.org/en/instruments-mechanisms/instruments/international-covenant-economic-social-and-cultural-rights.

[59] Turan Kayaoglu. "The Organization of Islamic Cooperation's Declaration on Human Rights: Promises and Pitfalls." Brookings. 28 September 2020. https://www.brookings.edu/research/the-organization-of-islamic-cooperations-declaration-on-human-rights-promises-and-pitfalls/.

Treating militancy and extremism as unrelated to Islamic law came at a price. It stifled debate about the reform of religious jurisprudence related to violence, extremism, and rights-enhancing social reforms. Viewed as a threat to autocratic control, reformists, intellectuals, and scholars ended up behind bars or, even worse, facing death penalties on trumped-up charges of being heretics or apostates. The securitisation of religious debate allowed autocrats like Bin Salman to take exclusive credit for reforms and discourage activism by condemning activists who advocated change to prison terms and travel bans. Finally, by preventing the emergence of a robust civil society, Bin Salman and other Middle Eastern autocrats unwittingly set the stage for a push for religious change from Asia rather than the Arab Muslim heartland.

Muhammad Abu Al-Fadl, the deputy editor of Egypt's influential state-controlled Al-Ahram newspaper, noted in Surabaya that "the majority of the Arab and Islamic delegations at the First International Convention on Islamic Jurisprudence for a Global Civilization expressed a traditional mindset that has become outdated. For they dealt with the centenary of Nahdlatul Ulama as if it were a carnival," Abu Al-Fadl wrote. "If the leadership of religious institutions in the Arab world continues to insist on burying their heads in the sand, then Arab states may require another 100 years to absorb the Nahdlatul Ulama project in Indonesia."

Abu Al-Fadl added that "the majority of Muslims look to the Arab world for guidance, and the failure of this region's ulama (Muslim religious scholars) to keep up with the transformations taking place will lead to the rug being pulled out from under them. For the openness adopted by Nahdlatul Ulama and its new Chairman, Yahya Cholil Staquf, will not stop at one specific country or region."[60] Abu Al-Fadl picked up on Nahdlatul Ulama's potential to outflank Arab proponents of Islam with its projection of a moderate interpretation of the faith. The Egyptian journalist warned that the "Arab face of Islam…was hopelessly contorted by extremism." He suggested, "certain elements in the West have become interested in 'Asian Islam,' which appears to be more moderate than Arab Islam (that is) less possessed by a genuine and sincere tendency to act with tolerance."[61]

Nahdlatul Ulama's call for the abolition of the caliphate challenged Muslim and non-Muslim world leaders who think in civilisational rather than national terms. These leaders imagine their countries' conceptual and/or physical boundaries as defined by history, ethnicity, culture, and/or religion rather than international law. They often deny the existence of the other and use their civilisational worldview to legitimise their authoritarian or autocratic rule. Russian President Vladimir Putin was in good company when he justified his 2022

---

[60] Muhammad Abu Al-Fadl. "الإسلام الإندونيسي.. مرة أخرى"(Indonesian Islam…Once Again)." 15 February 2023. https://gate.ahram.org.eg/daily/News/204398/4/888599/قضايا-وآراء/الإسلام-الإندونيسي-مرة-أخرى.aspx. R20 Indonesia 2022. https://r20-indonesia.org/.

[61] Muhammad Abu Fadil. "Political Horizons for Indonesian Islam (آفاق سياسية للإسلام الإندونيسي)." Al Arab. 15 June 2015. https://alarab.co.uk/آفاق-سياسية-للإسلام-الإندونيسي

invasion of Ukraine by asserting that Russians and Ukrainians were one people. In other words, Ukrainians as a nation did not exist. Neither did the Taiwanese or coastal states' maritime rights in the South China Sea, according to Chinese President Xi Jinping, nor Palestinians in the vision of Israeli Prime Minister Binyamin Netanyahu and his ultra-nationalist and religiously ultra-conservative coalition partners. Superiority and exceptionalism also guide Turkish President Recep Tayyip Erdogan, Indian Prime Minister Narendra Modi, and Hungary's Victor Orban.[62] In 2023, Xi expanded the definition of civilisationalism when he unveiled his Global Civilisation Initiative at a Beijing conference of 500 political parties from 150 countries.[63] The initiative redefined civilisation to incorporate the protection of autocracy. Taking a stab at the Western promotion of democracy and human rights, the initiative suggested that civilisations can live in harmony if they refrain from projecting their values and models globally.[64]

Xi's definition suited Al-Issa and Bin Salman, who declared himself the ultimate arbitrator of Islamic law.[65] Neither man intended to follow Nahdlatul Ulama's lead by confronting their history and revising their religious law, even if it was no longer fit for purpose. Since coming to office, Bin Salman has insisted that he was returning Saudi Arabia to a 'pure Islam' practised at the time of Prophet Mohammed and in the kingdom before the 1979 Iranian revolution. "The teachings of the Prophet and the four caliphs—they were amazing. They were perfect," Bin Salman told The Atlantic in 2022.[66]

Speaking to The Guardian four years earlier, Bin Salman attempted to rewrite history to fit his projection of Saudi Arabia as an enlightened, moderate Muslim-majority country by sweeping aside Wahhabism as an aberration…[67] "What happened in the last 30 years is not Saudi Arabia. What happened in the region in the last 30 years is not the Middle East. After the Iranian revolution in 1979, people wanted to copy this model in different countries, one of them is Saudi Arabia. We didn't know how to deal with it. And the problem spread all over the world. Now is the time to get rid of it," Bin Salman said. The

[62] James M. Dorsey. "Civilizationism vs the Nation State." The Turbulent World with James M. Dorsey. 24 March 2019. https://www.jamesmdorsey.net/post/civilizationism-vs-the-nation-state

[63] Outlook. "President Xi Moots Global Civilisation Initiative at World Political Parties Meet Held by CPC." 29 April 2023. https://www.outlookindia.com/international/president-xi-moots-global-civilisation-initiative-at-world-political-parties-meet-held-by-cpc-news-270457.

[64] CGTN. "Full Text of Xi Jinping's Keynote Address at the CPC in Dialogue with World Political Parties High-Level Meeting." 16 March 2023. https://news.cgtn.com/news/2023-03-16/Full-text-Xi-s-speech-at-CPC-in-Dialogue-with-World-Political-Parties-1id6MvcS8E0/index.html.

[65] Graeme Wood. "Absolute Power." The Atlantic. April 2022. https://www.theatlantic.com/magazine/archive/2022/04/mohammed-bin-salman-saudi-arabia-palace-interview/622822/.

[66] Ibid. Wood. "Absolute Power."

[67] Ibid. Chulov.

crown prince asserted that "we are simply reverting to what we followed – a moderate Islam open to the world and all religions. Seventy per cent of Saudis are younger than thirty; honestly, we won't waste thirty years of our life combating extremist thoughts; we will destroy them now and immediately."

Bin Salman's reforms have less to do with religion and more with social and economic change. In 2020, the Washington-based Cato Institute ranked Saudi Arabia as the Muslim-majority country with the least religious freedom.[68] The kingdom remains the only Gulf state to ban non-Muslims, including 1.4 million Christians, from public worship, displaying religious symbols, and building houses of worship. Non-Muslims congregate clandestinely in private homes or foreign embassies. When Bin Salman invited an Egyptian Coptic bishop to hold a mass in the kingdom, he did so in a fellow Copt's home.[69]

The ban on non-Muslim worship has long hampered Saudi efforts to project the kingdom as religiously tolerant. King Abdullah, King Salman's predecessor, set the stage for Bin Salman's outreach by co-sponsoring with King Juan Carlos of Spain a three-day interfaith dialogue in a royal palace on the outskirts of Madrid in 2008. Three hundred Jews, Christians, Buddhists, Hindus, and Sikhs participated in the first such event under Saudi auspices. Abdullah could only do it with Juan Carlos. Organising the event in the kingdom would have been impossible because of a ban on Jewish and Israeli travel to the kingdom. It took another six years for the kingdom to announce Jews were no longer barred from visiting the country.[70] The ban on Jews was written into Saudi Arabia's long-standing visa regulations that have since been changed to lift the ban.

The Madrid conference almost got off to a false start when Jewish invitees threatened to boycott the conference if the organisers failed to withdraw an invitation to a fringe, staunchly anti-Zionist, ultra-conservative Jewish sect. "It became patently clear that for the Saudi organizers, these were uncharted waters. The preparations, list of invitees, invitations, and even the program itself all betrayed the lack of familiarity with the interfaith territory at large and with specific religious communities in particular... It was clear that the hosts had decided to deliberately avoid inviting any official Israeli or Palestinian representatives," said Rabbi David Rosen of the American Jewish Committee, one of the invitees.[71] Rosen, an American-born dual US-Israeli citizen, recalls

[68] Mustafa Akyol. "Freedom in the Muslim World." Cato Institute. 25 August 2020. https://www.cato.org/publications/economic-development-bulletin/freedom-muslim-world.

[69] Al Bawaba. "First Ever Coptic Mass Held in Saudi Arabia Goes Viral." 3 December 2018. https://www.albawaba.com/loop/first-ever-coptic-mass-held-saudi-arabia-goes-viral-1221104.

[70] Al Watan. "في المملكة السماح باستقدام معتنقي اليهودية للعمل (Permission to Bring Adherents of Judaism to Work in the Kingdom)." 30 December 2014. https://wtn.sa/a/248510.

[71] David Rosen. "Rabbi Reports on Saudi-led Interfaith Conference." Jewish Telegraphic Agency. 29 July 2008. https://www.jta.org/2008/07/29/israel/rabbi-reports-on-saudi-led-interfaith-conference.

that people around King Salman "almost had heart attacks on the spot" when he introduced himself to the monarch saying in Arabic: "I am Rabbi Rosen from Jerusalem, Israel."

Moreover, evidence of a seventh-century synod founded 40 years after Prophet Mohammed's death near Jubail in the oil-rich Eastern Province and memories of a twentieth-century Jewish community in the Saudi border city of Najran has done little to enhance arguments in favour of lifting restrictions on non-Muslims.[72] Speaking to American-Israeli evangelical author and activist Joel C. Rosenberg, Bin Salman warned that "building a church in Saudi Arabia right now is exactly what Al-Qaeda and the extremists would love. If that would happen, bombs would fall (on those churches), and there would be terrorist activity. I am sorry, but I have to keep in mind the safety of my people."[73]

On similar grounds, Bin Salman refused to describe his reforms as cultivating "moderate Islam" even though Saudi officials and government websites tout the notion. Bin Salman argued the description "would make terrorists and extremists happy" because it suggests that "we in Saudi Arabia and other Muslim countries are changing Islam into something new, which is not true."

In reality, Bin Salman was more concerned about conservative clerics who rejected moderate Islam as a concept and insisted that the faith was moderate by definition. "In contrast to activists, who have the West as their ally, the clerics have God. One cannot change or downplay their influence. Their influence is on full display with the millions who follow them on social media," said a Saudi official.

As a result, Bin Salman has sought to weaken ultra-conservatives by taking Abdul Wahhab, the eighteenth-century preacher, off his pedestal. He "is not a prophet, he is not an angel. He was just a scholar like many other scholars who lived during the first Saudi state... Ibn Abdul Wahhab is not Saudi Arabia," Bin Salman said.[74] In an earlier interview, Bin Salman argued that commitment to following a school of thought or one scholar amounted to "deifying human beings...There are no fixed schools of thought, and there is no infallible person."[75]

In doing so, Bin Salman shoved aside the eighteenth-century power-sharing pact between his forefather and founder of the first Saudi state, Muhammad bin Saud, and Abdul Wahhab, that gave the Al Sauds political and military

---

[72] The Economist. "Saudi Arabia May Relax Its Ban on Christian Churches." 2 April 2018. https://www.economist.com/middle-east-and-africa/2018/08/02/saudi-arabia-may-relax-its-ban-on-christian-churches.

[73] Joel C. Rosenberg. "Enemies and Allies: An Unforgettable Journey Inside the Fast-Moving & Immensely Turbulent Modern Middle East." Carol Stream, IL: Tyndale. 2021.

[74] Ibid. Wood. "Absolute Power."

[75] Al Arabiya English. "Transcript: Saudi Crown Prince Mohammed Bin Salman's Full Interview on Vision 2030." 2 April 2021. https://english.alarabiya.net/News/gulf/2021/04/28/Transcript-Saudi-Crown-Prince-Mohammed-bin-Salman-s-full-interview-on-Vision-2030-.

power and the scholar and his descendants' control of religious and social affairs.[76] Potentially, Bin Salman also opened the door to religious reform. In Abdul Wahhab's place, Bin Salman proposed a socially liberal but politically restrictive nationalist approach. "The new political myth transforms the state to a full-fledged 'mortal god … to which… we owe … our peace and defence'… Justice is the will of the state and has no other meaning," noted Saudi scholar Sultan Alamer.[77]

In Bin Salman's mind, religious ultra-conservatism had outlived its purpose. With the demise of the Soviet Union and Arab nationalism's failure, communism, and pan-Arabism no longer posed threats. The 9/11 Al-Qaeda attacks, perpetrated mostly by Saudi nationals, turned religious ultra-conservatism from an asset into a liability amid a frantic quest for a 'moderate' interpretation of Islam. Moreover, economic diversification required social liberalisation which religious ultra-conservatives opposed. In addition, enhanced security demanded a revamped military and security apparatus capable of defending the kingdom's borders and safeguarding the Al Sauds' rule. "The twin pillars of the Faisal Formula crashed with the Twin Towers," said journalist and scholar Hassan Hassan, referring to the power-sharing agreement with religious leaders and the 9/11 attack on New York's World Trade Tower.[78]

As a result, Bin Salman set out to engineer the death of Wahhabism by a thousand cuts by subjugating the clergy, rolling back the powers of religious institutions, emphasising nationalism instead of religion, and liberalising social norms. To drive the point home, Bin Salman nominated himself in 2022 as the primary interpreter of Islamic law. "In Islamic law, the head of the Islamic establishment is wali al-amr, the ruler," Bin Salman asserted.[79] The crown prince takes that role literally. In contrast to most Muslim rulers, he refuses to solicit Muslim scholars to justify his policies. "Bin Salman puts religion at the service of his politics while protesting against the use of religion by his opponents," said scholar and author of a book on the Muslim World League Louis Blin.

In a wide-ranging interview in 2021 with Al-Arabiya, Bin Salman laid out his approach to religious jurisprudence. "Our constitution is the Qur'an, has been, still is, and will continue to be so forever. Our basic system of governance stipulates this very clearly… But in social and personal matters, we are only obliged to implement stipulations that are clearly stated in the Qur'an…. I cannot enforce a Sharia punishment without a clear Quranic stipulation or an explicit stipulation from the Sunnah," Bin Salman said referring to Prophet Mohammed's sayings and deeds. The crown prince argued that he was bound

---

[76] Sultan Alamer. "The Saudi "Foundation Day" and the Death of Wahhabism." The Arab Gulf States Institute in Washington. 23 February 2022. https://agsiw.org/the-saudi-founding-day-and-the-death-of-wahhabism/.

[77] Ibid. Alamer. "The Saudi "Foundation Day"."

[78] Ibid. Hassan. "The 'Conscious Uncoupling'."

[79] Ibid. Wood. "Absolute Power."

only by the veracity of a saying or deed determined by the number of people who narrated it. "This is the main reference for jurisprudence, for reducing regulations, Sharia-wise."[80]

While not advocating jurisprudential reform, Bin Salman kept the door open. "One hundred years ago, when a scholar would issue a certain fatwa not knowing that the Earth was round and not knowing about continents or technology, etc., that fatwa would have been based on the then-available inputs and information and their understanding of the Qur'an and Sunnah, but these things change over time and are different right now," Bin Salman said.[81]

In The Atlantic interview, Bin Salman explained his way of applying Islamic law by recounting the story of a pregnant woman who confessed her fornication crime to the Prophet. She begged to be executed under Islamic law. Bin Salman said the Prophet repeatedly told her to leave, signifying Mohammed's leniency towards lawbreakers. The crown prince omitted the end of the story recounted in the record of the Prophet's sayings and deeds preserved through a chain of narrators. The narrators describe how the woman returns to the Prophet with her illegitimate son as evidence of her crime. The Prophet acquiesces and has her buried up to her chest and stoned to death. "We should not try to seek out people and prove charges against them. You have to do it the way that the Prophet taught us how to do it," Bin Salman said, suggesting that his imprisoned and executed critics had, in effect, demanded to be punished.

Recounting a visit to a mosque in Taif, the summer residence of the king and his family, where the Prophet is said to have prayed, journalist Graeme Wood found a building in disrepair, fenced off by rusty wire, with parts of it reduced to rubble. A sign posted by the Ministry of Islamic Affairs in Arabic, Urdu, Indonesian, and English noted that historical evidence for the Prophet's visit was uncertain. The sign reflected the Wahhabi doctrine that devotion to prophets, righteous people, shrines, and graves constituted heresy and could lead to polytheism.[82]

Asked about the sign, Al-Issa downplayed its significance. "If in the past there were some mistakes, now there is correction. Everyone has the right to visit the historic places, and there is a lot of care given to them," Al-Issa said. When pressed on why the sign was still there, Al-Issa suggested, "maybe they are there to remind people to be respectful. You see signs like that at sites all over the world: 'Don't touch or take the stones.'"[83]

Al-Issa's words carry weight. He oversees Bin Salman's religious and anti-extremist messaging at home and abroad. In addition to the Muslim World League, the cleric heads the Directorate General for the Fight Against

---

[80] Ibid. Al Arabiya English. "Transcript."

[81] Ibid. Al Arabiya English. "Transcript."

[82] Drshire Ahmed. "Who's Muhammad Bin Abdul Wahab?" Medium. 13 August 2021. https://medium.com/@drshireahmed/whos-muhammad-bin-abdul-wahab-ae3b92635ef.

[83] Ibid. Wood. "Absolute Power."

Terrorism in the State Security and the defence ministry's Center for Ideological Warfare, units created by the crown prince. Al-Issa also leads the High Committee for Ideology in the Global Center for the Fight against Extremism, which was established during US President Donald J. Trump's 2017 visit to Saudi Arabia. In addition, Al-Issa has a widely viewed talk show on Saudi-owned MBC, a pan-Arab broadcaster, and Shahid, a pay-TV channel. "The centralisation of the message under the leadership of Sheikh al-Issa is important to avoid confusion in a country used to an inflation of fatwas of all kinds and to ensure harmony with the content of other advocates of a Muslim revival. This strengthens its credibility and facilitates its dissemination abroad," Blin, the Middle East scholar, said.

Breaking tradition, King Salman affirmed Al-Issa's status by inviting the cleric in 2022 to deliver the Arafah sermon, a crucial part of the annual Haj pilgrimage to Mecca. The address had long been the preserve of the kingdom's grand mufti and head of the Council of Senior Religious Scholars, Abdulaziz bin Abdullah al-Sheikh, a descendant of Abdul Wahhab. Al-Sheikh is widely viewed as a conservative despite public support for the crown prince's reforms. Translated into 14 languages, Al-Issa's sermon was broadcast across the Muslim world.[84] By inviting Al-Issa, Salman signalled Saudi Arabia's determination to abandon its puritan version of Wahhabism, seemingly in favour of Wahhabism-lite, the interpretation of the faith practised in Qatar, the world's only other Wahhabi state.

Conservatives condemned Al-Issa's sermon delivery on social media with the hashtag, 'Remove Al-Issa from the pulpit.'[85] They dubbed the cleric the 'Zionist imam' and denounced him as a traitor who, by engaging with Jews, paved the way for Bin Salman to establish formal relations with Israel. One tweet featured a cartoon of Al-Issa standing on the pulpit of Mount Arafah's Nimrah Mosque, reading a sermon handed to him by a rabbi. Muhammad al-Saghir, a controversial cleric associated with the International Union of Muslim Scholars, a Qatar-based group aligned with the Muslim Brotherhood, issued a fatwa banning the faithful from following Al-Issa in prayer at the mosque. Muslims are not obligated to pray at the Nimrah Mosque as part of their pilgrimage.

To his credit, Al-Issa used his position to kick into high gear Saudi Arabia's torturous, snail-paced, and long overdue overhaul of schoolbooks replete with supremacist, misogynist, sectarian, and anti-Semitic references. The kingdom had been dragging its feet since revisions of its textbooks became a hot topic in the wake of the 9/11 attacks carried out predominantly by graduates of the Saudi school system. Human Rights Watch and Israeli textbook watchdog Impact-se reported significant progress in rewriting textbooks for

---

[84] Saudi Gazette. "Sheikh Mohammad Al-Issa to Deliver Arafat Sermon." 5 July 2022. https://saudigazette.com.sa/article/622617/SAUDI-ARABIA/Sheikh-Mohammad-Al-Issa-to-deliver-Arafat-sermon.

[85] Twitter. https://mobile.twitter.com/hashtag/انزلوا_العيسى_من_المنبر?src=hashtag_click&f=video.

the first time in 2021, 20 years after 9/11. In separate reports, the two groups noted that the improvements related primarily to attitudes and perceptions of non-Muslim minorities, in line with Bin Salman's promotion of interfaith dialogue, rather than Muslim sects such as Shiites. Long discriminated against and vilified, Shiites account for ten to 15% of the Saudi population.[86]

"They removed some of the more offensive stuff like pictures of Shiite shrines that were called shirk (polytheistic), and they removed some offensive language, but the kernel is still there… They are trying to make the language less offensive, but the whole idea is offensive," said Human Rights Watch Middle East researcher Adam Coogle. "It's not like the Saudis looked at their textbooks and saw a problem. Other people didn't like it, and the Saudis are trying to quell those concerns." In a similar vein, authorities arrested a social media influencer for posting a YouTube video asking God "not to leave any Shia on the face of earth, even if there are 99 million of them."[87]

The textbook revisions removed explicit references to Shia Islam but left untouched harsh criticism of Shiite practices and traditions, labelling them polytheism that threatens Islam. A schoolbook for fourth-grade and nine-year-olds advised that adherence to such practices would lead to the cancellation of a person's good deeds, God's rejection of their repentance, and eternal damnation. The practices include praying to saints and visiting tombs and shrines of prominent religious figures rejected by Wahhabism as idolatry. They also involve Shiite supplication to God via intermediaries, kneeling to anyone other than God, building mosques and shrines on top of graves, and wailing over the dead. "Any Saudi who reads this will understand what it means," Coogle said. In a similar vein, the reports implicitly suggested that the revisions failed to address long-standing ultra-conservative concepts such as a ban on bida'a or religious innovation and shirk or polytheism as well as the rejection of supplication, a thinly veiled reference to the Shia notion of mediation.

Moreover, the Supreme Council of Ulema of Al-Issa's Muslim World League has no Shiite members, nor do Shiite judges sit on the benches of national courts or serve in the police force or as ambassadors. Bin Salman moved quickly to rebuild the levelled town of Awamiyah in the Eastern Province after brutally cracking down on rebellious Shiites. Yet, Shiites accounted for the majority of the 37 people beheaded in April 2019 in a mass

---

[86] James M. Dorsey. "Saudi Schoolbooks: What Does It Take to Recontextualize Islam?" The Turbulent World of Middle East Soccer. 18 February 2021. https://www.jamesmdorsey.net/post/saudi-schoolbooks-what-does-it-take-to-recontextualize-islam.

[87] Trend Twitter. "Faisal bin Hijab bin Nahit Incites Shiites and the Prosecution Arrests Him (نحيت يحرض على الشيعة والنيابة تقبض عليه فيصل بن حجاب بن)." Twitter. 9 August 2020. https://www.youtube.com/watch?v=u1XAqMJ1jXQ.

execution.[88] Forty-one Shiites were among the 81 people executed in one day in 2022.[89]

"What matters is how the Saudis interpret the teachings related to how Muslims should treat anybody of a different sect or faith. The problem is how they believe the other should be treated. It doesn't matter what they call me. It doesn't matter if they call me a kafir, an infidel, as long as they truly believe that I should be treated equally. The problem is that the Saudis don't really want to change their established system of beliefs," said Staquf, the leader of Nahdlatul Ulama and a prominent Islamic scholar.

That was the message of a US$75 million Ramadan series broadcast in 2022 by the largely Saudi government-owned MBC television network.[90] The series glorified seventh-century Caliph Mu'awiya I, who Shiites believe deprived Prophet Mohammed's cousin and son-in-law, Ali bin Abi Talib, the last of the rightly guided caliphs, and his sons Hassan and Hussein, of their position as the rightful heirs of the Prophet. Mu'awiya's forces assassinated Ali. Reviled by Shiites, Yazed I, Mu'awiya's son and successor, ordered Hussein's killing. Under pressure from Mu'awiya, Hassan abdicated as caliph after eight months in office.

Similarly, the first group of foreign nationals to be naturalised in late 2021 under a new decree that opened the door to Saudi citizenship to high-end achievers in law, medicine, science, technology, culture, and sport suggested that Bin Salman saw religion as an equally important arena in the competition for foreign talent. About a quarter of the 27 adopted citizens were religious figures or historians of Saudi Arabia. They included Lebanese Shiite Mohammed Ali al-Husseini; Mustafa Ceric, a former Bosnian grand mufti; Hussein Daoudi, a Muslim community leader in Sweden; Mohammad Nimr El Sammak, secretary-general of Lebanon's National Islamic Christian Committee for Dialogue; and Lebanese Islam scholar Radwan Nayef al-Sayed. None adhered to other faiths. Many of the religious figures were either signatories of the 2020 Mecca Declaration that called for cultural and religious tolerance and understanding and/or members of the supreme council of Al-Issa's Muslim World League. The group's composition linked Bin Salman's economic and social reforms to his quest for religious soft power and leadership of the Muslim world.

Al-Husseini checked all the boxes needed to help the kingdom position itself as the beacon of 'moderate,' albeit autocratic, Islam. A resident of

---

[88] CNBC. "Saudi Arabia Beheads 37 for Terrorism Crimes, Most of Them Minority Shiites." 23 April 2019. https://www.cnbc.com/2019/04/24/saudi-arabia-beheads-37-for-terrorism-most-of-them-were-shiites.html.

[89] Leila Saad. "Saudi Arabia Executes Two Shi'a Bahrainis on Terrorism Charges." Amnesty International. 2 June 2023. https://www.hrw.org/news/2023/06/02/saudi-arabia-executes-two-shia-bahrainis-terrorism-charges.

[90] Amwaj.media. "Saudi TV Network Under Fire as Iraqis Clash Over Controversial New Series." 23 February 2022. https://amwaj.media/media-monitor/iraq-s-sadr-urges-saudi-s-mbc-to-drop-airing-of-controversial-tv-series.

Saudi Arabia since a fallout with Hezbollah, the Iranian-backed Lebanese Shiite militia, Al-Husseini is the scion of a select number of Lebanese Shiite families believed to be descendants of the Prophet Mohammed. Granting him Saudi citizenship supported the kingdom's claim that it had turned its back on its ultra-conservative strand of Islam that sees Shiites as heretics and has become religiously tolerant, inclusive, non-sectarian, pluralistic, and non-discriminatory. "The glowing truth that cannot be contested is that the Kingdom of Saudi Arabia is open to everyone…and does not look at dimensions of…a sectarian type,"[91] Al-Husseini said as he accepted his Saudi citizenship.

As head of the relatively obscure Arabic Islamic Council that advocates interfaith dialogue, particularly with Jews, Al-Husseini ticked off another box on the Saudi checklist. He was the first Arab Shiite religious figure to address Israelis publicly in broken Hebrew. "We believe that not all Jews are bad [just as] not all Muslims are terrorists. Let us cousins put our conflicts aside and stay away from evil and hatred. Let us unite in peace and love," Al-Husseini told Israeli listeners.[92]

What drives Bin Salman's reformist zeal is not change because it is the right thing to do. His primary concern is securing the survival of his autocratic regime. To do so, he needs to cater to youth aspirations, diversify the kingdom's oil export-dependent economy, create jobs, ease social restrictions, and project an image of tolerance. His reforms serve that purpose but go no further. Al-Issa has helped lay the ground for civil rather than religious law adaptations as the czar of anti-extremism.

As a result, Saudi Arabia's first-ever personal status law that came into effect in June 2022 remains rooted in orthodox Islamic jurisprudence. It codifies problematic practices inherent in the kingdom's male guardianship system by entrenching gender-based discrimination in most aspects of family life, including marriage, divorce, child custody, and inheritance. Under the law, women are required to obtain the consent of their male legal guardian to get married. The law obliges a wife to "obey" her husband. It conditions her right to financial support, such as food and accommodation, on her "submit(ting) herself" to her husband.

Moreover, men can initiate divorce without conditions, while women face legal, financial, and practical barriers. In divorce, a mother does not have equal rights to her children; the father is granted guardianship as a matter of principle. Finally, the law institutionalises discrimination between men and women

---

[91] Mona Alami. "Why Has Saudi Arabia Granted Citizenship to a Former Hezbollah Insider?" Amwaj Media. 25 November 2021. https://amwaj.media/article/mohammad-ali-husseini.

[92] James M. Dorsey. "Saudi Religious Moderation Is as Much pr as It Is Theology." The Turbulent World with James M. Dorsey. 30 November 2021. https://www.jamesmdorsey.net/post/saudi-religious-moderation-is-as-much-pr-as-it-is-theology-1.

in inheritance, giving men a much larger share of assets than their female counterparts.⁹³

Similarly, restrictions announced in 2022 on Ramadan public celebrations were self-serving. They were designed to shift Saudi identity from religion to nationalism. They were also intended to strengthen government surveillance and control. The new rules curtailed the time allotted to evening prayers, forbade worshipers to bring their children to the mosque, banned prayer filming and broadcasting, curbed donations for organising the breaking of the fast, and obliged mosque officials to organise fast-breaking in courtyards rather than inside the mosque. The measures resembled restrictions the government tried a year earlier. However, online uproar forced the government to retract a ban on broadcasting uninterrupted live Ramadan footage from the two Mecca's foremost mosques viewed by Muslims worldwide.⁹⁴

Looking for a silver lining in the restrictions, Indian Muslim thinker and Secretary-General of the Islamic Forum for the Promotion of Moderate Thought A. Faizur Rahman said Bin Salman likely saw the measures as a way to counter Islam's ritualisation.⁹⁵ Rahman described the Ramadan restrictions as "a bad imitation of Ataturk. It's an expression of power. It's saying I am the ruler." Like Mustafa Kemal Ataturk, the visionary who carved modern Turkey out of the ruins of the Ottoman empire, Bin Salman wants to remove religion from the public square and relegate it to the private sphere, Rahman argued.

For Bin Salman, reforming religious law as long as it does not challenge his grip on power may be a question of if rather than when. Salman allowed discussion of reform to surface briefly. In 2016 and again in 2022, controversial cleric Saleh al-Maghamsi, backed by Turki Aldakhil, the Saudi ambassador to the UAE and former general manager of the state-controlled Al-Arabiya television network, called for the creation of a new school of Islamic legal thought that would replace Sunni Islam's four traditional schools. "Something new dominates every stage of jurisprudential construction.... In this time, issues must be liberated," Al-Maghamsi said. Widely believed to be close to King Salman, Al-Maghamsi argued that existing legal schools, unlike the Qur'an, were human constructs that could be revised. "If you admit that the 'companions of the sects' are human, what prevents you from reviewing?" Al-Maghamsi asked.⁹⁶ The Council of Senior Scholars, Saudi Arabia's highest religious body, rejected Al-Maghamsi's proposal out of hand, insisting that

---

⁹³ Amnesty International. "Saudi Arabia: New Personal Status Law Codifies Discrimination Against Women." 8 March 2023. https://www.amnesty.org/en/documents/mde23/6431/2023/en/.

⁹⁴ Rayhan Uddin. "Saudi Arabia Confirms Mecca and Medina Broadcasts Will Continue After Backlash over Ban." Middle East Eye. 24 March 2022. https://www.middleeasteye.net/news/saudi-arabia-mecca-medina-broadcasts-continue-backlash.

⁹⁵ Interview with the author, 11 March 2023.

⁹⁶ Turki AlDakhil. "Maghamsi.. and the New Jurisprudential Discourse! (الجديدالمغامسي.. والخطاب الفقهي)." Okaz. 29 May 2016. https://www.okaz.com.sa/article/1059627

existing legal schools could respond to all requirements of modern life and align them with Islamic law.[97]

A student of Saudi Arabia's most influential grand mufti, Abdulaziz bin Baz, Al-Maghamsi is no stranger to controversy. He was fired in 2020 as imam of the Quba Mosque in Medina, the world's oldest Muslim house of worship, built in the seventh century at the time of Prophet Mohammed. Al-Maghamsi insisted he was dismissed by the Islamic affairs ministry, a bastion of conservatism, rather than the king or crown prince.[98] He was penalised for calling for the release of prisoners charged with 'minor violations.' Authorities interpreted the tweet as a call to release incarcerated reformist clerics, including Salman Al-Awda and Awad Al-Qarni.[99] In 2014, he asserted on his YouTube channel with 2.21 million subscribers that "Allah only gathered Jews in the land of Palestine to destroy them," adding that "the hatred of Jews toward Muslims is eternal."[100] Two years earlier, Al-Maghamsi suggested that Osama bin Laden had died with more "sanctity and honor" than any infidel or non-Muslim.

In 2020, Saudi Opinions, a news website, dropped journalist Ahmad Hashem's article, calling for grammatical and linguistic changes to the Qur'an, widely viewed by Muslims as the untouchable word of God. Hashem asserted that the holy text contained some 2,500 spelling, syntax, and grammar errors. He argued that the Qur'an's Uthmani calligraphy, developed in the seventh century and named after Uthman ibn Affan, one of Prophet Mohammed's sons-in-law and Islam's third caliph, needed to be updated with proper Arabic spelling and grammar. "The Quranic text is open to any amendment that will make Allah's book easier for Muslims to read and linguistically more correct," Hashem said.[101]

Months later, Elaph, a London-based Saudi website operated by Othman Al Omeir, a reportedly agnostic businessman and journalist with close ties to Bin Salman, removed an article by Kurdish journalist and politician Jarjis Gulizada, calling for a rewriting of the Qur'an. Gulizada suggested that the Coronavirus pandemic had opened the door to change by forcing the government to take public health measures that violated Islamic law.

---

[97] BBC News. "Saleh Al Maghamsi: 'How Did the Saudi Council of Senior Scholars Respond to His Call to Establish a "New Islamic School of Thought"? (دعوته لإقامة "مذهب إسلامي جديد"؟ صالح المغامسي: كيف ردت هيئة كبار العلماء السعودية على). 8 April 2023. https://www.bbc.com/arabic/trending-65222323.

[98] Ibid. BBC News. "Saleh Al Maghamsi."

[99] Al Jazeera. "Sheikh Al Maghamsi Was Dismissed as Imam of the Quba Mosque in Medina After He Deleted a Tweet and Apologized for It (إمامة مسجد قباء بالمدينة المنورة بعد تغريدة حذفها واعتذر عنها.. إقالة الشيخ المغامسي من تغريدة-غير-موفقة-للمغامسي/). 29 March 2020. https://www.aljazeera.net/politics/2020/3/29/

[100] Saleh al-Maghamsi. 'The Hatred of Jews Toward Muslims Is Eternal (الشيخ صالح المغامسي عداوة اليهود للمسلمين أزلية ـ)." YouTube. 13 July 2014. https://www.youtube.com/watch?v=o8I-_AILYOk.

[101] www.saudiopinions.org/ar.

"One of the most important changes made during the Coronavirus on the religious Islamic level involved stopping people from praying in tight rows, as accepted in the Islamic Shari'a.... Public prayers and Friday and holiday prayers were banned to protect the worshipers and prevent them from infecting one another with the virus. This is a clear violation of the religious texts, but it was permitted following in-depth study to save lives," Gulizada said.

"The important point is that there was room for flexibility... For the first time in history since the days of the Righteous Caliphs, this flexibility allowed making essential changes to the mode of worship... They constitute a first sign, a very encouraging one, that a re-examination of the Islamic texts and of Islamic ritual is taking place based on modern perceptions and objectives that benefit the Muslims in our modern world... It is time for the human mind to become the supreme judge and, freeing itself of mysticism and irrationality, amend the textual and ideological mistakes that exist in the religious texts due to human error and due to the undeveloped state of the writing one or two thousand years ago," Gulizada said.[102]

In late 2022, the Afghan Taliban's ban on women's education and employment by foreign aid organisations prompted a third cluster of trial balloons. "The Taliban government's decision suggests a crisis of thought, the extent to which jurisprudence needs to be revised and developed... All religious institutions must work to create contemporary jurisprudence... (that) instill(s) a spirit of tolerance, love of life..., and standards of quality of life," said Okaz newspaper columnist and Jeddah-based lawyer Osama Al-Yamani.[103] "The Islamic world is waiting for (Saudi Arabia) to lead it towards contemporary jurisprudence," Al-Yamani added.

Bin Salman is tempted. Embracing religious reform would turbocharge his claim to leadership of the Muslim world and position him as Islam's foremost reformer in competition with Nahdlatul Ulama. However, that could prove a double-edged sword. It would highlight governance, political pluralism, and human rights as the core differentiators in the rivalry for religious soft power. "That could prove to be tricky. I don't think MbS wants to go down that road anytime soon," said a Saudi scholar.

---

[102] The Middle East Media Research Institute. "Articles in Saudi Press Call to Amend Thousands of Scribal Errors in the Quran, Reexamine Islamic Texts in Light of Modern Perceptions." 18 August 2020. https://www.memri.org/reports/articles-saudi-press-call-amend-thousands-scribal-errors-quran-reexamine-islamic-texts-light.

[103] Osama Al-Yamani. " 'منع النساء من التعليم'(Barring Women from Education)." Okaz. 29 December 2022. https://www.okaz.com.sa/articles/authors/2122996.

CHAPTER 4

Emirati Gold Loses Its Shine

UAE President Mohammed bin Zayed, who goes by his initials, MbZ, and Abdullah bin Bayyah, a prominent Muslim jurist in his employ, expected opposition to the 2020 recognition of Israel by the UAE, Bahrain, and Morocco, but not in their tightly controlled backyard. Yet, the diplomatic move sparked a rift in an organisation created to brandish the Emirates' moderate religious credentials and project the country as a beacon of religious tolerance.

A statement by Bin Bayyah on the website of the Abu Dhabi-based Forum for Promoting Peace in Muslim Societies sparked the rift. The statement praised Bin Zayed's wisdom in reaching out to Israel.[1] One of several UAE-backed groups, the Forum has emerged as a prominent vehicle in Bin Zayed's war on political Islam and countering Qatar-supported organisations affiliated with the Muslim Brotherhood. The Forum defined its mission as promoting peace, tolerance, solidarity, justice, and other politically neutral values to counter religious violence.

Within hours of the posting, three board members—Abdullah al-Maatouq, a former Kuwait religious affairs minister, United Nations envoy, and government advisor; prominent American Muslim activist Aisha al-Adawiya, founder of the human rights group Women in Islam; and Jerusalem's grand mufti, Muhammad Hussein—resigned. Hussein banned Emirati Muslims from

---

[1] Emirates News Agency. "The Board of Trustees of the Forum for Promoting Peace Will Hold Its Seventh Forum in Abu Dhabi Next December (مجلس أمناء منتدى تعزيز السلم يعقد ملتقاه السابع في أبوظبي ديسمبر المقبل)". 6 August 2020. https://www.wam.ae/ar/details/1395302862666.

visiting and praying at Jerusalem's Al-Aqsa Mosque, Islam's third holiest site.[2] Earlier, Palestinian worshippers embarrassed an Emirati delegation visiting the Al-Aqsa Mosque in Jerusalem by heckling them.

Hamza Yusuf, the Forum's vice president, a member of Bin Bayyah's Emirati Fatwa Council that trains scholars and licenses them to issue religious opinions[3] and a popular Islamic scholar who heads Zaytuna College—the United States' first accredited Muslim liberal arts college—distanced himself from the statement. Yusuf, an Irish Catholic convert to Islam born as Mark Hanson, asserted that he did "not engage in or endorse geopolitical strategies or treaties."

The bad news did not stop there. Realising that recognition of Israel would not distract from criticism of the Emirates' troubled human rights record, creation of a surveillance state, lagging controls on money laundering by corrupt and criminal operators, and military interventions in countries like Yemen and Libya, Bin Zayed decided not to attend a White House ceremony with US President Donald J. Trump and Israeli Prime Minister Binyamin Netanyahu to cement their deal. He sent his foreign minister instead.

Aaron David Miller, a former US Middle East peace negotiator, and one-time State Department official Richard Sokolsky, cautioned Bin Zayed in an op-ed in The Washington Post. "We have watched in abject horror as the Trump administration gave the Saudis virtual carte blanche to repress at home, help create the world's greatest humanitarian catastrophe in Yemen, and run roughshod over US interests in the region. The United States cannot and should not allow the same behaviour with the UAE," they wrote.[4]

The setbacks dented more than just Bin Zayed's religious soft power quest. They threw a shadow over the effort by the UAE, a country that prides itself on being a cutting-edge home to some 200 nationalities, to project itself as an open and tolerant society at the forefront of Islamic moderation, respect for religious diversity, and interfaith dialogue.[5] For Bin Zayed, those were temporary setbacks. Bin Zayed was determined to roll back the achievements of the 2011 popular Arab revolts that toppled leaders in Egypt, Tunisia, Libya, and Yemen at any cost. The uprisings fuelled the worst fears of men like Bin Zayed,

---

[2] James M. Dorsey. "UAE Recognition of Israel Dents Emirati Religious Soft Power." The Turbulent World with James M. Dorsey. 10 September 2020. https://mideastsoccer.blogspot.com/2020/09/uae-recognition-of-israel-dents-emirati.html.

[3] The UAE Council for Fatwa. 4 February 2019. http://binbayyah.net/english/wp-content/uploads/2019/02/Popes-Visit-to-Abu-Dhabi-English.pdf.

[4] Aaron David Miller and Richard Sokolsk. "Don't Let the United Arab Emirates Play Us the Way Mohammed bin Salman Did." The Washington Post. 9 September 2020. https://www.washingtonpost.com/opinions/2020/09/08/dont-let-united-arab-emirates-play-us-way-mohammed-bin-salman-did/.

[5] United Arab Emirates. "The UAE Soft Power Strategy." 27 September 2017. https://u.ae/en/about-the-uae/strategies-initiatives-and-awards/strategies-plans-and-visions/strategies-plans-and-visions-untill-2021/the-uae-soft-power-strategy.

Saudi Crown Prince Mohammed bin Salman, and Egyptian general-turned-president Abdel Fattah al-Sisi. The revolts challenged their autocratic rule and raised the spectre of their replacement by Muslim Brotherhood affiliates. In response, Bin Zayed launched a zealot's counterrevolution. "Abu Dhabi has succeeded in establishing a reputation as the champion opponent of people's protest movements," said Colin Powers, author of a report on UAE efforts to influence US policy.[6]

Bin Zayed projected his obsessive anti-Islamism as an apolitical, tolerant, and moderate vision of Islam. Yet, his notion of an Islam that embraces autocracy rather than democracy is no less politicised than the vision of the Brotherhood and other non-violent and violent expressions of political Islam. The UAE "represents a third trend in Islam," alongside political Islam and jihadism, said Gulf scholar Gregory Gause. "Official Islam in the Emirates is tightly tied to state authority and subservient to it."[7]

Leaked US State Department cables reporting on diplomatic conversations with Bin Zayed and other members of his ruling family provide insight into what drives the UAE strongman's quest to control Islam. Echoing Orientalist and civilisationalist tropes, Bin Zayed cautioned US Undersecretary of State Nicholas Burns in 2007 that the Middle East could not afford greater democracy because it would bring groups like the Brotherhood, the Gaza Strip's Hamas, and Lebanon's Hezbollah to power. To make his point, Bin Zayed closed the UAE offices of US and European foundations that support democracy development, including the Washington-based National Democratic Institute and Germany's Konrad Adenauer Foundation.

Bin Zayed justifies autocracy with the assertion that Muslims cannot be trusted because they are instinctively attracted to ultra-conservatism and/or militancy. "The Middle East is not California," Bin Zayed told Burns. He argued that education would need 25–50 years to change a deeply rooted culture in which "the masses in the Middle East would tend to go with their hearts and vote overwhelmingly for the Muslim Brotherhood and the jihadists represented by Hamas and Hizballah… No Emirati household would refuse to send its sons to what he described as "Talebani Qurani schools."" Bin Zayed asserted that up to 80% of the UAE's military personnel would respond to a call from "some holy man in Mecca."

A military man, Bin Zayed insisted he understood how Middle Eastern culture worked. "I am an Arab, I am a Muslim, and I pray. And in the 1970s and early 1980s, I was one of them. I believe these guys have an agenda," he said. Bin Zayed warned that "free elections in the Middle East" could mean that the United States would "have to find somewhere else to get 17 million

---

[6] Colin Powers. "Dollars and Decadence, Making Sense of the US-UAE Relationship." Noria Research. April 2021. https://noria-research.com/wp-content/uploads/2021/03/Noria-Research_Dollars-and-Decadence_2021_ENG.pdf.

[7] F. Gregory Gause III. "What the Qatar Crisis Shows About the Middle East." The Washington Post. 28 June 2017. https://www.washingtonpost.com/news/monkey-cage/wp/2017/06/27/what-the-qatar-crisis-shows-about-the-middle-east/.

barrels (of oil) a day."[8] The US embassy noted in a separate cable, referring to Bin Zayed by his initials, that "being labelled a Muslim Brother is about the worst epithet possible in MBZ's vocabulary." The embassy said that Bin Zayed "sees Iranian Influence in the Brotherhood very clearly as both a way to agitate the Arab populace and render the traditional leaders of Arab society impotent."[9] Public intellectuals working for Emirati and Saudi media seconded Bin Zayed's assertions. Describing the Brotherhood as "an existential threat," Reza Parchizadeh, a member of Saudi Arabia's Iran-focused Al-Arabiya Farsi news agency, asserted that the group's "ideology inspired the Khomeinist movement in Iran, and Sayyid Qutb, one of the most influential Brotherhood theorists, has always been popular among Iranian Islamists."[10]

Bin Zayed's anti-Islamist instincts were fuelled by the presence of two Emirati nationals among the 19 perpetrators of the 9/11 attacks on New York and Washington. Elaborating on Bin Zayed's assertion that ultra-conservatives and militants had hijacked Islam, Yusuf al-Otaiba, a close associate of the president and the UAE's influential ambassador in Washington, argued two decades later that "religion was never about politics… was never about extremism… was never about violence. I think what we are trying to do here is to take the narrative back and recapture what our religion means, both to us and to the rest of the world." Al-Otaiba defined the UAE's religious soft power ploy as an attempt "to present to the rest of the world that religion has absolutely nothing to do with extremism or politics. It has to do with faith and respect."[11]

Bin Zayed's deepest fears became reality with the post-revolt 2012 election of Muslim Brother Mohammed Morsi as Egypt's first and only democratically chosen president and Islamist advances in Libya, Tunisia, and Syria as a result of the 2011 revolts. The threat was compounded by Iranian support for armed groups in Iraq and Yemen and Syrian President Bashar al-Assad. Bin Zayed saw political Islam as "an existential threat to (the UAE's) broadly secular approach to government as well as to the stability of the so-called 'status quo' powers in the region… (He) is said to regard political Islamism as a tool used by regional rivals…to project their own power and weaken Gulf monarchies and secular

---

[8] US Embassy in the United Arab Emirates. "U/S Burns' January 22 Meeting with Abu Dhabi Crown Prince and UAE Foreign Minister." WikiLeaks. 24 January 2007. https://wikileaks.org/plusd/cables/07ABUDHABI97_a.html.

[9] US Embassy in the United Arab Emirates, "Strong Word in Private from MBZ at IDEX—Bashes Iran, Qatar, Russia." WikiLeaks. 25 February 2009. https://wikileaks.org/plusd/cables/09ABUDHABI193_a.html.

[10] Reza Parchizadeh. "Iran's Muslim Brotherhood Ties Overshadow Rapprochement with Egypt." Gulf International Forum. 29 June 2023. https://gulfif.org/irans-muslim-brotherhood-ties-overshadow-rapprochement-with-egypt/.

[11] Khaleej Times. "UAE Is Vocal About Tolerance Because Religion Has Been Hijacked: Al Otaiba." 21 July 2020. https://www.khaleejtimes.com/news/government/uae-is-vocal-about-tolerance-because-religion-has-been-hijacked-al-otaiba.

republics alike," concluded Peter Salisbury in a report on UAE foreign policy published by Chatham House, a prestigious British think tank.[12]

To make things worse, the UAE's allies, Saudi Arabia and the United States, failed to see the threat as Bin Zayed did. Unlike Bin Zayed, they distinguished between violent and non-violent Islamists and were willing to engage with non-violent groups like the Brotherhood, even though the kingdom designated the Brotherhood and other Islamist groups as terrorists. In Bin Zayed's mind, Turkish and Qatari support for the Brotherhood enhanced the threat. Compounding Bin Zayed's woes was the writing on the wall: the United States proved less interested in the Middle East as it pivoted to Asia. It could no longer be blindly relied upon as the Gulf's reliable security guarantor.

A 2014 secret meeting in a Turkish hotel between the Quds Force, the foreign military arm of Iran's Islamic Revolutionary Guard Corps, and the Brotherhood, barely a year after the Egyptian coup drove the group underground and into exile, threatened to turn Bin Zayed's nightmare into reality. The Islamic State's advances in Iraq and Syria persuaded two of political Islam's most potent forces to explore an alliance against conservative Gulf monarchies. Ultimately, to Bin Zayed's relief, political and sectarian Shiite-Sunni Muslim differences proved stronger than a shared animosity towards Saudi Arabia and the jihadists.[13]

Bin Zayed's anti-Islamism and vision of an autocratic but socially liberal Islam is grounded in more than survival instinct and a determination to sustain the UAE's ability to punch beyond its weight. In a rare interview, Bin Zayed described to The New York Times how his father, Zayed bin Sultan al-Nahyan, the charismatic founder of the UAE, asked him in the 1980s what he had done to help the impoverished population of Tanzania after he visited the country. When he shrugged his shoulders and said Tanzanians were not Muslims, Al-Nahyan "clutched my arm and looked into my eyes very harshly." He said, 'We are all God's children,' Bin Zayed recounted.[14] Bin Zayed's concept of Islam reflects his father's pluralistic instincts, tolerance of other religions, and insistence on universal education for women. A bronze sculpture emblazoned with the word tolerance in English adorns the entry to his main office in Abu Dhabi.

To emphasise his social and religious tolerance concept, Bin Zayed created a Ministry of Tolerance, declaring 2019 the Year of Tolerance. The year kicked off with a visit to the UAE by Pope Francis I, the first time a pontiff set

---

[12] Peter Salisbury. "Risk Perception and Appetite in UAE Foreign and National Security Policy, Chatham House." 1 July 2020. https://www.chathamhouse.org/publication/risk-in-uae-salisbury.

[13] James Risen. "A Secret Summit." The Intercept. 18 November 2019. https://theintercept.com/2019/11/18/iran-muslim-brotherhood-quds-force/.

[14] Robert F. Worth. "Mohammed bin Zayed's Dark Vision of the Middle East's Future." The New York Times. 9 January 2020. https://www.nytimes.com/2020/01/09/magazine/united-arab-emirates-mohammed-bin-zayed.html.

foot on the Arabian Peninsula, and the placing of a 10-metre-high, three-dimensional statue of Buddha, perfectly postured with one leg folded, on the E11 Sheikh Zayed Road that links Abu Dhabi and Dubai. A reproduction of an approximately 1,100-year-old Chinese representation of Guanyin, the Buddhist deity associated with compassion, greets visitors to the Asian Trade Routes gallery of Abu Dhabi's dependance of France's Louvre Museum. It flouts ultra-conservative and Orthodox strands of Islam that condemn polytheism and the portrayal of deities as idolatry. "History will record that Bin Zayed was the first to return the idols to the Arabian Peninsula," charged Emirati writer Khaled Muqdad, one of many who kicked up a storm on social media.[15]

Personifying Emirati values, Bin Zayed attempted to write tolerance into the UAE's DNA. His frequent references to tolerance became a benchmark for Emiratis. Bin Zayed saw tolerance as ensuring social cohesion in a country where migrants constitute the vast majority of the population. Even so, non-Muslim organisations reported that hotels, citing government regulatory barriers, refused to rent space for non-Islamic religious purposes. Local media reported difficulties in obtaining bank loans to cover construction costs for new religious spaces, including for registered religious organisations. The US State Department reported in 2021 that construction of a new Anglican church in Abu Dhabi stalled "due to financial issues." The government kept in place a ban on bell towers and crosses on churches but failed to enforce it, while churches refrained in deference from ringing and chiming bells.[16]

Moreover, UAE founder Sheikh Zayed bin Sultan Al-Nahyan's sons and successors have confused notions of tolerance, coexistence, peace, and harmony on the ruler's terms with multiculturalism, even if Emirati law guarantees non-discrimination irrespective of race, religion, and creed. They have exploited the confusion to ensure that their petrodollar ex-pat haven of sleek skyscrapers and polished public relations campaigns stays ahead of competitors, positioning the UAE as a beacon of religious moderation.

To undergird the country's claim to primacy, the government funded the UAE's first synagogue as part of a larger project to build a mosque, church, and temple in one complex, representing the three Abrahamic faiths. It has also built temples for Hindus and Sikhs. As far back as the 1960s, years before the UAE was an independent federal state, Dubai opened a Christian missionary school and church. Similarly, Dubai's ornate three-story Guru Nanak Darbar Sikh Temple, the largest Sikh temple in the Arab world, stands on land in Jebel Ali, a port and resort area donated by Dubai's ruler, Mohammed bin Rashid Al Maktoum. The temple has a soup kitchen that feeds hundreds of Sikhs and non-Sikhs on weekdays and upwards of 10,000 on weekends.

---

[15] Khaled Muqdad. Twitter. 2 April 2019. https://twitter.com/Kalmuqdad/status/1113013454703558656.

[16] US Department of State. "International Religious Freedom Report 2022." 15 May 2023. https://www.state.gov/reports/2022-report-on-international-religious-freedom/.

Moreover, the UAE supported restoring Christian life in Iraq, devastated by war and the Islamic State's jihadist rampage. As part of a United Nations Educational, Scientific and Cultural Organisation (UNESCO) project to reconstruct the Iraqi city of Mosul in ways that recognise its pluralistic history at the crossroads of cultures and religions, the UAE funded the rebuilding of two historic churches and the iconic Al-Nouri Mosque. "We want to send out a clear message that the mayhem spread by extremist ideologies can be undone, and divisive forces can be countered," said UAE Culture and Youth Minister Noura Al Kaabi. "How? Through nurturing and channelling stronger forces of coexistence and harmony, and culture has a prominent role to play in this."[17]

Al Kaabi's message glossed over the fact that faith groups face restrictions to conform to Islamic norms and law. In line with Emirati and Islamic law, faith groups, including Christians, Hindus, and Sikhs, must refrain from proselytising or attempting to convert Muslims—a criminal act in the UAE. Apostasy by Muslims is punishable by death under Islamic law, although there is no known legal case or prosecution in UAE history. Historically, Hindu temples displayed images rather than physical idols in their shrines to comply with Muslim idolatry bans.

Al Kaabi's message further masked the fact that it is UAE strongman Bin Zayed who tolerates. Bin Zayed's notion of tolerance, like that of the Ottomans, is rooted in a power relationship that allows the ruler to threaten the withdrawal of tolerance from a group vulnerable by being only tolerated. Tolerance suggests an inequality in which the ruler determines whether a less powerful group can exist and to what degree it can publicly manifest differences. "Toleration is a 'means of rule, of extending, consolidating, and enforcing state power,' and cannot be confused with equality or multiculturalism," said Ottoman historian Marc David Baer.[18]

Al Kaabi's message is difficult to disagree with. It earned the UAE the number one ranking on the International Institute for Management Development's 2016 regional index and the number three slot on its global index as well as praise from human rights groups.

Nevertheless, Bin Zayed has no tolerance for deviation from the Emirates' autocratic form of moderate Islam. "There is no room whatsoever for any interpretation of Islam in the UAE other than their own," said Hiba Zayadin, UAE researcher at Human Rights Watch. "As soon as you are out of step or criticize the state's definition of moderate Islam, you are in trouble."[19]

---

[17] Knox Thames. "The UAE Is Restoring Christian life in the Persian Gulf." Religion News Service. 11 February 2022. https://religionnews.com/2022/02/11/uae-restoring-christian-life-in-the-persian-gulf/.

[18] Marc David Baer. "Sultanic Saviors and Tolerant Turks: Writing Ottoman Jewish History, Denying the Armenian Genocide." Bloomington, IN: Indiana University Press. 2020. Kindle edition.

[19] Email exchange with the author, 21 June 2022.

Bin Zayed stepped up his crusade against political Islam, the Muslim Brotherhood, and Qatar in 2017. He accused Qatar of being one of the Brotherhood's principle backers and instigated a 3.5-year-long UAE-Saudi-led diplomatic and economic boycott of the iconoclastic Gulf state. At the root of the conflict were differing visions of the Middle East's future. In contrast to the UAE and Saudi Arabia, Qatar, despite being an absolute monarchy, believed change was inevitable and saw Islamists as catalysts for an emerging post-authoritarian order. Embracing the Brotherhood promised to enhance Qatar's soft power and political influence and ensure the survival of the Al-Thani family's rule. Qatar's vision of a populist, bottom-up Sunni Islam posed an existential threat to the UAE and Saudi Arabia's ruling families. They viewed democratisation as a mortal danger, particularly if it involved Islamists questioning their religious credentials and legitimacy.

Three months into the boycott, polling confirmed Bin Zayed's deepest fears. The poll suggested that 52% of Emiratis opposed punitive measures against Qatar. In comparison, 72% favoured "a compromise, in which all the parties make some concessions to each other to reach a middle ground." A third of Sunni Muslim Emiratis said they had a "somewhat positive" view of the Brotherhood. At the same time, 44% believed that each Arab country had "every right to decide for itself what political and religious groups to host or support, no matter what others think."[20]

Bin Zayed's ability to persuade Saudi Arabia to join the boycott highlighted his influence in shaping Bin Salman's policies in the initial years after the prince's rise to power in 2015. Bin Zayed moved quickly to reverse Bin Salman's initial inclination to engage with the Brotherhood. The Emirati leader also counselled the de facto Saudi leader on shaving off the rough edges of Wahhabism and Salafism, the ultra-conservative interpretations of Islam that have shaped the kingdom since its founding in 1932. In doing so, Bin Zayed brought the UAE and Saudi Arabia's religious soft power endeavours closer together.

Weary of Saudi Arabia's past ultra-conservative religious outreach, Bin Zayed saw a need to counter the kingdom's global influence. He recognised the value of projecting a moderate image of an Islam willing to engage with non-Muslims. Al-Otaiba, the UAE ambassador in Washington, made no bones about the UAE's ambition to be a regional hegemon in leaked email traffic shared with this author and others by a shadowy group suspected of links to Qatar identifying itself as 'Global Leaks.'[21] In exchanges with former US officials such as Martin Indyk, who served in the Clinton and Obama administrations, Stephen Hadley, former President George W. Bush's national security

---

[20] David Pollock. "UAE Public Overwhelmingly Backs Tough Line on Iran—But Not on Qatar or Muslim Brotherhood." The Washington Institute for Near East Policy. 12 October 2017. https://www.washingtoninstitute.org/fikraforum/view/uae-public-overwhelmingly-backs-tough-line-on-iran-but-not-on-qatar-or-musl.

[21] Emails to the author from Global Leaks in August 2017.

advisor, and Elliott Abrams, who advised Presidents Bush and Ronald Reagan, as well as journalists, including Washington Post columnist David Ignatius, Al-Otaiba suggested that Bin Salman was the UAE's opportunity to get "the most results we can ever get out of Saudi."

For Bin Zayed and Bin Salman, survival was the name of the game. The decade before the September 11, 2001, Al-Qaeda attacks on New York and Washington that put Islam on the defensive was a period of religious resurgence. "Declining oil wealth and living standards, intensified urbanization, the spread and visibility of Western influences, growing social disparities, and the rise in Islamist activity in other parts of the Arab world all contributed to making the UAE and the Gulf a field of intense ferment," said Emirati scholar Fatima Al Sayegh. "This discontent usually originated within Islamist groups that wished to see an end to any Western domination or influence over their societies. The political authorities sought to respond to these challenges by organizing the Islamic establishment in such a manner as to further co-opt the religious authorities (ulema) and to attempt to control appointments and sermons delivered by clerics."[22]

Among the rivals for religious soft power, Bin Zayed excelled in merging his religious quest with his employment of private military and intelligence operatives to do his bidding and advance his hard power geopolitical ambitions. Building military bases in Yemen and the Horn of Africa and acquiring stakes in ports across the globe constituted cornerstones of Bin Zayed's strategy. "This is the integration of religion and politics and is clearly part of the UAE's efforts at consolidating the autocratic state," said Islamic studies scholar Usaama al-Azami.[23]

Bin Zayed's efforts have paid off. An Israeli NGO gave the UAE high marks in 2022 for mandating schoolbooks that teach tolerance, peaceful coexistence, and engagement with non-Muslims. "The Emirati curriculum generally meets international standards for peace and tolerance. Textbooks are free of hate and incitement against others. The curriculum teaches students to value the principle of respect for other cultures and encourages curiosity and dialogue. It praises love, affection, and family ties with non-Muslims," the 128-page study by the Institute for Monitoring Peace and Cultural Tolerance in School Education (IMPACT-se) concluded.

However, the report shied away from highlighting the autocratic aspects of Emirati religious moderation, including the principle of uncritical obedience to authority. That principle is embedded in the teaching of 'patriotism,' 'commitment to defending the homeland,' and the notion of leadership that the

---

[22] Fatima Al Sayegh. "Post-9/11 Changes in the Gulf: The Case of the UAE." The Free Library. 22 June 2004. https://www.thefreelibrary.com/Post-9%2F11+changes+in+the+Gulf%3A+the+case+of+the+UAE.-a0118417354.

[23] Usaama al-Azami. "Neo-traditionalist Sufis and Arab Politics: A Preliminary Mapping of the Transnational Networks of Counter-Revolutionary Scholars After the Arab Revolutions." In Francesco Piraino and Mark Sedgwick (eds.) Global Sufism: Boundaries, Narratives, and Practices. London: Hurst. 2019. Kindle edition.

report defined as a pillar of national identity. Similarly, the report noted the textbooks' endorsement of traditional gender roles while advocating women's integration into the economy and public life.[24]

Ryan Bohl, an American who taught in an Emirati public school a decade ago, could have told Impact-se about the unwritten authoritarian principles embedded in the country's education system. One of several Westerners hired by the UAE to replace Arab teachers suspected of sympathising with the Brotherhood, Bohl described teaching in Emirati classrooms as "following the autocratic method, very similar to the ruler and the ruled." It's in classrooms "where those political attitudes get formed, reinforced, enforced in some cases if kids like they do decide to deviate outside the line. They understand the consequences long before they can become a political threat or an activist threat to the regime. It's all about creating a chill effect," Bohl said.

The textbook reforms helped Bin Zayed promote a state-controlled Islam that styles itself as tolerant and apolitical despite ruling at home with an iron fist. They reinforced the Emirati leader's propagation of an authoritarian version of a moderate form of Islam that evades addressing outdated or intolerant concepts embedded in the faith, such as the notion of kafirs or infidels, slavery, and Muslim supremacy that remain reference points even if large numbers of Muslims do not heed them. Bin Zayed's success, backed by armies of paid Western lobbyists, is evidenced by the contrast with Bin Salman and Saudi Arabia's reputational problems. Saudi Arabia has been dogged by the 2018 killing in Istanbul of journalist Jamal Khashoggi and the arrests and alleged torture of dissidents and anyone deemed a potential threat. In contrast, the UAE is widely perceived as a religiously tolerant, pluralistic, and enlightened society.

Rather than resorting to targeted assassinations or high-profile renditions, the UAE invested millions of dollars in public relations and public affairs companies tasked with brandishing the country's image in Bin Zayed's mould and burying the incarceration of anyone who voices a critical note. He also put money into sophisticated surveillance technology and the hiring of former US intelligence and military officials and investigation and communication companies that waged the UAE's covert information wars against Qatar and alleged affiliates of the Muslim Brotherhood.

Speaking in 2017 in a public forum, UAE Foreign Minister Abdullah bin Zayed Al-Nahyan, a brother of Bin Zayed and a driving force in the country's religious soft power quest, warned that "there will come a day that we will see far more radical extremists and terrorists coming out of Europe because of lack of decision-making, trying to be politically correct, or assuming that they know the Middle East, and they know Islam, and they know the others far better than we do…I'm sorry, but that's pure ignorance." Abdullah bin Zayed

---

[24] Eldad J. Pardo. "When Peace Goes to School. The Emirati Curriculum 2016–21." Impact-se. 20 January 2022. https://www.impact-se.org/wp-content/uploads/When-Peace-Goes-to-School_The-Emirati-Curriculum-2016%E2%80%9321.pdf.

went further in remarks to a gathering of Bin Bayyah's peace forum in which he likened European Muslims to an ulcer that risked political violence.[25]

The foreign minister expressed similar disregard for Indian Muslims' plight, threatened by Hindu nationalism, and Chinese Uyghurs forcibly being Sinicized. Like Saudi Arabia, the UAE has publicly supported China's incarceration of an estimated one million Uyghurs in what it called vocational training camps as part of a campaign to counter Uyghur nationalism and reduce religiosity in the Turkic Muslim group.[26] Likewise, when rioting left more than 50 Muslims dead over six days of violence in India in 2020, the UAE officially remained silent while seemingly encouraging local media to absolve Prime Minister Narendra Modi and his ruling Bharatiya Janata Party (BJP) of responsibility. The Gulf News, an English-language newspaper that adheres to the government line, published an op-ed entitled "Stop Blaming Modi for Delhi Riots and All Things Evil in India" penned by Sanjib Kumar Das, one of its senior editors. "If even for one second you think that it is Indian Prime Minister Narendra Modi who is to be held responsible for this bloodshed, then think again," Das wrote.[27] The UAE also backed Modi's stripping of Muslim-majority Kashmir of its autonomy, arguing in concert with New Delhi that it would "improve social justice and security…and further stability and peace."[28]

Similarly, neither the UAE and Saudi Arabia nor Indonesia's Nahdlatul Ulama took exception to Evangelist Ralph Drollinger's anti-Muslim rhetoric as he organised a twice weekly White House study group attended by senior members of President Trump's cabinet and scores of Republican lawmakers. Drollinger charged "Islam and its Koran are nothing more than a plagiarism of OT (Old Testament) truths." Earlier he depicted Islam as seeking "nothing less than world conquest for Allah… Salvation per Islamic theology is not attained via a loving, self-sacrificing act of God (as per Christianity); it is attained by jihad, a sacrifice of self in combatting the infidels. Whereas in biblical Christianity, God gives His life for man, in Islam, man must give his life for his god," Drollinger said.[29]

---

[25] Abdullah bin Zayed al-Nahayan. YouTube. 21 October 2018. https://www.youtube.com/watch?v=_usazfmHKf8&fbclid=IwAR1my06oz_1n3r1DzlPeMrJohcXCHM-JfbiSM UENlkfJzVRGvYwQ9tjk3ls&app=desktop. The video has since been removed.

[26] James M. Dorsey. "China's Uyghurs: A Potential Time Bomb." In James Reardon-Anderson and Mehran Kamrava (eds.) China and the Middle East. New York: Oxford University Press. 2018.

[27] Sanjib Kumar Das. "Stop Blaming Modi for Delhi Riots and All Things Evil in India." Gulf News. 9 March 2020. https://gulfnews.com/opinion/op-eds/stop-blaming-modi-for-delhi-riots-and-all-things-evil-in-india-1.1583761983415.

[28] Gulf News. "UAE Ambassador to India Reacts to Kashmir Decision." 6 August 2019. https://gulfnews.com/world/asia/india/uae-ambassador-to-india-reacts-to-kashmir-decision-1.1565038437014.

[29] Ralph Drollinger. "How Would You Rate Your Level of Spiritual Discernment?" Capital Ministries. 24 March 2014. https://capmin.org/how-would-you-rate-your-level-of-spiritual-discernment/.

Bin Salman echoed Emirati warnings about European Muslims when he still walked in Mohammed bin Zayed's shadow. "You know what's the biggest danger? They're [the Brotherhood] not in the Middle East because they know that the Middle East is taking good strategy against them in Saudi Arabia, Egypt, UAE, Jordan, and a lot of countries. Their main target is to radicalize Europe. They hope that Europe in 30 years will turn into a Muslim Brotherhood continent, and they want to control the Muslims in Europe by manipulation. So, this will be much more dangerous than the Cold War, than ISIS, than al-Qaeda, than whatever we've seen in the last hundred years of history," Bin Salman told Time Magazine.[30]

Bin Zayed and Bin Salman's views were music in the ears of the political right in Europe with the blurring of the lines between the centre and the far right, despite the centre's rejection of French novelist Renaud Camus' Great Replacement conspiracy that incentivised extremists like the white nationalist who in 2019 attacked two mosques in Christchurch, New Zealand, killing 51 people. Less known but more notorious than his namesake, philosopher and writer, Albert Camus, Renaud Camus coined the phrase in a book published in 2011. Rooted in racist nationalist views, the theory asserts that the liberal elite conspires to replace white Europeans with African and Middle Eastern migrants in what Camus described as "genocide by substitution."

The theory traces its roots to the father of French nationalism, Maurice Barrès. Barres warned in 1900, amid mounting anti-Semitism that a new population would "ruin our homeland." In a frontpage article in Le Journal, Barres wrote, "the name of France might well survive; the special character of our country would, however, be destroyed, and the people settled in our name and on our territory would be heading towards destinies contradictory to the destinies and needs of our land and our dead."[31]

Starting in the 1970s, conspiracy theorists, like Egyptian-born British Jewish author Gisèle Littman, writing under the pen name Bat Ye'or (Daughter of the Nile), picked up on Barres' claims in the 1970s. Ye'or asserted Europe had "surrendered to Islam and is in a state of submission in which Europe is forced to deny its own culture, stand silently by in the face of Muslim atrocities, accept Muslim immigration, and pay tribute through various types of economic assistance."[32]

Abdullah bin Zayed did not say publicly that the UAE would act pre-emptively if Europe failed to counter the perceived threat. Like a puppeteer, the Emirates marshalled its religious soft power, commercial and economic

---

[30] Time. "Crown Prince Mohammed bin Salman Talks to TIME About the Middle East, Saudi Arabia's Plans and President Trump." 5 April 2018. https://time.com/5228006/mohammed-bin-salman-interview-transcript-full/.

[31] Maurice Barres. "The sinecures for litterateurs (The Sinecures for Writers)." Le Journal. 23 October 1900.

[32] Bat Ye'or. Eurabia: "The Euro-Arab Axis." Madison, NJ: Fairleigh Dickinson University Press. 2010. Kindle edition.

sway, and hard power to counter political Islam in ways that potentially threatened pillars of Western democracy and strategic interests. The UAE's footprint was visible globally, most prominently in Egypt,[33] Libya,[34] and Europe.

Building on French, Saudi, and Emirati support for Libyan rebel leader Field Marshal Khalifa Haftar in Libya, the UAE and the kingdom lobbied for a tougher French policy towards political Islam, emphasising common interests and giving French President Emmanuel Macron cover for policies that targeted the Muslim community in France.[35] The policies included a new security law mandating tighter legal control of Muslim organisations, imposing a wider ban on home schooling and controls on religious, sporting and cultural associations, and introducing degrees of surveillance and limits on freedom of expression.[36] Suspect mosques were closed. Islamic charity organisations channelling aid to Syria were disbanded. Muslim organisations were required to sign a 'Republican charter' that endorsed apostasy and condemned racism, anti-Semitism, homophobia, and misogyny, frequent hot-button issues in the Muslim community.

Speaking in the French city of Mulhouse in February 2020, Macron laid out his strategy to combat political Islam represented by the Muslim Brotherhood and Salafists, who, in his words, insisted that Islam's legal code supersedes the laws of the French Republic and emphasise what he called "Islamist separatism" and "Islamist supremacy." Macron asserted that "in the Republic, we cannot accept that we refuse to shake hands with a woman because she is a woman. In the Republic, we cannot accept that someone refuses to be treated or educated by someone because she is a woman. In the Republic, one cannot accept school dropouts for religious or belief reasons. In the Republic, one cannot require certificates of virginity to marry."[37]

---

[33] David D. Kirkpatrick. "Recordings Suggest Emirates and Egyptian Military Pushed Ousting of Morsi." The New York Times. 1 March 2015. https://www.nytimes.com/2015/03/02/world/middleeast/recordings-suggest-emirates-and-egyptian-military-pushed-ousting-of-morsi.html?_r=0.

[34] Sean W. O'Donnell, Matthew S. Klimow and Ann Calvaresi Barr. "East Africa Counterterrorism Operation/North and West Africa Counterterrorism Operation." US Department of Defence. 25 November 2020. https://media.defense.gov/2020/Nov/25/2002541626/-1/-1/1/LEAD%20IG%20EAST%20AFRICA%20AND%20NORTH%20AND%20WEST%20AFRICA%20COUNTERTERRORISM%20OPERATIONS.PDF.

[35] James M. Dorsey. "France, Belgium and Austria Move into the Frontline of a Battle for the Soul of Islam." The Turbulent World with James M. Dorsey. 6 December 2020. https://www.jamesmdorsey.net/post/france-belgium-and-austria-move-into-the-frontline-of-a-battle-for-the-soul-of-islam.

[36] Kim Willsher. "Concern over French Bill That Cracks Down on Photos Identifying Police." The Guardian. 9 November 2020. https://www.theguardian.com/world/2020/nov/09/french-law-protect-police-press-freedom-journalists-ban-intent-harm.

[37] Elysee. "Protéger les libertés en luttant contre le séparatisme islamiste: conférence de presse du Président Emmanuel Macron à Mulhouse (Protecting Freedoms by Fighting Against Islamist Separatism: President Emmanuel Macron's Press Conference in Mulhouse)." 18 February 2020. https://www.elysee.fr/emmanuel-macron/2020/02/18/proteger-les-libertes-en-luttant-contre-le-separatisme-islamiste-conference-de-presse-du-president-emmanuel-macron-a-mulhouse.

In support of Macron, UAE Minister of State for Foreign Affairs Anwar Gargash argued that Macron "does not want to see Muslims ghettoized in the West and he is right. They should be better integrated into society. The French state has the right to explore ways to achieve that."[38] Mohammed al-Issa, head of the Muslim World League, a one-time major vehicle for the global propagation of past Saudi ultra-conservatism that now projects the kingdom's autocratic notion of moderate Islam, insisted that the security law would defend French secularism against Islamic radicalism.[39] Earlier, he told an interfaith conference in Paris, co-hosted by the League, that religion needed to be protected from political exploitation to safeguard youth against extremist groups.[40]

The UAE didn't leave it to words. An Emirati financial services and asset management company with close ties to the country's ruler helped bail out far-right French politician Marie le Pen's Rassemblement National, the former National Front founded by her estranged father, Jean-Marie le Pen, by guaranteeing and transferring in 2017 a US$7.5 million loan. Because Noor Capital, established by former oil minister and presidential advisor Mana Saeed al-Otaiba, the father of the Emirati ambassador to the United States, Yusuf al-Otaiba, holds investors' assets in its name, it is unclear who originated the loan. French businessman Laurent Foucher said he loaned the money and used Noor Capital, his Emirati banker, to execute the transaction.[41]

The UAE initially offered to fund Le Pen's party in the run-up to the 2014 senate election. A senior Emirati intelligence official extended the offer during a meeting with Marie Le Pen at the family's Montretout residence in the leafy hillside Paris suburb of Saint-Cloud. The official told Le Pen the UAE wanted to support her in countering the Brotherhood and Qatar. A year later, the UAE funded Le Pen's visit to Egypt, her first to a Middle Eastern country. Le Pen met with Egyptian President Abdel Fatah Al-Sisi and Major General Khaled Fawzi, the head of Egypt's General Intelligence Directorate. Le Pen's

---

[38] Daniel-Dylan Böhmer. "Wenn die ihr Imperium wieder errichten wollen – bitte schön. Aber nicht bei uns (If They Want to Resurrect Their Empire—Please Do. But Not with Us)." Die Welt. 2 November 2020. https://www.welt.de/politik/ausland/plus21 9126402/Grossmachtplaene-der-Tuerkei-Wenn-die-ihr-Imperium-wieder-errichten-wollen-bitte-schoen-Aber-nicht-bei-uns.html.

[39] Arab News. "Muslim World League Chief Denounces Extremists in Response to Macron's 'Islamist Separatism' Speech." 12 October 2020. https://www.arabnews.jp/en/saudi-arabia/article_28851/.

[40] Saudi Press Agency. "Paris Conference Exhorts Religious Leaders to Challenge Ideologies That Threaten Peace." Arab News. 20 September 2019. https://www.arabnews.com/node/1556996/world.

[41] Karl Laske and Marine Turchi. "The 8-Million-Euro Loan via a UAE Bank That Saved Marine Le Pen's Far-Right Party." Mediapart. 6 October 2019. https://www.mediapart.fr/en/journal/france/061019/8-million-euro-loan-uae-bank-saved-marine-le-pens-far-right-party.

party said in a statement that Le Pen's visit intended "to demonstrate her support for President Sisi in his unfailing combat against the Islamists."[42]

Macron's thinking was informed by French Muslims who maintained close contact with the French and Emirati governments, including Hakim El Karoui, the French-born son of an anthropologist of Islamic law and nephew of a former Tunisian prime minister. El Karoui projected Islamists as secessionists or separatists. He argued that political Islam is a product of Middle Eastern funding and political manipulation of faith rather than a response to political, social, and economic concerns.[43] An advisor to former French Prime Minister Jean-Pierre Raffarin, university lecturer, investment banker, geographer, and author of reports on Islam in France, El Karoui has long presented the UAE as a model of best practice in countering political Islam and fostering a moderate interpretation of the faith.[44] "I think that France and the UAE must engage more in a religious debate. The positions of the moderate Muslims in France can be close to the ones of the UAE," El Karoui told an Abu Dhabi-based newspaper.[45]

The Emirati effort benefitted from a rift between France's two most influential scholars of political Islam, Olivier Roy, a reformed Maoist who fought in 1980 in Afghanistan with the Mujahideen against the Soviets, and Gilles Kepel, a one-time Trotskyist who kick-started his career with a study of an Egyptian jihadist group that in 1981 killed President Anwar Sadat for making peace with Israel. Policymakers solicited both men's views. They clashed over the roots of militant Islamist violence and the reasons why some European Muslims joined jihadist groups. At the core of their enduring feud in a country that relishes intellectual debate is whether social, economic, and political marginalisation rather than religion is the primary driver of radicalisation.

Roy argued it wasn't. He perceived radicalisation as a generational revolt that saw a warped interpretation of Islam as the best vehicle for rebellion. Roy compared European jihadists to youth in the 1970s who joined militant left-wing groups such as the Red Brigades in Italy and the Red Army Faction or Baader-Meinhof Group in Germany. More in line with Emirati thinking, Kepel believed that marginalisation had pushed young Muslims towards extreme forms of Islam, including Salafism, the ultra-conservative strand of the faith Saudi Arabia exported across the globe. Kepel insisted that non-violent forms

---

[42] Marine Turchi. "French Far-Right Front National Party's Links with the United Arab Emirates." Mediapart. 24 October 2016. https://www.mediapart.fr/en/journal/international/241016/french-far-right-front-national-party-s-links-united-arab-emirates?userid=9fb58175-9044-44d2-93fd-3fa893236c8a.

[43] The Brookings Institution. "Islam in France." 27 March 2017. https://www.brookings.edu/wp-content/uploads/2017/04/20170327_islam_france_transcript.pdf.

[44] Institut Montaigne. Hakim El Karoui. https://www.institutmontaigne.org/en/experts/hakim-el-karoui.

[45] Damien McElroy. "French Muslims Must Resist Islamist Extremists: Hakim El Karoui." The National. 13 September 2018. https://www.thenationalnews.com/world/french-muslims-must-resist-islamist-extremists-hakim-el-karoui-1.770152?fromNewsdog=1.

of Salafism and jihadism were two sides of the same coin. With Macron facing off with a right-wing xenophobe in the 2022 election, Kepel replaced Olivier as the government's favoured expert.

Echoing Kepel's position and by implication of the UAE and Saudi Arabia, journalist and novelist Marc Weitzmann asserted, "at the risk of simplifying a bit, one could argue that from the mid-1990s onward, the rise of Islamist violence in France that culminated with the terror wave of 2015–2016 was essentially a Salafi undertaking." Weitzmann blamed the Muslim Brotherhood and its Middle Eastern backers alongside the Saudis for France's problem.[46]

A leak in 2023 of 78,000 internal documents laid bare the dark side of the UAE's promotion of its staunch anti-Islamism. The documents revealed the UAE's hiring of Alp Services, a Swiss company, operated by former intelligence agent Mario Brero, specialised in what he described as 'dark PR.' Brero's notion of public relations earned him a French court conviction in 2014 on charges of illegally procuring summaries of telephone calls of the head of a French nuclear energy company.[47] Alp joined a painstakingly created network of consultancies, public relations firms, think tanks, and individuals who either worked directly for the UAE or sympathised with its agenda.[48] The network included DarkMatter, a UAE-based company employing former US National Security Agency officials. DarkMatter complimented Alp's activity by targeting the computers of dissidents, human rights activists, rival leaders, and journalists in the UAE and abroad.[49] The goal, said scholar Andreas Krieg, was the "weaponisation of narratives in an effort to incline target audiences to voluntarily make the predetermined decision desired by the information warrior."[50]

An internal July 2017 Alp memo defined 'dark PR' as a "highly aggressive/ offensive, not open source. After identifying their supporters, we should obtain negative information on them and destroy their reputations. This would also deter other people from supporting them. We should 'Terrorize the Terrorists.'" In his pitch, Brero promised to publish or influence 100 media articles a year, some written by fictitious bloggers, that would target the Brotherhood

---

[46] Marc Weitzman. "France's Great Debate Over the Sources and Meaning of Muslim Terror." Tablet. 25 May 2021. https://www.tabletmag.com/sections/news/articles/roy-kepel-marc-weitzmann.

[47] Valérie de Senneville. "Areva: le tribunal refuse de rentrer dans le scenario (Areva: The Court Refuses to Return to the Scenario)." Les Echos. 20 June 2014. https://www.lesechos.fr/2014/06/areva-le-tribunal-refuse-de-rentrer-dans-le-scenario-305233.

[48] Corporate Europe Observatory. "United Arab Emirates' Growing Legion of Lobbyists Support Its 'Soft Superpower' Ambitions in Brussels." 17 December 2020. https://corporateeurope.org/en/2020/12/united-arab-emirates-growing-legion-lobbyists-support-its-soft-superpower-ambitions.

[49] Christopher Bing and Jonathan Schechtman. "Secret Hacking Team of American Mercenaries." Reuters. 30 January 2019. https://www.reuters.com/investigates/special-report/usa-spying-raven/ ullah bin zay.

[50] Andreas Krieg. "Subversion: The Strategic Weaponization of Narratives." Washington, DC: Georgetown University Press. 2023. Kindle edition.

and its backer, Qatar. "We can seriously damage, if not destroy, the reputation and survival of the main European Muslim Brotherhood groups through our offensive and confidential viral communication," Brero asserted."[51] Brero set out to do just that on behalf of the UAE. Hired two months after Bin Zayed instigated the 2017 UAE-Saudi-led boycott of Qatar, which he accused of supporting political Islam, Brero was handsomely rewarded with US$6.25 million in contracts to identify Brotherhood and Qatari networks in Europe and destroy their alleged agents' reputations.

Brero cast his net far beyond the 85 organisations designated in 2014 by the UAE as terrorists.[52] Pinpointing some 1,000 people, including activists, journalists, and politicians, and 400, often Muslim, organisations in 18 European countries, Brero's strategy was to "discredit targets by discreetly and massively distributing embarrassing information," using fake social media profiles, websites, and email addresses; journalists; and tendentious whisper campaigns. He called his employees "mercenaries with ethics" and dubbed the targets "a mafia-like network." In some instances, Brero characterised the targets as "openly critical" of the UAE but "not directly Muslim Brotherhood."

Tellingly, many of Brero's victims were non-Muslims, who would have had little affinity with a group that favours the rule of Islamic law. Brero's targets included former French presidential candidates Benoît Hamon and Jean-Luc Melenchon, Belgian Climate and Environment Minister Zakia Khattab, former UK Labour Party leader Jeremy Corbyn, one-time French senator Samia Ghal, researchers at the French National Centre for Scientific Research, and former Le Monde Diplomatique editor Alain Gresh as well as convicted Al-Qaeda operatives.[53]

In one instance, Brero proudly pointed to an Alp website that smeared Femyso, a European Union-subsidised Muslim youth network, as anti-Semitic and supportive of Hamas, the Islamist Muslim Brotherhood offshoot that governed the Gaza Strip until the Gaza war in 2023. In 2018, the website topped French-language Google searches for the Brotherhood. The campaign prompted two French ministers and far-right European parliamentarians to question European support for Femyso and convinced the European Commission to stop funding the group.

[51] Giovanni Tizian and Stefano Vergin. "Il Times, La Verità e "Mr Brero". La rete al servizio degli Emirati (The Times, The Truth and "Mr Brero." The Network at the Service of the Emirates)." Domani. 11 July 2023. https://www.editorialedomani.it/fatti/times-verita-mr-brero-la-rete-al-servizio-degli-emirati-jg9ln575.

[52] WAM. "UAE Publishes List of Terrorist Organisations." Gulf News. 15 November 2014. https://gulfnews.com/uae/government/uae-publishes-list-of-terrorist-organisations-1.1412895.

[53] Daraj, "أسرار أبو ظبي" : ألف أوروبي مسجّلون كـ"إخوان مسلمين" لدى أجهزة الأمن الإماراتيّة" (Abu Dhabi Secrets: A Thousand Europeans Registered as 'Muslim Brotherhood' with UAE Secret Services)." 7 July 2023. https://daraj.media/109749/.

Averroes, France's largest Muslim school, voted in 2013 as the country's best high school, faced closure in 2023 after local authorities terminated state funding. The decision made Averroes the first French private school to be defunded. The authorities initially suspended funding in 2019 after a book, Qatar Papers,[54] authored by two French journalists, Georges Malbrunot and Christian Chesnot, claimed Averroes had received US$3.2 million from Qatar Charity and had links to the Brotherhood.[55]

Atmane Tazaghart, a former French journalist, was more than just Malbrunot and Chesnot's book agent. Leaked emails disclosed that Tazaghart was in touch with Alp Services' primary Emirati intelligence contact. In one email exchange, Tazaghat offered information on alleged links between the former French Prime Minister and 2017 presidential candidate and Qatar and the Brotherhood. On behalf of the authors, Tazaghart arranged the French-language publication of their book. He also bought the book's foreign language rights and facilitated its translation and publication in English and Arabic. Based on documents leaked by a shadowy group calling itself Qatar Charity, the book detailed alleged Qatari funding of 140 projects, including mostly Brotherhood-linked schools, mosques, and Islamic centres in France and elsewhere in Europe.[56]

Like in the case of Averroes, a crusade against Islamic Relief Worldwide, a charity with operations in 40 countries, forced the resignation of charity executives accused of Brotherhood affiliations and persuaded the Dutch and German governments to halt the group's funding. Britain and Sweden investigated the organisation. The UAE designated the charity a terrorist organisation in 2014 because of its alleged ties to the Muslim Brotherhood. Egypt followed suit in 2015. The designations were also informed by Israeli assertions that the charity had donated funds to Hamas.

The crusade kicked into high gear with an article in the British newspaper, The Times, accusing Heshmat Khalifa, a trustee and director of the charity, of anti-Semitic postings on Facebook.[57] Khalifa's Facebook postings describing Jews as the "grandchildren of monkeys and pigs," asserting insulting fellow Muslims by labelling them a "pimp son of the Jews" and a "Zionist pig," and identifying Hamas as "the purest resistance movement in modern history and

[54] Christian Chesnot and Georges Malbrunot. "Qatar Papers." Paris: Michel Lafon. 2019.

[55] Anna Rabemanantsoa. "France's Largest Muslim School Threatened with Closure Amid Scrutiny of Funding, Courses." Yahoo News. 14 December 2023. https://www.yahoo.com/gma/frances-largest-muslim-school-threatened-101224446.html?guccounter=1.

[56] Yann Philippin and Antton Rouget. "Leaked Data Shows Extent of UAE's Meddling in France." Mediapart. 4 March 2023. https://www.mediapart.fr/en/journal/france/040323/leaked-data-shows-extent-uaes-meddling-france?userid=9fb58175-9044-44d2-93fd-3fa893236c8a.

[57] Andrew Norfolk. "Muslim Charity Islamic Relief Feels the Heat Again." The Times. 24 July 2020. https://www.thetimes.co.uk/article/muslim-charity-islamic-relief-feels-the-heat-again-q63vvplhh.

a symbol of honour, resistance and the real Islam," were taken down days before The Times article's publication.

Leaked Brero documents suggested that The Times' source was Lorenzo Vidino, a prominent, Italian-born, US-based expert on the Islamist group and an Alp consultant. Vidino has long asserted that the Brotherhood penetrated European institutions.[58] European politicians, intelligence services, and counterterrorism officials often sought Vidino's advice. Like Abdullah bin Zayed's warning, Vidino's alarmist, black-and-white messaging found a receptive audience with the rise of anti-Muslim populist and nativist sentiment in Europe. A 2017 report by Vidino on the Muslim Brotherhood in Austria,[59] commissioned by Austria's domestic intelligence agency and the Austrian Integration Fund, alongside other publications, persuaded UAE ambassador Al-Otaiba to arrange a meeting for Vidino and one of his associates, Mokhtar Awad, with the Emirati foreign minister.[60]

Vidino's Austria report was a major source for discussing Muslim extremism in the intelligence agency's 2018 annual report.[61] In July 2020, Vidino was appointed to the board of experts of the Austrian Chancellor's Documentation Center for Political Islam, which was created to monitor, surveil, and map Muslims in Austria.[62] Two months later, authorities conducted sweeping

[58] David D. Kirkpatrick. "The Dirty Secrets of a Smear Campaign." The New Yorker. 3 April 2023. https://www.newyorker.com/magazine/2023/04/03/the-dirty-secrets-of-a-smear-campaign. Clément Fayol, Yann Philippin, Antton Rouget and Antoine Harari. "Plus de 200 Français ont été fichés pour le compte des services secrets des Émirats arabes unis (More Than 200 French People Have Been Put on File on Account of the United Arab Emirates' Secret Services)." Mediapart. 7 July 2023. https://www.mediapart.fr/journal/international/070723/plus-de-200-francais-ont-ete-fiches-pour-le-compte-des-services-secrets-des-emirats-arabes-unis/. Kasper Goethals Roeland Termote and Nikolas Vanhecke. "De oude spion, de emir en hun Europese lastercampagnes: 'Ik wilde naar Genève rijden om hen allemaal te vermoorden' (The Old Spy, the Emir, and Their European Smear Campaigns: I Wanted to Travel to Geneva to Kill All of The)." De Standaard. 7 July 2023. https://www.standaard.be/cnt/dmf20230706_95804908/. Wilmer Heck and Andreas Kouwenhoven. "Dit schimmige bedrijf vernietigde reputaties van Europese moslims (This Shadowy Company Destroyed Reputations of European Muslims)." NRC Handelsblad. 7 July 2023. https://www.nrc.nl/nieuws/2023/07/07/dit-schimmige-bedrijf-vernietigde-met-succes-de-reputaties-van-europese-moslims-a4169074?utm_campaign=share&utm_medium=social&utm_source=twitter&utm_term=inbyline.

[59] Lorenzo Vidino, "Muslim Brotherhood in Austria." George Washington University/University of Vienna. August 2017. https://extremism.gwu.edu/sites/g/files/zaxdzs5746/files/MB%20in%20Austria-%20Print.pdf.

[60] Middle East Monitor. "EXCLUSIVE: UAE Works to 'Defeat Voices of Islamism' in the West, Reveal Leaked Emails." 9 November 2017. https://www.middleeastmonitor.com/20171109-exclusive-uae-works-to-defeat-voices-of-islamism-in-the-west-reveal-leaked-emails/.

[61] Federal Interior Ministry. "Verfassungsschutzbericht 2018 (Protection of the Constitution Report 2018)." 2019. https://www.bvt.gv.at/bmi_documents/2344.pdf.

[62] Michael Simoner. "Staatliche Dokustelle für politischen Islam soll Vereine und Moscheen durchleuchten (State Doucmentation Offcie for Political Islam Tasked with Investigating Associations and Mosques)." Der Standard. 15 July

raids, dubbed Operation Luxor, targeting dozens of people suspected of ties to terrorist and criminal organisations, forming a terrorist organisation, financing terrorism, and money laundering.

Prosecutors said the raids followed a year-long terrorism probe that identified "the Muslim Brotherhood (as) a globally active, radical Islamist, extremely anti-Semitic organization." They said the Brotherhood aimed to "set up an Islamic state on the basis of Islamic law in all countries on Earth." Prosecutors insisted the raids were not connected to the killing of four people in Vienna days earlier by an Islamic State operative.[63] In the aftermath of the attack, Chancellor Sebastian Kurz announced a package of measures to fight terrorism, including stripping suspects of their citizenship, closing mosques, and criminalising political Islam.

Farid Hafez, an Austrian professor and author of an annual report on European Islamophobia, recalled being "awoken by special forces crushing in my door, levelling their guns at me and waking up my children. I was targeted alongside 29 others, accused of being an enemy of the state and financing terrorist activity." Ten months later, a high court ruled that the raids lacked a legal base because the Brotherhood was not a proscribed organisation in Austria. More than a year later, the Austrian Supreme Court dropped terrorism charges against Hafez.

Beyond Austria, Vidino's analysis inspired European Union counterterrorism chief Gilles de Kerchove's creation of the Radicalization Awareness Network (RAN), a network linking thousands of practitioners seeking to counter extremism and militant recruitment proactively. De Kerchove was also inspired by the Hedayah Center of Excellence for Countering Violent Extremism, an Emirati counterterrorism think tank that, in line with Emirati and Saudi policy, blurs the lines between violent jihadism, extremism, and non-violent Islamist civil society groups. Chaired by Ali Rashid al-Nuaimi, a member of the UAE's Federal National Council, a partially elected parliamentary advisory body, the centre helps promote the narrative, as articulated by the Emirati embassy in Washington, that "the UAE has a new vision for the Middle East region — an alternative, future-oriented ideology grounded in respect, inclusion, and peace. It is a vision that rejects extremism and factionalism and instead embraces diversity, empowers women, encourages innovation, and welcomes global engagement. These values are reflected throughout the country's vibrant and diverse society, where over 200 nationalities and countless faiths live and worship side-by-side."[64]

2020. https://www.derstandard.at/story/2000118721151/staatliche-dokustelle-fuer-politischen-islam-soll-vereine-und-moscheen-durchleuchten.

[63] Deutsche Welle. "Austria Police Raid Muslim Brotherhood, Hamas Targets." 11 September 2020. https://www.dw.com/en/austria-police-raid-muslim-brotherhood-hamas-linked-targets/a-55542480.

[64] Embassy of the United Arab Emirates Washington DC. Society. Undated. https://www.uae-embassy.org/discover-uae/society.

The UAE-Saudi-inspired EU Radicalization Awareness Network's "framing meant that adherence to Muslim conservative values was inherently suspect, seen as a potential first step toward terrorist activity. It is inherently discriminatory because it fails to address the persistence of these exact same values among 'native' Europeans. The framing, by focusing disproportionately on Muslims, risked stigmatising Muslims. As a result, the European Union has become an unwitting promoter of the UAE's geopolitical interests," said Eldar Mamedov, a former European Parliament staffer dealing with Gulf affairs, who was caught up in a Belgian police investigation into alleged Qatari and Moroccan influence-peddling.[65] The network was modelled on Hedayah's vast web of counter-extremism policymakers, practitioners, and researchers who advise governments and civil society groups.

Simultaneously, the UAE successfully projected itself as a secular state, even though its constitution requires Islamic law-compatible legislation. In doing so, UAE leaders walked a fine line. Islamic scholars with close ties to the Emirati government rushed to defend Al-Otaiba, the UAE ambassador in Washington, against accusations of blasphemy for telling talk show host Charlie Rose that "what we would like to see is more secular, stable, prosperous, empowered, strong government."[66] To avert criticism, the government rolled out prominent Mauritanian philosopher Adballah Seyid Ould Abah, who insisted it was "obvious" that (Al-Otaiba) did not mean secularism in the Western sense. Like Saudi Arabia and other Middle Eastern countries, the UAE was keen to sponsor religion, maintain its role in public life, and protect "it from ideological exploitation, which is a hidden manifestation of secularization," Ould Abah said.[67]

The UAE scored one of its most significant successes with Pope Francis' visit to the Emirates. In Abu Dhabi, the pope signed a Document on Human Fraternity with Al-Azhar's Grand Imam, Ahmad El-Tayeb, at a conference attended by Muslim, Christian, Jewish, Hindu, Buddhist, and Sikh leaders.[68] The pope acknowledged the UAE's growing influence by publicly crediting Mohamed Abd al-Salam, El-Tayeb's legal aid, and a Bin Zayed advisor, with drafting the document.[69] The United Nations General Assembly adopted the

---

[65] Interview with the author. 14 July 2023.

[66] Charlie Rose. "Qatar and the Middle East." 26 July 2017. https://charlierose.com/videos/30799.

[67] Adballah Seyid Ould Anah. "What Does the UAE Envoy to Washington Mean by 'Secularism?'" Al Arabiya. 12 August 2017. https://english.alarabiya.net/en/views/news/middle-east/2017/08/12/What-does-the-UAE-envoy-to-Washington-mean-by-secularism-.html.

[68] Muslim Council of Elders. "Global Conference of Human Fraternity." February 2019. https://www.muslim-eldes.com/en/page/12/HumanFraternity.

[69] Gerard O'Connell. "An Inside Look at How Pope Francis and the Grand Imam of Al-Azhar Have Revolutionized Catholic-Muslim Relations." America. 13 April 2021. https://www.americamagazine.org/faith/2021/04/13/pope-francis-grand-imam-catholic-muslim-abdel-salam-240436.

document a year later and urged the international community to observe February 4 as the annual International Day of Human Fraternity.

The document served multiple purposes. Beyond projecting the UAE as a beacon of religious tolerance, it bolstered El-Tayeb in his power struggle with Egyptian President Al-Sisi over control of Al-Azhar, the more than 1,000-year-old citadel of Islamic learning, and boosted religious discourse to counter extremism. Al-Sisi worried that Al-Azhar's close ties to the UAE and mushrooming international activities undermined the state's grip on the institution. "The president seems to be uncomfortable with Al-Azhar's independence and the international role that the grand imam plays. (El-Tayyeb) behaves as though he is not subordinate to the presidency — an issue that clearly bothers the president," said a government official.[70] Former Egyptian Culture Minister Gaber Asfour charged, "The current leadership of al-Azhar does not believe in the need for renewal and is comfortable with things as they are. Keeping things unchanged serves the interests of this leadership, which will not allow any renewal to happen."[71]

Days before meeting the pope, El-Tayeb clashed with Cairo University President Mohamed al-Khosht, an Al-Sisi associate, at an Al-Azhar conference on renovating Islamic thought held under Al-Sisi's auspices. El-Tayeb rejected Al-Khost's assertion that a new religious discourse required discarding past thought that "was made to suit a different age" and scrapping religious education based on Islamic heritage. Al-Khost argued that Muslims were held hostage by the thoughts of people who lived long ago.[72] Adding fuel to the fire, Al-Khost infuriated El-Tayeb by publicly handing the cleric a copy of one of his books, laying out his vision.[73] Earlier, El-Tayeb rejected Al-Sisi's call for an amendment of Egypt's personal status law to eliminate the Sharia-based right of a husband to divorce his wife by verbally announcing his repudiation. Instead, Al-Azhar's Supreme Council of Scholars urged the state to improve living standards, charging that economic struggles were responsible for the country's high divorce rate.[74]

---

[70] Asmahan Soliman. "How Al-Azhar's Grand Imam Survived the Constitutional Amendments." Mada Masr. 11 April 2019. https://www.madamasr.com/en/2019/04/11/feature/politics/how-the-grand-imam-of-al-azhar-survived-the-constitutional-amendments/

[71] Interview with the author. 15 March 2020.

[72] Al. Ghad TV. " تجديد الفكر الإسلامي يشعل الجدل بين شيخ الأزهر ورئيس جامعة القاهرة" (The Renewal of Islamic Thought Ignites the Controversy Between the Sheikh of Al-Azhar and the President of Cairo University)." YouTube. 28 January 2020. https://www.youtube.com/watch?v=_EOW9XYzwf4.

[73] BBC News. " شيخ الأزهر يحرج رئيس جامعة القاهرة وينتقد الزعماء" (Sheikh Al-Azhar Embarrasses the President of Cairo University and Criticizes the Leaders)." YouTube. 30 January 2020. https://www.youtube.com/watch?v=aUGOKeiWZ5g.

[74] Al-Monitor. "Egypt's Presidency Clashes with Religious Institutions Over Verbal Divorce." 17 September 2020. https://www.al-monitor.com/originals/2020/09/egypt-sisi-calls-annul-verbal-divorce-dispute-al-azhar.html.

Two months after the papal visit, Abd al-Salam and Abbas Abd Allah Abbas Shoman, a senior Al-Azhar cleric, were dismissed from Al-Azhar in a deal mediated by UAE Foreign Minister Bin Zayed and former Egyptian Interim President Adly Mansour. Al-Sisi hoped El-Tayeb's loss of two influential and trusted aides would weaken the imam. Rumours suggested that the two dismissed men had ties to the Brotherhood. "The presidency spread the rumours. Everybody knows there's no truth in them," said an Egyptian official.[75]

In exchange for the firing, Al-Sisi dropped a proposed amendment to the 2014 post-revolt constitution that would have given him the authority to appoint Al-Azhar's grand imam. The amendment would have abolished Al-Azhar's status as an "independent Islamic scientific institution, with exclusive competence over its own affairs." Also, it would have done away with the provision that "Al-Azhar's Grand Sheikh is independent and may not be dismissed" and that "the Law shall regulate the method of selecting the Grand Sheikh among the members of Council of Senior Scholars."[76] Ironically, toppled Egyptian President Hosni Mubarak appointed El-Tayeb in 2010. The council confirmed El-Tayeb's appointment in 2012 to prevent a Brotherhood power grab while Morsi, the Muslim Brother, was president. Al-Sisi, Mubarak's military intelligence director, and El-Tayeb are among the few senior officials from the Mubarak period still holding office.

Differences between Al-Sisi and El-Tayeb over religious discourse went to the heart of the Muslim world's debate about religious reform. El-Tayeb, backed by the UAE, rejected the president's insistence that Al-Azhar remove elements of historical texts that appear to endorse violence and supremacy. El-Tayeb argued that he had no right to do so. Instead, El-Tayeb reinterpreted problematic texts to counter extremist interpretations. Bin Zayed's support for El-Tayeb enhanced Emirati influence in Al-Azhar, long a preserve of Saudi ultra-conservatives, and its ability to shape religious discourse across the Muslim world. To boost its impact, the UAE donated tens of millions of dollars to Al-Azhar months before Al-Sisi's removal of Morsi from office.[77] The UAE opened its Al-Azhar-affiliated Zayed Center for Culture and Technology in Cairo a year later. In 2015, the UAE's General Authority of Islamic Affairs and Endowments funded the opening in the Emirates of Al-Azhar's first overseas branch and, in 2021, the construction of a new library.[78] "Control

---

[75] Interview with the author. 16 March 2020.

[76] Constitution of the Arabic Republic of Egypt 2014. Constitutionnet. Undated. https://constitutionnet.org/sites/default/files/dustor-en001.pdf.

[77] Sky News Arabia. " ‎66 مليون دولار تمويل إماراتي للأزهر‎ Emirates Donates 66 Million Dollars to Al-Azhar)." 30 April 2013. https://www.skynewsarabia.com/business/213369-66-‎الأزهر‎-‎بملايين‎-‎لمشروعات‎-‎إماراتي‎-‎تمويل‎-‎دولار‎-‎مليون‎.

[78] WAM. " ‎الإمارات ومصر.. أخوة راسخة وقيم مشتركة جسدها دعم الأزهر الشريف‎ (The UAE and Egypt... Solid Brotherhood and Common Values Embodied in the Support of Al-Azhar Al-Sharif)." Emirates Today. 22 October 2022. https://www.emaratalyoum.com/local-section/other/2022-10-24-1.1680843.

of Al-Azhar is a powerful tool. It lends significant authority to one's voice," said an Emirati diplomat.[79]

In 2023, the UAE capitalised on the visit and Emirati chairmanship of the United Nations Security Council to invite the pope and El-Tayeb to address the Council in a meeting dubbed "The Importance of Human Fraternity Values in Promoting and Sustaining Peace." Invitations for the gathering noted that "the United Arab Emirates (which will be holding the Security Council's presidency) will highlight pressing and urgent humanitarian issues and try to take serious steps toward establishing security and ending conflicts around the world." It was the first time the council hosted two of the world's foremost religious leaders.[80] The UAE saw the Council meeting as a way of taking the wind out of the sails of a call by Nahdlatul Ulama, the world's largest, Indonesia-based Muslim civil society movement, to position religion as part of the solution to the world's problems rather than as part of the problem through jurisprudential reform, the promotion of an Islam that unambiguously embraces human rights and pluralism, and confronts the faith's ugly truths.

The Council meeting was a milestone in Mohammed bin Zayed's multi-pronged geopolitical and religious offensive to bolster his version of Islam and counter political Islam and its backers. Bin Zayed drew a line in the sand when, in 2013, he helped orchestrate the military coup that toppled Morsi, the Muslim Brother president.[81] He unsuccessfully attempted to fortify the battle lines in 2014 by engineering the 10-month withdrawal of ambassadors of the UAE, Saudi Arabia, and Egypt from Doha and in 2017, the debilitating boycott of Qatar.[82] The battle lines were as much in the realm of ideology and ideas as in war theatres like Libya, where the UAE funded and armed Libyans fighting the elected, internationally recognised, Islamist-tinted Government of National Accord based in Tripoli.

The mantle of quietist Sufism, a mystical strand of Islam, provided the UAE the theological framework and moral justification for its assault on Wahhabism and Salafism, the crackdown on dissent and civil society, and the lumping together of non-violent Islamism and jihadism. The UAE saw quietist Sufism as an anti-dote to Wahhabism and Islamism. In the run-up to inviting Bin Bayyah and other Sufi scholars, including Aref Ali Nayed, a former Libyan ambassador to the UAE, Yemeni scholar Habib Ali Al-Jifri, and prominent American Muslim leader Hamza Yusuf, to do its bidding, the UAE sought to

---

[79] Interview with the author. 16 June 2022.

[80] Mohammed Magdy. "UN Security Council Invites Pope Francis, Al-Azhar imam for Joint Speech." Al-Monitor. 9 May 2023. https://www.al-monitor.com/originals/2023/05/un-security-council-invites-pope-francis-al-azhar-imam-joint-speech.

[81] Guido Steinberg. "Regional Power United Arab Emirates: Abu Dhabi Is No Longer Saudi Arabia's Junior Partner." German Institute for International and Security Affairs. 10 June 2020. https://www.swp-berlin.org/10.18449/2020RP10/.

[82] Ibid. Steinberg. "Regional Power United Arab Emirates."

establish Sufism as part of Gulf history. Starting in 2011, the Dubai-based Al-Mesbar Studies and Research Center published studies asserting that Yemeni scholars brought Sufism to the Gulf centuries ago. The publications argued that Sufism was repressed after Wahhabism's rise in the eighteenth century but re-emerged in the late nineteenth century.[83]

"The UAE has adopted a new definition of Islam as an apolitical religion that obeys oppressive rulers, justifies their actions, and delegitimizes their adversaries. Scholars and observers describe such a brand of Islam as a neo-traditionalist interpretation that embraces Sufism as its prime ideology…" "The UAE adopted a multifaceted and assertive strategy that follows three key tactics: creating a network of religious institutions to disseminate its version of Islam, co-opting religious leaders who tend to embrace and advance the Islamist vision, and positioning itself as the beacon of tolerance in the Muslim world," said Middle East scholar Khalil al-Anani.[84]

The strategy set the stage for a battle of the clerics.

---

[83] Haytham Mouzahem. "The Return of Sufism to the UAE." Al-Mesbar Studies and Research Center. 16 April 2018. https://mesbar.org/the-return-of-sufism-to-the-uae/.

[84] Khalil al-Anani. "The UAE's Manipulative Utilization of Religion." Arab Center Washington DC. 29 September 2020. https://arabcenterdc.org/resource/the-uaes-manipulative-utilization-of-religion/#_ftnref2.

CHAPTER 5

Muslim Clerics Battle It Out

Like most first-time travellers to the Gulf, Yusuf al-Qaradawi's first impression of Qatar was overshadowed by heat and humidity. The Gulf's desert climate assaulted him as he disembarked at Doha airport in 1961. Qaradawi was on a mission to introduce the education curriculum of his alma mater, Al-Azhar, the Cairo-based, constitutionally recognised citadel of Islamic learning, to the British protectorate a decade before independence. Doha was "a large village…uncorrupted by modern life," Qaradawi recalled in his four-volume, 2,000-page autobiography.[1]

The scion of a religious family who memorised the Qur'an by age nine, and a Muslim Brotherhood member, who spent time in Egyptian President Gamal Abdul Nasser's prisons, Qaradawi quickly mingled with the Qatari elite. He was chaperoned by Abdallah bin Turki al-Subaie, the head of Islamic Sciences in the protectorate's newly established education ministry and a disciple of Qatar's foremost Wahhabi scholar, Mohammed bin Mani. Qaradawi befriended Suhaim bin Hamad al-Thani, a cousin of the emir. Al-Thani represented Qatar in Egypt in the late 1950s and became foreign minister in 1972, a year after Qatar's independence. Qaradawi also forged a close relationship with Ahmad bin Ali al-Thani, Qatar's emir. Qaradawi's social circle further included fellow Al-Azhar graduates, many of whom were Muslim Brothers who, like him, had served time in Egyptian prisons and fled into exile.

---

[1] Yusuf al-Qaradawi. "Ibn al-Qkarya wa Al-Kuuttab: Sira wa Masira" (Son of the Village and Books: Biography and Career, Cairo). Cairo: Dar-al-Shuruq, Vol. 2, pp. 351–353.

© The Author(s), under exclusive license to Springer Nature Singapore Pte Ltd. 2024
J. M. Dorsey, *The Battle for the Soul of Islam*,
https://doi.org/10.1007/978-981-97-2807-7_5

Al-Subaie first met Qaradawi in 1957 on a visit to Cairo to recruit Islamic scholars. He invited the Egyptian to his hotel after hearing his Friday sermon at a mosque in the upper-class neighbourhood of Zamalek, an island in the Nile River. The two men bonded over a discussion of historical religious texts and figures.[2] Even so, it took Qaradawi three years to qualify to take up Al-Subaie's job offer. Qaradawi used those years to write his most popular and influential book, 'The Lawful and the Prohibited in Islam.' A moral guide for the uninitiated, written at the request of Hassan al-Hudaybi, the then Muslim Brotherhood leader, the book anticipated societal changes that decades later helped shape the Islamist awakening in the Gulf and the 2011 popular Arab protests. The book's impact made Qaradawi a welcome figure in Qatar's religious, political, and tribal elites.

Qaradawi's book, one of more than 100 he authored, and his down-to-earth approach to religious jurisprudence helped him reform the education system created by Qatar's indigenous scholars, followers of Saudi Arabia's ultra-conservative Wahhabi strand of Islam and ultimately marginalise them. In doing so, Qaradawi ensured that Qatar, long before the kingdom, which post 9/11 had a target on its back, as a fountain of extremism and violent jihad, shed the rough edges of its puritan religious worldview. In Qaradawi's educational world, mathematics, foreign languages, and social and natural sciences were as significant as Islamic disciplines. "Rather than understanding Qatari affinity for Qaradawi in terms (of) I have no doubt, of 'being religious,' instead…it was his effort to make Islamic jurisprudence relevant and responsive to realities of everyday life that was appealing," said Islam scholar David H. Warren.[3]

Qaradawi shared his hosts' desire to avoid grooming a class of clerics who, like in Saudi Arabia, would want to share power with the country's tribal leaders. He encouraged his students to embark on careers beyond religion. Many became diplomats and senior bureaucrats. He encouraged women to study at Al-Azhar in Cairo. So many went that the emir rented a building to accommodate them in the Egyptian capital.

Qaradawi's international moment emerged with the 2011 popular Arab revolts that toppled the autocratic leaders of four countries—Tunisia, Egypt, Libya, and Yemen—and shook the pillars of autocratic governance in the Middle East. The revolts sparked sharp arguments among prominent Muslim scholars on the virtues of democracy as opposed to autocracy and notions of 'Islamic democracy,' with Qatar supporting the revolts. For their part, the UAE and Saudi Arabia sought to roll back the clock. In those debates, Qaradawi emerged as the most vocal and globally recognised, albeit controversial, Muslim scholar supporting the revolts and advocating a degree of

---

[2] Idem. Warren, p. 24.

[3] David H. Warren. "Rivals in the Gulf, Yusuf al-Qaradawi, Abdullah Bin Bayyah, and the Qatar-UAE Contest Over the Arab Spring and the Gulf Crisis." London: Routledge. 2021, p. 29.

democracy. "Understanding Qaradawi is key to understanding the discourse and struggle within modern Islam today," said Islam scholar Bettina Gräf, whose Ph.D. thesis analysed Qaradawi's social media strategy.[4]

Qaradawi claimed a middle ground by opposing literal interpretations of the Qur'an and the Sunnah, the traditions and practices of Prophet Mohammed, as well as secularism. He advocated a religiously guided form of democracy, opposed the principle of absolute obedience to the ruler, insisted on clerical independence, and defended political rights such as the right to protest. Yet, he sparked controversy by adopting positions on several issues that violated those principles. These included legitimising Palestinian suicide bombings; employing harsh, often anti-Semitic language against Israelis and Jews; approving the execution of homosexuals; and adopting, at times, misogynist views, including justifying wife-beating while endorsing coeducation.

Moreover, questions remained about his relation to Qatar, which gave him a powerful platform on its state-owned Al Jazeera television network, where he attracted millions of viewers worldwide. Qatar also helped him establish influential transnational organisations such as the European Council for Fatwa and Research, founded in 1997, and the International Union of Muslim Scholars (IUMS), established in 2004. Even so, the IUMS was founded in London rather than Doha, according to Qaradawi, "because we couldn't find an Islamic country close to our region that would welcome us."[5] Sharjah, one of the UAE's constituent emirates and its most conservative, was dissuaded by its big brother, Abu Dhabi, not to grant the groups sanctuary.[6]

Much like the founding rationale of Indonesia's Nahdlatul Ulama, the IUMS, claiming a membership of 100,000 religious scholars, was an attempt to fill a void in a fractured and fragmented Muslim world. However, in contrast to religious figures and institutions aligned with the UAE that propagated a socially liberal, politically autocratic interpretation of Islam, the IUMS, led by representatives of multiple sects, sought to be an umbrella that would promote trust among differing Muslim communities and constitute a platform for legal pluralism and religious tolerance. The union prided itself on its independence, arguing that state control of clerics and institutions undermined their credibility and authority.[7] Yet, it also helped Qatar achieve its foreign policy goals. The group's Secretary-General, Ali Al-Qaradaghi, valued the role his group

---

[4] Bettina Gräf. "Qaradawi and the Struggle for Modern Islam." New Lines Magazine. 25 October 2022. https://newlinesmag.com/first-person/qaradawi-and-the-struggle-for-modern-islam/.

[5] Motaz al-Khateeb, "The Union of Scholars: The Role, The Reference, The Future." Al-Manar-Al-Jadeed. Vol. 36. Autumn 2006, p. 102 (electronic copy provided by Al-Khateeb).

[6] Interview with a source close to Qaradawi. 24 March 2022.

[7] Muhammad al-Atawneh, "In Search of Religious Authority: The International Union Of Muslim Scholars." In Daphne Ephrat and Meir Hatina (eds.) Religious Knowledge, Authority and Charisma, Islamic and Jewish Perspectives. Salt Lake City: University of Utah Press. 2014, Kinde Edition.

played in US-Taliban negotiations that led to the American troop withdrawal from Afghanistan and the facilitation of the Taliban's relations with Turkey, Malaysia, Indonesia, Kuwait, Oman, and Iraq. Praising the Taliban regime as a model Islamic state, Qaradaghi noted that "we have been steadfast in our efforts to foster connections between the (Afghan) Islamic government and other Islamic nations."[8]

In Qaradawi's view, the union would embrace the spectrum of non-jihadist Muslim thought, find common ground based on coexistence, advocate for the Muslim public interest, and fend off challenges to clerical authority by American-style televangelists. Conservatives and critics accused the televangelists of propagating an "air-conditioned" version of Islam that views the hijab as a fashion item and celebrates personal success and getting rich rather than spirituality.[9]

Speaking at the IUMS' launch in London, Qaradawi projected the group as a platform that would serve as a reference point for Islamic jurisprudence and culture. His audience included the heads of official fatwa bodies in several Muslim countries, Sunni and Shiite Muslim leaders, and the Riyadh-based Organization of Islamic Cooperation (OIC) secretary-general.[10] The IUMS insists that it "does not follow a certain country, group, or sect," and that it "derives its strength from the confidence it earns from the world's citizens and the Muslim masses,"[11] the group said in its founding document. Yet, Qaradawi's support for popular revolts and conciliatory attitudes towards Shiites failed the IUMS' litmus test when majority Shiite Bahrain in 2011 demanded the removal of the island's minority Sunni Muslim ruling family. Afraid that a successful revolt would turn Bahrain into an Iran-like Islamic republic, Qaradawi supported a Saudi-led intervention that included Qatari forces to suppress the revolt.

Even so, Qaradawi's advocacy of religiously guided democracy, coupled with his roots in the Muslim Brotherhood, put him in the crosshairs of autocrats. In contrast to clerical supporters of autocracy, Qaradawi argued, "The essence of democracy ... is that people choose who rules over them and

---

[8] Middle East Information and Research Project. "In Interview With Pro-Afghan Taliban Media, Secretary-General of Qatar-Funded International Union of Muslim Scholars (IUMS) Dr. Ali Al-Qaradaghi, Alleges Zionist Propaganda Against Muslims, Cites Quran to Argue That 'Allah Has Called Media Jihad as the Greatest Jihad'; 'We Should Not Neglect The Significance Of Effective [TV] Channels in Languages Like Pashtu, Farsi, And Urdu.'" 19 December 2023. https://www.memri.org/reports/interview-pro-afghan-taliban-media-secretary-general-qatar-funded-international-union-muslim.

[9] Patrick Haenni and Husam Tammam, "Egypt's Air-conditioned Islam, Le Monde Diplomatique." September 2003. https://mondediplo.com/2003/09/03egyptislam.

[10] Amjad Ashlatouni, "An Islamic Conference of Muslim Scholars in London" (المسلمين في لندن مؤتمر إسلامي للعلماء). BBC Arabic. 11 July 2004. http://news.bbc.co.uk/hi/arabic/middle_east_news/newsid_3876000/3876047.stm.

[11] International Union of Muslim Scholars. "Introduction, International Union of Muslim Scholars Project." 4 November 2015. http://iumsonline.org/en/ContentDetails.aspx?ID=8151.

manages their affairs.... Whoever contemplates the essence of democracy finds that it accords with the essence of Islam. Islam rejects the idea that people be led in prayer by someone they do not accept and, indeed, despise. If this is the case with ritual prayers, it's all the more so in matters of life and politics... The virtue of democracy is that it has found forms and means...that still compromise the best guarantees for protecting people from tyrants."[12]

Liberal critics charged that Qaradawi's understanding of democracy was shallow because the cleric assumed a Muslim-majority society would adopt a majoritarian approach. "Qaradawi's understanding of democracy and its institutions is superficial. He treats democracy as an expression of the will of the majority. He assumes that the majority of the citizenry of an Islamic state will be Muslim. As a result, he sees no problem in applying Sharia law in a democratic state," said Islam legal scholar Khaled Abou El Fadl.[13] "Democracy is not religious tolerance, justice, or any other religious value. "Democracy is a civil principle, not a religious value," added Jordanian author Shaker Al-Nabulsi.[14] David Warren noted that in Qaradawi's concept, "though the people may choose their rulers, they may not choose to forbid that which Islam has permitted or permit that which Islam has forbidden. Consequently, they remain in need of the ulama to maintain those boundaries."[15]

The revolts brought to the fore the differing religious soft power strategies of prominent religious scholars and their Gulf state backers. In 2011, Qaradawi moved the IUMS headquarters from Dublin to Doha. The move sealed Qatar's embrace of Qaradawi's support of the revolts, even if it exempted itself from his democracy vision. Qaradawi's advocacy bolstered Qatar's effort to turn the revolts to its advantage and differentiate itself from Emirati and Saudi post-9/11 attempts to garner soft power brownie points with lofty declarations projecting religious moderation. Qatar's support put the Gulf state at odds with the UAE and Saudi Arabia, which were determined to stymie the revolts and reverse their initial successes.

The UAE-backed campaign to defeat political Islam and reverse the achievements of the popular revolts culminated in the 2013 military coup against Mohammed Morsi, a Muslim Brother who was Egypt's first and only democratically elected head of state. The UAE's opportunity to recruit a prominent Islamic scholar of its own who could compete with the IUMS and its rejection of a politically autocratic interpretation of Islam emerged when the Qatari-backed group condemned the military takeover, and differences spilt into the open between Qaradawi and his 87-year-old deputy, Abdullah Bin Bayyah, an

---

[12] Yusuf al-Qaradawi. "Islam and Democracy." In Roxanne L. Euben and Muhammad Qasim Zaman (eds.) Princeton Readings in Islamist Thought: Texts and Contexts from al-Banna to Bin Laden. Princeton: Princeton University Press, 2009, pp. 232, 235.

[13] Interview with the author. 7 November 2016.

[14] Shaker Al-Nabulsi. "Two Qaardawis, Not One Qaradawi" .قرضاويّان، لا قرضاوي واحد Elaph.com, 14 June 2004. https://elaph.com/ElaphWriter/2004/7/175.htm.

[15] Ibid. *Warren*, Rivals in the Gulf, p. 33.

Islamic jurist, politician, and former minister who supported the religious principle of absolute obedience to the ruler. In his native Mauritania, Bin Bayyah was one of a small cohort of religious scholars who created the foundations of state-controlled Islam in which clerics were subservient to the state.[16]

The differences between Qaradawi and Bin Bayyah initially erupted over the IUMS and Qaradawi's support for the protests[17] as well as the rights of citizens as expressed by prominent Saudi scholar Salman al-Awda, another IUMS scholar, who has lingered in Saudi prison since 2017.[18] The UAE, Saudi Arabia, and Egypt demanded the handover of figures accused of terrorism, including Qaradawi, during their failed 3.5-long diplomatic and economic boycott of Qatar that was lifted in January 2021.[19]

Qaradawi developed his notion of the right to protest with Sunni Muslim-majority countries in mind. He assumed that a majority of Sunnis would support his quest for majoritarian rule guided by independent Muslim scholars. Qaradawi hit a wall when, in 2011, protests erupted not only in Sunni-majority countries like Tunisia and Egypt but also in Bahrain, a Shiite-majority nation governed by a minority Sunni ruling family. Unwilling to question his own assumptions and break with Qatar's willingness to exempt the Gulf from its support for popular revolts sweeping the Middle East and North Africa, Qaradawi denounced the Bahrain protests as part of an imaginary sectarian Iranian plot and falsely alleged that they were violent rather than peaceful. In doing so, the cleric set aside his long-standing advocacy of the burying of the hatchet by Sunni and Shiite Muslims and the fact that prominent Shiite religious figures were part of his International Union of Muslim Scholars.

Once a welcome guest in Western capitals as a voice of moderation, Qaradawi, known for his trademark beatific smile and folksy speaking style, was barred entry after he drew in 2001 a distinction between the jihadism of Al-Qaeda and the Islamic State and suicide bombings targeting Israel and Israeli nationals. Qaradawi had been celebrated for his advocacy of wasatiyya, a centrist view of Islam that rejects both secularism and extremism, and the development, together with Taha Jabir al-Alwani, an Iraqi-born American scholar and Al-Azhar graduate, of a legal doctrine that would help

---

[16] Alexander Thurston. "Clerical Independence and the Religious Field in Post-Colonial Mauritania." Journal of Islamic Studies, 19 December 2022.

[17] International Union of Muslim Scholars. "The Legitimacy of Peaceful Demonstrations" (السلميةشرعية المظاهرات),. 23 November 2011. http://iumsonline.org/ar/ContentDetails.aspx?ID=1717.

[18] International Union of Muslim Scholars. "Claiming Rights.. Fatwa by Dr. Salman Al-Awda" (بالحقوق.. فتوى للدكتور سلمان العودةالمطالبة). 22 March 2011. http://iumsonline.org/ar/ContentDetails.aspx?ID=1718.

[19] The Associated Press. "List of Demands on Qatar by Saudi Arabia, Other Arab Nations." 23 June 2017. https://apnews.com/article/bahrain-qatar-iran-saudi-arabia-united-arab-emirates-3a58461737c44ad58047562e48f46e06.

Muslim minorities, particularly in the United States and Europe, manage their integration into a non-Muslim society.

Mockbul Ali, the head of the British Foreign Office's Middle East desk, noted in 2004 before Qaradawi's banning from the UK, that the cleric was "regarded by most as a pragmatic conservative in the classic Muslim Brotherhood mould rather than a fanatic or extremist."[20] In an email to the Home Office, Ali warned that banning Qaradawi would "alienate significant and influential members of the global Muslim community" and "have a negative impact on our relations with British Muslim communities."[21] In a setback to Qatari religious soft power, the ban ended a period of engagement with a man who, according to Chief Constable of the Metropolitan Police Ian Blair, could "command an audience of 50,000 young people at the drop of a hat."[22]

Blair favoured engagement even though Qaradawi's justification of suicide bombings legitimised attacks by militant Islamist groups such as Hamas and Islamic Jihad on the grounds that Palestinians had no other way of resisting Israeli occupation. Qaradawi said Israelis were legitimate targets because "Israeli society is completely military in its make and does not include civilians."[23]

Earlier, Qaradawi issued a fatwa that appeared to justify Israel's claim that anti-Zionism constituted a form of anti-Semitism by asserting that there was no distinction between Judaism and Zionism and that Jewish targets were Israeli targets. The cleric refused to attend Qatar-sponsored interfaith conferences to which Jewish leaders were invited. "How can we conduct a dialogue in a time when they seize lands, shed blood, burn farms, and demolish houses? Palestine's conundrum has to be resolved first before we sit together at the same table," he said.[24]

In 2015, Qaradawi reversed his fatwa justifying suicide attacks on the grounds that Palestinians had enhanced their capabilities with the acquisition of missiles but did not withdraw his justification of attacks on civilian

---

[20] Martyn Frampton and Shiraz Maher. "Between 'Engagement' and a 'Values-Led' Approach: Britain and the Muslim Brotherhood from 9/11 to the Arab Spring." Al-Mesbar Studies & Research Center. 3 October 2014, https://mesbar.org/engagement-values-led-approach-britain-muslim-brotherhood-911-arab-spring/.

[21] Martin Bright. "When Progressives Treat with Reactionaries: The British State's Flirtation with Radical Islamism." Policy Exchange. July 2006, p. 53. https://policyexchange.org.uk/wp-content/uploads/2006/07/when-progressives-treat-with-reactionaries-jul-06.pdf.

[22] Sir Ian Blair. "Connecting Counter-Terrorism and Community Policy." Citizens Crime Commission of New York. 18 April 2006. http://www.nycrimecommission.org/pdfs/blair.pdf.

[23] The official channel of Sheikh Yusuf al-Qaradawi "The Palestinian Intifada and the Martyrdom Operations" (الانتفاضة الفلسطينية والعمليات الاستشهادية). YouTube. 2001. https://www.youtube.com/watch?v=pIlgndap5S4.

[24] Ahmed el-Beheri. "Sheikh Boycotts Interfaith Conference Due to Attendance of Jews." Egypt Independent. 19 October 2010. https://egyptindependent.com/sheikh-boycotts-interfaith-conference-due-attendance-jews/.

targets.[25] Qaradawi's reversal corresponded with the policy of Hamas, the militant Islamist Palestinian group that controlled the Gaza Strip, expressed by its late founder and spiritual leader, Sheikh Ahmad Yasin, a wheelchair-bound quadriplegic who was nearly blind. "Once we have warplanes and missiles, then we can think of changing our means of legitimate self-defense. But right now, we can only tackle the fire with our bare hands and sacrifice ourselves," Yasin said before he was killed in an Israeli strike in 2004.[26]

Similarly, Qaradawi also never backed down from his defence in 2004 of the Holocaust as "divine punishment" of the Jews and hoped that "the next time will be at the hand of the believers." To be fair, Qaradawi's approach to Jews vacillates throughout his career between hostility and prejudice and a willingness to find common ground. He sees Jews alongside colonialism, Zionism, Crusaders, Communists, idolaters, and the Islamic world's 'hypocritical' rulers as conspiring to destroy Islam.[27] Yet, he quotes the Qur'an as calling on Muslims to see points of agreement and understanding on issues such as atheism, materialism, nudism, sexual promiscuity, and gender diversity.

In the same vein, Qaradawi was unequivocal in his condemnation of the 9/11 attacks and endorsement of American Muslims serving in the US military in Afghanistan. "The Palestinian who blows himself up is a person who is defending his homeland. When he attacks an occupier enemy, he is attacking a legitimate target. This is different from someone who leaves his country and goes to strike a target with which he has no dispute," Qaradawi declared.

Qaradawi applied that logic when, three years later, When his International Union of Muslim Scholars issued a fatwa authorising the abduction and killing of Americans in Iraq to force a US withdrawal from the country.[28] Bin Bayyah, who served as the union's vice president at the time of the fatwas on the Palestinians and Iraq, took no exception to Qaradawi's justifications and distinction between what he called legitimate "martyrdom operations" and terrorism.

That did not stop the UAE from seeking to exploit Qaradawi's loss of standing in the West a decade later by projecting Bin Bayyah as the world's foremost moderate Muslim cleric with unrivalled convening power. The UAE hoped that Bin Bayyah's change of colours, which earned him the epitaph

[25] The Middle East Media Research Institute. "Sheikh Al-Qaradhawi: Permission Previously Given To Palestinians To Carry Out Suicide Attacks—No Longer Valid; They Now Have Missiles That Can Strike Deep Inside Israel." 28 July 2016. https://www.memri.org/reports/sheikh-al-qaradhawi-permission-previously-given-palestinians-carry-out-suicide-attacks-%E2%80%93-no.

[26] Haim Malka. "Must Innocents Die? The Islamic Debate Over Suicide Attacks." Brookings. 1 March 2003. https://www.brookings.edu/articles/must-innocents-die-the-islamic-debate-over-suicide-attacks/

[27] Yusuf al-Qaradawi. "Al sahwa al-islāmiyya bayna al-juhud wal-tafarruq." Cairo: Dar al-Shuruq, 2001, pp. 94–95/Yusuf al-Qaradawi. "A'da al-hall al-islāmī." Cairo: Maktabat al-Wabha, 2000.

[28] Ayman Al-Masri. "IAMS Backs Iraqi Resistance, Opposes Killing Civilians." Islam Online. 20 November 2004. https://web.archive.org/web/20041121151504/http://www.islamonline.net/English/News/2004-11/20/article02.shtml.

"counter-revolutionary Islam's most important scholar,"[29] would position the country as a centre of moderate Muslim scholarship. In a policy-setting speech designed to help the UAE institutionalise its autocratic version of moderate Islam, Bin Bayyah asserted Muslims' "right and obligation to find a better political solution than democracy and to establish a system based on the principles of consultation and higher justice." The cleric warned that "the call for democracy is essentially a call for war" in societies that were not ready for democratic governance.[30]

Critics of Bin Bayyah's legitimisation of a politically autocratic but socially liberal Islam dismissed it as shallow and incapable of withstanding independent scrutiny. "The counterrevolutionary Islamic political thought that is being developed and promoted by Bin Bayyah and the UAE suffers from certain fundamental structural problems that mean its very existence is precariously predicated on the persistence of autocratic patronage," asserted Usaama Al-Azami, a British Middle East scholar of South Asian descent who trained as a classical Islamic scholar. "Its lack of independence means that it is not the organic product of a relatively unencumbered engagement with political modernity that might be possible in freer societies than counterrevolutionary Gulf autocracies."[31]

More bluntly, Yahya Birt, a scholar of British Islam and a Muslim convert, who has researched UAE-backed clerics, argued that there is a discrepancy between how scholars like Bin Bayyah project their sponsors abroad and the reality on the ground. "The extracted price of government patronage is high for ulema (religious scholars) in the Middle East. Generally speaking, they have to openly support or maintain silence about autocracy at home, while speaking of democracy, pluralism, and minority rights to Western audiences," Birt said.[32]

Bin Bayyah legitimised an Emirati approach geared towards ingratiating the UAE with the international community as the model of moderate Islam in the aftermath of 9/11 and the emergence of the Islamic State. To do so, the UAE adopted social and economic liberalism and promoted separation of mosque and state. At the same time, it repressed dissent, depoliticised civil society, and concentrated power in the hands of Mohammed bin Zayed. The moves sought to eliminate political expressions of Islam that threatened the Emirati autocracy. Bin Bayyah's legitimisation strengthened the UAE's efforts

---

[29] Usaama al-Azami, "Abdullāh bin Bayyah and the Arab Revolutions: Counter-Revolutionary Neo-traditionalism's Ideological Struggle against Islamism." The Muslim World, Vol. 109, Issue 3. July 2019.

[30] Abdullah Bin Bayyah. "Framework Speech for Promoting Peace om Muslim Societies, Forum for Promoting Peace in Muslim Societies." 2014, p. 32. https://drive.google.com/file/d/1TOts39QzfEg-QQGZ-I0WD731KlSy_nL7/view.

[31] Ibid. Al-Azami, 'Abdullāh bin Bayyah and the Arab Revolutions.'

[32] Yahya Birt, "Blowin' in the Wind: Trumpism and Traditional Islam in America." Medium. 14 February 2017. https://yahyabirt.medium.com/https-medium-com-yahyabirt-blowin-in-the-wind-trumpism-and-traditional-islam-in-america-40ba056486d8.

to install or support regimes across the Middle East and North Africa that contained civil society, championed military rule, and countered the appeal of political Islam.

Toeing the UAE's line of downplaying the role of religion, Ed Husain, a former advisor to British Prime Minister Tony Blair and co-founder of Quilliam, a controversial far-right counter-extremism think tank that reinforced Islamophobic positions,[33] gushed after attending a conference in Abu Dhabi in 2014 about Bin Bayyah as "a man who has no contemporary rival… I have not seen so many Muslim thought leaders gathered in one place. Imams and muftis from Morocco to India to Bosnia to Chechnya to Pakistan to Saudi Arabia to war-torn Syria – Shia, Sunni, Salafi, Sufi, and others. Not only was the convening power of Bin Bayyah on display as a popular senior scholar but the emerging importance of the UAE as a potential home for moderate Muslim scholarship."

Husain argued that "Bin Bayyah's genius is to bring his sterling Islamic knowledge and mastery of French and European political thought expressed in language that simplifies complicated history and religion. Extremists demand 'our rights as Muslims' to 'overthrow governments and establish an Islamic state'. In this absolute pursuit, unjust violence is justified as 'jihad.'… Rather than try to engage hardliners only on their own aims and declarations, Sheikh bin Bayyah's fresh approach changes the conversation."

Husain praised Bin Bayyah's reference to a compromise forged by Prophet Mohammed to restore peace as evidence that social peace supersedes the quest for human and other rights. "Sheikh bin Bayyah reminds us that Prophet Mohammed signed the treaty of Hudaibiyah with his oppressors to keep peace in society. When his opponents rejected the first line of the treaty drafted by Muslims, the Prophet erased references to Allah as 'compassionate and merciful' in line with demands from Mecca's non-Muslims. Not content, they then required the Prophet to delete mention of 'Mohammed, the Prophet of God' – in other words, the Prophet's entire raison d'être was rejected. The Prophet made the changes, and the Hudaibiyah agreement was signed. At what price? The very basis of belief in God's characteristics and the Prophet's purpose was dismissed – but agreed by the Prophet himself for maintaining wider peace in society. Peace is the first right – once that is secured, other rights can be considered," Husain noted.[34]

Competing with Qaradawi was no mean feat. Qaradawi had a powerful pulpit at Doha's Umar al-Khattab mosque in addition to a weekly talk show and other appearances on Qatar's influential global Al Jazeera television network, during which he discussed topics ranging from popular Arab

---

[33] Malia Bouattia. "The Quilliam Foundation Has Closed But Its Toxic Legacy Remains." Al Jazeera. 20 April 2021. https://www.aljazeera.com/opinions/2021/4/20/the-quilliam-foundation-has-closed-but-its-toxic-legacy-remains.

[34] Ed Husain. "One Cleric's War on Radicals is the Hope for Moderate Islam." The National. 12 March 2014. https://www.thenationalnews.com/one-cleric-s-war-on-radicals-is-the-hope-for-moderate-islam-1.265770.

revolts to female masturbation that were beamed into tens of millions of Muslim households. To counter the cleric's sway, the UAE helped Bin Bayyah create institutions such as the Forum for Promoting Peace in Muslim Societies (FPPMS) under the auspices of UAE Foreign Minister Abdullah bin Zayed, and the Muslim Council of Elders that were designed to win hearts and minds in the Muslim world, position the UAE as a beacon of religious moderation, and forge links to non-Muslim faith groups.

Established in 2014, the Forum positioned itself as a body of state-aligned religious scholars that reached out to philosophers and social scientists. The Forum's annual conference brings together hundreds of Muslim, Jewish, and Christian leaders, scholars, and thinkers to forge alliances based on virtues that promote the UAE's image as a safe haven for minorities and religious tolerance. In 2015, the government extended a law that criminalised blasphemy and hate speech against Islam to apply to all religions. But proselytising by non-Muslims and conversion from Islam remains illegal in the UAE.[35]

Meanwhile, the Forum was instrumental in the issuance in 2016 of the Marrakech Declaration on the Rights of Religious Minorities in Predominantly Muslim Majority Communities, and the UAE's appointment of ministers of tolerance and happiness and its designation of 2019 as a Year of Tolerance.[36] "We have…learned from hundreds of thousands of dead and millions of refugees in our region that sectarian, ideological, cultural and religious bigotry only fuel the fires of rage. We cannot and will not allow this in our country (…) When the Arab world was tolerant and accepting of others, it led the world," said UAE Prime Minister and Dubai ruler Mohammed ibn Rashid Al Maktoum.[37]

The Emiratis sought to reassure non-Muslims that they would be welcomed and safe in the UAE, and that blue chips would be boosted rather than threatened by Emirati investment. By projecting itself as tolerant, cutting edge, and open to the world, the UAE wanted to avoid a repeat of the debacle in 2006 when Dubai-owned DP World strove to acquire Peninsular and Oriental Steam Navigation Company (P&O). The acquisition sparked controversy over national security in the United States. Many questioned the handover of six major US ports to a Middle Eastern company as part of the takeover. A

---

[35] US Department of State. "United Arab Emirates 2017 International Religious Freedom Report." January 2019. https://www.state.gov/wp-content/uploads/2019/01/United-Arab-Emirates-2.pdf.

[36] Forum for Promoting Peace in Muslim Societies. "Historic Marrakesh Declaration" (التاريخي إعلان مراكش),. Undated. https://peacems.com/initiatives/marrakesh-declaration/.

[37] United Arab Emirates Government Portal. "Anti-discrimination/Anti-hatred Law." 18 May 2022. https://www.government.ae/en/about-the-uae/culture/tolerance/anti-discriminationanti-hatred-law.

humiliating debate forced DP World to sell the US portion of the acquisition involving port management to an American finance and insurance company.[38]

The P&O experience is one reason why the UAE's notion of tolerance and associated policies are guided by political and economic expediency rather than religious law decades after Sheikh Rashid ibn Saeed Al Maktoum, the father of Mohammed, Dubai's current ruler first articulated the approach. "We build mosques for the Muslims, churches for the Christians, and bars for everyone else. All will be free to worship as they choose," he told visiting American officials in 1982. Rashid defined his philosophy as freedom of religion and social life but without public expressions of dissent. "Literally, anything was allowed in private – sex, drugs, and rock and roll). But tribal autocracy simply does now allow any public dissent for the ruling elite," said a US official who participated in the meeting with Rashid.[39]

Four decades later, freedom of religion and social liberalisation are facts of Emirati life; political freedoms are not. The release in June 2022 of Lightyear, a Disney and Pixar animated production, highlighted of social liberalisation's boundaries and fragility. Emirati censors banned Lightyear, allegedly because of a same-sex kiss scene,[40] six months after the UAE announced it would end the censorship of films. Instead, the country's Media Regulatory Office said it would introduce a viewer 21+ age classification policy.[41] That wasn't evident when the office tweeted an image of Buzz Lightyear, crossed out with a red line.[42]

Bin Zayed needs his subjects to replicate his tolerance and project his notion of moderate Islam to ensure that the UAE, despite its autocracy and repression of political rights, is perceived as a progressive cutting-edge and forward-looking country worthy of foreign investment, international support, and the protection of the international community.

Parallel to the Forum, the UAE created the Muslim Council of Elders made up of religious scholars who support the notion of obedience to the ruler, to focus on the Muslim world and high-level outreach to non-Muslim communities. Co-led by Bin Bayyah and the grand imam of Al-Azhar, Sheikh Ahmed al-Tayeb, the Council aims to institutionalise cooperation between the

---

[38] James M. Dorsey. "UAE Nation Branding Encounters Early Headwinds." The Turbulent World of Middle East Soccer. 21 September 2021. https://www.jamesmdorsey.net/post/uae-nation-branding-encounters-early-headwinds.

[39] Email to the author. 5 February 2022.

[40] BBC News. "Buzz Lightyear Film Banned from Cinemas by UAE." 14 June 2022. https://www.bbc.com/news/entertainment-arts-61786355.

[41] Josh Wilson. "What The United Arab Emirates New Censorship Policy Means For The Film And TV Industry." Forbes. 29 December 2021. https://www.forbes.com/sites/joshwilson/2021/12/29/what-the-united-arab-emirates-new-censorship-policy-means-for-the-film-and-tv-industry/?sh=35d9926a5e83.

[42] Media Regulatory Office. Twitter. 13 June 2022. https://twitter.com/uaemro/status/1536251764202164224.

UAE and Al-Azhar and give Emirati religious soft power efforts the imprimatur of the revered Egyptian institution. The Council further defines its mission as "extinguishing the fires" of violence, extremist ideologies, and sectarianism sweeping the Muslim world.[43] The Council played a central role in arranging Pope Francis' visit to the UAE in 2019, which culminated in the Declaration of Human Fraternity issued together with Al-Tayeb at a conference attended by Muslim, Christian, Jewish, Hindu, Buddhist, and Sikh leaders.[44]

Council members appear to have been chosen as much for their religious qualifications as for their political fealty. They include Muhammad Quraish Shihab, an Al-Azhar-educated, socially liberal Muslim scholar who served for two months as Indonesia's religious affairs minister; Sheikh Sharif Ibrahim Saleh Al-Hussaini, head of the Nigerian Supreme Council for Islamic Affairs; Jordan's Prince Ghazi bin Muhammad. A religious affairs advisor to King Abdullah who has long been a critic of Saudi ultra-conservatism; prominent Malaysian scholar and former mufti and Religious Affairs Minister Zulkifli bin Mohamad Al-Bakri; Organisation of Islamic Cooperation (OIC) Secretary-General Yousef Al-Othaimeen, and Emirati scholar Ahmed Abdulaziz al-Hadda.

Egyptian scholar Hassan al-Shafei is the exception that confirms the rule. Shafei, a widely respected Al-Azhar scholar and former advisor to Al-Tayeb, was removed from various official posts after he criticised the brutal crackdown on protesters against the 2013 UAE-backed military coup that toppled Mohammed Morsi, the democratically elected Muslim Brotherhood president. A Muslim Brother in his youth, Al-Shafei also called for withdrawing the military from politics.[45] Equally remarkably, Saudi Arabia honoured Al-Shafei by awarding him the King Faisal International Prize in 2022 for the second time in a decade.[46] Al-Shafei sought to pre-empt the coup by suggesting that Morsi should be persuaded to hold early elections in response to UAE-backed mass protests against his presidency.

The Forum and the Council's close association with Al-Azhar strengthened links between the UAE and Egypt cemented by Emirati support for the 2013 military coup and massive financial aid that kept the country afloat. The association also bolstered Emirati inroads among Al-Azhar scholars that

[43] Muslim Council of Elders. "Who We Are." Undated. https://www.muslim-elders.com/en/page/7/who-we-are.

[44] Muslim Council of Elders. "Global Conference of Human Fraternity." February 2019. https://www.muslim-eldes.com/en/page/12/HumanFraternity.

[45] Middle East Monitor. "An Eminent Egyptian Scholar Persecuted in Egypt But Honoured Abroad." 7 January 2022. https://www.middleeastmonitor.com/20220107-an-eminent-egyptian-scholar-persecuted-in-egypt-but-honoured-abroad/.

[46] Mohammed Abdullah, he achieved the difficult equation and won everyone's warmth. "Sheikh Hassan Al-Shafei Wins the King Faisal Prize Again" (حسن الشافعي يفوز بجائزة الملك فيصل مجدداً..أيّد ثورة يناير وسُجن في عهد عبد الناصر.. الشيخ). AlJazeera Arabic. 10 January 2022. https://www.aljazeera.net/news/cultureandart/2022/1/9/جامعة-

aimed to undercut empathy for Saudi Arabia's ultra-conservative strand of Islam developed over decades of Saudi funding and sympathy among clerics for the Muslim Brotherhood and other expressions of political Islam. The UAE greased palms by funding Al-Azhar hospitals and encouraging the institution to establish a branch in the Emirates.

According to one Islam scholar, the Emirati funding amounted to "a movement of renewal of Islamic jurisprudence… It's a movement that is funded by the wealthy Gulf countries. Don't forget that one reason for the success of the Salafis is the financial power that backed them for decades. This financial power is now being directed to the Azharis, and they are taking advantage of it… Don't underestimate what is happening. It might be a true alternative to Salafism."[47]

A prominent Islamic legal scholar, who rejected a nomination for Saudi Arabia's prestigious King Faisal International Prize, recalled El-Tayeb, the Al-Azhar grand imam, effusively thanking the kingdom for its numerous donations to the university. Al-Azhar scholars competed "frantically" for sabbaticals in the kingdom that could last anywhere from one to 20 years, paid substantially better, and raised a scholar's status.

"Many of my friends and family praise Abdul Wahhab in their writing," the scholar said referring to Mohammed ibn Abdul Wahhab, the 18th-century religious leader whose puritan interpretation of Islam became the basis for the power-sharing agreement between the ruling Al Saud family and the country's religious establishment. "They shrug their shoulders when I ask them privately if they are serious… When I asked El-Tayeb why Al Azhar was not seeing changes and avoiding dogma, he said: 'my hands are tied.'"

To illustrate Saudi inroads, the scholar recalled watching Muhammad Sayyid Tantawy, a former grand mufti of Egypt and imam of the Al-Azhar Mosque, being interviewed about Saudi funding. "What's wrong with that?" the scholar recalled Tantawy as saying. Irritated by the question, he pulled a check for US$100,000 from a drawer and slapped it against his forehead. "Alhamdulillah (Praise be to God), they are our brothers," Tantawy said.[48]

The UAE's projection of itself as the beacon of a moderate Islam, bolstered by the prestige of Al-Azhar, helped the Gulf state position itself with influential segments of the counterterrorism and intelligence communities in countries as diverse as the United States, Britain, France, India, Russia, and China as a partner of choice. Emirati officials succeeded in convincing many of its closest allies in foreign intelligence and security services that non-violent political Islam was part of the problem.

To do so, it embedded its socially moderate religious discourse in institutions like the Hedayah Center of Excellence for Countering Violent Extremism, which was founded in 2012. Chaired by Ali Rashid al-Nuaimi,

---

[47] Interview with the author. 7 July 2021.
[48] Interview with the author. 9 November 2016.

a member of the UAE's Federal National Council, a partially elected parliamentary advisory body, the centre helps promote the narrative that "the UAE has a new vision for the Middle East region – an alternative, future-oriented model that supports moderate Islam, empowers women, embraces diversity, encourages innovation, and welcomes global engagement… It explains why over 200 nationalities call the UAE home and why different religions have built approximately 40 churches, two Hindu temples, a Sikh temple, and a Buddhist temple, which welcome multi-national congregations."[49]

The UAE's positioning benefitted from differentiating itself from the ultra-conservatism long propagated by Saudi Arabia, the region's behemoth. UAE officials believed that Mohammed bin Salman's rise would serve their goal of becoming a regional hegemon alongside the kingdom. In leaked email exchanges, Yousef al-Otaiba, the UAE's ambassador in Washington, made no bones about the UAE's ambition. In exchanges with former US officials such as Martin Indyk, who served in the Clinton and Obama administrations, Stephen Hadley, former President George W. Bush's national security advisor, and Elliott Abrams, who advised Presidents Bush and Ronald Reagan, as well as journalists, like Washington Post columnist David Ignatius, Al-Otaiba, suggested that Saudi Arabia would be instrumental in achieving Emirati goals. He went out of his way to promote Bin Salman, the powerful son of King Salman and the rising star in Saudi Arabia's ferment.

"Jeez, the new hegemon! Emirati imperialism! Well, if the US won't do it, someone has to hold things together for a while." Abrams quipped about the UAE's newly found assertiveness. "Yes, how dare we! In all honesty, there was not much of a choice. We stepped up only after your country chose to step down," Al-Otaiba. said He was referring to perceptions that the United States was reducing its security commitment to the Middle East, if not disengaging.

Discussing the UAE's relationship with Saudi Arabia and Bin Salman, Al-Otaiba told Abrams that "I think in the long term we might be a good influence on KSA (Kingdom of Saudi Arabia), at least with certain people there. Our relationship with them is based on strategic depth, shared interests, and most importantly the hope that we could influence them. Not the other way around." In his exchanges with Indyk and Ignatius, Al-Otaiba was unequivocal about UAE's backing of the likely future king as an agent of change who would adopt policies advocated by the Emirates.

"I think MBS is far more pragmatic than what we hear is Saudi public positions," Al-Otaiba told Ignatius, referring to Bin Salman by his initials. "I don't think we'll ever see a more pragmatic leader in that country. Which is why engaging with them is so important and will yield the most results we can

---

[49] Embassy of the United Arab Emirates Washington, DC, Society, Undated. https://www.uae-embassy.org/discover-uae/society.

ever get out of Saudi," the ambassador said. "Change in attitude, change in style, change in approach."⁵⁰

A decade after the revolts, autocrats and counterrevolutionaries have gained the political upper hand in the battle over governance, but reform-minded clerics retain the discursive high ground. The debate shapes the struggle for dominance in the Muslim world and the rivalry for religious soft power.

The debate's key geographical nodes say much about the way winds are blowing in centres that wield religious influence. The protagonists are in Doha, Abu Dhabi, and Jakarta, not Cairo, home to Al-Azhar, one of the oldest seats of Islamic learning; Medina, where the Islamic University served as the intellectual fountain of Saudi Arabia's four-decade-long global campaign propagating Muslim ultra-conservatism; Istanbul, where the last Caliph resided; or Qom, the theological capital of the Muslim world's only revolutionary states with remnants of what was once may have qualified as an Islamic democracy.

The shift may be temporary. Qatar and the UAE will likely struggle to maintain their centrality in the religious debate once prominent but elderly scholars die. At best, two names pop up as potential heirs of the UAE's Bin Bayyah, a high priest of autocratic rule. Both are foreigners with no indigenous roots in the Gulf state. No one capable of fitting into Qaradawi's shoes comes to mind since the cleric died at age 96 in 2022.

In contrast to Qaradawi, who spent most of his life in Qatar, Bin Bayyah only hooked his fortunes to the UAE a decade ago. Despite long-standing relations with Abu Dhabi's ruling Al-Nahyan family, Bin Bayyah long aligned with its nemesis as vice president of Qaradawi's International Union of Muslim Scholars and European Council for Fatwa and Research. The Council aimed to guide European Muslims through the labyrinth of religious opinions. Members of the Al-Nahyan, including then Crown Prince Mohammed and Foreign Minister Abdullah bin Zayed, began courting Bin Bayyah in early 2013. They invited the cleric to the Emirates at the time Morsi, the post-2011 revolt Muslim Brother Egyptian president, was toppled.⁵¹

In a letter Bin Bayyah sent three months later to the IUMS, he announced his resignation because "the humble role I am attempting to undertake towards reform and reconciliation (among Muslims) requires a discourse that does not sit well with my position at the International Union of Muslim Scholars."⁵² Published to demonstrate to Emirati leaders that he had ended

---

⁵⁰ James M. Dorsey, Reducing Middle East tensions? Saudi-UAE moves hint at willingness to engage with Iran, "The Turbulent World of Middle East Soccer." 16 August 2017. https://www.jamesmdorsey.net/post/reducing-middle-east-tensions-saudi-uae-moves-hint-at-willingness-to-engage-with-iran.

⁵¹ The Official Website of His Eminence Shaykh Abdallah Bi Bayyah. In his second episode on Saudi TV, "Scholar Bin Bayyah: Community and Family Are Fundamentals of Religion, and Branches are Sacrificed for Its Sake" (بالفروع حلقته الثانية على التلفزيون السعودي / العلامة ابن بيه: الجماعة والألفة أصل من أصول الدين يضحى في سبيلهافي). 11 February 2014. https://binbayyah.net/arabic/archives/category/news/page/15.

⁵² Ibid. Al-Azami, 'Abdullāh bin Bayyah and the Arab Revolutions.

his association with Qatari-supported Islamic groups, Bin Bayyah wrote his letter after the IUMS bitterly denounced the coup and condemned the subsequent brutal repression of the Brotherhood. Mohammed bin Zayed needed Bin Bayyah to religiously legitimise the UAE's involvement in the coup and its subsequent military interventions in Yemen and Libya.

Ultimately, Bin Bayyah could pass his baton to Hamza Yusuf, a media-savvy convert to Islam who runs an Islamic college in California, or Ali al-Jifri, a young Saudi-born Yemeni scholar and another Bin Bayyah disciple. Yusuf already serves as Bin Bayyah's deputy in the Forum and the Emirates Fatwa Council. The Council was established in 2018 to counter what Bin Bayyah described as 'the chaos of the fatwa' and the need "to take the fatwa out of the hands of terrorists and extremists."[53] Hamdan Al Mazroui, the head of the General Authority of Islamic Affairs and Endowments, said the Council had been created to "ensure alignment of fatwas in the country and ensure preaching of moderate Islam."[54]

Al-Jifri is known for his smile and gentle demeanour. His Tabah Foundation has emerged as a prominent promoter of what Al-Azmi, the Islam scholar, terms 'autocratic Islam.' The foundation aims to help Muslim discourse tackle the international community's concerns. Its Senior Scholar Council includes Bin Bayyah as well as Ali Gomaa, the former grand mufti, who shocked even the most conservative Muslim scholars when he legitimised the killing by security forces of hundreds of people protesting against the 2013 military coup that toppled Morsi.[55]

To close the circle, Aref Ali Nayed, a former Libyan ambassador to the UAE, Islamic intellectual, post-2011 presidential candidate, and a close friend of Mohammed Bin Zayed, facilitated Emirati military support for Libyan rebel general Khalifa Haftar. Nayed's heritage garnered him the support of two prominent Libyan tribes, the Warfalla and the Tarhuna, and enabled him to build a network that he put at Bin Zayed's disposal. Nayed and Bin Zayed wanted Haftar, like them, an avowed anti-Islamist who has been accused of torturing and executing his opponents, to capture Tripoli, the Libyan capital, and depose the internationally recognised government.

The UAE and Haftar charged that members of the government were linked to the Brotherhood. Yet, Haftar's militia, populated by followers of quietist Saudi ultra-conservative religious scholar Raba'a al-Madkhali, sought

---

[53] Binbayyah.net, Mulakhas Ajwibat al-Allama Abdullah Bin Bayyah fi Awwal al Mu'tamr Suhufi li-Majlis al—Imarat li-l=ifta al-Shar'I (Summary of Answers by Scholar Abdullah Bin Bayyah During the First News Conference of the Emirates Fatwa Council). Binbayyah.net, 10 July 2018. http://binbayyah.net/arabic/archives/4014.

[54] Samir Salama. "Fatwa Council to Spread Moderate Values of Islam." Gulf News. 31 May 2017. https://gulfnews.com/uae/government/fatwa-council-to-spread-moderate-values-of-islam-1.2036258.

[55] Ali Gomaa's message to Egyptian security forces delivered prior the 2013 Rabaa Massacre Part 2 of 2. YouTube. 21 September 2014. https://www.youtube.com/watch?v=fIGYRu6thyg&t=24s.

to impose ultra-conservative Islamic rule in Benghazi, Libya's second-largest city, and other areas of eastern Libya they controlled. The UAE liked Madkhali's philosophy, despite his being a Salafii, because it preached public loyalty to the ruler. It was willing to look the other way as the Madkhalis sought to ban other schools of Islamic thinking, demolished mausoleums, burned books, and restricted women's movements.

The founder of Kalam Research & Media, a UAE-backed media company and think tank with offices in Dubai and Tripoli, Nayed sees himself as engaged in an "existential struggle" for "the soul of Islam" between two Middle Eastern camps. "On one side, the Saudis, the Emiratis, and the Egyptians. On the other, Qatar, Iran, and Turkey. It's not a secret. To me, this is a struggle for the soul of Islam. What Islam do we want?" Nayed asked, describing Islamists as a "fascist political movement."[56]

The mantle of quietist Sufism, a mystical strand of Islam, provided the UAE the theological framework and moral justification for its crackdown on dissent and civil society, and the lumping together of non-violent Islamism and jihadism. The UAE further saw quietist Sufism as an anti-dote to Wahhabism and Islamism. In the run-up to inviting Bin Bayyah and other Sufi scholars, the UAE sought to establish that Sufism was a part of Gulf history. Starting in 2011, the Dubai-based Al-Mesbar Studies and Research Center published studies asserting that Yemeni scholars brought Sufism to the Gulf centuries ago. The publications argued that Sufism was repressed in the wake of Wahhabism's rise in the eighteenth century but re-emerged in the late nineteenth century.[57]

Talking about the kingdom before the rise of King Salman and his son, Mohammed bin Salman, UAE ambassador to the United States Yousef al-Otaiba asserted that "Abu Dhabi fought 200 years of wars with Saudi over Wahhabism. We have more bad history with Saudi than anyone."[58] The UAE initially signalled its post-independence theological differences with Saudi Arabia in the 1980s when Emirati officials and scholars targeted the Wahhabi rejection of celebrating the Prophet Mohammed's birthday. Isa al-Mani al-Humayri, the head of Dubai's Office of Religious Endowments and Islamic Affairs, issued a fatwa insisting that the birthday should be celebrated "every

---

[56] Frédéric Bobin, "Aref Ali Nayed: 'Libyan Security Is Threatened by Qatar, Turkey and Iran'" (Aref Ali Nayed: 'La sécurité libyenne est menacée par le Qatar, la Turquie et l'Iran'). Le Monde, 24 August 2018. https://www.lemonde.fr/afrique/article/2018/08/24/aref-ali-nayed-la-securite-libyenne-est-menacee-par-le-qatar-la-turquie-et-l-iran_5345724_3212.html.

[57] Haytham Mouzahem. "The Return of Sufism to the UAE." Al-Mesbar Studies and Research Center. 16 April 2018. https://mesbar.org/the-return-of-sufism-to-the-uae/

[58] Leaked email exchange between Yousef al-Otaiba and New York Times columnist Thomas Friedman shared with media, including this author, by a shadowy group calling itself with DC Leaks or Global Leaks.

year and every month and every week and every hour and every moment!"[59] Al-Humayri turned the fatwa into a full-length book. At the same time, the Emirati minister of endowments and Islamic affairs, Ahmad ibn Hasan al-Khazraji, wrote a volume of his own in defence of the commemoration.[60]

However, the UAE waited for more than three decades to frontally attack Wahhabism and Salafism, ultra-conservative revivalist strands of Islam advocating a return to the practices of early Islam that shaped Saudi Arabia. The UAE launched its assault in 2016, a year after Saudi Crown Prince Mohammed bin Salman's rise, at a UAE-sponsored gathering of prominent Sunni Muslim leaders in the Chechen capital of Grozny. In a resolution, the conference effectively excommunicated Wahhabism by defining Sunni Muslims as followers of the four traditional schools of religious jurisprudence and praising Sufi practices, implying that Wahhabis and Salafis fall outside the pale.[61] Western officials refrained from publicly commenting but privately commended the UAE's efforts to confront a worldview that they feared provided a breeding ground for social tensions, militancy, and extremism.[62]

In many ways, the Grozny assault on Wahhabism was long in the making. Bin Zayed visited Al-Azhar's sprawling mosque and university complex in Cairo a year after the Egyptian coup to demonstrate his determination to steer the institution towards adopting Emirati concepts of moderate Islam and countering extremism and fanaticism. Bin Zayed spelled out his view of Wahhabism in a conversation a decade earlier with US Ambassador James Jeffrey. He compared Saudi Arabia's religious leaders to "somebody like the one we are chasing in the mountains," a reference to Osama bin Laden who was believed to be hiding in a mountainous region of Afghanistan at the time.[63] In an email to New York Times columnist Thomas Friedman, twelve years later, UAE ambassador Al-Otaiba asserted that "Abu Dhabi fought 200 years of wars with Saudi over Wahhabism." He claimed the Emirates had more "bad history" with Saudi Arabia than anyone else.[64]

Participants in the Grozny conference included El-Tayeb, Egyptian Grand Mufti Shawki Allam, Allam's Indian and Jordanian counterparts Abubakr Ahmad and Abdul Karim Khasawneh, former Egyptian Grand Mufti and Sufi

[59] Isa al-Mani al-Humayri, "Dubai Fatwa: Should We Celebrate Mawlid—The Prophet's (s) Birthday? As-Sunnah Foundation of America." 24 February 2014. https://sunnah.org/2014/02/24/dubai-fatwa-mawlid/

[60] Marion Holmes Katz. "The Birth of the Prophet Mohammed, Devotional Piety in Sunni Islam." Abingdon, UK: Routledge. 2007, pp. 186–187.

[61] James M. Dorsey. "Fighting for the Soul of Islam: A Battle of the Paymasters, RSIS Commentary No. 241." 20 September 2016. https://www.rsis.edu.sg/wp-content/uploads/2016/09/CO16241.pdf.

[62] Interviews with the author in September and October 2016.

[63] United States Embassy in the United Arab Emirates. "MBZ Meeting with Senior Advisor on Iraq Jeffrey, WikiLeaks." 15 October 2005. https://wikileaks.org/plusd/cables/05ABUDHABI4308_a.html.

[64] Leaked emails of Yusuf al Otaibah shared in 2017 with this author by Global Leaks.

authority Gomaa, a strident supporter of Egyptian President Abdel Fattah Al-Sisi, Al-Sisi's religious affairs advisor Usama al-Azhari, the mufti of Damascus Abdul Fattah al-Bizm, a close confidante of Syrian President Bashar al-Assad, and Al-Jifri, the head of the Abu Dhabi-based Islamic Tabah Foundation.[65] The foundation co-organised the Grozny conference. Gomaa, like Bin Bayyah, is a member of the foundation's senior scholar council.

The participation of El-Tayeb, a political appointee and salaried Egyptian government official, and other Egyptian religious luminaries supportive of Al-Sisi's military coup said much about the UAE's inroads into Al-Azhar, an institution that was for decades a preserve of Saudi ultra-conservatives. El-Tayeb signalled his shifting alliance when, in 2013, he accepted the Sheikh Zayed Book Award for Cultural Personality of the Year in recognition of his "leadership in moderation and tolerance." El-Tayeb was lauded "for encouraging a culture of tolerance, dialogue, and protection of civil society" when Morsi, the embattled Egyptian president, was fighting for his political life, and Bin Zayed was cracking down on the Emirati Muslim Brothers.[66]

[65] James M. Dorsey. "Fighting for the Soul of Islam: A Battle of the Paymasters." RSIS Commentary No. 241. 30 September 2016. https://www.rsis.edu.sg/wp-content/uploads/2016/09/CO16241.pdf.

[66] Mohammed Eissa. "Azhar Grand Imam el-Tayyeb Wins Cultural Personality Award." Ahram Online, 30 April 2013. http://english.ahram.org.eg/NewsContent/18/0/70444/Books/Azhar-Grand-Imam-ElTayyeb-wins-Cultural-Personalit.aspx.

CHAPTER 6

Turkey Seeks Lost Glory

Turkic archers on horseback gallop as they unsheathe their arrows. World War I Ottoman infantry repels an attack, and modern Turkey's army shows off its prowess. All in a four-minute video depicting a 1,000-year-long religious, military, and nationalist endeavour that frames Turkish President Recep Tayyip Erdogan's quest for leadership of the Islamic world.[1]

Fahrettin Altun, the president's communications director, launched the clip as Turkey celebrated the 949th anniversary of the 1071 Battle of Manzikert. In the battle, the Seljuk Turks inflicted their first significant victory over the Byzantines in Anatolia, took Byzantine Emperor Diogenes prisoner, and opened the region to Turkification. On Twitter, Altun asserted that oppressed peoples "from Gibraltar to Hejaz (in Saudi Arabia), from the Balkans to Asia," clamoured for Turkey's protection.

Laced with Ottoman martial music, the clip meshes religious and Ottoman symbolism. It mixed images of Ottoman horses and swordsmen and Sultan Mehmet the Conqueror with Erdogan against the backdrop of modern Turkey's powerful military. Mehmet conquered Constantinople in 1453 and converted Istanbul's Hagia Sophia, one of Istanbul's most iconic Byzantine monuments, into a mosque. Erdogan was forced to resign in 1998 as mayor of Istanbul after a court sentenced him to 10 months in prison for reciting a

---

[1] T.C. Communications Ministry. "Kizil Elma (Red Apple)." YouTube. 25 August 2020. https://www.youtube.com/watch?v=lTQ-KD-RMiA.

poem that asserted, "The mosques are our barracks, the domes our helmets, the minarets our bayonets, and the faithful our soldiers."[2]

Published just after Erdogan returned the Hagia Sofia, a sixth-century Orthodox church-turned-mosque-turned-museum, to its original status as a Muslim house of worship, the clip put the Turkish president on par with Mehmet. It projected Erdogan's rule and the Turkish republic as the latest phase of a Turkish quest for greatness that started with the Seljuks and peaked with the Ottomans, and the thwarting of a military coup on 15 July 2016.

Entitled Red Apple, the clip ended with a panorama view of Jerusalem's Al-Aqsa Mosque, Islam's third holiest site. It reinforced Erdogan's claim to leadership in defending Muslim rights in Jerusalem and the Palestinians' struggle for statehood. "For us, the Red Apple is a big and strong Turkey. It is the happy march of our nation which wrote epics from Manzikert to 15 July," Altun said in his tweet.

With Turkey embroiled in military conflicts in Syria, Libya, and northern Iraq and projecting its influence in the Eastern Mediterranean, the Balkans, the Horn of Africa, and Central Asia, the clip identified Turkish Islam with the country's militant nationalism and flexing of its military muscle.[3] It was a message that was likely to go down well with significant segments of the Turkish electorate and Diaspora, and groups like the Palestinians and Kashmiris, who have few powerful friends to turn to.

To drive the point home, a nationalist Turkish television station with close ties to Erdogan dug up a 12-year-old map projecting Turkey's sphere of influence in 2050. It stretched from southeastern Europe on the northern coast of the Mediterranean and Libya on its southern shore across North Africa, the Gulf, and the Levant into the Caucasus and Central Asia.[4] The broadcasting of the map, first published in a book authored by George Freidman,[5] the founder of Stratfor, an influential American corporate intelligence group, followed calls by the pan-Turkic daily Turkiye, Turkey's fourth largest newspaper, for the creation of a military alliance of Turkic states.[6]

The call came on the back of Turkish support that helped Azerbaijan defeat Armenia in a 2021 war. The victory positioned Azerbaijan, and by extension Turkey, as an alternative westward transportation route that would

---

[2] James Dorsey. "Turkey Seeks Ban on Islamic Party Set to Win Poll." The Scotsman. 24 October 2002.

[3] Fahrettin Altun. Twitter. 25 August 2020. https://twitter.com/fahrettinaltun/status/1297971223591358465

[4] TGRT Haber. "Golge CIA'nin 2050 Turkiye Map (The CIA's covert map of Turkey)." 9 February 2021. https://www.facebook.com/watch/?v=912342479506473.

[5] George Friedman. "The Next 100 Years: A Forecast for the 21st Century." New York: Anchor. 2009.

[6] James M. Dorsey. "Ceasefire in the Caucasus Opens Door to Rebalancing of Regional Power." The Turbulent World with James M. Dorsey. 10 November 2020. https://www.jamesmdorsey.net/post/ceasefire-in-the-caucasus-opens-door-to-rebalancing-of-regional-power.

allow Central Asian nations to bypass corridors dominated by Russia or Iran.[7] Erdogan ruffled Iranian feathers by reciting a nationalist poem at a military parade in Azerbaijan, calling for the reunification of two Iranian ethnic Azeri provinces with Azerbaijan and the publication by state-run Turkish Radio and Television's Arabic service of a map on Instagram depicting Iran's oil-rich province of Khuzestan with its large population of ethnic Arabs as separate from Iran.[8]

Erdogan staked his claim as the advocate for Muslim rights far beyond the erstwhile Ottoman Empire's boundaries. His Vice President Fuat Oktay and Foreign Minister Mevlut Cavusoglu were the first high-level foreign dignitaries to visit Christchurch after in 2019 a white supremacist gunman killed 51 people in mass shootings at two mosques in New Zealand's South Island city.[9] In a chapter of his rambling 74-page manifesto, entitled 'To Turks,' Brenton Tarrant, the gunman, warned, "If you attempt to live in European lands, anywhere west of the Bosphorus. We will kill you and drive you roaches from our lands. We are coming for Constantinople, and we will destroy every mosque and minaret in the city."[10]

In response, Erdogan showed footage of the Christchurch rampage at an election rally. "There is a benefit to watching this on the screen. Remnants of the Crusaders cannot prevent Turkey's rise," Erdogan declared. "We have been here for 1,000 years, and God willing, we will be until doomsday. You will not be able to make Istanbul Constantinople. Your ancestors came and saw that we were here. Some of them returned on foot, and some returned in coffins. If you come with the same intent, we will await you too."[11]

Jerusalem stands at the core of Erdogan's donning of the mantle of Muslims' shining White Knight. Erdogan didn't mince his words at the opening of parliament in 2020. In his first claim to a lost non-Turkic part of the Ottoman Empire, Erdogan declared that Jerusalem was Turkish. "In this city, which we had to leave in tears during the First World War, it is still

---

[7] Paul Goble. "Growing Azerbaijani–Central Asian Ties Likely to Trigger Conflicts With Russia and Iran." Eurasia Daily Monitor. 18 February 2020. https://jamestown.org/program/growing-azerbaijani-central-asian-ties-likely-to-trigger-conflicts-with-russia-and-iran/.

[8] James M. Dorsey. "Turkish Shadow Boxing Reflects Growing Rivalry with Iran." The Turbulent World with James M. Dorsey. 17 December 2020. https://www.jamesmdorsey.net/post/turkish-shadow-boxing-reflects-growing-rivalry-with-iran.

[9] Derek Cheng. "High-Level Turkish Delegation Visits Two Days After Shootings." New Zealand Herald. 17 March 2019. https://www.nzherald.co.nz/nz/high-level-turkish-delegation-visits-two-days-after-shootings/4N6HS3I4XW3QVXAETYH76SCV3Q/?c_id=1&objectid=12213579.

[10] Brenton Tarrant. "The Great Replacement." Undated. https://www.great-replacement.com/text/brenton-tarrant-the-great-replacement-manifesto.pdf.

[11] Borzou Daragahi. "How the New Zealand terror attack has become a key factor in Turkey's upcoming elections." Independent. 18 March 2019. https://www.independent.co.uk/news/world/middle-east/new-zealand-terror-attack-turkey-elections-erdogan-christchurch-mosques-islam-crusades-a8828396.html.

possible to come across traces of the Ottoman resistance. So Jerusalem is our city, a city from us," Erdogan said. "The current appearance of the Old City, which is the heart of Jerusalem, was built by Suleiman the Magnificent, with its walls, bazaar, and many buildings. Our ancestors showed their respect for centuries by keeping this city in high esteem." Erdogan was referring to the 16th-century Ottoman sultan, a sponsor of monumental architectural development, who is widely viewed as having protected his Jewish subjects.[12] Three months earlier, Erdogan asserted that the return of Istanbul's Hagia Sofia to its status as a Muslim house of worship would pave the way for the "liberation" of Jerusalem's Al-Aqsa Mosque, Islam's third holiest site.[13]

The president, who embeds his often-raw nationalism in a religious mantle, can have no illusion that Jerusalem will return to Turkish rule. Yet, by putting forward his claim, Erdogan hoped to put his quest for leadership of the Muslim world on par with that of one of Turkey's staunchest religious soft power rivals, Saudi Arabia. The kingdom is home to Islam's two most sacred cities, Mecca and Medina.

Rather than seeking to regain lost Ottoman territory, Erdogan is staking a claim to custodianship of Jerusalem's Haram ash-Sharif or Temple Mount and Al-Aqsa Mosque compound that currently rests with a Jordanian-controlled religious endowment known as the Waqf.

Erdogan's claim added to Jordan's worries that Israel, in the wake of formalising its ties to Gulf states, could support Saudi ambitions to join the Hashemite kingdom, if not replace it, as the holy site's administrator. Israel Hayom, Israel's most widely read newspaper long supportive of Prime Minister Binyamin Netanyahu, quoted an unidentified Saudi diplomat as saying that Saudi funds were needed to counter Turkish influence in Jerusalem. "If the Jordanians allow the Turks to operate unhindered at the Al-Aqsa Mosque compound, within a matter of years, their special status in charge of the Waqf and Muslim holy sites would be relegated to being strictly 'on paper,'" the diplomat said.[14]

Raed Daana, a former director of preaching and guidance at the Al-Aqsa Mosque Directorate, said in 2018, in the wake of US President Donald J. Trump's recognition of Jerusalem as Israel's capital, that Saudi Arabia had secretly invited Palestinian Muslim dignitaries to garner support for a Saudi

---

[12] Republic of Turkey Presidency. "TBMM 27. Dönem 4. Yasama Yılı Açılış Konuşmaları (Grand National Assembly of Turkey 27th Term 4th Legislative Year Opening Speeches)." 1 October 2020. https://www.tccb.gov.tr/konusmalar/353/122222/tbmm-27-donem-4-yasama-yili-acilis-konusmalari.

[13] The New Arab. "Hagia Sophia Resurrection Paves Way for 'Al-Aqsa liberation', Erdogan Says." 11 July 2020. https://www.newarab.com/news/hagia-sophia-resurrection-paves-way-al-aqsa-liberation-erdogan.

[14] The Jerusalem Post. "Saudi Arabia, Israel Negotiating Temple Mount Control—Report." 1 June 2020. https://www.jpost.com/middle-east/saudi-arabia-israel-negotiating-temple-mount-control-report-629917.

role in the Waqf. Daana attributed the secrecy in part to a refusal by Palestinian religious figures to accept the invitation.[15]

In 2019, Jordan increased the number of Waqf members from 11 to 18 to give it a more Muslim than exclusively Jordanian flavour and to fend off attempts by regional powers to muscle their way into the body. The new members included officials of Palestinian President Mahmoud Abbas's Palestine Authority as well as figures with links to Turkey and Gulf states like Sheikh Ekrima Sabri, a former grand mufti of Jerusalem and Holocaust denier who has defended Erdogan's militancy regarding Jerusalem, and Sabri's successor, Muhammad Hussein, who had close ties to the UAE until he barred Emiratis from visiting Al-Aqsa in protest against the UAE's recognition of Israel.[16]

Saudi Arabia never officially announced its quest to wrest control from Jordan of the Haram al-Sharif. Even so, the writing appeared to be on the wall. Saudi Arabia first signalled its interest when, in 2015, it allowed Iyad Madani, a Saudi national and secretary-general of the Jeddah-based, 57-nation Organization of Islamic Cooperation (OIC), to pay an unprecedented visit to Jerusalem and pray at the Dome of the Rock despite Israel's control of the city. "It is our right to come here and pray here. No occupation authority should take this right from us," Madani said.[17]

Flexing the kingdom's financial muscle, Saudi King Salman told an Arab summit in Dhahran three years later that he was donating US$150 million to support Islam's holy places in Jerusalem.[18] The donation constituted a multitude of Turkish bequests to Islamic organisations in Jerusalem and efforts to acquire real estate. A year earlier, Saudi Arabia, unlike Jordan, backed Israel's installation of metal detectors following an attack that killed two Israeli policemen.[19] The Saudi donation came months after the kingdom unsuccessfully challenged Jordanian custodianship of Haram al-Sharif at a meeting of the Arab Inter-parliamentary Union.[20]

---

[15] Rasha Abou Jalal. "Is Riyadh Really Pushing for Control of Jerusalem Holy Sites?" Al-Monitor. 2 July 2018. https://www.al-monitor.com/originals/2018/07/saudi-arabia-holy-sites-jordan-jerusalem-pa-guardianship.html.

[16] Daoud Kuttab. "New Aqsa Council Gives Palestinians Greater Control in Jerusalem." Al-Monitor. 20 February 2019. https://www.al-monitor.com/originals/2019/02/jordan-waqf-new-council-changes-al-aqsa-mosque-jerusalem.html.

[17] The Associated Press and Rawhi Razim. "In Jerusalem, Islamic Leader Urges Muslims to Visit Al-Aqsa. Haaretz. 5 January 1015.

[18] Saeed Haider. "King Salman Donates $150m for Jerusalem Islamic Endowments." Saudi Gazette. 18 April 2018. https://saudigazette.com.sa/article/532764.

[19] Dov Lieber. "Saudi King Said to Intervene in Reopening of Temple Mount." The Times of Israel. 15 July 2017. https://www.timesofisrael.com/saudi-king-said-to-personally-intervene-in-reopening-temple-mount/.

[20] Al Quds Al_Arab. «البرلماني العربي سابقة سعودية في الاعتراض على «الوصاية الهاشمية» على القدس ومواجهة مع الوفد. Saudi Precedent in Objecting to 'Hashemite Custodianship' of Jerusalem and a Confrontation with the Jordanian Delegation in the "Arab Parliamentary Conference")." 18 December 2017. https://www.alquds.co.uk/%ef%bb%bf‫سابقة-سعودية-في-الاعتراض-على-الوصاي‬/.

Erdogan attempted to lay the groundwork for his claim with millions of dollars in donations to local Islamic organisations and support of thousands of Turkish religious activists and pilgrims visiting Jerusalem whom Israel has accused of instigating Palestinian protests after Turks participated in demonstrations. Diyanet lists Al-Aqsa as a site for Umrah, the lesser Muslim pilgrimage. Turkey's cultural centre in Jerusalem and a Turkish-renovated coffee shop two minutes from the city's Western Wall, adorned with Turkish and Palestinian flags as well as portraits of Erdogan and Ottoman Sultan Abdul Hamid II, served as a meeting point for activists and pilgrims.[21] "Turkey is working diligently to deepen its involvement and influence on the Temple Mount, in the Old City of Jerusalem, and in east Jerusalem neighbourhoods. It is encouraging welfare-religious (dawa) activities…aimed at drawing the Palestinian public toward the Turkish-Islamic heritage and at weakening Israel's hold on the Old City and east Jerusalem," said conservative Israeli journalist and analyst Nadav Shragai.[22]

In Yeni Safak, a newspaper that echoes the ruling Justice and Development Party (AKP), Yusuf Kaplan, a commentator with close ties to Erdogan, laid out the sharp, civilisationalist edge of Turkey's religious soft power effort. Erdogan has refrained from unambiguously articulating Kaplan's positions for geopolitical and domestic political reasons. By the same token, Erdogan has not taken public distance from the hegemonic anti-Western, anti-Shiite Muslim views expressed by people like Kaplan.

"Turkey faces two important sieges that will determine the Islamic world's destiny in particular and the world's destiny in general…. Western imperialists settled in our region and turned it into hell. Turkey, confined to the Anatolian continent, could not be physically colonized, but it colonized itself mentally… It stopped its own civilization march!… Turkey was pushed into Westernization, secularization; secularism was imposed top-down, using Jacobean methods, as if to change religion in this grand nation that has been the flag-bearer of Islamic civilization for a millennium… The more it became secular, the more ethnic identities came to the forefront; the Islamic identity and sensitivities that kept the society together corroded," Kaplan said, condemning Kemalism, the secular ideology that informed Mustafa Kemal Ataturk's post-Ottoman creation of modern Turkey and shaped the republic for much of its almost a century-long history.[23]

---

[21] Pinhas Inbari. "Erdogan's Turkey Intensifies Involvement in Gaza and Jerusalem." Jerusalem Center for Public Affairs. 14 June 2018. https://jcpa.org/article/erdogans-turkey-intensifies-involvement-in-gaza-and-jerusalem/.

[22] Nadav Shragai. "Turkey's Intrusion into Jerusalem." Jerusalem Center for Public Affairs. 15 June 2020. https://jcpa.org/article/turkeys-intrusion-into-jerusalem/.

[23] Yusuf Kaplan. "Destiny of Islam, humanity depends on Turkey." Yeni Safak. 8 March 2020, https://www.yenisafak.com/en/columns/yusufkaplan/destiny-of-islam-humanity-depends-on-turkey-2047374.

Singling out Shiites as Turkey hosted some four million refugees and attempted to fend off a new wave of migrants fleeing war and economic deprivation, Kaplan warned that "the second siege is the sectarian/Shi'ite siege from outside. If we fail to break this siege, the destiny of Islam – not only us but all Muslims – as well as the destiny of the Islamic world will be left to the mercy of Western imperialists and their servants' evil plots… This is the Shi'ite-Persian empire attempt that imperialists have been striving greatly to turn into a reality. This attempt is invading the Sunni Arab world, which constitutes the heart of the Islamic world, step by step; it is enslaving it and carrying out unbelievable massacres such as the ones in Syria, Iraq, and Yemen."

Kaplan's views took on significance given not only the author's ties to the president and the party but also the fact that they were published without pushback or repercussion in a strictly state-controlled media environment and in a country that ranks among the foremost jailers of journalists. Kaplan's views further suggest that Turkey's soft power strategy is driven as much by nationalist as religious motives and targets Turkish Diaspora Sunni Muslims rather than Kurds or Alevis.

The targeting bodes ill for Shiite Alevis, who account for approximately 20 per cent of the Turkish population, and risks fuelling division rather than cohesion in the Diaspora, potentially complicating integration into the home or host countries of Turkish Muslim communities. In 2020, a Dutch parliamentary commission held controversial hearings about "unwanted influencing by unfree countries"[24] that focused on Turkish and Gulf support for Dutch Muslim communities and an unnuanced view of political Islam. The commission contemplated following in the footsteps of Austria[25] and France[26] that have banned foreign funding for Muslim organisations.

Diyanet, Erdogan's Religious Affairs Department, one of modern Turkey's first institutions created by Ataturk under the same law that in 1924 abolished the Caliphate and allowed for the closure of madrassas or religious seminaries, shot itself in its foot in its effort to win hearts and minds in the Turkish Diaspora with the way it handled the Coronavirus crisis at home. Inconsistencies in its policy contributed to a deepening, if not widening, of Turkey's social and political fault lines. Diyanet's approach to the Umrah was criticised by both AKP members and the opposition. While the government quarantined

---

[24] Tweede Kamer der Staten-Generaal. "Parlementaire ondervragingscommissie vraagt gerechtshof om uitspraak (Parliamentary inquiry commission asks court for ruling)." 4 March 2020. https://www.tweedekamer.nl/nieuws/kamernieuws/parlementaire-onderv ragingscommissie-vraagt-gerechtshof-om-uitspraak.

[25] Bundesministerium Europaeische und Internationale Angelegenheiten. "Islamgesetz 2015 – Zusammenfassung (Islam Law 2015—Sumnmary)." 2015. https://www.bundes kanzleramt.gv.at/dam/jcr:a0466509-1c32-4e9c-82c4-586444068dcc/islamgesetz_2015_ -_zusammenfassung.pdf.

[26] Benjamin Dodman. "Will Banning Foreign Funds for French Mosques Help Combat Terrorism?" France 24. 29 July 2016. https://www.france24.com/en/20160729-foreign-financing-mosques-valls-france-secularism-islam.

Turkish nationals evacuated from China and halted all flights to and from Iran, Diyanet failed to push for the immediate return of 21,000 mostly elderly Turks who performed Umrah. Less than a third of the pilgrims were quarantined upon return. Pilgrimages constitute a major revenue source for the directorate. Diyanet was also late in introducing social distancing to Friday prayers.

Diyanet was further taken to task for backing and distributing video clips of VIP Friday prayer on the grounds of Erdogan's presidential palace at a moment when ordinary Turks were asked to pray at home. An exclusive VIP prayer violated concepts of the Friday prayer that is open to all and representative of Islam's unifying nature, irrespective of social class or ethnicity. In addition, Diyanet came under fire for issuing a fatwa supporting Erdogan's national fundraising campaign for the needy while banning a similar effort by the opposition. Like the VIP prayer, Diyanet appeared to go against the principle that Muslims have the freedom to choose recipients of their zakat or obligatory almsgiving.

"Diyanet has come to represent the concerns of AKP elites rather than ordinary Muslims in Turkey. The gap between Diyanet and the public has become more visible… Many have come to question whether the institution is contributing enough to society, especially in the time of a pandemic," said journalist Pinar Tremblay.[27]

As with Diyanet's handling of the Coronavirus crisis, leaked transcripts of the tapping of the phone of Hasan Dogan, Erdogan's chief of cabinet, illustrated the political drivers of Turkey's religious soft power campaign and effort to position itself as an Islamic leader. Speaking by phone in July 2013, a day after Egyptian President Morsi was toppled, to Osama Qutb, a representative of Yusuf al-Qaradawi, a prominent but controversial Doha-based Islamic scholar widely viewed as a major influence in the Muslim Brotherhood, and a nephew of Said Qutb, one of the group's most militant thinkers who was executed in 1996, Dogan predicted the Brotherhood's return to power. He pointed out that Erdogan's rise, first as prime minister in 2003, came six years after the military pushed his predecessor, Necmettin Erbakan, out of office. "God willing, I predict that this will lead to an explosion, a bigger and more dynamic change in Egypt within three to five years," Dogan said, referring to Morsi's ouster.[28]

If Ataturk converted the 6th-century Hagia Sophia, Istanbul's cathedral-turned-mosque, into a museum, Erdogan, a former Istanbul mayor, intended his legacy to be one of converting churches and museums into mosques and

---

[27] Pinar Tremblay. "Turkey's State Religious Body Undermines Anti-coronavirus Efforts." Al-Monito. 7 April 2020, https://www.al-monitor.com/pulse/originals/2020/04/turkey-religious-body-diyanet-mired-coronavirus-controversy.html.

[28] Abdullah Bozkurt. "Erdoğan Government Believed Muslim Brotherhood Would Make a HUGE comeback in Egypt in Few Years." Nordic Monitor. 2 April 2020. https://www.nordicmonitor.com/2020/04/erdogan-government-believed-muslim-brotherhood-would-make-a-huge-comeback-in-egypt-in-few-years/.

building Muslim houses of worship at home and in places as far-flung as Latin America where Islam is the fastest-growing religion. He returned the Hagia Sophia to its former status as a Muslim house of worship, renaming it the Hagia Sophia Grand Mosque. A former academic, foreign minister, and onetime associate of Erdogan, Ahmet Davutoglu, argued, in anticipation of the Red Apple clip and the change of Hagia Sophia's status, that Turkey's geography, history, and religious cultural agency empowered it to be a regional hegemon.[29]

Erdogan underlined the importance of religious soft power by granting Diyanet, which employs Turkey's imams, pays their salaries, organises the country's religious life, and acts as the highest religious authority in questions of doctrine and practice, a key role in soft power, foreign, and aid policy in the wake of the failed coup. Religious scholars, chanting Allahuekber or God is Great, joined crowds that took to the streets to thwart the coup. Imams used minarets to call on the faithful to resist the attempted government takeover. "Turn on the lights of every mosque and encourage the people to join the independence struggle! Our people should be at ease! We should all pray! Tonight, together we will eliminate the biggest act of murder and betrayal against our people!" the imams shouted.[30] Diyanet President Mehmet Gormez took credit for defeating the coup, claiming "with the prayer in its ears, Allahuekber in its mouth, and the flag in its hand, the nation defeated the traitors."[31]

While Turkey continued to, at least nominally, adhere to its secular republican origins, it was no different from its Gulf rivals when it came to grooming state-aligned clergymen, whose ability to think outside the box and develop new interpretations of the faith was impeded by a religious education system that stymied critical thinking and creativity. Like Gulf states, Turkey emphasised the study of Arabic and the memorisation of the Qur'an and other religious texts, creating a religious and political establishment that discouraged, if not penalised, innovation. Following in the footsteps of the Byzantine and Ottoman empires, Turkey's "brand of secularism fundamentally relates not to the separation of religion and state but to the state's control over the influence that religion has on society in order to advance the interests of the state," said scholar Ahmet Erdi Ozturk.[32]

---

[29] Ahmet Davutoglu. "The Clash of Interests: An Explanation of the World (Dis)order." Perceptions Journal of International Affairs. Vol. 2, Issue 4. December 1997–February 1998, p. 1.

[30] Hudaibiya. "AKSARAY—Darbe sonrası ezan sesleri." YouTube. 16 July 2016. https://www.youtube.com/watch?v=7ceZ9nDXRxk.

[31] Akit. "Babam 'minareye çık ve sala oku' demişti" (My Father Said, 'Go Up to the Minaret and Recite Prayer,' He saId). 30 August 2016. https://www.yeniakit.com.tr/haber/babam-minareye-cik-ve-sala-oku-demisti-207145.html.

[32] Ahmet Erdi Ozturk. "Turkey's Ambivalent Religious Soft Power in the Illiberal Turn." In Peter Mandaville (ed.) The Geopolitics of Religious Soft Power: How States Use Religion in Foreign Policy. New York: Oxford University Press. 2023. p. 83.

Erdogan infused Diyanet, established in 1924 to replace the Ottoman ministry of Sharia and endowments and the grand mufti, and propagate a statist, moderate form of Islam that endorsed secularism, with his version of political Islam. In a since-removed mission statement posted after the coup, Diyanet said the authority saw itself as "historically rooted" in its imperial predecessor and sought to advance the "traditional mission" of the Ottoman Sheikh al-Islam.[33] Erdogan turned it into one of the government's most influential and best-funded agencies. Today, Diyanet operates some 90,000 mosques, 23 Qur'an schools in Turkey, and another 2,000 houses of worship worldwide at a cost of more than US$500 million.[34] In 145 countries, Diyanet's Turkiye Diyanet Foundation (TDV) manages many of the overseas mosques. TDV positioned its mosque activity as the perpetuation of Seljuk and Ottoman culture.

Erdogan and Diyanet's ambitions didn't stop there. They worked to position Istanbul's May 29 University, funded by the Diyanet Foundation, as a rival to premier institutions of Islamic learning, including Egypt's more than 1,000-year-old Al-Azhar University, the Islamic University of Medina, Pakistan's Saudi-funded International Islamic University, Iran's Al-Mustafa International University, and Malaysia's International Islamic University. These institutions were "unable to find solutions to problems in the world," Gormez said. Rather than seeking peaceful solutions, Gormez charged that "Muslims bring suffering, violence, and sorrow to each other… The scholars who graduate from these universities are becoming the problem themselves, rather than solving the problems."[35] Diyanet expected to benefit from Turkey's hosting of more than 1,000 religious scholars who have sought refuge from Iran and wars in Syria, Libya, and Yemen. An earlier attempt to create an International Eurasian Islamic University under the auspices of the moribund Eurasian Islamic Council failed.[36]

Alongside Diyanet, Turkey's aid agency, the Turkish Cooperation and Coordination Agency (TIKA), has emerged as a key vehicle for garnering soft power, often with a religious taint. With Turkish development aid ballooning from USD 85 million a year in 2002 to 8.8 billion in 2022 and 30,000 projects in 170 countries, TIKA often packages its humanitarian and other assistance in Islamic terms.[37] Taking Africa as a case study, scholars Buğra Süsler and

[33] https://diyanet.gov.tr/tr/icerik/kurulus-ve-tarihce/8.

[34] Diyanet Isleri Baskanligi. "Statistics." 1 June 2020, https://stratejigelistirme.diyanet.gov.tr/sayfa/57/istatistikler.

[35] Fatma Aksu. "Turkey Aims to Open Islamic university: Top Religious Head." Hurriyet Daily News. 2 October 2014. https://www.hurriyetdailynews.com/turkey-aims-to-open-islamic-university-top-religious-head-72418.

[36] Mehmet Ozkan. "Turkey's Religious Diplomacy." The Arab World Geographer, Vol. 17, Issue 3. Fall 2014, pp. 223–238.

[37] Organisation for Economic Cooperation and Development. "Development Co-operation Profiles. Turkiye." 24 June 2023. https://www.oecd-ilibrary.org/sites/714276e8-en/index.html?itemId=/content/component/714276e8-en.

Chris Alden noted that "frameworks that are co-constituted in ideational terms offer a broader basis from which Turkey and African counterparts negotiate. Ideationally based exchanges typically invoke shared moral precepts and aspirational forms of social cooperation that impact upon the content and outcome of negotiations... A distinctive aspect of Turkey's relationship with Africa... is the use of religious references, namely the notion of Muslim kinship, aimed to develop closer relations with communities following the same faith."[38] Turkey employed the Qur'anic Verse of Brotherhood (49: 10) that declares universal brotherhood among Muslims irrespective of their race or tribe to argue that developing closer ties with non-Turkish Muslims was a moral imperative that distinguished its engagement from the intentions of past Western colonisers.

Turkey's religious packaging of aid and economic cooperation benefitted from Saudi Crown Prince Mohammed bin Salman's rollback of global funding of Muslim ultra-conservatism, the UAE' abstention from proselytisation, and Iranian handicaps in bridging the Sunni-Shiite and propagating their activist interpretation of the faith. In the Middle East, Iran, the world's foremost Muslim theocracy, drew battle lines by sponsoring Shiite militias in the Middle East. Initially, militias served as tools to export the revolution. Over time, they became an integral part of Iran's forward defence strategy. They also bolstered Iranian support for President Bashar al-Assad in the Syrian civil war. At the same time, Iran sought to mobilise Muslims elsewhere to counter US, Saudi, and Israeli interests. In Africa, Iran's religious soft power effort contributed to inter-communal disputes between Muslims and Christians, and among Muslims.

Portraying its Islam as moderate and inclusive, Iran exploited its position as the most populous Shiite nation and a prominent centre of Islamic learning to counter Sunni Muslim ultra-conservative prejudice, particularly in the form of Wahhabism, and promote Iranian culture and the Persian language. Like Saudi Arabia, Iran's religious and cultural outreach was managed by governmental and non-governmental religious, humanitarian, and educational organisations such as the Imam Khomeini Relief Committee (Emdad), the Islamic Culture and Relations Organization (ICRO), the Ahl al-Bayt World Assembly, and branches of Al-Mustafa University.[39]

Moreover, competing with Turkey, Saudi Arabia, and Al-Azhar, Iran offered scholarships to thousands of religious scholars and aspiring clerics for study in the holy city of Qom and other Iranian educational institutions. At the same time, organisations like the relief committee operated not only in Shiite communities but also in Sunni-majority countries. Iranian cultural diplomacy frequently sought to project the Islamic Republic, in competition with Turkey,

---

[38] Buğra Süsler and Chris Alden. "Turkey and African Agency: The Role of Islam and Commercialism in Turkey's Africa Policy." The Journal of Modern African Studies. Vol. 60, Issue 4. 9 March 2023, pp. 597–617.

[39] Banafsheh Keynoush. "Iran's Africa-Pivot Policy." Middle East Policy. Vol. 28, Issue 3–4. Fall–Winter 2028, pp. 228–248.

as the defender of Muslim communities in jeopardy by emphasising Iran's role in the Axis of Resistance which groups various Tehran-backed militias.

The breadth, scope, and intensity of Turkey's religious soft power campaign have forced the country's often state-controlled rivals to take notice. Established more than a century ago, Cairo-based Dar al-Ifta Al-Missriya, a centre for Islamic legal research that issues authoritative religious edicts, has, like Diyanet, become a tool of Egyptian foreign policy. Building on a history of support for successive Egyptian governments, Dar al-Ifta has embraced the UAE's propagation of a statist interpretation of Islam to rally support for Egyptian general-turned-president Abdel Fattah al-Sisi. The embrace has transformed the centre from a respected pro-government religious institution into a government public affairs asset. "Since Sisi became president in 2014, Dar Al-Ifta has turned into a mouthpiece of the state and has been employed as a political pawn to legitimize Sisi's internal and external policies," said Egypt scholar Khalil al-Anani.[40]

As the Egyptian leader threatened military intervention in Libya in the summer of 2020, the centre opined that criticism or opposition to the president's policy was forbidden under Islamic law. It advised its more than 800,000 Twitter followers that Egyptians had a religious obligation to obey and support the country's leadership. Those that fail to do so "do not deserve the honour of belonging to the country," the centre said.[41]

The centre's Observatory for Monitoring Takfiri Fatwas and Extremist Ideologies regularly condemned Turkish military operations in northern Syria as terrorism.[42] In the run-up to Ramadan in 2020, the Muslim holy month of fasting, the centre banned Arabic-dubbed Turkish soap operas that glorify the Ottoman Empire and Turkish state-controlled Islam from Egypt's pro-government television channels. Dar al-Ifta charged that the TV series was a Turkish attempt to carve out an "area of influence."[43]

The Turks "export to the people and nations the notion that they are the leaders of the caliphate, responsible for supporting Muslims worldwide and are their salvation from oppression and injustice while also seeking to implement Islamic law. The Turkish president and his followers are not immune from

---

[40] Khalil al-Anani. "An Old, Ongoing Struggle: Domesticating Religious Institutions in Egypt." Arab Center Washington, DC. 2 April 2021. https://arabcenterdc.org/resource/an-old-ongoing-struggle-domesticating-religious-institutions-in-egypt/.

[41] Dar al-Ifta Al-Masriya. Twitter. 19 July 2020. https://twitter.com/EgyptDarAlIfta?ref_src=twsrc%5Etfw%7Ctwcamp%5Etweetembed%7Ctwterm%5E1274781113056137216%7Ctwgr%5E&ref_url=https%3A%2F%2Farabic.cnn.com%2Fmiddle-east%2Farticle%2F2020%2F06%2F21%2Fazhar-ifta-egypt-libya-lna-gna.

[42] MENA. "Darul Iftaa's Observatory Condemns Turkish Attack on Afrin City in Aleppo Countryside." 29 April 2020. https://www.egypttoday.com/Article/1/85214/Darul-Iftaa-s-observatory-condemns-Turkish-attack-on-Afrin-city.

[43] Yeni Safak. "Following in UAE, Saudi Footsteps, Egypt Issues Fatwa Banning Turkish TV Series." 10 February 2020. https://www.yenisafak.com/en/news/following-in-uae-saudifootsteps-egypt-issues-fatwa-banning-turkishtv-series-3511681.

using religious discourse in general, and fatwas in particular, as a cover for their military operations," Dar al-Ifta said.

The ban singled out the award-winning Resurrection Ertugrul series based on a depiction of the 13th-century warrior Ertugrul Ghazi, the father of Osman who founded the Ottoman Empire, as fighting the Crusaders and Byzantines for Islam. The fatwa also named Valley of the Wolves that features a Turkish intelligence agent who hides his identity to infiltrate the Turkish mafia, in Turkey and neighbouring countries. Instead, Dar al-Iftar advised viewers to watch a US$40 million Saudi production, Kingdoms of Fire, designed to counter the Turkish projection of the Ottomans and "expose Ottoman tyranny."[44]

Starting in 2021, Dar al-Ifta toned down its criticism as Egypt, Saudi Arabia, and the UAE sought to de-escalate regional tensions by freezing their differences to ensure that they did not spin out of control. Turkish soap operas 'Noor' and 'Forbidden Love' became popular in Egypt and across the Muslim world because they extolled shared cultural and family values yet catered to changing winds by tackling sensitive issues such as forced marriages, rape, divorce, and extramarital affairs. Women often identified actresses who on screen made their own choices in life about whom they marry, whether to work or not, and whether to have children. The operas propelled Turkey into the ranks of the world's top TV series exporters, accounting for annual revenues of US$350 million.[45]

Like Dar al-Ifta, Saudi Arabia, sought to stymie Turkey's soft power efforts before the kingdom opted to freeze differences and focus on economic cooperation and collaboration on issues on which rivals found common ground. The kingdom blocked the state-run Turkish Anadolu news agency's website and the Arabic-language broadcasts of Turkish Radio and Television,[46] banned Turkish TV series,[47] and produced its own programs to counter the Turks.

In 2019, Diyanet opened Ottoman-style mosques in Japan, Tanzania, Djibouti, the Netherlands, Cambridge, Cyprus, Albania, Macedonia, and Kosovo.[48] Moreover, Diyanet funded the construction of mega mosques

---

[44] Saudi Gazette. "MBC to Air Biggest Drama Exposing Ottoman Tyranny." 4 November 2019. https://saudigazette.com.sa/article/581674.

[45] Daily Sabah. "Turkish TV Series Exceed $350 Million in Exports." 4 January 2018. https://www.dailysabah.com/business/2018/01/04/turkish-tv-series-exceed-350-million-in-exports.

[46] Anadolu Agency. "Saudi Arabia Bans Anadolu Agency Website: Reports." 13 April 2020. https://www.aa.com.tr/en/middle-east/saudi-arabia-bans-anadolu-agency-website-reports/1803101.

[47] Umut Uras. "Saudi Network Ban on Turkey TV Shows Is 'Political': Minister." Al Jazzera. 6 March 2018. https://www.aljazeera.com/news/2018/3/6/saudi-network-ban-on-turkey-tv-shows-is-political-minister.

[48] Diyanet Isleri Baskanligi. "2019 Annual Report." 2020. https://stratejigelistirme.diyanet.gov.tr/Documents/2019%20Y%C4%B1l%C4%B1%20Faaliyet%20Raporu.pdf.

in Moscow, Germany's Duisburg, Kosovo's Pristina and Kosovo Mitrovica, Bosnia's Gorazde, Bucharest, Bulgaria's Kardzhali, Tirana, Budapest, Minsk, Cambridge, Utrecht, Turkish Cyprus' Nicosia, Crimea's Simferopol, Georgia's Batumi, Gaza, Kazakhstan's Turkistan, Haiti's Cap-Haitien, Havana, Bamako, and Bishkek.[49] Many rank as the largest in their host country or region. A US$110 million mosque and cultural centre in the US state of Maryland is the biggest Muslim house of worship in the Western Hemisphere. All told, Diyanet established a presence in 81 countries by 2011.[50] The mosques are often built with the agreement of the host government but without public consultation. They are endowed with cultural centres, places of learning, shops, and cafes to project Turkish Sunni Islam as modern, moderate, and forward-looking.

In Syria, Diyanet sought to enhance Turkish influence in rebel-held areas by repairing war-ravaged mosques and training Syrian imams and female Qur'an instructors.[51] At the same time, Diyanet opened religious advisory offices staffed by Syrian imams in refugee camps in Turkey[52] and printed four million Arabic-language schoolbooks to "shield" children against "manipulation" by militants.[53]

In Africa and parts of Eastern Europe, Turkish-built mosques are located on the frontline of Islam's competition with Christianity for souls. Albania found itself without houses of worship after the downfall of Albanian communist strongman Enver Hoxha, who banned the public practice of religion, demolished or repurposed places of worship, jailed and executed clerics, and persecuted their families in a country that is 60 per cent Muslim.[54]

---

[49] Michael Bird and Zeynep Şentek. "Turkey Global Mega-Mosque Bonanza List." The Black Sea. Undated. https://theblacksea.eu/blogs/turkey-global-mega-mosque-bonanza-list/.

[50] TC Baskanlik Diyanet Isleri Baskanlig. "2013 Faaliyet Raporu," March–April 2014. https://stratejigelistirme.diyanet.gov.tr/Documents/2013%20Y%C4%B1l%C4%B1%20Faaliyet%20Raporu.pdf.

[51] Diyanet Isleri Baskanligi. "Suriye'de terörden temizlenen bölgeye koordinatör müftüler (Regional Coordinating Muftis Cleared of Terrorism in Syria)." 12 June 2017. https://www.diyanet.gov.tr/tr-TR/Kurumsal/Detay/10176/suriyede-terorden-temizlenen-bolgeye-koordinator-muftuler.

[52] Haber Turk. "Diyanet İşleri Başkanlığı Suriyeli 100 imam istihdam edecek (Diyanet Presidency Will Employ 100 Syrian Imams)." 7 November 2017. https://www.haberturk.com/suriyeli-100-imam-istihdam-edilecek-1703025.

[53] Hurriyet. "Suriyeli öğrencilere 4 milyon ders kitabı (4 Million Textbooks for Syrian Students)." 21 December 2016. https://www.hurriyet.com.tr/egitim/suriyeli-ogrencilere-4-milyon-ders-kitabi-40313436.

[54] Valbona Bezati. "How Albania Became the World's First Atheist Country." BalkanInsight. 28 August 2019. https://balkaninsight.com/2019/08/28/how-albania-became-the-worlds-first-atheist-country/.

Christians were quick to fill the void. Pope John Paul II laid the cornerstone for a Roman Catholic cathedral in 1993[55]; a few years later, the Greek Orthodox Church began work on its own, one of Europe's largest.[56] Initially, Muslims appeared to have been left behind. Tirana's 19th-century Et'hem Bey Mosque, with room for a few dozen worshippers at a time, was the only Muslim house of worship to survive the Hoxha era. In 2010, Turkey constructed the city's mega mosque, the largest in the Balkans, on George W. Bush Street, near the Albanian Parliament and not far from the two churches, to ensure Muslims kept up with the pace of change.[57] "There's religious competition. Different countries and religious bodies converge here," said Albanian historian Auron Tare.

Diyanet's mosques are frequently built by a TDV-owned construction company, Kocatepe Modern Retailing Enterprises Industry and Trade Joint Stock Company or KOMAS, part of the authority's mushrooming business and real estate empire.[58] Critics dubbed the empire, with its more than 2000 properties and significant tax-exempt pilgrimage, halal slaughter, and meat packing businesses, Diyanet Holding. "Diyanet resembles a gigantic holding company — or even more sinister: a state within a state," said theologian Cemal Kilic.

Turkey's religious soft power campaign is as much about rolling back the Hizmet movement, headed by Fethullah Gulen, an exiled one-time government-employed preacher and Erdogan ally accused of instigating a failed 2016 military coup against Erdogan, as it is about exercising control over the Turkish Diaspora, countering the religious soft power of its rivals, Saudi Arabia, the UAE, and Egypt, and establishing Turkey as a regional power. As part of the agreement to build a mosque, Albania handed Turkey religious seminaries operated by Gulen, who lives in exile in the United States. Gulen operated six of Albania's seven Muslim religious seminaries as part of a global network of more than 1,000 acclaimed, gender-segregated, pre-university schools in 100 countries[59] that shared Erdogan's goal of raising a pious generation. Following the rupture between the two men, the need to counter Gulen's global reach put Erdogan's quest for religious soft power in sharp relief.

Until the early 2010s, Gulen's educational network, media empire, and backing by influential conservative businessmen enhanced Turkey's religious

[55] Religiana. "St. Paul's Cathedral." Undated. https://religiana.com/st-pauls-cathedral-tirana.

[56] Religiana. "Cathedral of the Resurrection of Christ." Undated. https://religiana.com/cathedral-resurrection-christ-tirana.

[57] Daily Sabah. "Erdoğan, Rama to Inaugurate Ethem Bey Mosque in Tirana." 17 January 2022. https://www.dailysabah.com/politics/erdogan-rama-to-inaugurate-ethem-bey-mosque-in-tirana/news.

[58] https://www.komasas.com/.

[59] Helen Rose Ebaugh. "The Gülen Movement: A Sociological Analysis of a Civic Movement Rooted in Moderate Islam." Berlin: Springer. 2009. p. 4.

soft power, even if the cleric was a divisive figure. Believers asserted that the cleric, who before the coup was one of Turkey's most popular religious leaders, preached a new, Westernized Islam, a precursor of the interpretation of the faith propagated by Saudi Arabia's Bin Salman and UAE President Mohammed bin Zayed. "Fethullah's advocacy of obedience to the state was a response to radical Islam," said Rusen Cakir, author of numerous books on the politics of Turkish Islam.[60]

Erdogan's secular predecessors viewed Gulen, with his appeal among urban conservative youth and left-wing intellectuals, as their most effective weapon in countering Islamists. Critics suggested Gulen's alliance with secularists was part of a long-term strategy of preparing for control of the state through gradual infiltration of the military, the police, and other state institutions that was initially endorsed by Erdogan when he became prime minister in 2003. Gulen's quest came to a screeching halt when a Turkish court in 2014 issued an arrest warrant, accusing him of running "an armed terrorist group."[61] Following the failed coup, Erdogan purged some 125,000 alleged Gulen followers.[62]

A doleful 82-year-old diabetic with a heart ailment often dressed in a crumpled sports jacket and slacks, Gulen doesn't look like a religious firebrand—nor does he talk like one. In the immediate years before the coup and in exile, Gulen devoted himself to writing tracts on Islam that shied away from advocating theological renewal and regurgitated traditional attitudes towards women. In conversation, Gulen, a committed bachelor, conceded that women made him uncomfortable.

Even so, his advocacy of tolerance, dialogue, and worldly education, as well as his endorsement of Turkey's close ties to Europe, positioned him alongside secular Turkish leaders and politicians and against Refah, the Islamist party to which Erdogan belonged before it was banned in 1998 by the country's Constitutional Court. "We can build confidence and peace in this country if we treat each other with tolerance," Gulen said in his first interview with a foreign journalist. "There's no place for quarrelling in this world."[63]

The Albanian handover of Gulen's educational facilities was a node in Turkey's global campaign to place Gulen's far-flung network of schools under the auspices of its Turkish Maarif Foundation once Erdogan turned on the preacher. Created for that purpose, the foundation oversees the introduction of a curriculum whose Islamic aspects are administered by Diyanet. The

---

[60] Interview with the author. 18 December 1995.

[61] BBC News. "Turkey Issues Fethullah Gulen Arrest Warrant." 19 December 2014. https://www.bbc.com/news/world-europe-30552148.

[62] Joseph Hincks. "Here's a Time Line of the Insane Number of People Turkey's President Has Fired Since July." Time. 23 November 2016. https://time.com/4581070/turkey-erdogan-fired-dismissed-suspended-sacked-officials-total/.

[63] James M. Dorsey. "Islamic Leader Bridges Gap in Turkey— Ciller Looks to Fethullah Gulen as Vote Nears." The Wall Street Journal Europe. 22 December 1995.

foundation has offices in 52 countries. Some 40,000 students attend its 465 schools, training centres, and universities in 67 countries and/or live in 42 dormitories managed by the foundation.[64]

The foundation works alongside the government-backed Hudayi Foundation that operates Imam Hatip schools in 14 countries and offers scholarships to study Islam at its Distant Training Faculty of Theology and the Suleymancılar, a controversial Sufi group. Russian security forces cracked down on the Suleymancılar in 2023. Russia's Federal Security Service (FSB) accused the group of propagating a Turkic state in Eurasia that included parts of Russia, converting to Islam Russian Orthodox believers, and applying corporal punishment in its dormitories and religious boarding schools.[65]

Erdogan lobbied heads of state and government to close Gulen-affiliated schools and/or turn them over to the Maarif Foundation. The Gulen movement charged in a report that schools put under Maarif Foundation management would be run by "pro-AKP Islamist association," the 27-page report said, referring to Erdogan's ruling Justice and Development Party by its initials. The report asserted that "the "Maarif Foundation was not set up for its stated aims of increasing education quality and particularly not providing education abroad… The obvious aim is to replace and become an alternative to the schools of the Gülen Movement."[66]

As Turkey, a NATO member aspiring to European Union membership, focused on education, schoolbooks used in Turkey and abroad were scrutinised by an education watchdog. A report by the Institute for Monitoring Peace and Cultural Tolerance in School Education (Impact-se), an Israeli research group that monitors educational materials in the Middle East and the Muslim world, and Britain's Henry Jackson Society concluded that Turkey's latest school books had replaced concepts of evolution, cultural openness, and tolerance towards minorities that included Kurdish as a minority language, with notions of jihad, martyrdom in battle, and a neo-Ottoman and pan-Turkist ethnoreligious worldview. They asserted that recent curricula include anti-American and anti-Armenian attitudes, display "sympathy for the motivations of ISIS and Al-Qaeda," focus exclusively on Sunni Muslim teachings, and replace electives such as Kurdish with religious courses. Moreover, the schoolbooks refer to Jews and Christians as infidels rather than as 'People of the Book,' the common Muslim reference, despite portraying Jewish civilisation and Hebrew positively and discussing the Holocaust for the first time.

---

[64] https://turkiyemaarif.org/dunyada-maarif.

[65] Massimo Introvigne. "Süleymancılar: Russia Cracks Down on Turkish Sufi Organization." Bitter Winter. 7 July 2023. https://bitterwinter.org/suleymancilar-russia-cracks-down-on-turkish-sufi-organization/.

[66] Erkan Toguslu. "The Turbulence Between AKP and Hizmet. The African Case." Centre for Hizmet Studies. 2017. https://www.hizmetstudies.org/assets/docs/The_Turbulence_between_AKP_and_Hizmet.pdf.

The textbooks promote concepts such as "Turkish World Domination" and the Turkish or Ottoman "Ideal of the World Order," the report said. "Education is a prime pillar in Erdogan's efforts to drape the country in the cloak of Sharia… The Ministry of Education has been pressuring citizens to conform to conservative Islamic practices in public schools," commented Turkey scholar Soner Cagaptay in a forward to the study.[67]

In Gaza, Mehmet Gormez, a one-time Diyanet president, recalled seeing plaques on mosques that read, 'Invaders devour it, but Turkey comes and repairs it,' when he visited the territory as Diyanet president.[68] "Our mosque and its complex will hopefully lead to the revival of the religion, language, history, culture and love that existed in the past between Anatolia and Central Asia," Erdogan said as he inaugurated a mosque in the Kyrgyz capital.[69] Erdogan's strategy proved more successful in Central Asia than the Middle East, where Arab countries once ruled by the Ottoman Empire still see Turkey as an imperial power. Erdogan's Islamist-laced policy and support for the 2011 popular revolts reinforced Arab autocrats' suspicion of Turkey. European governments shared autocrats' misgivings about Turkish religious outreach as Erdogan rolled back democratic freedoms in the wake of mass 2013 anti-government protests and the failed 2016 coup.[70]

Diyanet's 2017–2021 Strategic Plan defined the goal of the mosque-building program as "increase(ing) the Presidency's (Diyanet's) recognition and influence in the international community as a reference institution producing Islamic religious knowledge and religious education."[71] Beyond religious subjects, students at Diyanet mosques are taught Turkish in support of enhancing Turkey's soft power. Islam scholar Mashuq Kurt argued that Diyanet "aims to monopolize Islam and form an imagined Muslim ummah at the service of the Turkish state's political interests."[72] Former US State

---

[67] Hay Eytan Cohen Yanarocak. "The Erdoğan Revolution in the Turkish Curriculum Textbooks." Impact-se. March 2021. https://www.impact-se.org/wp-content/uploads/The-Erdogan-Revolution-in-the-Turkish-CurriculumTextbooks.pdf.

[68] Meltem Özgenç. "Top Cleric Delivers Friday Sermon in Mardin." Hurriyet Daily News. 5 February 2016. https://www.hurriyetdailynews.com/top-cleric-delivers-friday-sermon-in-mardin-94823.

[69] Ozge Ozdemir. "Türkiye yurt dışında nerelerde cami inşa etti, bu camilerin maliyeti ne?" (Where Did Türkiye Build Mosques Abroad and How Much Did These Mosques cost?). BBC News Türkçe. 17 May 2019. https://www.bbc.com/turkce/haberler-turkiye-48294387.

[70] AFP. Europe's Rights Chief Urges Turkey's Erdogan to Respect Law." France 24. 3 September 2020. https://www.france24.com/en/20200903-europe-s-rights-chief-urges-turkey-s-erdogan-to-respect-law.

[71] Diyanet Islerin Baskanligi. "Strateji Plan 2017–2021." Strategic Budget Presidency. 2016, http://www.sp.gov.tr/upload/xSPStratejikPlan/files/wHF4q+diyanet_stratejik-plan-2017-2021.pdf.

[72] Mashuq Kurt. "Allah, Bread, Freedom: Turkey's Muslim Others and Transnational Mosques in Europe." Contemporary Islam, 12 September 2023, https://link.springer.com/article/10.1007/s11562-023-00538-5.

Department advisor and Columbia University human rights scholar David L. Phillips charged that "Turkish financed mosques are not legitimate places of worship. They propagate political Islam as sources of division and proponents of discord... Diyanet is Erdogan's vehicle for spreading political Islam. It is not staffed by imams and religious scholars. Rather, Diyanet is run by bureaucrats and political henchmen."[73]

Many Turkish-built mosques deliver the same state-mandated weekly sermon heard in every city, town, and village in Turkey. In 2017, Diyanet distributed a Friday prayer sermon read in mosques in Germany and elsewhere, highlighting the importance of mosque building in Turkey's religious soft power campaign. It stressed that mosques were not only places of worship but also educational, cultural, and social spaces that reinforced unity and solidarity among the faithful. The sermon asserted that Turkish migrant workers' first endeavour after arriving in Germany in the 1960s was to build mosques in emulation of Prophet Mohammed and his companions.[74] Turkish workers prayed for at least the first decade of their presence in Europe in makeshift mosques in basements, canteens, garages, and railroad cars.[75] They only began building proper mosques in the 1980s when it was evident they had moved to Germany permanently and were unlikely to return to their country of origin.[76]

Turkey's religious soft power drive originated in an effort in the 1970s to cater to the needs of a growing Turkish Diaspora in Europe, largely made up of migrant workers, and counter emerging Kurdish nationalist communities. European governments encouraged the drive. They saw Turkish imams as products of a secular government that would serve as buffers against radicalism, including Turkish Muslim groups considered militants by Turkey's Kemalist political elite. Moreover, European leaders believed Turkish imams would shield their countries from the influence of clerics trained in Saudi Arabia and other Arab countries who propagated more rigid interpretations of Islam. Turkish officials capitalised on European perceptions. "Asked what Islam and Sharia mean to him, a man from Saudi Arabia will repeat: having a thief's hand cut off. Asked what Islam and Muslimdom represent for him,

---

[73] David L. Phillips. "Turkish-Financed Mosques Are Embassies of Political Islam." Politurco. 1 October 2018. https://politurco.com/turkish-financed-mosques-are-embassies-of-political-islam.html.

[74] Diyanet Işleri Türk İslam Birliği Hutbe Komisyonu, "Masjids and Mosques: The Houses of Mercy (Mescit ve Camiler: Rahmân'ın Evleri)." 29 September 2017. https://ditib.de/detail_predigt2.php?id=372&lang=en.

[75] Elisabeth Becker. "Good Mosque, Bad Mosque: Boundaries to Belonging in Contemporary Germany." Journal of the American Academy of Religion, Vol. 85, Issue 4. December 2017, pp. 1050–1088.

[76] 2 Ossama Hegazy, "Towards a German Mosque: Rethinking the Mosque's Meaning in Germany by Applying Socio-Semiotics." In Erkan Toguslu (ed.) Everyday Life Practices of Muslims in Europe. Leuven: Leuven University Press. 2015, p. 204.

a Turk will answer: sincerity and moral conduct," noted former Diyanet President Ali Bardakoglu.[77]

Turkey's Islam branding as Anatolian rather than Turkish appealed to Europeans. Anatolian Islam was rooted in the Maturidi school of theology that rejects the superiority of religious sciences over natural sciences, the Hanafi legal school defined by its flexibility and ability to address a wide range of problems across ages and cultures, and Sufi traditions that embrace tolerance.[78] Men like former Prime Minister and President Turgut Ozal, who in the 1980s and early 1990s put Turkey on a path towards an export-driven free market economy; Necmettin Erbakan, an anti-Western Islamist prime minister in the 1990s who was forced to resign by the military; and Erdogan were close to the Naqshbandi Sufi brotherhood that is widely seen as the cradle of political Islam in Turkey.[79]

The Turkish religious soft power effort was further aided by the appointment of religious affairs officials in Turkish consulates in the late 1970s and the creation of a foreign affairs department within Diyanet in 1984. Following the failed coup, religious attaches, concerned about the influence of Gulen followers, started limiting mosque volunteers' activities and imposing their will on affiliates of the Diyanet-controlled Turkish-Islamic Union for Religious Affairs (DITIB), one of the largest Islamic organisations in Germany. "The attaches were ordered by Ankara to closely monitor mosques and restrict the activities of those who were not DITIB staff or imams paid by the government," said a volunteer who migrated to a mosque that was not Turkish-controlled.[80]

Diyanet's international footprint expanded with the 1989 demise of the Soviet Union and the independence of Turkic republics in Central Asia and the Caucasus, which had been cut off from contact with the Muslim world for some 70 years. Underlining Diyanet's growing role, Erdogan boosted the department's status by ranking its head in state protocol above that of many cabinet ministers.[81] Meanwhile, Diyanet's budget has increased twentyfold

---

[77] Günter Seufert. "Religion: Nation-Building Instrument of the State or Factor of Civil Society? The AKP Between State- and Society-Centered Religious Politics." In Hans-Lukas Kieser, Turkey Beyond Nationalism. Towards Post-Nationalist Identities. London: I.B. Tauris. 2006, Kindle Edition.

[78] Iulia-Alexandra Oprea. "An Assessment of DİTİB's Role in the Prevention of Violent Radicalization." German Institute for International and Security Affairs. 1 June 2020. https://www.swp-berlin.org/fileadmin/contents/products/arbeitspapiere/CATS_Working_Paper_Nr.1__Iulia_Alexandra_Oprea.pdf.

[79] Angel Rabasa and F. Stephen Larrabee. "The Rise of Political Islam in Turkey." Rand Corporation. 2008. https://www.rand.org/pubs/monographs/MG726.html.

[80] Interview with the author. 21 January 2019.

[81] Hurriyet Daily News. "Turkish PM Seeks Restitution of Top Religious Body's 'Honor.'" 5 September 2014. https://www.hurriyetdailynews.com/turkish-pm-seeks-restitution-of-top-religious-bodys-honor--71328.

since Erdogan first became prime minister in 2002.[82] The budget exceeded that of eight of the government's 16 ministries, including home and foreign affairs, energy, agriculture, the environment, and tourism.[83] Following in the footsteps of Saudi Arabia, the department had by 2019 distributed globally eight million Qur'ans translated into 23 languages.[84]

Similarly, like Saudi Arabia, where Crown Prince Mohammed bin Salman reduced the religious establishment to parrot-like endorsers of government policy, Diyanet ensured its fatwas supported Turkish government policies and socially conservative views popular in Erdogan's AKP party.[85] Diyanet rails against contraception, calls abortion 'murder,' advises couples not to hold hands before marriage, condemns tattoos as sinful, discourages men from wearing jewellery, claims illegal downloading on the Internet is against Islam, and charges that having a pet pooch is un-Islamic because the Prophet Muhammad said angels will not enter a house where there is a dog. The authority initially endorsed girls' marriage and pregnancy at nine years of age but subsequently raised the age limit online to 17. In response to a question, Diyanet refrained from banning intimate relations between father and daughter.[86]

Turkey, alongside Qatari and Emirati religious soft power and aid efforts, gained importance as Saudi Arabia, under Bin Salman's leadership, retreated from religiously packaged foreign funding activity.[87] With a staff exceeding

---

[82] Serkan Talan. "The Budget of the Religious Affairs Directorate Has Increased by 2 Thousand 90 Percent!" (Kaynak Yeniçağ: Diyanet İşler Başkanlığı'nın bütçesi yüzde 2 bin 90 arttı!). Yenicag. 15 January 2020. https://www.yeniCaggazetesi.com.tr/diyanet-isler-baskanliginin-butcesi-yuzde-2-bin-90-artti-264325h.htm.

[83] BirGun. "Diyanet's 2020 Budget Surpasses Eight Ministries (Diyanet' in 2020 bütçesi sekiz bakanlığı geride bıraktı). 24 October 2019. https://www.birgun.net/haber/diyanet-in-2020-butcesi-sekiz-bakanligi-geride-birakti-273683.

[84] Ozan Cepni. "They Printed More Books Than Students (Öğrenciden fazla kitap bastılar)." Cumhuriyet. 30 July 2019. https://cumhuriyet.com.tr/haber/ogrenciden-fazla-kitap-bastilar-1512276.

[85] DemokratHaber., "İhsan Eliaçık: Diyanet Legitimizes the Actions of the State (İhsan Eliaçık: Diyanet devletin icraatlarını meşrulaştırıyor)." 3 March 2020. https://www.demokrathaber.org/guncel/ihsan-eliacik-diyanet-devletin-icraatlarini-mesrulastiriyor-h125271.html.

[86] MEMRI. "Turkey's Religious Affairs Ministry, Authority Over Hagia Sophia Mosque and 2,000 Mosques Around The World, Part II—Statements on Women, Children: Girls Are Permitted to Marry, Become Pregnant at Age Nine; If 'A Father Lustfully Kisses His Daughter or Lustfully Hugs Her, the Mother... Becomes Forbidden' to Him; 'If He Beats You... Say: 'I Will Do Whatever You Like'." Special Dispatch 8882. 7 August 2020. https://www.memri.org/reports/turkeys-religious-affairs-ministry-authority-over-hagia-sophia-mosque-and-2000-mosques-0.

[87] Jonathan Benthall. "The Rise and Decline of Saudi Overseas Humanitarian Charities." Georgetown University Qatar. 2018. https://repository.library.georgetown.edu/bitstream/handle/10822/1051628/CIRSOccasionalPaper20JonathanBenthall2018.pdf?sequence=1&isAllowed=y.

100,000, Diyanet reported that it had organised more than 200,000 symposiums, conferences, panels, and meetings across the globe, including the first African Muslim summit. At the third such gathering in 2019, Erdogan charged that Christian missionaries were changing Africa's demographics and converting African Muslims under the protection of Western powers. "Although only seven percent of the African population was Christian in the early 1900s, today Christians constitute 55 percent of the continental population. ... Muslims have become minorities in many African countries," Erdogan asserted.[88]

Targeting Pakistani and Indian Muslims, Erdogan established the South Asia Strategic Research Center (GASAM) headed by Ali Sahin, an AKP member of parliament and former deputy minister who studied in Pakistan. GASAM invites South Asian Muslim clerics, politicians, and community leaders to conferences in Turkey that build on historic Indian Muslim support for the Ottoman Caliphate. The meetings regularly feature Yunus Husaini, a son of militant pro-Erdogan Indian Muslim preacher Salman Nadwi, who studied at Istanbul's Fatih Sultan Mehmet Vakfi University. Turkish-Indian Muslim relations date to the nineteenth century when the Ottomans gave shelter to Indian Muslims fleeing British persecution in the wake of the 1857 revolt against colonial rule. Supported by Mahatma Gandhi, the leader of the Indian independence campaign, Indian Muslims launched the popular Khilafat movement in the early twentieth century to defend the Ottoman Caliphate against dismemberment by the British.[89]

Diyanet further reported in 2013 that it had sent eighty delegations to Muslim-majority countries or countries with significant Muslim minorities, initiated joint projects with more than 70 countries, and enrolled 3,700 students in Qur'anic courses, Imam Hatip schools, and Islam-related postgraduate programs in Turkey. In 2020, Diyanet reported that 15,531 students had enrolled in 25 overseas Imam Hatip schools in Azerbaijan, Kazakhstan, Kyrgyzstan, Romania, Bulgaria, Somalia, Malaysia, Bangladesh, Haiti, North Cyprus, Mongolia, Palestine, Georgia, and Pakistan.[90]

In addition, the education ministry donated staff educational materials for local religious schools in Russia and Greece. Convened by Diyanet, a summit of African Muslim religious leaders concluded that "educational institutions

---

[88] Nordic Monitor. "Turkey's Politicized Religious Authority Diyanet Expands Its Activities with More Cash and Manpower Amid Economic Crisis." 28 August 2020. https://www.nordicmonitor.com/2020/08/turkeys-state-religious-body-diyanet-continues-growing/.

[89] Abhinav Pandya. "Caliph Erdogan? Why Turkey's President Is Quietly Courting Indian Muslims." Haaretz. 27 December 2018. https://www.haaretz.com/middle-east-news/2018-12-27/ty-article-opinion/.premium/is-turkeys-erdogan-quietly-courting-indian-muslims-to-crown-him-caliph/0000017f-f2b9-d223-a97f-fffda8230000.

[90] Diyanet Burslari. "International Imam Hatip School Scholarship Program." January 2020. https://diyanetburslari.tdv.org/wp-content/uploads/2020/01/%C4%B0HL-Ba%C5%9Fvuru-K%C4%B1lavuzu-2020-ENG.pdf.

similar to the Imam Hatip schools in Turkey should be used as an example for schools in Africa and backed with faculties providing higher religious education like (Turkey's) theology faculties."[91] Some European countries, including France and Austria, thwarted the opening of Imam Hatip schools in cities like Strasbourg and Vienna. Turkey created the Imam Hatip school system, designed to train preachers, in 1951 to replace madrassas banned by the government.

A product of Turkey's first state-run Imam Hatip school, Erdogan expected the religious education system to produce "a pious generation that will work for the construction of a new civilisation." The Turkish leader pumped billions of dollars into the education system that excludes Charles Darwin's evolution theory from science lessons. In 2006, a glossy, 768-page, easy-to-read "Atlas of Creation" found its way into school libraries. On some 500 pages, it featured images comparing fossils with present-day animals to argue that Allah created all life as it is and evolution never happened. Advocating the principle of 'survival of the fittest,' the book asserted that evolution was the root of terrorism and had sprouted un-Islamic and destructive doctrines such as racism, Nazism, and communism.[92] Adnan Oktar, aka Harun Yahya, a cult leader, preacher, creationist, conspiracy theorist, and pamphleteer, authored the Atlas. Oktar was sentenced in 2022 to 8,658 years in prison for heading a criminal gang, espionage, and sexual abuse of minors.[93] A local Istanbul authority released in 2012 a series of books for primary schoolchildren, falsely asserting that Charles Darwin was a Jew, who "had two problems: first he was a Jew; second, he hated his prominent forehead, big nose, and misshapen teeth." The book claimed that Darwin preferred feeding monkeys nuts rather than going to school.[94]

Erdogan's boosting of the Imam Hatip schools, at times at the expense of providing other services, was an investment that has yet to yield sustainable results. A mere 18 per cent of applicants from Imam Hatip schools secured a place in a full degree universities in 2017, compared to 35 per cent from regular state schools and 45 per cent from private ones.[95] Bulut

---

[91] Hurriyet. Daily News. "Africa Seeks Turkish Islamic Education." 25 November 2011. https://www.hurriyetdailynews.com/africa-seeks-turkish-islamic-education-7725.

[92] Tom Heneghan. "Creation vs. Darwin Takes Muslim Twist in Turkey." Reuters. 10 August 2007. https://www.reuters.com/article/us-religion-turkey-evolution-idUSL0926554120061122/.

[93] Al Jazeera. "Turkish 'Cult Leader' Oktar Sentenced to 8,658 Years in Prison." 17 November 2022. https://www.aljazeera.com/news/2022/11/17/turkey-court-sentences-tv-preacher-to-8658-years-in-prison.

[94] Daniel Dombey and Funja Guler. "Turkish Book on Darwin Sparks Outrage." Financial Times. 19 October 2012. https://www.ft.com/content/f27adba8-1a01-11e2-a179-00144feabdc0.

[95] Daren Butler. "With More Islamic Schooling, Erdogan Aims to Reshape Turkey." Reuters. 25 January 2018. https://www.reuters.com/investigates/special-report/turkey-erdogan-education/.

Can Okuducu, an opposition politician for the secular Republican People's Party founded by Ataturk, complained his Istanbul Umraniye neighbourhood had three Imam Hatip schools 200 metres from each other but no kindergarten. He said one of the schools had been opened despite a petition signed by 5,000 people demanding that the building be used for what it was intended, a kindergarten.[96]

Turkish Diaspora opposition groups, Kurds, and Western governments challenged Erdogan's religious soft power campaign. Thousands of supporters and opponents of Erdogan took to the streets of Cologne in 2018 as he inaugurated DITIB's new central mosque, the largest in the country.[97] The German government stopped funding DITIB a month before the inauguration even though the group packages Turkey's religious soft power diplomacy in terms of countering extremism.[98] Even so, Germany's intelligence service, the Federal Office for the Protection of the Constitution, classified DITIB as a nationalist rather than a religious organisation.[99]

Turkish support of foreign mosques and state-backed organisations like DITIB, which operates some 900 of the country's 2,600 mosques, and the Diyanet Foundation of The Netherlands, which controls 147 Muslim houses of worship, has sparked controversy and investigations by law enforcement and intelligence services. DITIB was founded in 1984 when Diyanet created a foreign affairs department.

DITIB, whose imams are trained in Turkey, classified as Turkish civil servants, and paid by Turkish consulates, admitted in 2018 that some of its clerics spied on behalf of the Turkish government.[100] Turkey recalled in 2016 Yusuf Acar, the religious affairs attaché at its embassy in The Hague, after Dutch authorities accused him of gathering intelligence on alleged followers of Gulen, the exiled preacher charged by Erdogan with attempting to remove him from office. Belgian authorities rejected the visa applications of 12 Turkish imams seeking to work in the country on suspicion that they would operate as government agents rather than clerics.[101] France closed in

---

[96] Bulut Can Okuducu. Twitter. 19 September 2021. https://twitter.com/bulutcanokuducu/status/1439611847230083077.

[97] Al Jazeera. "Erdogan Opens Huge Mosque in Germany Amid Rival Rallies." 30 September 2018. https://www.aljazeera.com/news/2018/09/erdogan-opens-huge-mosque-germany-rival-rallies-180930074443295.html.

[98] Deutsche Welle. "Germany Cuts Funding to Largest Turkish-Islamic Organization, DITIB." 30 August 2018. https://www.dw.com/en/germany-cuts-funding-to-largest-turkish-islamic-organization-ditib/a-45297763.

[99] Domradio.de. "They Are Nationalists (Das Sind Natonalisten)." 8 November 2018. https://www.domradio.de/themen/islam-und-kirche/2018-11-08/verfassungsschutz-zur-tuerkisch-islamischen-ditib.

[100] Chase Winter. "Turkish Islamic Organization DITIB Admits Preachers Spied in Germany." Deutsche Welle. 12 January 2017. https://www.dw.com/en/turkish-islamic-organization-ditib-admits-preachers-spied-in-germany/a-37106126.

[101] Ibid. Nordic Monitor.

2020 Diyanet-related groups' bank accounts as part of President Emmanuel Macron's campaign against political Islam.[102]

Much like the UAE's blending of hard power with religious soft power in Libya where the Gulf state backed a rebel military force whose backbone were Salafist militants, Erdogan harnessed the Diyanet to legitimise his military escapades in Syria, Libya, and Iraq.[103] DITIB mosques were instructed to pray for the success of Turkey's military intervention in Syria, prompting allegations that the group violated German law. The religious affairs directorate regularly ordered imams to recite a Qur'anic verse, Sura Al-Fath or the Verse of the Conquest, to legitimise the Turkish president's foreign adventures. The sura conveys a message of victory and conquest for Muslims and the favour God conferred upon the Prophet Mohammed and his followers. It promises increased numbers of monotheists as well as forgiveness of mistakes by those who do jihad on the path of God.

Mosques and the dispatch of Diyanet personnel who serve as imams, religious counsellors, and political commissars were a pillar of a multi-pronged soft power strategy that included development and humanitarian aid, infrastructure funding and building, Turkish private sector investment, and university openings. Religious soft power, coupled with aid, served Turkey well in its bid to project power. Perhaps nowhere more so than in Somalia, where US$1 billion in aid channelled through Diyanet and other NGOs funded the building of the Recep Tayyip Erdogan Hospital in the capital, Mogadishu,[104] and facilitated the establishment of Turkey's foremost foreign military base.[105] The price tag attached to Turkish largesse often persuaded beneficiaries to hand over schools operated by Gulen, the exiled preacher. It also included the extradition of suspected Gulen followers and looking the other way when Turkish intelligence agents kidnapped alleged followers of the preacher and returned them to Turkey.[106]

Turkey's quest for soft power kicked into high gear in the wake of the failed coup, with Erdogan defining Turkish identity as essentially Ottoman. It is an identity built on a nationalist spin already woven into the fabric of Turkish

[102] Daily Sabah. "France Shuts Diyanet's Bank Accounts." 20 February 2020. https://www.dailysabah.com/politics/2020/02/20/france-shuts-diyanets-bank-accounts.

[103] Hurriyet Daily News. "Conquest' Prayers Performed Across Turkey's Mosques for Afrin Operation." 21 June 2018. https://www.hurriyetdailynews.com/conquest-prayers-performed-across-turkeys-mosques-for-afrin-operation-126072.

[104] Pınar Akpınar. "From Benign Donor to Self-Assured Security Provider: Turkey's Policy in Somalia." Istanbul Policy Center, IPC Policy Brief. 3 December 2017, https://www.researchgate.net/publication/323219525_From_Benign_Donor_to_Self-Assured_Security_Provider_Turkey's_Policy_in_Somalia.

[105] Ash Rossiter and Brendon J. Cannon. "Re-examining the 'Base': The Political and Security Dimensions of Turkey's Military Presence in Somalia." Insight Turkey. Vol. 21, Issue 1. Winter 2019.

[106] Die Morina. "Kosovo Minister and Spy Chief Sacked Over Turkish Arrests." Politico. 30 March 2018. https://balkaninsight.com/2018/03/30/kosovo-intelligence-director-and-internal-minister-dismissed-over-turkish-arrested-men-03-30-2018/.

education under successive Kemalist governments. Journalist Burak Bekdil recalled being instructed in school in the 1970s that "our textbooks taught us that the supreme Turkish race dominated the entire world for centuries; that the Ottoman Empire collapsed only after a coalition of world powers attacked it; that we lost World War Two because we had allied with the Germans, who were defeated (not us); and that one day, we will make the entire planet Turkish. We were taught that an Ottoman warrior could keep on fighting even after having been beheaded by the (Byzantine) enemy."[107]

Erdogan's Turkish identity obliged Turkey to defend Muslims, starting with the 45 modern-day states that once were Ottoman territory. Erdogan supported Palestinian nationalist aspirations and groups like Hamas, the Islamist group that controlled the Gaza Strip, as well as the independence of Kosovo because they were majority Muslim entities. The faithful at the Al-Aqsa Mosque in Jerusalem, Islam's third most holy site, frequently display portraits of Erdogan as they perform Friday prayers under a gleaming gold crescent on the Dome of the Rock which was funded by Turkey.

Erdogan is not the first Turkish leader to root Turkey's Islamic identity in its Ottoman past. So did former President Ozal, whose liberal economic policy helped Turkey capitalise on the emergence of independent post-Soviet Turkic states in the Caucasus and Central Asia and encouraged Turkish investment in the Middle East and North Africa while simultaneously emphasising the country's ties to the West. Erdogan went further than Ozal by breaking with Turkey's Kemalist past and projecting Islam not only as a religion but also as a foundational civilisation in Turkish education and social life as well as globally. If Ozal, a former World Banker, was the more cosmopolitan expression of Turkish Islamism, Erdoğan veered towards its more exclusivist, anti-Western bent. Ozal embraced Westernisation as empowering Turkey. Erdogan rejected it believing that Westernisation deprived the state of its religious legitimacy, ruptured historical continuity, and produced a shallow identity. It is a strategy that has paid dividends. Erdogan emerged as the most trusted regional leader in a 2017 poll that surveyed public opinion in 12 Middle Eastern countries. Forty per cent of respondents also recognised Erdogan as a religious authority even though he was not an Islamic scholar.[108] The Islam Erdogan promoted shared a foundational principle with Kemalism and proponents of an autocratic version of moderate Islam that is subjugated by and integrated into the state bureaucracy rather than a faith that is adopted voluntarily and evolves independently.

[107] Burk Bekdil. "Give War a Chance: Turkish Leader Finesses Political Defeat." The Begin-Sadat Center for Strategic Studies. 30 July 2021. https://besacenter.org/give-war-a-chance-turkish-leader-finesses-political-defeat/.

[108] Yusuf Sarfatip. "Religious Authority in Turkey: Hegemony and Resistance." Baker Institute for Public Policy, Rice University. March 2019. https://www.bakerinstitute.org/media/files/files/c873dd82/cme-pub-luce-sarfati-031119.pdf.

Similarly, the irony of Erdogan's fallout with Gulen was that both Gulen and Erdogan were nurtured in Saudi-backed organisations associated with the Muslim Brotherhood. Gulen played a key role in the 1960s in the founding of the Erzurum branch of the Associations for the Struggle against Communism, an Islamist-leaning Cold War Turkish group that had ties to Saudi Arabia.[109] Erdogan, former President Abdullah Gul, and former parliament speaker Ibrahim Karatas, among many others, were formed in nationalist and Islamic politics in their days as members of the Turkish National Students Union, which represented the Muslim World League in Turkey. Prominent assassinated journalist Ugur Mumcu mapped connections between Erdogan and his inner circle with Saudi Arabia in a book first published in 1987.[110]

Turkey has a leg up on its competitors in the Balkans, Central Asia, and Europe. Centuries of Ottoman rule, as well as voluntary and forced migration, have spawned close ethnic and family ties. Millions of Turks pride themselves on their Balkan roots. The names of Istanbul neighbourhoods, parks, and forests reflect the Balkans' Ottoman history. Central Asians identify as Turkic, speak Turkic languages, and share cultural attributes and culinary delights with Turks. In Europe, Turkish operatives often enjoy the goodwill of large, well-integrated Diaspora communities, even if the fault lines run deep between Turks and Kurds opposed to the Turkish government's repression of Kurdish political aspirations.

Turkey's Achilles heel may be that the Ottoman-style Islam it projects is based on a misreading of the empire's history. In a twist of irony, Erdogan embraced a Kemalist vision of the Ottomans as a religiously driven empire rather than one that perceived itself as both Muslim and European, pragmatic and not averse to aspects of secularism. That misreading has produced, in the words of Turkey scholar Soner Cagaptay, "an ahistorical, political Islam-oriented, and often patronising foreign policy concoction" and has informed Turkey's religious soft power strategy.[111]

It also fuels the grandness of its associated architecture, including the Camlica Mosque, the largest in Turkey with six minarets, and Erdogan's purpose-built US$615 million presidential complex in Ankara. The mosque and the presidential complex denoted Erdogan's ambitions and sense of grandeur. Erdogan's sponsorship of the mosque emulated Ottoman sultans who sought a legacy in grandiose mosque construction. The presidential complex, a mesh of Ottoman architecture inspired by the Ottoman-era Dolmabahce and Topkapi palaces and giant columns favoured by 20th-century

---

[109] Ertuğrul Meşe. "Komünizmle Mücadele Dernekleri." İstanbul: İletişim. 2016. pp. 134–135.

[110] Uğur Mumcu. "Rabıta." Ankara: UMAG. 2014. p. 199.

[111] Soner Cagaptay. "Erdogan's Empire." London: I.B. Tauris. 2020 p. 54.

European autocrats, includes a mosque that can accommodate 4,000 worshippers. A video clip of the palace, seemingly posted online with Erdogan's endorsement, associated the complex with Turkey's Ottoman past by adding martial drumming and brass instruments to its rendition of Turkey's national anthem.[112]

---

[112] Erdoğan Gönüllüleri. "AK-Saray'ın Tanıtım Filmi." YouTube. 30 October 2014. https://www.youtube.com/watch?v=ouCnd73OaeE.

CHAPTER 7

Trouble Brews in Islam's Backyard

Little did Elianu Hia know that a video he posted on Facebook in early 2021 would shape Indonesian policy and turn his life upside down. A Christian in the world's largest Muslim-majority nation and democracy, Hia objected to vocational school authorities in the West Sumatran city of Padang, obliging his daughter to wear a hijab. In a secretly taped video, his daughter's teacher insisted that wearing a hijab was mandatory. The teacher demanded that Hia put his daughter's refusal in writing, which would have created a first step to expelling her. The video went viral.[1]

In response, Indonesian Religious Affairs Minister Yaqut Cholil Qoumas and his home affairs and education counterparts threatened to sanction state schools seeking to impose religious garb violating government rules and regulations. "Religions do not promote conflict, neither do they justify acting unfairly against those who are different," said Qoumas, a leader of Nahdlatul Ulama, the world's largest Muslim civil society movement and foremost advocate of theological reform in line with the Universal Declaration of Human Rights.[2] The school complied. Over the last two years, the number of Christian girls who shed the hijab has grown.

---

[1] Andreas Harsono. "Forced from Home for Protesting Indonesia's Mandatory Hijab Rules." Human Rights Watch. 17 March 2023. https://www.hrw.org/news/2023/03/17/forced-home-protesting-indonesias-mandatory-hijab-rules.

[2] James M. Dorsey. "Battle for the Soul of Islam.'" Horizons. Winter 2021. https://www.cirsd.org/en/horizons/horizons-winter-2021-issue-no-18/battle-for-the-soul-of-islam.

But at the same time, Hia received threatening messages on Facebook and WhatsApp. "I lost count," he said. "Hundreds of them." Hia's air conditioning business lost customers. "Some customers asked me whether I was the one who was protesting the mandatory hijab rule. And they stopped requesting my services," Hia said. Struggling to repay a bank loan, he fired five employees and sold his truck and minibus. Almost two years later, Hia and his wife decided to sell their house while waiting for their daughter to finish high school. "I cannot earn enough money now. We have to move out of West Sumatra," he said.

Hia's story pinpointed primary and secondary schools as one frontline in the battle for the soul of Islam and the struggle to define the boundaries of religious expression and behaviour. The Indonesian government's response contrasted starkly with Egyptian schoolgirls' experience. Mada Masr, Egypt's foremost independent news outlet, documented how, in 2020, Egyptian schoolgirls who refused to wear a hijab were coerced and publicly shamed in the knowledge that the education ministry would not enforce its policy of mandating the wearing of a headdress. "The model, decent girl is expected to dress modestly and wear a hijab to signal her pride in her religious identity since hijab is what distinguishes her from a Christian girl," said Lamia Lotfy, a gender consultant and rights activist. Teachers at public high schools said they were reluctant to take boys to task for violating dress codes because they were more likely to push back and create problems.[3]

Hia's experience and Mada Masr's disclosure tell the story of changes in youth attitudes towards religion and religiosity across large chunks of the Muslim world that often resemble a seesaw with conservatism on the one side, and more critical, individualistic attitudes on the other. Hia's story speaks to a broad trend towards less tolerant, more conservative religious outlooks, or in some cases, more militant interpretations of Islam, deism, a belief in a God that does not intervene in the universe and that is not defined by organised religion, and atheism. All in all, the changes in attitude run the gamut from quests for more personal understandings of religion, scepticism towards religious and temporal authority, and demands for religious reform to support for greater public adherence to religious mores and clerics who legitimise autocratic rule. They are often driven by discontent with autocratic intolerance, repression of dissent, failure to deliver public services and goods, and/or corruption.

"This generation of Arabs grew up in the midst of a far-reaching civilisational upheaval with access to increasingly advanced technologies… Consequently, the religious cultural heritage of Muslim Arabs, which was formulated in the 7th Century, lost its relevance to them, leading them to live in a state of confusion as they constantly contrast between what they were taught at home and current enlightenment and knowledge… They hold on to their religion,

---

[3] Nada Gamal. "'Cut It, Dye It, Cover It': How Schools Control Girls' Hair." Mada Masr. 1 February 2021. https://www.madamasr.com/en/2021/02/01/feature/society/cut-it-dye-it-cover-it-how-schools-control-girls-hair/.

unable to pinpoint the problem areas they know exist. We see them hesitate at times and push for reform at others," said civil engineer and Islam scholar Mohammed Shahrour.[4]

Taking as a case study post-autocracy -pre civil war Sudan, a year after mass protests ended Islamist President Omar al-Bashir's 26 years in office, Michael Robbins, director and co-principal investigator of Arab Barometer, a group that regularly surveys public opinion in the Middle East, and international affairs scholar Lawrence Rubin, illustrated in a 2020 Washington Post op-ed the fragility of public support for a separation of religion and state. As the post-revolt government declared a separation and ended the ban on apostasy and alcohol consumption by non-Muslims, and prohibited corporal punishment, including public flogging, Robbins and Rubin noted that 61% of those they surveyed on the eve of the uprising believed that Sudanese law should be based on Sharia. Two-thirds of their respondents believed Sharia would guarantee provision of essential services and eradicate corruption. At the same time, Robbins and Rubin concluded that Sudanese youth favoured a reduced role for religious leaders in political life. They said the youth had soured on the idea of religion-based governance because of widespread corruption in the region of Al-Bashir, who professed his adherence to religious principles.

"If the transitional government can deliver on providing basic services to the country's citizens and tackling corruption, the formal shift away from Sharia is likely to be acceptable in the eyes of the public. However, if these problems remain, a new set of religious leaders may be able to galvanize a movement aimed at reinstituting Sharia as a means to achieve these objectives," Robbins and Rubin warned.[5]

Writing at the outset of the revolt, Islam scholar and former Sudanese diplomat Abdelwahab El-Affendi noted that "for most Sudanese, Islamism came to signify corruption, hypocrisy, cruelty, and bad faith. Sudan is perhaps the first genuinely anti-Islamist country in popular terms. But being anti-Islamist in Sudan does not mean being secular."[6]

The Muslim world's clinging to religious precepts was mirrored in European minority communities. A 2018 report by the Dutch government's Social and Cultural Planning Bureau noted that the number of Muslims of Turkish and Moroccan descent who strictly observe traditional religious precepts had

---

[4] Mohammad Shahrour. "Opinion: Arab Youth Struggle with Religious Values and Institutions Trapped in the Past." Arabian Business. 30 April 2019. https://www.arabianbusiness.com/politics-economics/419026-opinion-arab-youth-struggle-with-religious-values-institutions-trapped-in-the-past.

[5] Michael Robbins and Lawrence Rubin. "Islamic Law Has Long been the Basis of Law in Sudan." The Washington Post. 27 August 2020. https://www.washingtonpost.com/politics/2020/08/27/sudans-government-seems-be-shifting-away-sharia-law-not-everyone-supports-these-moves/.

[6] Abdelwahab El-Affendi. "Sudan Protests: How Did We Get Here?" Al Jazeera. 28 December 2018. https://www.aljazeera.com/opinions/2018/12/28/sudan-protests-how-did-we-get-here.

increased by approximately eight per cent. Dutch citizens of Turkish and Moroccan descent account for two-thirds of the country's Muslim community. The report suggested that in a pluralistic society in which Muslims are a minority, "the more personal, individualistic search for true Islam can lead to youth becoming more strict in observance than their parents or environment ever were."[7]

For clerics in Muslim-majority countries, the shift is tricky. The clerics are on thin ground. They offer religious cover for far-reaching social reforms like those enacted by Saudi Crown Prince Mohammed bin Salman that are exclusively anchored in civil rather than Islamic law. They also legitimise brutal political repression that accompanies the social reforms of men like Bin Salman and UAE President Mohammed bin Zayed. Since coming to office, Bin Salman has curbed the mandate of the religious police, lifted a ban on women's driving, enhanced women's professional opportunities and social rights, loosened restrictions on gender mixing, and kick-started a Western-style entertainment industry. Bin Zayed decreed a major overhaul of his country's Islamic personal laws, allowing unmarried couples to cohabitate, loosening alcohol restrictions, and criminalising 'honour killings' that punish with death a woman for behaviour that allegedly tarnishes a family's reputation.

The popularity of Bin Salman's social reforms and multiple public opinion polls indicate a reduced willingness among Muslim youth to accept ritualistic forms of Islam that have long been upheld by governments of various Muslim-majority countries with the support of state-controlled conservative and ultra-conservative Islamic scholars. The polls suggest that Muslim youth could be receptive to a reconceptualisation of religious precepts frozen in time. A 2019 survey of Arab youth showed that two-thirds of those polled felt that religion played too large a role in their lives, up from 50% four years earlier. Seventy-nine per cent argued that religious institutions needed to be reformed, while half said that religious values hold the Arab world back.[8]

Arab Barometer surveys over the last decade revealed that a growing number of youths were turning their backs on religion.[9] Similarly, polls conducted by Middle East scholar David Pollock over the last decade suggested that a significant number of Saudis would endorse a more contemporary interpretation of Islam. Asked in 2015 and again in 2017 what they thought of the statement that Saudis "should listen to those among us who propose interpreting Islam in a more moderate, tolerant, and modern way,"

---

[7] Willem Huijnk. "De religieuze Beleving Van Moslims in Nederland (The Religious Experience of Muslims in the Netherlands)." Sociaal en Cultureel Planbureau. 7 June 2018. https://www.scp.nl/publicaties/publicaties/2018/06/07/de-religieuze-beleving-van-moslims-in-nederland.

[8] asda'abcw. 2010. 11th "Annual asda'abcw Arab Youth Survey 2019." https://www.arabyouthsurvey.com/index.html.

[9] Arab Barometer. https://www.arabbarometer.org/survey-data/.

Pollock noted that the number of respondents who agreed had doubled in the two years between the surveys from 15% to 30%.[10]

The various polls contrast starkly with attitudes expressed in a survey of the world's Muslims conducted several years earlier by the Pew Research Center. Pew's polling in 2013 suggested that ultra-conservative attitudes promoted by Saudi Arabia, the UAE, and Qatar legitimised authoritarian and autocratic regimes. More than 70% of those surveyed in South Asia, Southeast Asia, the Middle East, and North Africa favoured making Sharia the law of the land and granting Sharia courts jurisdiction over family law and property disputes. However, those numbers varied broadly when respondents were asked about specific issues like apostasy and corporal punishment. Three-quarters of South Asians favoured the death sentence for apostasy as opposed to 56% in the Middle East and only 27% in Southeast Asia, while 81% in South Asia supported physical punishment compared to 57% in the Middle East and North Africa and 46% in Southeast Asia.[11]

Changing attitudes towards religion coupled with rejection by anti-government protesters in Lebanon and Iraq of sectarianism propagated by politicians as well as Sunni and Shiite Muslim clerics led to calls for a separation of religion and state in countries as different as Saudi Arabia and Sudan. Saudi columnist Wafa al-Rashid sparked a fiery debate on social media after calling in a local newspaper for a secular state in the kingdom. "How long will we continue to shy away from enlightenment and change? Religious enlightenment, which is in line with reality and the thinking of youth, who rebelled and withdrew from us because we are no longer like them… We no longer speak their language or understand their dreams," Al-Rashid wrote.[12]

"People are sick and tired of organized religion and being told what to do. That is true for all Gulf states and the rest of the Arab world," added a Saudi businessman.[13] Social scientist Ellen van de Bovenkamp described Moroccans she interviewed for her Ph.D. thesis as living "a personalized, self-made religiosity, in which ethics and politics are more important than rituals."[14]

Bin Salman has sought to fortify his social reforms by balancing religion's place in Saudi identity with a dose of nationalism. He hoped nationalism

---

[10] David Pollock. "New Saudi Views of Jews—and of Israel." The Washington Institute for Near East Policy. 12 September 2018. https://www.washingtoninstitute.org/fikraforum/view/new-saudi-views-of-jewsand-of-israel.

[11] Pew Research Center. "The World's Muslims: Religion, Politics and Society." 30 April 2013. https://www.pewforum.org/2013/04/30/the-worlds-muslims-religion-politics-society-overview/.

[12] Wafa Al-Rashid. "Is the Civil State Not Religious? (الدولة المدنية.. هل لا دينية؟)." Okaz. 14 June 2020. https://www.okaz.com.sa/articles/authors/2028295.

[13] Email exchange with the author. 14 October 2020.

[14] Ellen Van de Bovenkamp. "La popularité de Tariq Ramadan au Maroc." Amsterdam: Vrije Universiteit. Ph.D. Thesis 2017.

would counter a more recent revival of conservatism. The seesaw of greater conservatism and changing attitudes towards religion appeared to swing in Bin Salman's favour when Saudis on social media welcomed in late 2023 a new emphasis on pre-Islamic pagan Arabian deities such as Al-Uzza, one of three major ancient goddesses acknowledged in the Qur'an. Bin Salman positioned the deities as part of preserving the kingdom's history and national heritage.[15]

Even so, a recent swing towards greater conservatism is troubling news for Bin Salman, Bin Zayed, and Nahdlatul Ulama. The group's efforts to reform Islamic law in Indonesia, the world's largest Muslim-majority country and democracy, may encounter greater resistance beyond the group's Javan stronghold. The group's push for religious reform comes as an increasing number of Indonesians want religion to play a bigger role in public life. Just over half, 51% of the respondents in a 2023 survey by Singapore's ISEAS–Yusof Ishak Institute agreed or strongly agreed that Islam should be prioritised. Thirty-seven per cent favoured Islamic scholars playing a greater role in politics, while 33% disagreed.[16]

Moreover, greater conservatism could signal a revival of political Islam after a decade in which groups like the Muslim Brotherhood suffered significant setbacks, particularly in the Middle East. A 2023 Pew Research poll graphically depicts what Nahdlatul Ulama's moderate leadership is up against. It also lays bare contradictions in attitudes towards religiosity in Indonesia and elsewhere in the Muslim world. On the plus side, 82% of Indonesians surveyed described Islam as a religion one chooses to follow. Yet, at the same time, 82% defined the faith as part of their culture, 81% perceived it as a family tradition they were obliged to uphold, and 77% portrayed Islam as an ethnicity they had been born into. Ninety-two per cent rejected the freedom to abandon Islam or convert to another religion. Eighty-six per cent said adhering to Islam was an important element of being an Indonesian. One hundred per cent professed belief in God, and 98% identified religion as a significant part of their lives. Sixty-four per cent believed Sharia should be the law of the land. Fifty-eight per cent wanted religious leaders to publicly endorse politicians and political parties.[17]

---

[15] Middle East Monitor. "Outrage as Saudi Accounts Promote Ancient Arabian Goddesses Amid Attempt to Revive National Heritage." 3 December 2023. https://www.middleeastmonitor.com/20231203-saudi-social-media-accounts-promote-ancient-arabian-goddesses-sparking-religious-outrage-amid-attempts-to-revive-national-heritage/.

[16] Burhanuddin Muhtadi, Hui Yew-Foong and Siwage Dharma Negara. "The Indonesia National Survey Project 2022: Engaging with Developments in the Political, Economic and Social Spheres." Singapore: ISEAS-Yusof Ishak Institute. 2023. https://bookshop.iseas.edu.sg/publication/7841.

[17] Jonathan Evans, Kelsey Jo Starr, Manolo Corichi and William Miner. "Buddhism, Islam and Religious Pluralism in South and Southeast Asia." Pew Research. 12 September 2023. https://www.pewresearch.org/religion/2023/09/12/buddhism-islam-and-religious-pluralism-in-south-and-southeast-asia/.

Islamists, with the Muslim Brotherhood in the forefront, initially emerged as winners from mass anti-government protests in 2011 that toppled autocratic leaders of Tunisia, Egypt, Libya, and Yemen. They won free and fair elections and formed governments but failed to deliver once in power. They also were unprepared for a ruthless UAE-Saudi-led effort to roll back the achievements of the revolts that, like the Islamists, threatened autocratic monarchies in the Gulf. The effort sparked a military coup in Egypt in 2013 that overthrew Mohammed Morsi, a Muslim Brother, and the country's first and only democratically elected president, and contributed to civil wars in Libya, Yemen, and Syria.

"Results from nationally representative public opinion surveys…strongly suggest that political Islam is making a comeback. In most countries surveyed, young and old citizens demonstrate a clear preference for giving religion a greater role in politics. This is the first time that support for political Islam has increased meaningfully…since the Arab Uprisings of 2011," said Robbins, the Arab Barometer director.[18] Like with Hia's story, support for political Islam provides texture for the increased religious conservatism reflected in polling in the Middle East and Southeast Asia.

A survey by New York-based consultancy Wunderman Thompson Intelligence suggested that the trend towards greater religiosity was stronger in Southeast Asia, home to 307 million Muslims who account for almost half of the region's population than in the faith's Arab heartland. Ninety-one per cent of respondents described a strong relationship with Allah as very important. Eighty-four per cent said they prayed five times daily. Thirty-three per cent described themselves as more observant than their parents, 45% said they were just as observant as their parents, and 21% stated that they were less observant.[19]

In a poll conducted at about the same time by UAE-based public relations agency Asda'a BCW,[20] 41% of 3,400 young Arabs in 17 Arab countries aged 18–24 said religion was the most important element of their identity, with nationality, family and/or tribe, Arab heritage, and gender lagging far behind. Similarly, the Arab Barometer reported a stark increase in the number of Muslim youths in several Arab countries that wanted clerics to have greater influence on government decisions. "In 2021–2022, roughly half or more in five of ten countries surveyed agreed that religious clerics should influence decisions of government," Robbins said. "While youth ages 18–29 have led the return to religion across MENA (the Middle East and North Africa), the rise in support for religion in politics is more widespread across society. In

---

[18] Michael Robbins. "A New Dawn for Political Islam?" Arab Barometer. 8 May 2023. https://www.arabbarometer.org/2023/05/a-new-dawn-for-political-islam/.

[19] Wunderman Thompson Intelligence. "The New Muslim Consumer." 21 September 2022. https://www.wundermanthompson.com/insight/the-new-muslim-consumer.

[20] Arab Youth Survey. "Charting a New Course." 14th Annual Asda'a BCW Arab Youth Survey 2022. https://arabyouthsurvey.com/en/findings/?utm_source=substack&utm_medium=email.

most countries, both older and younger members of society are shifting their views in concert."

In the same vein, more than half or 56% of those surveyed by Arab Barometer said their country's legal system should be based on Sharia or Islamic law. Seventy per cent expressed concern about the loss of traditional values and culture. Sixty-five per cent argued that preserving their religious and cultural identity was more important than creating a globalised society. Yet at the same time, incongruously, 73% insisted that religion played too much of a role in the Middle East. That was up from 58% in 2018. In addition, 77% believed Arab religious institutions should be reformed, up from 50% in 2015.

Contradictory attitudes may be part and parcel of attitude swings and a gradual process of change. The contradictions arose in an unpublished 2016 survey[21] of the aspirations of 100 male Saudi 20-year-olds. The survey highlighted the limits of their quest for greater freedom and a more individual religious experience. Some 50% said they wanted to have fun, date, enjoy mixed-gender parties, dress freely, and drive fast cars. The men "wanted social change, but they pulled back when they realised this has consequences for their sisters," said Abdul Al Lily, a Saudi scholar who conducted the survey and authored a book on rules that govern Saudi culture.[22] "People ended up not doing anything when confronted with the idea that someone might want to go on a date with their sister," Al Lily said.

Gulf scholar Eman Alhussein argued that seemingly contradictory attitudes emerging from polls reflect dilemmas facing Arab youth rather than conflicting views about religion. She noted that political Islam, jihadist violence, and the harnessing of religion by the state have shaped youth perceptions. The state's manipulation of religion is "no longer deceptive to the youth who can now see through it," Alhussien said. The state's "current interpretation of religion and the way it influences the legislative system in many Arab countries can depict an outdated reality," she added.[23] The prominence in identity of religion, as opposed to nationality, family, and gender, suggested that increasing conservatism constituted a search for an unaltered form that enables more individual spiritual experiences.

As a result, the stakes in managing shifting attitudes could not be higher. Particularly decisive is likely to be Indonesia's management of the swings. Indonesia represents everything the UAE and Saudi Arabia feared in the 2011

---

[21] James M. Dorsey. "Reformist Saudi Prince Bounces up Against Flawed Education System and Ingrained Social Mores." The Turbulent World with James M. Dorsey. 8 November 2016. https://www.jamesmdorsey.net/post/reformist-saudi-prince-bounces-up-against-flawed-education-system-and-ingrained-social-mores.

[22] Abdul Al Lily. "The Bro Code of Saudi Culture: Describing the Saudi from Head to Toe." CreateSpace Independent Publishing Platform, Amazon, 2018.

[23] Eman Alhussein. "Arab Youth View Religion as Important But Feel Alienated from Its Current Form." In A Voice For Change, 14th Annual Asda'a BCW Arab Youth Survey 2020. http://arabyouthsurvey.com/wp-content/uploads/whitepaper/2020-AYS-whitepaper.pdf.

Arab uprisings. It is a Muslim-majority nation which successfully replaced decades of autocratic rule with democracy in a popular revolt in 1998. Indonesia is "where the removal of constraints imposed by an authoritarian regime has opened up the imaginative terrain, allowing particular types of religious beliefs and practices to emerge… The Indonesian cases study…brings into sharper relief processes that are happening in ordinary Muslim life elsewhere," said Indonesia scholar Nur Amali Ibrahim.[24]

Even so, Indonesian democracy also illustrates the delicate balance between ingrained traditional social and religious norms and greater pluralism, tolerance, and embrace of human rights. Political scientist Ronald F. Inglehart noted in 2019 that "the populations of the 18 Muslim-majority countries for which data are available in the World Values Survey…have stayed…strongly religious and committed to preserving traditional norms concerning gender and fertility. Even controlling for economic development, Muslim-majority countries tend to be somewhat more religious and culturally conservative than average."[25]

If successful in its management of shifting attitudes, Indonesia holds out the promise of a pluralistic, tolerant, and more democratic alternative to state-controlled interpretations of Islam that autocratic rulers want to maintain as the Muslim world's dominant religious narrative. For autocrats, control of the religious narrative and managing a widening gap between youth religious aspirations and state-imposed interpretations of Islam is key to securing their survival and carving out a place for themselves in a new world order. Yet, youth in much of the Muslim world, question state-controlled religion, not religion itself.

The questioning challenges long-standing approaches towards religion. According to Mustafa Akyol, a prominent Turkish Muslim intellectual, the questioning amounted to a rejection of Ash'arism,[26] the theological basis for centuries of religiously legitimised autocratic rule in the Muslim world. A major school of Muslim philosophy, Ash'arism stresses scriptural and clerical authority. Akyol argued that Ash'arism has dominated Muslim politics at the expense of more liberal strands of the faith "not because of its merits, but because of the support of the states that ruled the medieval Muslim world."[27] As a result, "no topic has impacted the Middle East more profoundly than religion. It has changed the geography of the region, it has changed its language, it has changed its culture. It has been shaping the region for thousands of

---

[24] Nur Amali Ibrahim. "Improvisational Islam: Indonesian Youth in a Time of Possibility." Ithaca, NY: Cornell University Press. 2018.

[25] Ronald F. Inglehart. "Giving Up on God." World Values Survey. May 2022. https://www.worldvaluessurvey.org/WVSContents.jsp.

[26] Britannica. "Ashʿariyyah." https://www.britannica.com/topic/Ashariyyah.

[27] Mustafa Akyol. "Reopening Muslim Minds: A Return to Reason, Freedom, and Tolerance." New York: St. Martin's Essentials. 2021. Kindle edition.

years. [...] Religion controls every aspect of people who live in the Arab world," noted Nadia Oweidat, a student of the history of Islamic thought.[28]

Against that backdrop, renewed support for political Islam and a greater role for religion in politics constitute the most significant shifts in public attitudes. Support for clerical influence on policy in the 2021–2022 Arab Barometer poll seemed to reverse outlooks expressed five years earlier in a 2017 poll by Washington-based John Zogby Associates. A majority of Zogby respondents in Saudi Arabia, the UAE, Egypt, Lebanon, Jordan, Turkey, and Iran said they wanted religious movements to focus on personal faith and spiritual guidance and not involve themselves in politics. Reconciling the various surveys is complicated by pollsters failing to explore what type of clerics respondents thought of when discussing whether they should exercise political influence.

"The youth are not interested in institutions or organizations. These do not attract them or give them any incentive; just the opposite, these institutions and organizations, and their leadership take advantage of them only when they are needed for their attendance and for filling out the crowds," asserted Naser Adeen Al-Shaer, a Palestinian scholar and former education minister of Gaza, the Palestinian strip along the Mediterranean coast that was controlled by Hamas, an Islamist group affiliated with the Muslim Brotherhood.[29]

"Youth have [...] witnessed how religious figures, who still remain influential in many Arab societies, can sometimes give in to change even if they have resisted it initially. This not only feeds into Arab youth's scepticism towards religious institutions but also further highlights the inconsistency of the religious discourse and its inability to provide timely explanations or justifications to the changing reality of today," added Alhussein, the Gulf scholar.[30]

In Syria, clerical support for President Bashar al-Assad's brutal crackdown on anti-government protesters and decade-long civil war was a watershed. "The young men and women had to swallow the bitter pill and realize that religious and political establishments are intimate allies. They had to discover the extent to which religion was involved in politics, which made them sceptical of everything that arrived to them through the regime, including its official variety of Islam," said journalist Sham al-Ali, describing the evolution of his own family.[31] In response, Syrian Sunni Muslim youth rallied around clerics who backed the call for greater freedom.

The return in the 2020s to conservative religious values harks back to a strengthening of traditional religious values in the Muslim world in the

---

[28] University of Oxford Podcasts. "The Place of Religion After the Uprisings." 26 February 2021. https://podcasts.ox.ac.uk/place-religion-after-uprisings.

[29] Interview with the Author. 22 February 2020.

[30] Ibid. Alhussein. Arab Youth View Religion as Important But Feel Alienated from Its Current.

[31] Sham al-Ali. "The Surge of Religion in Syria: A Family Portrait." Al-Jumhurriya. 25 January 2017. https://aljumhuriya.net/en/2017/01/25/the-surge-of-religion-in-syria-a-family-portrait/.

1990s and 2000s.[32] "The indices of Islamic reawakening in personal life were many: increased attention to religious observances (mosque attendance, prayer, fasting), proliferation of religious programming and publications, more emphasis on Islamic dress and values, the revitalization of Sufism (mysticism). This broad-based renewal was accompanied by Islam's reassertion in public life: an increase in Islamically oriented governments, organizations, laws, banks, social welfare services, and educational institutions," Islam scholar John Esposito noted at the time.[33] Another scholar, Jean-Paul Carvalho, argued that an economic "growth reversal which raised aspirations and led subsequently to a decline in social mobility which left aspirations unfulfilled among the educated middle class (and) increasing income inequality and impoverishment of the lower-middle class" drove the revival.[34] The same factors fuel the current trend towards traditional, more conservative religious values and norms of religiosity.

The shift symbolises the failure of the 2011 revolts and mass anti-government protests in various Arab countries in 2019 and 2020, as well as Iran in 2022, to achieve sustainable change. The revolts' failure to produce what Oweidat, the Islamic thought scholar, described as 'dawla madiniya,' a civic state "where the laws are written by people so that we can challenge them, we can change them, we can adjust them. It's not God's law, it's madiniya, it's people's law," shined a spotlight on the role of religion.

"Too many terrible things have recently happened in the Arab world in the name of Islam. These include the sectarian civil wars in Syria, Iraq, and Yemen, where most of the belligerents have fought in the name of God, often with appalling brutality. The millions of victims and bystanders of these wars have experienced shock and disillusionment with religious politics, and more than a few began asking deeper questions," said Akyol, the Turkish Muslim intellectual.[35]

Many found answers that led them away from traditional Islam. Some changed their religious practice. Others secretly converted to other religions even though apostasy is punishable by death. Yet, others abandoned organised religion in favour of deism, agnosticism, or atheism. Atheists and converts often attribute their search to perceived discriminatory provisions in Islam's legal code regarding Muslim sects, non-Muslims, and women.

"The primary thing that led me to atheism is Islam's moral aspect. How can, for example, a merciful and compassionate God, said to be more merciful

---

[32] World Values Survey. "Wave 3 1996." https://www.worldvaluessurvey.org/WVSDocumentationWV3.jsp.

[33] John L. Esposito. "The Islamic Threat: Myth or Reality?" New York: Oxford University Press. 1999, p. 35.

[34] Jean-Paul Carvalho. "A Theory of the Islamic Revival." Economics Series Working Papers 424. University of Oxford. Department of Economics. 2009. https://ora.ox.ac.uk/objects/uuid:e3ee0e39-763c-4459-9baf-9e01bb7693e2.

[35] Mustafa Akyol. "How Islamists are Ruining Islam." Current Trends in Islamist Ideology. Hudson Institute. 12 June 2020. https://www.hudson.org/national-security-defense/how-islamists-are-ruining-islam.

than a woman with her baby, permit slavery and the trade of slaves in slave markets? How come He permits rape of women simply because they are war prisoners? These acts would not be committed by a merciful human being much less by a merciful God," said Hicham Nostic, a Moroccan jihadist-turned-atheist, writing under a pen name.[36] A fighter in Bosnia in the 1990s, Nostic referred to the atrocities the Islamic State committed and justified by citing Islamic law that, for example, keeps slavery on its books even though it has been abolished across the Muslim world.

For Muslim autocrats, the questioning of religion constituted a double-edged sword. Rolling back the achievements of the 2011 revolts enabled them to weaken and fracture Islamist groups, including the Muslim Brotherhood, and drive them into exile. The 3.5-year-long diplomatic and economic boycott of Qatar because it supported revolts and Islamist groups that challenged autocracy blocked access in Saudi Arabia, the UAE, Bahrain, and Egypt to the Gulf state's popular Al Jazeera television network. The blockage helped Saudi Crown Prince Mohammed "recapture (the) mandate of change, wrap it in a national mantle, and sever it from its Arab Spring associations. The boycott and ensuing nationalist campaign against Qatar became central to achieving that," said Gulf scholar Kristin Smith Diwan.[37]

Simultaneously, Bin Salman sought to stymie an abandonment of religion by youths that could weaken the religious legitimacy he and his father, King Salman, enjoy as custodians of Islam's holiest cities, Mecca and Medina. A WIN/Gallup International survey reported in 2012 that five per cent of Saudis—or more than one million people—identified themselves as "convinced atheists," while 19% described themselves as non-religious. The Saudi figure contrasted starkly with the absence of non-believers in other Muslim-majority countries surveyed, except for Turkey, which ranked second with two per cent.[38] To counter the trend, Bin Salman maintained the Saudi legal definition of terrorism as including "calling for atheist thought in any form."[39] Rafi Badawi, a Saudi dissident and founder of the Free Saudi Liberals website, was sentenced to ten years in prison and 1,000 lashes on charges of apostasy

---

[36] Hicham Nostik. "Mudakkirat Kafir Maghribi (Memoirs of a Moroccan Apostate)." Rabat: Dar al-Watan. 2019, p. 162.

[37] Kristin Smith Diwan. "Why the Saudis Ended the Dispute With Qatar." The Arab Gulf States Institute in Washington. 8 February 2021. https://agsiw.org/why-the-saudis-ended-the-dispute-with-qatar/.

[38] WIN Gallup International and Red C Research. "Global Index of Religion and Atheism." 2012. https://www.redcresearch.ie/wp-content/uploads/2015/10/RED-C-press-release-Religion-and-Atheism-25-7-12.pdf.

[39] U.S. Embassy and Consulates in Saudi Arabia. "2022 Report on International Religious Freedom for Saudi Arabia." 30 May 2023. https://sa.usembassy.gov/2022-report-on-international-religious-freedom-for-saudi-arabia/#:~:text=The%20counterterrorism%20law%20criminalizes%2C%20among,Prince.%E2%80%9D%20The%20law%20also%20bans.

for questioning why Saudis should be obliged to adhere to Islam and asserting that the faith did not have answers to all questions.[40]

A decade later, Saudi Arabia no longer sees exceptional. Mass anti-government protests in Iraq in 2019 rejected sectarianism and called for a secular national Iraqi identity.[41] Almost 70% of those polled a year earlier in an Arab Opinion Index poll believed that "no religious authority is entitled to declare followers of other religions to be infidels."[42] Fadhil, a 30-year-old from the southern port city of Basra, complained that religious leaders "overuse and misuse God's name, police human bodies, prohibit extramarital sex, and police the bodies of women."[43] One-time Shiite cleric Gaith al-Tamimi concluded that "Iraqis are questioning the role religion serves today."[44]

Challenging attempts by governments and religious authorities to suppress changing attitudes rather than engaging with groups groping for greater religious freedom, Kuwaiti writer Sajed al-Abdali noted in 2012 that "it is essential that we acknowledge today that atheism exists and is increasing in our society, especially among our youth, and evidence of this is in no short supply."[45] Al-Abdali sounded his alarm three years before the Pew Research Center published a study that predicted the growth trajectories of the world's religions by the year 2050. The study suggested that the number of people among the 300 million inhabitants of the Middle East and North Africa who were unaffiliated with any faith would remain stable at about 0.6% of the population.[46]

The Egyptian government's religious advisory body, Dar al-Ifta Al-Missriya, published a 2014 scientifically disputed survey that sought to project the number of atheists in the region as negligible. The survey identified 2,293 atheists, including 866 Egyptians, 325 Moroccans, 320 Tunisians, 242 Iraqis, 178 Saudis, 170 Jordanians, 70 Sudanese, 56 Syrians, 34 Libyans, and 32 Yemenis. It defined atheists as not only those who did not believe in God

---

[40] BBC News. "Raif Badawi: Saudi Blogger Freed After Decade in Prison." 11 March 2022. https://www.bbc.com/news/world-middle-east-60714086.

[41] Harith Hasan. "Iraq Protests: A New Social Movement Is Challenging Sectarian Power." Malcolm H. Kerr Carnegie Middle East Center. 4 November 2019. https://carnegie-mec.org/2019/11/04/iraq-protests-new-social-movement-is-challenging-sectarian-power-pub-80256.

[42] Arab Center Washington DC. "Arab Opinion Index 2017–2018. Main Findings." July 2018. https://arabcenterdc.org/wp-content/uploads/2018/07/Arab-Opinion-Index-2017-2018-1.pdf.

[43] Nazli Tarzi. "Iraq's Growing Community of Atheists No Longer Peripheral." The Arab Weekly. 20 July 2019. https://thearabweekly.com/iraqs-growing-community-atheists-no-longer-peripheral.

[44] Ibid. Nazli. "Iraq's Growing Community of Atheists No Longer Peripheral."

[45] Sajed al-Abdali. " الإلحاد..لماذا يتزايد؟(Atheism. Why Is It Spreading?" Al Bayan. 8 August 2012. https://www.albayan.ae/opinions/articles/2012-08-08-1.1704026.

[46] Pew Research Center. "The Future of World Religions: Population Growth Projections, 2010–2050." 2 April 2015. https://www.pewresearch.org/religion/2015/04/02/religious-projections-2010-2050/.

but also converts to other religions and advocates of a secular state.[47] A poll conducted that same year by Al-Azhar, Cairo's ancient citadel of Islamic learning, concluded that Egypt counted 10.7 million atheists. Al-Azhar's Grand Imam, Ahmad al-Tayyeb, warned on state television that flight from religion constituted a social problem.[48]

Similarly, in Libya, many gravitated towards secretive atheist Facebook pages. The trend signalled the UAE's inability to align support for rebel Field Marshal Khalifa Haftar with its claim to be a beacon of a forward-looking moderate version of Islam. Said, a 25-year-old student from Benghazi, Haftar's stronghold, turned his back on religion after his cousin was beheaded in 2016 for speaking out against militants. "My cousin's death occurred during a period when I was deeply religious, praying five times a day and studying ten new pages of the Qur'an each evening," Said said.[49] Haftar's rebel forces were populated by Madkhalists, a branch of Salafism named after a Saudi scholar who preached absolute obedience to the ruler and projected Saudi Arabia, stretching back to the kingdom's pre-2015 ultra-conservative days, as a model of Islamic governance.

Referring to the 2011 uprisings, Moroccan journalist and human rights activist Ahmed Benchemsi suggested that "the Arab Spring may have stalled, if not receded, but when it comes to religious beliefs and attitudes, a generational dynamic is at play. Large numbers of individuals are tilting away from the rote religiosity Westerners reflexively associate with the Arab world." In 2015, Benchemsi counted 250 Arab atheism-related pages or groups on the Internet, with memberships ranging from a few to more than 11,000. "And these numbers only pertain to Arab atheists (or Arabs concerned with atheism) who are committed enough to leave a trace online," Benchemsi noted.[50]

Benchemsi argued that "in today's Arab world, it's not religiosity that is mandatory; it's the appearance of it. Nonreligious attitudes and beliefs are tolerated as long as they're not conspicuous. As a system, social hypocrisy provides breathing room to secular lifestyles while preserving the façade of religion. Atheism, per se, is not the problem. Claiming it out loud is. So those who publicize their atheism in the Arab world are fighting less for freedom of conscience than for freedom of speech." The same could be said for the

---

[47] Louay Ali. "مرصد دار الإفتاء: مصر الأعلى عربيا فى الإلحاد بـ866 ملحدا"(Dar Al-Iftaa Observatory: Egypt Tops the Arab World in Atheism, with 866 Atheists)." Youm7. 10 December 2014. https://www.youm7.com/story/2014/12/10/مرصد-دار-الإفتاء-مصر-الأعلى-عربيا-فى-الإلحاد-بـ866-ملحدا.

[48] Ahmed Hassan. "شيخ الأزهر يحذر من انتشار الإلحاد في مصر"(The Sheikh of Al-Azhar Warns of the Spread of Atheism in Egypt)." Elaph. 14 October 2014. https://elaph.com/Web/News/2014/10/949085.html.

[49] Jack Jeffery. "Young Libyan Atheists Seeking Refuge Online." Al-Monitor. 22 June 2020. https://www.al-monitor.com/originals/2020/06/libya-youth-atheists-muslim-islamic-state-extremism.html.

[50] Ahmed Benchemsi. "Invisible Atheists." The New Republic. 24 May 2015. https://newrepublic.com/article/121559/rise-arab-atheists.

right to convert or opt for alternative practices of Islam. Echoing journalist Benchemsi, Saudi ambassador to the United Nations Abdallah al-Mouallimi argued that "if (a person) was disbelieving in God, and keeping that to himself, and conducting himself, nobody would do anything or say anything about it. If he is going out in the public, and saying, 'I don't believe in God,' that's subversive. He is inviting others to retaliate."[51]

Al-Ali, the Syrian journalist, recounts the story of a female relative who escaped the civil war to Germany, where she decided to remove her hijab. Her father, who lives in Turkey, accepted his daughter's decision but threatened to disown her if she posted pictures of herself uncovered on Facebook. "His issue was not with his daughter's abandonment of religious duty, but with her publicizing that before her family and society at large," Al-Ali said.[52]

Nowhere in the Muslim world is the gap between state-imposed religion and popular aspirations wider than in Iran. Pooyan Tamimi Arab, a co-organiser of online surveys in Iran, noted in his polling a stunning rejection of state-imposed adherence to conservative religious mores and the role of religion in public life. The widening gap "becomes an existential question. The state wants you to be something that you don't want to be [...]. Political disappointment steadily turned into religious disappointment [...]. Iranians have turned away from institutional religion on an unprecedented scale,"[53] Arab said. He argued that his polling "shows that there is a social basis" for the concern of autocrats, who use religion to further their geopolitical goals and maintain their grip on potentially restive populations.

Autocrats were not the only ones threatened by changing attitudes towards religion and religiosity. So were leaders of Muslim-majority democracies, however flawed. Autocrats and authoritarians long feared faith becoming a platform for dissent. As far back as 1989, David Cashin, a Bangladesh scholar resident in Dacca, recalled Bangladeshis looking for a copy of Salman Rushdie's Satanic Verses as soon as it was banned by Iran's Ayatollah Khomeini, who condemned the British author to death. "It was the allure of forbidden fruit. Yet, I also found that many were looking for things to criticize, an excuse to think differently," Cashin said.[54]

In a similar vein, Turkish art historian Nese Yildiran warned that a fatwa issued by Turkish President Recep Tayyip Erdogan's Directorate of Religious Affairs or Diyanet declaring popular talismans to ward off "the evil eye" as forbidden by Islam fueled criticism of one of the best-funded branches of government. The fatwa followed the issuance of similar religious opinions

---

[51] Al Jazeera English. "UpFront—What Is Saudi Arabia's Endgame in Yemen and Syria?" 26 March 2016. https://www.youtube.com/watch?v=8z8ME2O5XdY.

[52] Sham al-Ali. "'On Rising Apostasy Among Syrian Youths." Al-Jumhurriyah. 15 March 2017. https://aljumhuriya.net/en/2017/03/15/on-rising-apostasy-among-syrian-youths/.

[53] Interview with the Author. 8 March 2021.

[54] Email exchange with the author. 27 January 2021.

banning dying of men's moustaches and beards, feeding dogs at home, tattoos, and playing the national lottery, as well as statements that were perceived to condone or belittle child abuse and violence against women.[55]

By the same token, Malaysia's top religious regulatory body, the Malaysian Islamic Development Department (Jakim), which is responsible for training Islamic teachers and preparing weekly state-controlled Friday sermons and is widely seen as a conservative bastion, portrayed liberalism and pluralism as threats. In 2006, Jakim condemned liberalism as heretical in a fatwa.[56] "The pulpit would like to state today that many tactics are being undertaken by irresponsible people to weaken Muslim unity, among them through spreading new but inverse thinking like Pluralism, Liberalism, and such. The pulpit would like to state that the Liberal movement contains concepts that are found to have deviated from the Islamic faith and shariah," read a 2014 Friday sermon drafted and distributed by Jakim.[57]

The fatwa echoed a similar opinion issued in 2005 by Indonesia's semi-governmental Indonesian Ulama Council (MUI). MUI labelled the opinion SIPILIS, an acronym for equating secularism, pluralism, and liberalism, which it likened to a venereal disease. The council was headed at the time by Ma'ruf Amin, a prominent Nahdlatul Ulama figure and former Indonesian vice president. "Pluralism, secularism, and religious liberalism...are concepts that are contrary to the teachings of Islam. It is illegal for Muslims to follow pluralism, secularism, and religious liberalism. In matters of faith and worship, Muslims must be exclusive, in the sense that it is forbidden to mix the faith and worship of Muslims with the faith and worship of followers of other religions," the fatwa ordained.[58]

Arab's surveys suggested that Iranians were on the frontline of the quest for religious change.[59] Their quest runs the gamut from changes in personal religious behaviour to secret conversions to abandoning religion in favour of agnosticism or atheism. After months of protests in 2022 against the imposition of the hijab, women in parts of Tehran no longer even pretend to comply

[55] Andrew Wilks "Turkey's Religious Authority Denounces 'Evil-Eye' Charms." Al Jazeera. 21 January 2021. https://www.aljazeera.com/news/2021/1/23/turkeys-religious-authority-bans-on-evil-eye-charms.

[56] JAKIM. "Aliran Pemikiran Liberal: Hukum dan Implikasinya Kepada Islam di Malaysia (Liberal Thought: Law and Its Implications for Islam in Malaysia)." 25–27 July 2006. http://e-smaf.islam.gov.my/e-smaf/fatwa/fatwa/find/pr/16319.

[57] Malaysia Today. "LI Beral Thinking Is Deviant Teaching, Says Malaysia's Islamic Authority." 24 October 2014. https://www.malaysia-today.net/2014/10/24/liberal-thinking-is-deviant-teaching-says-malaysias-islamic-authority/.

[58] Majelis Ulama Indonesia. "Pluralisme, liberalisme dan sekularis agama (Pluralism, Liberalism and Religious Secularism)." 26–29 July 2005. https://mui.or.id/baca/fatwa/pluralisme-liberalisme-dan-sekularisme-agama.

[59] Ammar Maleki and Pooyan Tamimi Arab. "Iranians' Attitudes Toward Religion: A 2020 Survey Report." The Group for Analyzing and Measuring Attitudes in Iran August 2020. https://gamaan.org/wp-content/uploads/2020/09/GAMAAN-Iran-Religion-Survey-2020-English.pdf.

with government regulations. "The picture on the streets of parts of Tehran is a forest of thick women's hair," said a Tehran resident.[60]

Responding to Arab's 2020 survey, 80% of the participants said they believed in God, but only 32.2% identified themselves as Shiite Muslims—a far lower percentage than asserted in official figures of predominantly Shiite Iran. Sixty-eight per cent said they opposed the inclusion of religious precepts in national legislation, 70% rejected public funding of religious institutions while 56% opposed mandatory religious education in schools. Almost 60% admitted that they do not pray, and 72% disagreed with women being obliged to wear a hijab in public. An unpublished slide from the survey shows the change in religiosity is reflected in an increasing number of Iranians no longer naming their children after religious figures.

A five-minute YouTube clip uploaded by an ultra-conservative channel allegedly related to Iran's Revolutionary Guards attacked the survey once the pollsters disclosed in their report that the poll was supported by an exile human rights group, despite initially distributing the questionnaire.

In yet another sign of rejection of state-imposed expressions of Islam, Iranians sought to alleviate the social impact of COVID-19-related lockdowns and restrictions on face-to-face human contact by acquiring dogs, cats, birds, and even reptiles as pets. Tehran Police Chief Hossein Rahimi banned walking dogs even before the pandemic.[61] The Islamic Republic has long viewed pets as a fixture of Western culture.[62] The pets suggested that many Iranians no longer accept long-standing cultural, religious, and doctrinal taboos as God's unalterable words of God. "This shift towards deconstructing old taboos signals a transformation of the Iranian identity—from the traditional to the new," said psychologist Farnoush Khaledi.

Pets are one form of dissent; clandestine conversions are another. Exiled Iranian Shiite scholar Yaser Mirdamadi noted that "Iranians no longer have faith in state-imposed religion and are groping for religious alternatives."[63]

"Tehran may well be the least religious capital in the Middle East. Clerics dominate the news headlines and play the communal elders in soap operas, but I never saw them on the street except on billboards. Unlike most Muslim countries, the call to prayer is almost inaudible [...]. Alcohol is banned, but home delivery is faster for wine than for pizza [...]. Religion felt frustratingly hard to locate, and the truly religious seemed sidelined, like a minority,"

---

[60] Interview with the Author. 15 October 2022.

[61] BBC News. "Tehran Bans Dog Walking in Public Spaces." 29 January 2019. https://www.bbc.com/news/blogs-news-from-elsewhere-47041611.

[62] Reuters. "Iran Cleric Says Dogs "Unclean" and Not to be Kept as Pets." 19 June 2010. https://www.reuters.com/article/idUSTRE65I0M220100619/#:~:text=TEHRAN%20(Reuters)%20%2D%20A%20senior,a%20newspaper%20reported%20on%20Saturday.

[63] The Economist. "Disenchanted Iranians Are Turning to Other Faiths." 21 January 2021. https://www.economist.com/middle-east-and-africa/2021/01/21/disenchanted-iranians-are-turning-to-other-faiths.

added journalist Nicholas Pelham based on a visit in 2019 during which he was detained for several weeks.[64]

A former Israeli army human intelligence official, retired Lt. Col. Marco Moreno, put the number of converts in Iran, a country of 83 million, at about one million. Other studies estimated conversions between 100,000 and 500,000. Whatever the number may be, the conversions fit a trend not only in Iran but across the Muslim world of changing attitudes towards religion, a rejection of state-imposed interpretations of Islam, and a search for more individual and varied religious experiences. Iranian press reports about the discovery of clandestine church gatherings in homes in the holy city of Qom suggested conversions to Christianity began more than a decade ago.[65] "The fact that conversions had reached Qom was an indication that this was happening elsewhere in the country," added Mirdamadi.

Seeing converts as an Israeli asset, Moreno backed the production of a two-hour documentary, Sheep Among Wolves Volume II, produced by two American evangelicals, one of whom resettled on the Israeli-occupied Golan Heights. The documentary asserts that Iran's underground community of converts to Christianity is the world's fastest-growing church.[66]

"What if I told you the mosques are empty inside Iran?" said a church leader in the film, his identity masked and his voice distorted to avoid identification. Based on interviews with Iranian converts while travelling abroad, the documentary opens with a scene on an Indonesian beach where they meet with the filmmakers for a religious training session.

"What if I told you that Islam is dead? What if I told you that the mosques are empty inside Iran? [...] What if I told you no one follows Islam inside of Iran? Would you believe me? This is exactly what is happening inside of Iran. God is moving powerfully inside of Iran?" the church leader added. Unsurprisingly, given the film's Israeli backing and the filmmaker's affinity with Israel, the documentary emphasised the converts' break with Iran's staunch rejection of the Jewish state by emphasising their empathy for Judaism and Israel.

Even so, Iran's religious leadership was concerned. Prominent cleric Mohammad Abolghassem Doulabi, a member of the Assembly of Experts that appoints Iran's supreme leader and an advisor to President Ebrahim Raisi, claimed in June 2022 that 50,000 of the country's 75,000 mosques had closed because of lack of attendance. While it was impossible to confirm the figure, Doulabi said it was a "worrying admission." He cited it as causing "the humiliation of people in the name of religion," "falsification of religious concepts

[64] Nicholas Pelham. "Trapped in Iran." The Economist. 20 January 2019. https://www.economist.com/1843/2020/01/20/trapped-in-iran.

[65] PIME Asia News "Ayatollah in Qom Wants to Bring Converts to Christianity (and Other Faiths) Back to Islam." 3 November 2023. https://www.asianews.it/news-en/Ayatollah-in-Qom-wants-to-bring-converts-to-Christianity-(and-other-faiths)-back-to-Islam-57942.html.

[66] Fai Studios. "Sheep Among Wolves Volume II." YouTube. 24 August 2019. https://www.youtube.com/watch?v=9SAPOLKF59U.

and teachings," and "depriving people of a decent life and creating poverty in the name of religion."[67]

Multiple Turkish surveys suggested that Erdogan's goal of raising a religious generation had backfired, despite pouring billions of dollars into religious education. Students often rejected religion, described themselves as atheists, deists, or feminists, and challenged Islam's interpretation taught in schools. A 2019 polling and data company IPSOS survey reported that only 12% of Turks trusted religious officials and 44% distrusted clerics.[68] "We have declined when religious sincerity and morality expressed by the people is taken into account," said Ali Bardakoglu, who headed Diyanet from 2003 to 2010.[69]

Counterintuitively, that may be the unintended result of Erdogan's Islamization policy and crackdown on dissent since the failed 2016 military coup. Mehmet, a 37-year-old government employee and supporter of Erdogan's ruling Justice and Development Party (AKP), lost faith when he was one of the thousands fired from their jobs on suspicion of sympathising with exiled preacher Fethullah Gulen's movement. Erdogan accused Gulen followers in the Turkish military of staging the coup on the preacher's orders.

"I didn't know what to do. I couldn't make ends meet. This couldn't be God's will. I started to question God. I'd like to return to Islam, but that may no longer be possible," said Mehmet, identifying himself only by his common first name. The crackdown persuaded Celik, another erstwhile AKP supporter, that oppression breeds revolution, and revolution breeds oppression. The crackdown initially radicalised Celik, turning him into an Islamic State and Al-Qaeda sympathiser. "Today, I'm an atheist. Islam in whatever form didn't provide answers," Celik said.[70]

For others, politics has little to do with their epiphany. Cigdem teaches religion in an elementary school but no longer cares whether God exists or not. A one-time conservative who would not shake a man's hand, she still wears a headdress in school but says it is the only thing that still connects her to Islam. She realised that she had lost her faith when she one day woke up depressed. "I was going crazy," Cigdem recalled. "That's when I realized that I no longer believed."

Unaware that microphones had not been muted, Erdogan, a year before Bardakoglu, the former Diyante head, issued his warning, expressed concern to his education minister about the spread of deism among Turkish youth during a meeting of his party's parliamentary group. "No, no such thing

---

[67] Iran International. "Senior Cleric Claims Religion In Iran Weak, 50,000 Mosques Closed." 2 June 2022. https://www.iranintl.com/en/202306027255.

[68] Ipsos. "Global Trust in Professions. Who Do Global Citizens Trust?" September 2019. https://www.ipsos.com/sites/default/files/ct/news/documents/2019-09/global-trust-in-professions-trust-worthiness-index-2019.pdf.

[69] Interview with the author. 15 April 2020.

[70] Selin Girit. "The Young Turks Rejecting Islam." BBC. 10 May 2018. https://www.bbc.com/news/world-europe-43981745.

can happen," Erdogan thundered against the backdrop of Turkish officials painting deism as a Western conspiracy designed to weaken Turkey. Erdogan's comments came in response to the publication of an education ministry report that, in line with the subsequent survey, warned that popular rejection of religious knowledge acquired through revelation and religious teachings and a growing embrace of reason was on the rise.

The report noted that increased enrolment in a rising number of state-run religious Imam Hatip high schools had not stopped mounting questioning of orthodox Islamic precepts. Neither had increased the study of religion in mainstream schools that deemphasised the teaching of evolution. The greater emphasis on religion failed to advance Erdogan's dream of a pious generation with a Qur'an in one hand and a computer in the other.[71] Instead, reflecting on a discussion on faith and youth among some 50 religion teachers, the report suggested that lack of trust in educators had fueled the rise of deism. Teachers could not answer the often-posed question: why does God not intervene to halt evil and why does he remain silent? The report's cautionary note was bolstered by a flurry of anonymous confessions and personal stories by deists and atheists recounted in newspaper interviews.

Acting on Erdogan's instructions, Ali Erbas, Diyanet's president, declared war on deism. The government's top cleric, Erbas, blamed Western missionaries seeking to convert Turkish youth to Christianity for deism's increased popularity. Erbas' declaration followed a three-day consultation with 70 religious scholars and bureaucrats convened by Diyanet that identified "Deism, Atheism, Nihilism, Agnosticism" as the enemy. Erdogan's alarm and Erbas' spinning of conspiracy theories constituted attempts to detract attention from the fact that youth in Turkey, like in Iran and the Arab world, were turning their back on orthodox and classical interpretations of Islam against the backdrop of the Turkish president's increasingly authoritarian and autocratic rule. When protesting students displayed a poster depicting one on Islam's holiest sites, the Kaaba shrine in Mecca, with LGBT flages, Erdogan thundered that "there is no such thing" as LGBT. Adding that and "this country is national and spiritual, and will continue to walk into the future." [72]

"There is a dictatorship in Turkey... This drives people away from religion," said Temel Karamollaoglu, the leader of the Islamist Felicity Party, which opposes

---

[71] Evrensel.:Erdogan reiterated his dream of a "pious generation", connecting the solution of social problems to religion (Erdoğan "dindar nesil" hayalini yineledi, toplumsal sorunların çözümünü dine bağladı)." 6 June 2019. https://www.evrensel.net/haber/390428/erdogan-dindar-nesil-hayalini-yineledi-toplumsal-sorunlarin-cozumunu-dine-bagladi.

[72] Ali Kucukgocmen, Ezgi Erkoyun and Tuvan Gumrukcu. "Erdogan Says Will Not Let Turkish University Protests Swell." Reuters. 4 February 2021. https://www.reuters.com/article/turkey-security-bogazici-int/erdogan-says-will-not-let-turkish-university-protests-swell-idUSKBN2A30SX/.

Erdogan's AKP because of its authoritarianism.[73] Turkey scholar Mucahit Bilici described Turkish youths' rejection of Orthodox and politicised interpretations of Islam as "a flowering of post-Islamist sentiment" by a "younger generation (that) is choosing the path of individualized spirituality and a silent rejection of tradition."[74]

Bilici's colleague, Murat Cokgezen, took a step further with his conclusion that Erdogan's Islamisation policy had backfired and failed to achieve the president's goal of raising a "pious generation" in Turkey. Cokgezen's research detected "a significant decline in belief in God and trust in clergy, irrespective of the age cohorts and gender.… As the government is identified with religion in the eye of the public, dissatisfaction with the government turned to dissatisfaction with religious values," Cokgezen said.[75]

Scholar Volkan Ertit noted that "contrary to claims of societal Islamization…praying rates have decreased, extramarital sexual relationship has become prevalent, the number of mosques per person has decreased, the belief in virginity is a point of honour for fewer people, people's clothes have become more flatteringly formfitting and more attractive, including women's headscarves; secular experts rather than religious officials are being sought for help concerning problems in daily life, homosexuality has become more socially acceptable visible, traditional family structures has been shattered."[76]

Even so, Arab Barometer's polling showed that more people thought honour killings were more acceptable than homosexuality. In most countries polled, young Arabs appeared more likely than their parents to condone honour killings.[77] Social media and occasional protests bear that out. Thousands rallied in early 2020 in Hebron, a conservative city on the West Bank, after the Palestinian Authority signed the UN Convention on the Elimination of All Forms of Discrimination Against Women.[78]

---

[73] Temel Karamollaoglu. "Karamollaoğlu: Deizmin yükselme nedeni iktidar (Deism Is Rising Due to the Government). " Gazete Duvar. 23 July 2019. https://www.gazeteduvar.com.tr/politika/2019/07/23/karamollaoglu-deizmin-yukselme-nedeni-iktidar.

[74] Mucahit Bilici. "The Crisis of Religiosity in Turkish Islamism." Middle East Research and Information Project. No. 288, Fall 2018. https://merip.org/2018/12/the-crisis-of-religiosity-in-turkish-islamism/.

[75] Murat Cokgezen. "Can the State Make You More Religious? Evidence From Turkish Experience." Journal for the Scientific Study of Religion. Vol. 61, Issue 2. June 2022. pp. 349–373.

[76] Volkan Ertit. "God Is Dying in Turkey as Well: Application of Secularization Theory to a Non-Christian Society." Open Theology. 2018:4, 17 May 2018. pp. 192–211.

[77] Arab Barometer. "Arab Governments Are Doing Too Little to End Honour Killings." 5 February 2021. https://www.arabbarometer.org/media-news/arab-governments-are-doing-too-little-to-end-honour-killings/.

[78] Mohanad Adam. "CEDAW Faces a Fierce Battle in Palestine." Mediterranean Network for Feminist Information. 22 March 2021. https://medfeminiswiya.net/2021/03/22/cedaw-faces-a-fierce-battle-in-palestine/?lang=en.

Muslim youths' more critical attitude towards religion is hardly the exception that proves the rule. In fact, it is reinforced by recognition that Muslim youth are part of a global trend that reaches beyond Islam. In the United States, more than half of 10,000 young American Muslims, Christians, Jews, and Buddhists aged 13–25 surveyed in 2019 professed to be affiliated with an organised religion but conceded that they had little or no trust in organized religion. Twenty per cent went further to say that they were not personally religious even though they were affiliated with an organized religion.[79] "They're checking the box that says they are Muslim, Jewish, Catholic or whatever, but over half of them are saying, 'even though I checked the box, I don't trust organized religion,'" said Josh Packard, the religion sociologist who conducted the poll.[80]

Packard suggested that what was true for non-Muslim religious leaders seeking to keep youth engaged in institutionalized religion was also true for Muslim clerics, particularly ones aligned with the state. "Religion has not disappeared; it's just become more diffuse. What used to happen via programs in houses of worship has moved outward into the wider world," he said.

Packard's conclusion that youth are less inclined to take guidance from clerics because of their title or status and more likely to follow priests who show genuine interest in them is particularly relevant for Muslim youth attempting to free themselves from the shackles of a fossilized Islam promoted either at the behest of autocratic or authoritarian leaders or by ultra-conservative scholars who refuse to adapt to change. "There are five characteristics that determine youths' attitudes towards religious authority: listening, transparency, integrity, care, and expertise," Packard noted. None of those come naturally to autocrats and ultra-conservatives.

---

[79] Springtide Research Institute. "The State of Religion & Young People 2020." December 2020. https://www.springtideresearch.org/the-state-of-religion-young-people/.

[80] Interview with the Author.

CHAPTER 8

Epilogue: The Prabowo Presidency

The 2023 Gaza war was in its nineth month as I finished the manuscript of this book. The war's fallout is likely to reverberate for years, potentially swinging the pendulum in the Battle for the Soul of Islam with newly elected Indonesian President Prabowo Subianto as a joker.

Prabowo vowed to walk in the footsteps of his immediate, widely popular predecessor, Joko Widodo, who maintains close ties to Nahdlatul Ulama. He owed his third-time success, after twice failing to defeat Widodo, to his predecessor and Nahdlatul Ulama's tacit support. Prabowo cemented that support by choosing Widodo's son, Gibran Rakabuming Raka, as his vice presidential running mate.

However, it remains to be seen whether Prabowo feels obliged to continue outsourcing Indonesia's religious soft power campaign to Nahdlatul Ulama, even if the group is too powerful a player for him to ignore.

While Prabowo turned away from his erstwhile hardline Islamist supporters, whom Widodo banned, when he joined the government in 2019 as defence minister, the potential fault lines in his relationship with Nahdlatul Ulama are multiple.

A scion of one of Indonesia's wealthiest and most influential families and a former special forces general with a chequered human rights record under Suharto, the country's autocratic leader, and the new president's one-time father-in-law who was toppled in a 1998 popular revolt, Prabowo has an at best illiberal view of democracy that could clash with centre-right Nahdlatul Ulama's concept of pluralism.

A populist who a decade ago campaigned in uniforms that evoked the Sukarno era but has since rebranded himself as a cuddly grandfather, Prabowo

© The Author(s), under exclusive license to Springer Nature Singapore Pte Ltd. 2024
J. M. Dorsey, *The Battle for the Soul of Islam*,
https://doi.org/10.1007/978-981-97-2807-7_8

was expelled from the Indonesian army over allegations his men tortured dissidents. For years, he was banned from travelling to the United States and Australia. Prabowo never faced a trial and vehemently denies most of the charges, although several of his men were tried and convicted.

Known for his temper, unease with criticism, and fiery speeches, Prabowo and his running mate were the only candidates in the 2024 election not to respond to a Human Rights Watch questionnaire, or attend an event where candidates pledged to protect press freedom.

A decade ago, Prabowo used his first presidential campaign to unveil a plan to dismantle Indonesia's hard-fought democracy. A one-time proponent of "strong" leadership, the former general asserted that elections were a Western construct that was incompatible with Indonesian culture. Prabowo compared elections to an addiction to smoking.

"We need a new consensus. Political leaders, intellectuals, religious and cultural leaders, even workers. I don't want this abnormality to allow us to abandon the cultural values of our ancestors," Prabowo said.

Prabowo suggested replacing elections in which "in the name of democracy, all policies have to be via voting, including direct elections" with a vague concept of a large-scale national meeting that would create a "new consensus," a term that harks back to Suharto's dictatorship.[1]

Prabowo likely had in mind eliminating local government elections that he long had opposed and election of the president by parliament rather than by popular vote. Earlier, Prabowo said he would create a "productive" rather than "destructive" democracy that "exhausts us" and called for a return to Indonesia's original 1945 Constitution that concentrated power in the hands of the president.[2]

To be sure, Prabowo has since insisted he will preserve Indonesia's democracy. Moreover, his government will be a coalition of parties that will not want to see a system of checks and balances dismantled that remains robust despite Widodo's moves to weaken it.

Even so, strains between Nahdlatul Ulama and the National Awakening Party (PKB), the political grouping aligned with the movement, will likely complicate Nahdlatul Ulama's ability to influence the Prabowo government's policy. The PKB had four Cabinet seats in the Widodo government, including the religious affairs ministry, but aligned itself with Prabowo's Islamist rival in the 2024 election from which it emerged as Indonesia's fourth largest party with 11.7% of the vote.

---

[1] Arimbi Ramadhiani. "Prabowo Sebut Indonesia Produk Barat yang Susah Diperbaiki (Prabowo Calls Indonesia a Western Product That Is Difficult to Improve)." Kompas. 29 June 2014. https://nasional.kompas.com/read/2014/06/29/0824212/Prabowo.Sebut.Indonesia.Produk.Barat.yang.Susah.Diperbaiki.

[2] Merdeka.com. "Prabowo: We build a productive democracy, not a wani piro (Prabowo: We Build a Productive Democracy, not a 'how Much Can You Pay Me')." 9 June 2014. https://www.merdeka.com/politik/prabowo-kita-bangun-demokrasi-produktif-bukan-wani-piro.html.

Prabowo may be a politician with authoritarian tendencies but, like Widodo, he is not an Islamist. Even so, the Gaza war may give him greater leeway given that it could force Nahdlatul Ulama's autocratic soft power rivals and much of the international community to temper their hardline rejection of Islamists. That is if Hamas, the Muslim Brotherhood-linked group that controlled the Gaza Strip before the war, survives as a player in the postwar administration of Gaza and the West Bank, a competitor in long overdue Palestinian elections, and a partner in efforts to resolve the Israeli-Palestinian conflict.

Coming to grips with Hamas, and potentially political Islam, would not necessarily constitute a paradigm shift for either Saudi Arabia and the UAE, which in the past backed Islamists in Syria in the 2010s, or Prabowo but would go against Nahdlatul Ulama's grain. The movement was founded in 1926 in opposition to ultra-conservative and political Islam.

Even so, Prabowo and Nahdlatul Ulama may find common ground. Prabowo's inclinations are likely to steer him closer to Saudi Arabia and the UAE' autocratic version of 'moderate Islam.' Similarly, Nahdlatul Ulama is engaged in a subtle tug of war with the two Gulf states and Cairo's Al-Azhar University over who will define 'moderate Islam' in the twenty-first century. The question is whether one side will co-opt the other.

Nahdlatul Ulama has so far held its ground as it accepted significant Emirati financial support and was showered with honours by the UAE and Al-Azhar.

In late January 2024, Widodo and Emirati Energy and Infrastructure Minister Emirates Suhail Mohamed Al Mazrouei laid the foundation for a high rise on the campus of Nahdlatul Ulama University of Yogyakarta. The building will house the Mohamed Bin Zayed College for Future Studies backed by a US$100 million Emirati investment in the university's development.

The UAE awarded Nahdlatul Ulama days later the Zayed Award for Human Fraternity, alongside Muhamadiyya, Indonesia's second-largest Muslim civil society movement. At about the same time, Al-Azhar, a beneficiary of UAE largesse, honoured Nahdlatul Ulama's legendary Al-Azhar-educated leader, Abdurrahman Wahid, Indonesia's first post-dictatorship democratically elected president.

"Nahdlatul Ulama/UAE strategic engagement deepens," said LibForAll, a Nahdlatul Ulama US-based non-profit in a report on the foundation ceremony at the Yogyakarta university.

Nahdlatul Ulama officials insist that engagement with their rivals does not come at the price of compromising on principles. On the contrary, they argue, it enhances the group's prestige in the Muslim Middle East and beyond.

As I submitted my book manuscript, the jury was out on the outcome of the Nahdlatul Ulama-Gulf states tug of war, the Gaza carnage, and whether President Prabowo would prove to be a wolf in sheep's clothes or an autocrat who had made his peace with democracy.

Index

A

Abbas Abd Allah Abbas Shoman, 119
Abd al-Aziz-al-Rayes, 65
Abdallah bin Bayyah, 26
Abdallah bin Turki al-Subaie, 123
Abdallah I bin Al-Hussein, 4
Abdel Fattah al-Sisi, 99, 142, 154
Abdel Raziq, Ali, 81
Abdelwahab El-Affendi, 173
Abdulaziz al-Sheikh, 13
Abdulaziz Bin Baz, 3, 94
Abdullah Azzam, 2
Abdullah bin Zayed, 106, 108, 115, 133, 138
Abdulrahman al-Sudais, 65
Abou El Fadl, Khaled, 65, 127
Abu al-Hasan al-Mawardi, 16
Abu Ishaq al-Shatibi, 19
Aceh, 43
Adballah Seyid Ould Abah, 117
Afghanistan, 1–3, 68, 111, 126, 130, 141
Africa, 2, 3, 8, 10, 72, 105, 152, 153, 156, 164, 165
Ahmad bin Ali al-Thani, 123
Ahmadi, 34, 49
Ahok. *See* Purnama, Basuki Tjahaja
AKP. *See* Justice and Development Party
Akyol, Mustafa, 37, 85, 179, 181
Al-Ahram, 83
al-Assad, Bashar, 8, 100, 142, 153, 180
Al-Azami, Usaama, 78, 105, 131
Al-Azhar, 15, 38, 54, 78, 79, 117–119, 123, 124, 128, 134–136, 138, 141, 142, 152, 153, 184, 195
al-Baghdadi, Abu Bakr, 78
Albania, 155–157
Alevis, 149
Al-Farabi, 16
Al-Ghazali, Abu Hamid, 16, 19
al-Ibrahim, Badr, 70
Ali Goma, 78
Al-Jifri, Habib Ali, 120, 139, 142
Al Kaabi, Noura, 103
Al-Mesbar Studies and Research Center, 121, 140
al-Nuaimi, Ali Rashid, 116, 136
al-Otaiba, Yusuf, 100, 104, 105, 110, 115, 117, 137, 140, 141
Alp Services, 112, 114
Al-Qaeda, 3, 7, 35, 67, 73, 87, 128
al-Qaradawi, Yusuf, 123, 124, 127, 130, 150
Al Saud, Turki AlFaisal, 2, 12
al-Tayyeb, Ahmad, 38, 39, 184
American Jewish Committee (AJC), 57–59, 76, 85
Amin, Ma'ruf, 48, 49, 56, 186
Amnesty International, 14, 91, 93
A. Mostafa Bisri, 35
Anglican, 21, 72, 102
Ansor Youth Movement. *See* Gerakan Pemuda Ansor
Anwar Gargash, 110

© The Editor(s) (if applicable) and The Author(s), under exclusive license to Springer Nature Singapore Pte Ltd. 2024
J. M. Dorsey, *The Battle for the Soul of Islam*,
https://doi.org/10.1007/978-981-97-2807-7

Arab Barometer, 30, 173, 174, 177, 178, 180, 191
As'ad Said Ali, 45, 50
ASEAN. *See* Association of Southeast Asian Nations
Ashoka approach, 60–62
Association of Southeast Asian Nations, 60
Asy'ari, Hasyim, 14, 51
Ataturk, Mustafa Kemal, 4, 14, 18, 20, 51, 81, 93, 148–150, 166
Atheism, 130, 172, 181, 183, 184, 186
Atmane Tazaghart, 114
Austria, 115, 116, 149, 165
Autocracy, 7–9, 13, 26, 52, 81, 84, 99, 124, 126, 131, 134, 173, 182
Ayatollah Mohammed Beheshti, 6
Ayatollah Sadegh Khalqali, 6
Aydin, Mehmet S., 17, 18
Azra, Azyumardi, 70

B
Baker, James, vii
Banser. *See* Multipurpose Ansor Front
Bardakoglu, Ali, 162, 189
Barrès, Maurice, 108
Basgil, Ali Fuad, 17
Baswedan, Anies, 49
Bat Ye'or. *See* Gisèle Littman
Benchemsi, Ahmed, 184, 185
Bennabi, Malik, 44
Bey, Seyyid, 4, 15, 17
Bharatiya Janata Party, 23, 107
BJP. *See* Bharatiya Janata Party
Brzezinski, Zbigniew, 1, 2, 30
Buddhism, 39, 41, 58, 61
Buddhist Intellectual Association, 48
Burns, Nicholas, 99
Bush, George W., 23, 30, 32, 50, 104, 137, 157

C
Cairo Declaration on Human Rights in Islam, 82
Caliphate, 3–5, 14, 15, 17, 20, 33, 34, 37, 51, 52, 77, 78, 80, 81, 83, 149, 154, 164

Centre for Shared Civilisational Values (CSCV), 35, 60
Centrist Democrat International (CDI), 21, 23, 36, 59
C-Fam, 23
China, 23, 27, 62, 66, 107, 136, 150
Cholil, Mohammed. *See* C. Holland Taylor
C. Holland Taylor, 14, 23, 35, 36, 41, 42, 50, 60, 62
Christian Chesnot, 114
Christianity, 33, 77, 107, 156, 188, 190
Christian nationalism, ix
Christopher, Warren M., 1, 2
Church of England, 72, 73
CIA, 31, 32
Clinton, Hilary, 8, 9, 104, 137
Communism, 1, 11, 20, 32, 45, 68, 87, 165, 169

D
Dar al-Ifta Al-Missriya, 154, 183
Darkmatter, 112
Dasgupta, Sri Swapan, 25, 26
Davutoglu, Ahmet, 151
Declaration of Human Fraternity, 38, 135
Deism, 172, 181, 189, 190
de Kerchove, Gilles, 116
Directorate for Religious Affairs, 17
DITIB. *See* Turkish-Islamic Union for Religious Affairs
Diyanet. *See* Directorate for Religious Affairs
Durham, W. Cole, 26

E
Egypt, 1, 7, 15, 30, 31, 68, 83, 98, 100, 108–110, 114, 118–120, 123, 124, 126–129, 135, 136, 150, 152, 154, 155, 157, 172, 177, 180, 182, 184
El Karoui, Hakim, 111
Emirati Fatwa Council, 98
Ennahada, 43
Erbas, Ali, 190
Erdogan, Recep Tayyip, 9, 17, 84, 143–152, 157–170, 185, 189–191

European Council for Fatwa and Research, 125, 138
Extremism, 3, 7, 10, 29, 35, 52, 53, 67, 76, 81, 83, 100, 115, 116, 118, 128, 141, 166

F

Federal Office for the Protection of the Constitution, 166
Federal Security Service, 159
Fernando, Eric, 48
Fiqh, 14, 19, 20, 52, 80, 81
Forum for Promoting Peace in Muslim Societies, 26, 97, 131, 133
France, 108, 109, 111, 112, 114, 136, 149, 165, 166
Francis, Pope, 22, 38, 76, 101, 117, 135
Freedom of religion, 10, 27, 46, 134
FSB. *See* Federal Security Service

G

G20. *See* Group of 20
G20 Interfaith Forum Association, 24
Gender equality, 8, 17, 35
Geneva Consensus Declaration on Promoting Women's Health and Strengthening the Family, 23
Geopolitics, 5, 6, 8
Gerakan Pemuda Ansor, 37, 50, 52, 53
Germany, 99, 111, 156, 161, 162, 166, 185
Ghannouchi, Rachid, 43, 44
Gisèle Littman, 108
Gormez, Mehmet, 151, 152, 160
Gräf, Bettina, 125
Great Replacement Conspiracy, 108
Group of 20, 21, 27, 60, 63
Group of Friends of the Family, 23
Gulen, Fethullah, 157–159, 162, 166, 167, 169, 189
Gus Dur. *See* Wahid, Abdurrahman

H

Hadith, 18, 74
Hafez, Farid, 116
Hagia Sofia, 144, 146

Halakha, 57
Hanson, Mark. *See* Yusuf, Hamza
Haram ash-Sharif, 146
Hassan al-Shafei, 135
Haysim Muzad, 34
Hedayah Center of Excellence for Countering Violent Extremism, 116, 136
Henry Ndukuba, 72
Heshmat Khalifa, 114
Hindu, 7, 21, 24–27, 36, 41, 42, 58, 82, 103, 107, 117, 135, 137
Hinduism, 24, 39, 41, 58, 61
Hindutva, 25
Hippocratic Oath, viii
Hizb ut-Tahrir, 33, 35, 45, 47
Hojatoleslam Akbar Hashemi Rafsanjani, 6
Hudayi Foundation, 159
Humanitarian Islam, 9, 15, 25, 26, 36, 38, 50–53, 55, 64, 70, 79
Human rights, 8, 10, 35, 45, 48, 53, 54, 59, 62, 82, 84, 95, 97, 98, 103, 112, 120, 161, 179, 184, 193
Human Rights Watch, 45, 46, 90, 103, 171, 194
Husain, Ed, 132

I

Ibn Abd al-Wahhab, Mohammed, 13, 20
Ibn Sina, 16
Ilyas, Yunahar, 40, 43
Imam Hatip schools, 159, 164–166
India, 21, 23–27, 30, 36, 66, 82, 107, 132, 136
Indonesia, 3, 5, 8, 9, 11, 15, 17, 18, 21–24, 27–30, 33–37, 39–42, 44, 46–49, 51, 53–56, 58, 60, 64, 70, 71, 83, 125, 126, 135, 176, 178, 179, 186, 193–195
Indonesian Communist Party (PKI), 11, 46
Indonesian Ulama Council (MUI), 34, 49, 56, 186
Indosphere, 60, 61
Infidel, 14, 19, 33, 38–40, 80, 82, 91, 94, 106, 107, 159, 183

Institute for Monitoring Peace and Cultural Tolerance in School Education (Impact-se), 90, 105, 106, 159
International Covenants on Civil and Political Rights (ICCPR), 36, 82
International Union of Muslim Scholars (IUMS), 89, 125–128, 130, 138
Iran, 1, 5, 6, 8, 15, 16, 21, 45, 52, 53, 68, 69, 100, 101, 126, 140, 145, 150, 152–154, 180, 181, 185, 187, 188, 190
Iraq, 5, 6, 30–32, 78, 80, 100, 101, 103, 126, 130, 144, 149, 167, 175, 181, 183
ISIS. *See* Islamic State
Iskandar, Muhaimin, 23, 48, 49
Islam, 2–16, 18, 20–22, 24, 30–45, 49–61, 63–70, 72, 75, 79, 80, 82, 83, 86, 87, 90–95, 97–109, 111, 115, 120, 121, 124–128, 130, 131, 133, 136, 139–141, 144, 146, 147, 149–153, 155, 156, 158–163, 168, 169, 172–174, 176, 179–192
Islamic and Arabic College of Indonesia, 43
Islamic Brotherhood Front, 79
Islamic Defenders Front (FPI), 34, 35, 47, 54, 79
Islamic law, 4, 10, 12, 14, 15, 17–19, 21, 44, 50–53, 61, 65, 72, 74, 77–84, 87, 88, 94, 103, 111, 113, 116, 117, 154, 174, 176, 178, 182
Islamic Relief Worldwide, 114
Islamic Revolutionary Guard Corps, 101
Islamic State, 3, 37, 42, 51, 52, 66, 73, 78–81, 101, 103, 116, 126–128, 131, 132, 182, 189
Israel, 6, 7, 26, 30, 57–59, 76, 86, 89, 97, 98, 111, 128, 129, 146–148, 188
Israel Lau, 58

J
Jakim. *See* Malaysian Islamic Development Department
Java, 11, 33, 46–48, 52, 61, 71

Jerusalem, 57, 58, 75, 86, 97, 98, 144–148, 168
Jews, 14, 26, 53, 57–59, 74, 77, 85, 89, 92, 94, 114, 125, 129, 130, 159, 192
Jihad, 1–3, 68, 107, 129, 132, 159, 167
Jihadism, 3, 4, 7, 10, 13, 79, 99, 112, 116, 120, 128, 140
John Zogby Associates, 180
Jordan, 108, 135, 146, 147, 180
Judaism, 33, 57–59, 85, 129, 188
Justice and Development Party, 17, 148, 159, 189

K
Kafir. *See* Infidel
Kalam Research & Media, 140
Kemalism, 148, 168
Kepel, Gilles, 111, 112
Khaled bin Mahfouz, 67
Khalifa Haftar, 109, 139, 184
Khalifa, Rashad, 74
Khashoggi, Jamal, 9, 65, 76, 106
Kuran, Timur, 17
Kuru, Ahmet, 5, 16–19

L
Laden, Osama bin, 2, 3, 30, 94, 141
LGBT, 23, 190
LibForAll, 50, 58, 195
Libya, 7, 98, 100, 109, 120, 124, 139, 140, 144, 152, 154, 167, 177, 184
LIPIA. *See* Islamic and Arabic College of Indonesia

M
Maarif, Ahmad Syafi'i, 40, 41
Macron, Emmanuel, 109–112, 167
Madhav, Ram, 24–27
Madrid Conference, 85
Mahmoud Mohammed Taha, 74
Maimonides, 57
Malaysian Islamic Development Department, 186
Malbrunot, Georges, 114
Maqashid al-shari'a, 19

Marie le Pen, 110
Mario Brero, 112
Marsudi, Retno, 55
Masorti Judaism, 59
Mecca, 1–4, 6, 14, 24, 43, 63, 65, 70, 89, 93, 99, 132, 146, 182
Medina, 2, 6, 14, 15, 24, 43, 54, 94, 138, 146, 152, 182
Melloni, Alberto, 22
Middle East, 1, 2, 5, 6, 9, 12, 15, 17, 22, 28, 30, 42, 44, 52, 54, 55, 61, 62, 68, 84, 89, 90, 98, 99, 101, 104, 106, 108, 116, 124, 128, 129, 131, 132, 137, 153, 159, 160, 168, 173–179, 183, 187, 195
Moderate Islam, 5–8, 12, 14, 15, 19, 21, 26–29, 43, 44, 51, 54, 56, 66, 72, 75, 78, 81, 85, 86, 103, 110, 131, 132, 134, 136, 137, 139, 141, 168, 195
Mohamed Abd al-Salam, 117
Mohamed al-Khosht, 118
Mohammad Abolghassem Doulabi, 188
Mohammed Abdelkarim al-Issa, 63
Mohammed Ali al-Husseini, 91
Mohammed bin Salman, 8, 36, 56, 63, 99, 137, 140, 141, 153, 163, 174
Mohammed bin Zayed, 8, 26, 29, 36, 56, 97, 108, 120, 131, 139, 158, 174
Moreno, Marco, 188
Morsi, Mohammed, 100, 119, 120, 127, 135, 138, 139, 142, 150, 177
Mosque, Al-Aqsa, 98, 144, 146, 168
Muhamadiyya, 22, 195
Muhammad Abu Al-Fadl, 83
Muhammad bin Saud, 19, 63, 87
Multipurpose Ansor Front, 46
Muslim Brotherhood, 2, 10, 15, 18, 27, 30, 34, 37, 43, 45, 52, 66, 71, 78, 89, 97, 99, 104, 106, 108, 109, 112–116, 123, 124, 126, 129, 135, 136, 150, 169, 176, 177, 180, 182, 195
Muslim Council of Elders, 76, 117, 133–135
Muslims, 3, 5, 8, 19, 21, 23–27, 32, 34, 37–39, 41, 43, 44, 49, 52, 55, 57, 61, 65, 66, 70, 72, 74, 75, 79–83, 89, 91–95, 97, 99, 101, 103, 106–108, 110, 111, 114, 115, 117, 118, 126, 128, 130–132, 134, 138, 145, 149, 150, 152–154, 157, 161, 164, 167, 168, 173–175, 177, 186, 187, 192
Muslim World League, 3, 24, 26–28, 36, 56, 63, 65–67, 71, 75, 87, 89–91, 110, 169
Mutaween, 16

N
Nahdlatul Ulama, 9–11, 13–30, 33–56, 58–62, 64–66, 70–73, 77–81, 83, 84, 91, 95, 107, 120, 125, 171, 176, 186, 193–195
Narendra Modi, 21, 23, 36, 59, 84, 107
National Awakening Party, 23, 34, 48, 50, 194
National Commercial Bank, 67
Nayed, Aref Ali, 120, 139, 140
Netherlands, 155, 166, 174
Nigeria, 72, 73
Novel Bamukmin, 79
Nusantara Islam, 51

O
Obama, Barak, 32, 104, 137
Observatory for Monitoring Takfiri Fatwas and Extremist Ideologies, 154
OIC. *See* Organisation for Islamic Cooperation
Operation Luxor, 116
Organisation for Islamic Cooperation, 82
Osama bin Mohammed Abdullah Al-Shuaib, 70
Ottoman, 4, 20, 34, 41, 51, 81, 93, 103, 143–146, 151, 152, 155, 159, 164, 167–170
Ozal, Turgut, 162, 168
Ozturk, Ahmet Erdi, 151

P
Packard, Josh, 192
Pakistan, 1, 2, 15, 21, 30, 31, 44, 52, 67, 68, 132, 152, 164

Palestinian, 2, 6, 32, 57, 58, 71, 76, 84, 85, 98, 125, 129, 130, 144, 146–148, 168, 180, 195
Pancasila, 34, 39, 42, 45, 46, 51
Pentagon, 3, 30
Pew Research Center, 11, 60, 175, 183
PKB. *See* National Awakening Party
PKS. *See* Prosperous Justice Party
Pluralism, 7, 8, 10, 21, 22, 32, 34–36, 43, 47, 51, 53, 61, 64, 65, 95, 120, 125, 131, 179, 186, 193
Political Islam, 9, 15, 29, 30, 52, 66, 71, 97, 99–101, 104, 109, 111, 113, 115, 116, 120, 127, 132, 136, 149, 152, 161, 162, 167, 176–178, 180, 195
Pompeo, Mike, 22, 23
Prosperous Justice Party, 10, 27, 34, 45, 49, 71
Purnama, Basuki Tjahaja, 48

Q

Qatar, 21, 52, 53, 55, 69, 89, 97, 104, 106, 110, 113, 114, 120, 123–125, 127–129, 132, 138, 140, 175, 182
Qoumas, Yaqut Cholil, 48, 55, 56, 171
Quds Force, 101
Qur'an, 12, 18, 38, 40, 79, 81, 87, 88, 93, 94, 123, 125, 130, 151, 152, 156, 176, 184, 190

R

R20. *See* Religion Forum 20
Raba'a al-Madkhali, 139
Radicalism, 10, 29, 45, 110, 161
Radicalization Awareness Network (RAN), 116, 117
Ralph Drollinger, 107
Rashtriya Swayamsevak Sangh, 21, 36
Religion, 5, 7, 8, 10, 11, 14, 15, 18–22, 24, 25, 30, 32, 35, 39, 42, 45, 46, 48, 57, 58, 60–62, 64, 66, 69, 71, 72, 80–83, 85, 87, 91, 93, 100–103, 105, 110, 111, 117, 120, 121, 124, 132, 133, 137, 138, 148, 151, 156, 160, 168, 172–192
Religion Forum 20, 21, 27, 60, 63, 72

Religious law, 8, 14, 38, 57, 60, 65, 78, 79, 82, 84, 92, 93, 134
Religious reform, 10, 18, 23, 26, 30, 50, 55, 60, 72, 81, 87, 95, 119, 172, 176
Religious soft power, 2, 4–7, 20, 28, 54, 55, 71, 91, 95, 98, 100, 104–106, 108, 127, 129, 135, 138, 146, 148, 150, 151, 153, 154, 157, 158, 161–163, 166, 167, 169, 193
Renaud Camus, 108
Riyanto, 47
Rosen, David, 85, 86
Roy, Olivier, 111
RSS. *See* Rashtriya SwayamsevakSangh
Rushdie, Salman, 73, 74, 185
Russian Orthodox church, ix

S

Sahin, Ali, 164
Salafism, 63, 65, 66, 104, 111, 112, 120, 136, 141, 184
Saleh al-Luhaidan, 13
Saleh al-Maghamsi, 93
Salman al-Awdah, 13
Salman bin Abdulaziz Al Saud, 3
Saudi Arabia, 1, 2, 5, 6, 8–13, 15, 16, 19–21, 23, 24, 27, 28, 30, 34, 43–45, 52–55, 63, 65–70, 75–78, 82, 84–86, 89–95, 100, 101, 104, 106–108, 111, 112, 117, 120, 124, 127, 128, 132, 135–138, 140, 141, 143, 146, 147, 153, 155, 157, 158, 161, 163, 169, 175, 178, 180, 182–184, 195
Saudi High Commission for Aid to Bosnia, 67
Savarkar, Vinayak Damodar, 25
Sharia. *See* Islamic law
Shawki Allam, 78, 141
Sid-Ahmed, Mohamed, 20
Simon Wiesenthal Center, 21, 57
Sirajd, Said Aqil, 48
South Asia Strategic Research Center, 164
Staquf, Yahya Cholil, 11, 13–15, 20–23, 36, 37, 41, 42, 48–51, 55–59, 61, 62, 64, 70, 83, 91

State Department, 23, 30, 31, 67, 73, 98, 99, 102, 161
Subianto, Prabowo, 193
Sudan, 173, 175
Sufism, 120, 121, 140, 181
Suharto, 34, 193, 194
Sukarno, 47, 193
Suleymancılar, 159
Sunan Kalijogo, 41
Sunni Muslims, 53, 141, 149
Supremacism, 3, 65, 67
Syria, 5, 16, 45, 78, 80, 100, 101, 109, 132, 144, 149, 152, 154, 156, 167, 177, 180, 181, 195

T
Tabah Foundation, 139, 142
Taqi ad-Dīn Ahmad ibn Taymiyyah, 16
TDV. *See* Turkiye Diyanet Foundation
Temple Mount. *See* Haram ash-Sharif
Textbooks, 77, 90, 105, 106, 160, 168
TIKA. *See* Turkish Cooperation and Coordination Agency
Tolerance, 7, 8, 27, 29, 32, 36, 39, 45, 51, 53, 60, 61, 63, 74, 83, 91, 92, 95, 97, 101–103, 105, 118, 121, 125, 127, 133, 134, 142, 158, 162, 179
Trump, Donald J., 32, 68, 89, 98, 107, 108, 146
Turkey, 4, 5, 8, 15–18, 21, 51, 52, 93, 126, 140, 143–170, 180, 182, 185, 190, 191
Turkish Cooperation and Coordination Agency, 152
Turkish-Islamic Union for Religious Affairs, 162
Turkish Maarif Foundation, 158
Turkiye Diyanet Foundation, 152

U
Ultra-nationalism, 84
United Arab Emirates (UAE), 5, 8–10, 15, 21, 23, 24, 26, 28, 29, 52, 55, 56, 66, 76, 78, 82, 93, 97–121, 124, 125, 127, 128, 130–142, 147, 153–155, 157, 158, 167, 174, 175, 178, 180, 182, 184, 195

United Nations (UN), 23, 55, 77, 81, 82, 97, 185
United States (US), 1, 3, 5, 6, 8–10, 12, 30–32, 35, 50, 57, 67–69, 73, 75, 76, 89, 98–101, 104, 106, 110, 112, 129, 130, 133, 134, 136, 137, 140, 141, 146, 153, 156, 157, 192, 194
Universal Declaration of Human Rights, 8, 36, 51, 54, 62, 82, 171
US National Strategy for Combating Terrorism, 32

V
van Bruinessen, Martin, 55, 56
Vidino, Lorenzo, 115, 116

W
Wahhabism, 20, 24, 53, 63, 65, 66, 84, 87, 89, 90, 104, 120, 121, 140, 141, 153
Wahid, Abdurrahman, 11, 15, 36, 37, 47, 49–51, 58, 195
Wahid, Hidayat Nur, 71
Wali al-amr, 87
Wali Songo, 41–43, 51
WAMY. *See* World Assembly of Muslim Youth
Warren, David H., 2, 124, 127
Wasatiyyah, 10
Widodo, Joko, 10, 22, 28, 29, 35, 36, 47–51, 54–56, 60, 63, 80, 193–195
Widya Priyahita Pudjibudjo, 56
World Assembly of Muslim Youth, 71
World Evangelical Alliance, 21

X
Xi Jinping, 84

Y
Yusanto, Muhammad Ismail, 33
Yusuf, Hamza, 26, 98, 120, 139

Z
Zia ul-Haq, 2
Zionism, 129, 130

GPSR Compliance

The European Union's (EU) General Product Safety Regulation (GPSR) is a set of rules that requires consumer products to be safe and our obligations to ensure this.

If you have any concerns about our products, you can contact us on

ProductSafety@springernature.com

In case Publisher is established outside the EU, the EU authorized representative is:

Springer Nature Customer Service Center GmbH
Europaplatz 3
69115 Heidelberg, Germany